T0360857

Imperial Borderlands

What are the institutions that govern border spaces and how do they impact long-term economic and social development? This book focuses on the Habsburg military frontier zone, which originated in the sixteenth century as an instrument for protecting the empire's southern border against the threat of the Ottoman Empire and which lasted until the 1880s. The book outlines the conditions under which this extractive institution affected development, showing how locals were forced to work as soldiers and exposed to rigid communal property rights, an inflexible labor market, and discrimination when it came to the provision of public infrastructure. While the formal institutions set up during the military colony disappeared, their legacy can be traced in political attitudes and social norms even today with the violence and abuses exercised by the imperial government transformed into distrust in public authorities, limited political involvement, and low social capital.

Dr. Bogdan G. Popescu is Assistant Professor at John Cabot University, Rome, Italy. He completed his PhD in the Department of Political Science at the University of Chicago and has held postdoctoral positions at Princeton University and Bocconi University.

Cambridge Studies in Economic History - Second Series
Cambridge Studies in Economic History

Cambridge Studies in Economic History comprises stimulating and accessible economic history which actively builds bridges to other disciplines. Books in the series will illuminate why the issues they address are important and interesting, place their findings in a comparative context, and relate their research to wider debates and controversies. The series will combine innovative and exciting new research by younger researchers with new approaches to major issues by senior scholars. It will publish distinguished work regardless of chronological period or geographical location

A complete list of titles in the series can be found at:

www.cambridge.org/economichistory

Imperial Borderlands

Institutions and Legacies of the Habsburg Military Frontier

Bogdan G. Popescu
John Cabot University

Shaftesbury Road, Cambridge CB2 8EA, United Kingdom

One Liberty Plaza, 20th Floor, New York, NY 10006, USA

477 Williamstown Road, Port Melbourne, VIC 3207, Australia

314–321, 3rd Floor, Plot 3, Splendor Forum, Jasola District Centre,
New Delhi – 110025, India

103 Penang Road, #05-06/07, Visioncrest Commercial, Singapore 238467

Cambridge University Press is part of Cambridge University Press & Assessment,
a department of the University of Cambridge.

We share the University's mission to contribute to society through the pursuit of
education, learning and research at the highest international levels of excellence.

www.cambridge.org
Information on this title: www.cambridge.org/9781009365161

DOI: 10.1017/9781009365215

First published 2024

A catalogue record for this publication is available from the British Library.

*A Cataloging-in-Publication data record for this book is available
from the Library of Congress*

ISBN 978-1-009-36516-1 Hardback

Contents

Figures

Tables

Acknowledgments

This book focuses on an understudied topic that has remained somewhat elusive of extractive institutions. The literature in the past twenty years has mostly concentrated on the ways in which European colonial empires created institutions in their territories overseas for monetary gains. Yet much less literature discussed the possibility that European empires could use similar extractive strategies only on part of their population. Thus, this book attempts to fill that gap by paying close attention to the modus operandi of extractive institutions in a particular space – the Habsburg Empire – and within a particular context – the forced military enrollment of borderland dwellers.

The idea of this project came in the last two years of my PhD at the University of Chicago, while trying to question the usual tropes about the legacies of the Habsburg and Ottoman empires: the Ottoman Empire had "bad" institutions, which is why Ottoman successor states should feature lower development, while the Habsburg Empire had "good" bureaucracy and institutions, and thus, Habsburg successor states should be better off in the long run. A simple visual examination using satellite luminosity within the two empires showed substantial variation within the two polities. The pattern that got my attention is the lower luminosity in the region which constituted the Habsburg border with the Ottoman Empire, which I subsequently discovered was not coincidental. The southwestern part of the Habsburg Empire was a military encampment for over three centuries, acting as a buffer zone between the two empires. This led me to further dig into the intricate history of the regions that today coincide with Croatia, Serbia, and Romania. The institutional setup and the hierarchies created by the state match very closely the hierarchies created by colonial empires overseas. Some might dismiss and find problematic the comparisons between the sea-based and land-based empires on the grounds that hierarchies describing the two imperial models are fundamentally different, with the former usually being based on race. As some economic historians have argued, race is only one of the many characteristics that might create power asymmetries. Other characteristics could be religion, social stata, affiliation to a particular group, or possession of specific sociopolitical privileges defined by the center. The creation of the legal category – the Grenzer and the subsequent association with negative characteristics such as "savage and wild," together with the imperial needs of having troops always ready to act – is what kept this institution in place for over 300 years on the southwestern side. Thus, borderland dwellers in the Habsburg frontier experienced particular kinds of discrimination in the form of limited access to public goods and incomplete property rights.

I write this book aspiring to make a theoretical contribution to both political science and economics by unpacking the notion of extractive institutions and examining its components: use of violence, limited property rights, and under-provision of public goods. These three components together help us understand why extractive historical institutions can have negative long-term effects. The book contributes to the historical literature on the Habsburg Empire, which mostly focuses on the whole of the Habsburg Empire or its multiethnic and multireligious composition, which was meant to put substantial pressure on the capital. The book is a crafting project. I scanned and georeferenced a variety of maps from the Austrian Archives. I geolocated historical districts, villages, and cantons in what is today Croatia, Serbia, and Romania and made maps which show us different socioeconomic characteristics of the region. To keep a certain level of parsimony, not all the maps made it into this book. I also consulted a variety of archival documents: letter exchanges, cadastral plans, travel books from the eighteenth and nineteenth centuries, legal documents from the eighteenth and nineteenth centuries documenting the rights and obligations of border inhabitants.

The project, which was initially only one chapter in my PhD dissertation, grew into a book during my postdoctoral fellowships at Princeton and Bocconi universities. I am very grateful to the Bobst Center for Peace and Justice at Princeton, specifically, Carles Boix and Amaney Jamal, who believed in this project and supported me for one year. My research and the writing of this monograph was supported by the European Research Council Horizon 2020 Starting Grant "Spoils of War," led by Prof. Tamás Vonyó as a principal investigator, and the Dondena Centre for Research on Social Dynamics and Public Policy at Bocconi University, where I was postdoctoral research fellow from 2019 to 2022.

I also revised the manuscript at Magdalen College, Oxford, where I worked as a lecturer. In the fall of 2021, I organized a book workshop at Bocconi, where Mark Dincecco, Grigore Pop-Eleches, Kristin Fabbe, Tomáš Cvrček, and Tamás Vonyó provided incredible feedback on the project. They took the time to read the draft manuscript and provided thoughtful comments, which allowed me to write a much better book as a result.

I am also very appreciative of the support of the Executive Publisher for History at Cambridge, Michael Watson, and the Economic History Series editors who supported the project. To be published by the flagship book series in economic history at the world's oldest university press is indeed an honor.

Beyond funders and publishers, a number of individuals deserve special praise for their graciousness. I am grateful to Miroslav Birclin, director of the Pančevo Museum in Serbia, who gave me permission to use Paja Jovanović's "The Great Migration of the Serbs" as a cover for the book, and to the Austrian Archives in Vienna, who allowed me to reproduce the letter from Joseph II in Chapter 3 and the map of Zelcin in Chapter 5.

In the long and arduous road of writing *Imperial Borderlands*, a few mentors deserve special recognition. Robert Gullotty was an incredibly helpful mentor in my final year at the University of Chicago, who allowed me to get more clarity on my theoretical framework and gave me advice on navigating the intricate, sinuous ways of academia. Mike Albertus at the University of Chicago was also very supportive and believed in the originality of the historical data and the quantitative historical approach. I am also thankful to Monika Nalepa and James Robinson, who chaired my dissertation and who pushed me to write a more interesting project.

My intellectual interlocutors – too many to name them all – have contributed directly or indirectly to this project in essential ways: Scott Abramson, Andrea Bartoletti, Michael Bernhard, John Brehm, Volha Charnysh, Maura Cremin, Francisco Garfias, Jacob Hariri, Melissa Lee, Isabela Mares, Yusuf Magiya, Daniel Mattingly, Steve Monroe, Stefan Nikolic, Tom Pavone, Mircea Popa, Beth Simmons, Fer Sobrino, Joan Ricart, Holly Shissler, Andres Uribe, Steven Wilkinson, Mihnea Zlota, and Christina Zuber.

Some of these individuals may not remember it, but they shaped my growth as a social scientist by supplying inspiring conversations, thoughtful written feedback, essential contacts, and invaluable friendship when I needed it most. I am also very grateful to Hector Salvador for proofreading the manuscript and providing valuable comments and support.

Finally, I must acknowledge those whose love has warmed my spirit and kept me going: my parents, Virgil and Elena Popescu, who supported me in becoming the first person in my family to get an undergraduate degree, and subsequently obtain a PhD.

1   Historical States, Imperialism, and Development

Western Europe and North America have been commonly associated with economic development, a multifaceted process which manifests itself in high levels of income, productivity, consumption, investment, education, life expectancy, employment, etc. All these are factors which make for a better life. Many of these outcomes have been attributed to the existence of good institutions, in particular the existence of democracy, which encourages investment by safeguarding property rights, the efficient allocation of resources through the free flow of ideas, and incentivizing governments to make good policy decisions given the threat of not being re-elected (Przeworski, 2012).

Other studies in political science and economics attribute such economic outcomes to the institutions that were created by historical empires. For example, some scholars contend that historical states such as the Habsburg Empire, a political entity which governed parts of Western and Central Europe for over four centuries, facilitated trust in government institutions and enforced rules and property rights. These in turn provided the "cultural and legal underpinnings for groups to achieve mutually productive outcomes" (Becker *et al.*, 2016, p. 41). Other empires which governed in Europe for a similar amount of time, such as the Ottomans, are associated with negative economic outcomes (Dimitrova-Grajzl, 2007; Grosjean, 2011; Kuran, 2012). Scholarship investigating why the Middle East lagged behind Western Europe focused on a variety of Islamic legal institutions which blocked the emergence of some of the features of modern economic life. These have to do with inheritance of property, lack of trade organizations, lack of impersonal exchange, etc. (Kuran, 2012). Research examining specifically the legacies of the Ottoman Empire also discussed the role of the prohibition of interest lending (Grosjean, 2011) or the delay in the adoption of the printing press (Popescu and Popa, 2022) as key factors explaining developmental outcomes in Ottoman successor states. The focus on the legacies of these two empires rests on the assumption that they had institutions which were homogeneously enforced within their territory. The empirical reality, however, reveals a more nuanced picture: patterns of

1

economic versus under-development do not start at the border of these two empires.

The legacies of the Habsburg and Ottoman empires in Central and Southeast Europe have long been studied and debated. Historians have argued that development in terms of urbanization and industrialization diffused from north-west to south-east in the Danube region (Good, 1984; Pollard, 1986) and economic historians of Austria-Hungary show persistent gaps and lack of convergence between the lands of Central Europe (Cvrček, 2013; Klein *et al.*, 2017; Schulze, 2007). One of the main factors explaining under-development in the eastern and southern regions of the Habsburg Empire is geography, particularly low population density and lack of urban concentration. Both were – in large part – legacies of Ottoman rule and extensive warfare between rival imperial powers during the early modern period. Less attention has been paid to the lasting developmental consequences of these historical patterns. One common way of visualizing such persistent effects has been through the use of nighttime satellite luminosity (Henderson *et al.*, 2012). This measure gained momentum in economic and political science in the absence of accurate official statistics or more conventional data including national or regional GDP, and has the added advantage of having very fine-grained data which is highly comparable across time and space (Donaldson and Storeygard, 2016). Satellite luminosity has been utilized as a way to examine the effects of pre-colonial ethnic institutions (Michalopoulos and Papaioannou, 2013), historical state-building efforts (Mattingly, 2017), or of pre-colonial conflict exposure (Dincecco *et al.*, 2022), etc. The superimposition of nighttime satellite luminosity over historical borders reveals some interesting regional asymmetries which go beyond the presumed dichotomies: the Habsburgs had good institutions which contributed to higher economic outcomes and the Ottomans had bad institutions which help explain lower developmental outcomes today.

Figure 1.1 displays patterns in regional luminosity pertaining to the Habsburg successor states: the north of the Habsburg Empire corresponding to Poland, Czechia, and Slovakia seems to be much more luminous compared to Habsburg successor states like Romania, Serbia, and Croatia. If we focus on the southern borderlands of the former Habsburg Empire, we see further evidence for divergent development at the regional level, too. Within modern-day Croatia, in particular, the south appears significantly less developed than the north. Even though this may reflect several confounding factors, I will demonstrate throughout this book that this pattern is the legacy of a peculiar historical institution – the Habsburg (or Austrian) military frontier. This is a buffer area which the Habsburgs created in 1553 in order to defend themselves

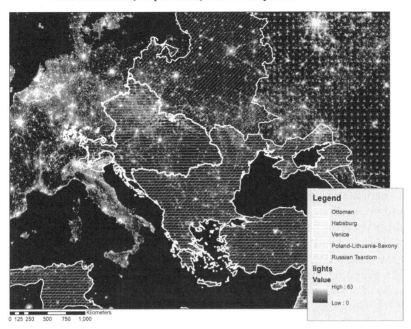

Figure 1.1 Political borders in 1739 and satellite luminosity
in 2013

against an inimical neighboring state, the Ottoman Empire. As the Habsburg armies gradually forced the Ottomans out of Hungary, the military frontier expanded, stretching through the territory of modern-day Croatia, Serbia, and Romania. The frontier remained in place in different forms until the second half of the nineteenth century (Ferguson, 1954; Lesky, 1957; Rothenberg, 1960a, 1960b). The buffer zone in the Habsburg military frontier zone acquired the name of the Habsburg military colony.

Military colonialism was not unique to the Habsburg Empire. As a definition, military colonialism was a widespread cost-effective method for territorial protection that many states adopted, including the Russian, French, and Roman empires. This method entailed the forceful recruitment of people located on the border of the state and their engagement in military activities for the defense of the state (Isaac, 1988; Pipes, 1950; Sumner, 1949). Within the Habsburg military colony, landed elites were removed and the local population forced to live under a strict communal property rights regime. To keep them subservient and keep expenditures low, the Habsburg state made very few investments in infrastructure (Blanc, 1957; Rothenberg, 1966). Similarly, people in the military colony were exposed to some violence including beatings and torture for disobeying the imperial authorities. At the same time, they were free from the feudal yoke that constrained the lives of the enserfed peasantry in the rest of the empire until the early 1800s (O'Reilly, 2006), while village communities in the military colony were self-sufficient.

Despite the formal abolition of the military colony in Croatia and Slavonia in 1881, and in Transylvania and the Banat almost three decades earlier, some of the institutions that were formally enshrined in law became informal and continued to exist. They outlived both the military colony and the Austro-Hungarian Empire itself. For example, while land inequality and an increasingly large landless rural proletariat characterized the economy of imperial Hungary after the abolition of serfdom in 1848, an equitable distribution of land and large communal properties remained predominant in the former borderlands. This went hand in hand with limited access to public goods, which can be observed to the present day. Public goods are goods that users cannot be excluded from accessing. At the same time, use by one person does not prevent access of other people or does not reduce availability to others (Oakland, 1987). Generally, examples of public goods include law enforcement, national defense, rule of law, access to clean air, (government-provided) roads, and schools. In the case of the legacy of the military colony, limited public goods can be observed when it comes to density of roads and railroads, historical access to hospitals, access to schools, and access to water and sanitation in the present day.

Similarly, the legacy of these institutions can also be traced at the level of political attitudes and social norms. These are transmitted over generations vertically from parents to children and can still be observed in differences right across the historical border. Such attitudes take the form of higher trust in family members and lower trust in outsiders. These are caused by exposure to communal properties which entailed segmentation across family clans and low inter-clan interaction. Equally, the violence and abuses exercised by the imperial government limited the ability of locals to participate politically, which is why locals are less likely to sign petitions and to participate in demonstrations. I demonstrate the persistence of such norms using historical data from qualitative primary and secondary sources as well as historical and modern statistical material. The quantitative results obtained from modern surveys are compatible with historical accounts by travelers and Habsburg bureaucrats that described the low level of social capital as a product of exposure to military colonialism. As such, the alienation from the state in modern times has historical roots. The results and the mechanisms of transmission shed new light on the relationship between centralized states and civil society. Unlike previous accounts according to which strong centralized states and village intermediation can have positive effects on long-term development (Dell *et al.*, 2018), the Habsburg example demonstrates a more sinister side to this relationship. Despite working with local villages, which would in principle empower local communities, the patron–client relationships between the center and the periphery negatively affected development. This has to do with the creation of a civil society which is much more trusting of family members and distrusting of outsiders.

The historical literature on the Habsburg Empire concentrated on some political and economic factors contributing to lower economic outcomes. Such factors include the dissolution of the empire or the effects of imperial external borders. For example, a vast literature focused on the negative impact of its dissolution and made propositions to reintegrate the successor states (Hodža, 1942; Jászi, 1929; Schacher, 1932). Economists writing after World War I (Hertz, 1947; Macartney, 1937; Pasvolsky, 1928) and historians since (Bachinger and Lacina, 1996; Berend, 1998; Berend and Ránki, 1960; Feinstein *et al.*, 2008; Karner, 1990; Mosser and Teichova, 1991) have recurrently emphasized the economic penalties of political fragmentation in Central Europe. Recent studies challenged the traditional view of economic integration and convergence within the empire and the damage that successor states suffered after its dissolution (Berger, 1990; Cvrček, 2013; Schulze, 2007; Schulze and Wolf, 2011; Wolf *et al.*, 2011). Older and newer monographs are at odds over the political viability of the Habsburg monarchy in the nineteenth century (Judson, 2016; Taylor, 1948). More generally, however, the literature on the legacies of the Habsburg Empire focuses extensively on the external borders of the empire and the new borders codified in the peace treaties that followed World War I. As such the historical literature pays less attention to the more complex legacies of internal borders within the Habsburg monarchy such as those around the former military colonies. Thus, the book highlights important legacies of well-documented historical institutions that largely eluded researchers and can inspire a more complex understanding of how historical borders affected local institutions and constrained nation building.

This book speaks to a large literature on legacies of colonialism. The comparison between Western colonialism and Habsburg military colonialism is justifiable for a variety of reasons. On the most basic level, generations of historians who studied the Habsburg military frontier utilized the term "colonialism" to refer to the Habsburg military frontier in English (Rothenberg, 1960a, 1960b, 1966; Wessely, 1973), in French (Blanc, 1957; Boppe, 1900; Perrot, 1869), or in German (Kaser, 1997; Vaníček, 1875a). On a more abstract level, there are a few additional reasons justifying such a comparison.

First, on a conceptual level, the basic institutional framework of the Habsburg military frontier matches closely the definition of colonialism proposed by philosophers. For example, Kohn and Reddy (2017) define colonialism as the "practice of domination, which involves the subjugation of one people to another."[1] Sociologists provide more specific definitions indicating that colonialism "entails settlement and institutional transplantation" (Mahoney, 2010, p. 23). Others use the term colonialism to describe dependencies that are directly governed by a foreign nation and contrast this with imperialism, which involves indirect forms of domination. Irrespective of the finer conceptual nuances, colonialism has existed since ancient times. The Greeks, the Romans, or the Ottomans are famous examples of states which set up colonies (Kohn and Reddy, 2017). With the advancement of sailing technology, colonialism and imperialism, have become terms used to refer closely to the process of European settlement and political control over the rest of the world, including the Americas, Australia, and parts of Africa and Asia. Closely related to colonialism, imperialism is also a "process that involves growing control of one state over another state or *people*" (emphasis added) (Kohli, 2020, p. 7). However, as Kohn and Reddy (2017) contend, "colonialism is not restricted to a specific time and place."

The second reason why the comparison with Western forms of colonialism is justifiable has to do with the stark distinctions that the Habsburg Empire made between the capital and people in the periphery. The subjects who were exposed to military colonial institutions were a distinct socio-legal category, in a similar way to many other cases of Western colonialism. Military colonists were formally called *grenzer* or *graničari* and were controlled by generals sent from Vienna, who were often perceived as "foreign," contributing to the stark de jure and de facto distinction between the center and the periphery. Hence, the relationship between Vienna and locals in the Habsburg frontier is compatible with John Stuart Mill's understanding of colonialism (Mill, 1861): a despotic government by outsiders which can lead to injustice and economic exploitation. The injustice and exploitation can take place through two mechanisms. First, external imperial delegates are unlikely to have the knowledge of local conditions and therefore would be unable to adopt effective public policies. Second, given the potential cultural, linguistic, and religious differences, the non-local imperial representatives are less likely to empathize with locals.

---

[1] Kohn and Reddy (2017) argue that there is extensive conceptual overlap between colonialism and imperialism, that latter involving "political and economic control over a dependent territory." However, they do contend that the distinction between colonialism and imperialism is not clear or consistently made in the literature.

Finally, the most important reason why the term "colonialism" can be used for the Habsburg military frontier has to do with the fact that military colonies constituted a model for the institutional framework developed by Western empires overseas. The French intellectual and military elites were discussing the suitability of adopting the Habsburg military colonial model to ensure the protection of the French settlers from belligerent local tribes. In Chapter 7, I provide an extensive qualitative analysis of the different French discourses focusing on the adoption of Habsburg military colonies to ensure the protection of their territories overseas. The French imperial elites in the early 1800s used the term "colonialism" both in reference to their project in Algeria and to the Habsburg military frontier giving further credence to comparisons between European empires and Western imperial territories overseas. More importantly, such elite discussions provide valuable insights indicating that some of the institutions that Western empires adopted in their territories overseas in fact had their roots in Europe. Therefore, sea-based and land-based empires have more common ground than might have been suggested by some scholars (Barkey, 2008).

I contend that settlements on the Habsburg frontier are expressions of both imperial and colonial enterprises. Having people exposed to institutions dictated by the center which entail removal of property rights, living within a communal property rights regime, and having to show up for battle and do military patrol are indeed the expression of exerting control over a population. At the same time, living in settlements dictated by military generals sent by the center or having to move to a new military settlement are also examples of colonialism.

Given the institutional similarities between cases of Western colonialism and the Habsburg military frontier, it is worth investigating whether some of the empirical regularities that some scholars identified for the former also hold for the latter. This is relevant when it comes to long-term effects of historical limited provision of public goods, specific property rights arrangements, and historical exposure to violence. These are the three broad categories that much of the social science empirical research would fall under.

A variety of studies in the social sciences, including political science and economics, suggest that historical colonial experiences undermine access to public goods and economic development more generally (Dell, 2010; Guardado, 2018; Kohli, 2020; Lowes and Montero, 2021). For example, Dell (2010); Guardado (2018) contends that forced labor conscription together with the sale of offices by the Spanish crown in Latin America to incompetent governors are two important factors contributing to under-development in the region. Lowes and Montero (2021) also focus on one aspect related to labor conscription which has to do with the exertion of violence in Africa and how that was the basis for lower trust in the authorities, which in turn caused collective action problems, further undermining economic development. More recent works, however, have found that under certain circumstances, historical colonialism can in fact be associated with positive economic outcomes, despite colonialism being an immoral practice of subjugation, and despite many locals having lost their lives in the fight against the colonial oppressors. For example, Donaldson (2018) discusses and finds strong empirical evidence that British investments in transportation infrastructure projects aimed at facilitating further extraction contributed to decreased trade costs and increased real price gaps. Mattingly (2017, p. 435) also finds positive effects in China associated with Japanese colonization, which include persistent increases in schooling, health, and bureaucratic density as a result of "considerable investments in local state institutions." Dell and Olken (2020) identify positive consequences associated with the construction of sugar cane factories in Dutch Indonesia which were aimed at processing sugar cane and transporting it to the capital. Such positive effects include provision of public education for locals, better transportation infrastructure, and a lower likelihood of work in agriculture. Recent studies on the economic history of colonialism, both in Africa and Asia, have presented more balanced accounts of legacies of colonization (Frankema and Booth, 2019; Gardner and Roy, 2020; Kohli, 2020).

This book engages directly with this literature by focusing on extractive institutions, typical for Western colonialism in the global south, which allowed the imperial elites to oppress and exploit their subjects. Extractive institutions are arrangements which cement the authority of one group to impose law and order at the expense of another. They contrast with inclusive institutions, which involve a wide stratum of society in economic and political life (Acemoğlu and Robinson, 2012). The book also contributes to debates on state formation (Boix, 2015; Dincecco, 2011; Fabbe, 2019; Herbst, 2000; Migdal, 1988; North *et al.*, 2009; Tilly, 1990), social capital (Putnam, 2000; Putnam *et al.*, 1993), and the function and legacies of borders (Scott, 2010).

On a theoretical level, this research provides a conceptual framework for how we should think about legacies of colonialism using an interdisciplinary approach. Colonialism is indeed a deplorable practice whereby a stronger agent takes over a weaker agent usually for economic gain. The theoretical framework does not ever make colonialism normatively good even if the consequences associated with it can be economically good. In other words, the goal of the theoretical framework is never to exonerate the abuses, violence, and killings that many

Western empires utilized as part of their colonial enterprises but rather to provide a lens through which to analyze the conditions under which imperialism affects development, drawing insights from both economics and political science. I posit that developmental consequences are largely contingent on imperial investment, the transformation of local society under changing property regimes, and the presence of physical coercion. By deconstructing extractive institutions in this manner and investigating their impact on development, the proposed theoretical framework fills a void in the empirical literature and helps explain the mixed results it has offered. Benefiting from a historical case study richly documented in primary and secondary sources, the book illustrates how these colonial interventions and their developmental impact evolved in the process of historical change. This motivates the chronological structure of the narrative, which begins in the era of military colonialism itself, followed by its immediate aftermath, and finishes with persistent legacies.

Some scholars classified colonialism based on whether the dominant unit governed directly or indirectly (Gerring *et al.*, 2011; Iyer, 2010; Mamdani, 1996). Direct rule depended on an integrated state apparatus, the dismantling of preexisting political institutions, and the construction of centralized, territory-wide, and bureaucratic legal-administrative institutions that were controlled by colonial officials. Indirect rule on the other hand was a form of colonial domination via collaboration with indigenous intermediaries who controlled regional political institutions. At the same time, scholars such as Doyle (1986) and Lange (2009) make the distinction between direct and indirect rule based on the origin of the political agents: direct rule entails the appointment of executive agents appointed by the center and who are not born in the area where they are appointed. While there can be some level of delegation at the very bottom of the political hierarchy, if above the local power holders there are still imperial authorities in place, then that would still be an example of direct rule. The Habsburg military colony entailed some amount of delegation of power to local power holders. For example, until 1754, locals could choose their own magistrates and captains, which meant that the Habsburgs used indirect rule to some extent. However, if we follow the definition proposed by Doyle (1986) and Lange (2009), the presence of imperial authorities who control and manage local leaders, together with the highly centralized decision-making of the Habsburg Empire, would indicate that the military colony should be regarded as a direct form of rule.

Irrespective of the direct–indirect rule distinction, much of the literature takes colonialism as a monolithic concept, assuming that it was homogeneously enforced throughout the subordinate state's territory. In other words, such literature pays less attention to the possibility that colonialism could be asymmetrically enforced throughout a country's territory. In addition, due to the exclusive focus on the effect of Western colonialism on non-Western states, the literature ignores that colonialism could be applied within the territory of the dominant state. One such example is military colonialism, which consisted of extracting labor from a designated territory and subjecting local populations to forced conscription. While originally, people might have had a choice about whether to be part of the designated territory of the military or not, this changed with time; thus, being part of the military colony was no longer a choice.

In problematizing extractive institutions and unpacking them in the Habsburg historical context, the book goes beyond mainstream interpretations of colonialism that draw primarily on the experience of Western imperialism in the non-European world. My narrative reveals that some of the colonial institutional practices commonly attributed to overseas imperialism had their roots in historical institutions within Europe. Extractive institutions can be associated with positive developmental outcomes when they entail substantial investment in local infrastructure and the protection of individual property rights. Positive examples include the case of forced labor in sugar factories in nineteenth-century Dutch Indonesia (Bosma, 2007; Dell and Olken, 2020) and forced labor in the construction of public works in Japanese Korea before World War II (Kohli, 2004). Sometimes, however, extractive institutions can thwart development when they generate violence (Mukherjee, 2018, 2021), remove or weaken property rights, and neglect public investment, as in the use of forced labor for rubber extraction in the Congo Free State in the late nineteenth century (Frankema and Buelens, 2013; Lowes and Montero, 2021), or under the forced labor regimes in silver mines of Spanish colonial Peru and Mexico (Brading and Cross, 1972; Dell, 2010).

Given that development is the outcome of interest in most of the analyses in this book, it is important to define it. Following Amartya Sen, development can be defined as "the expansion of 'capabilities' of people to lead the kind of lives they value – and have reasons to value" (Sen, 1999, p. 18). Under such conceptualization, development is more of a process which empowers individuals to accomplish the goals that they value. Components of development include wealth in the form of real income, growth of the economy, and the provision of public goods and services, which have the role of providing a basic infrastructure for individuals to create even more wealth. For example, access to education and health facilities further enables individuals to have long and informed lives. These are examples of public goods that are jointly used and where exclusion is infeasible.[2] Examples of public goods for joint use and where exclusion is feasible include telephone service, toll roads, cable TV, and electric power. These in turn offer opportunities for individuals to engage in activities which aim to achieve other kinds of freedoms such as democracy (Rueschemeyer *et al.*, 1992). The expansion of public goods will be the focus of this book, specifically understanding its causes and how it covaries with extractive practices.

The book speaks to a wide scholarship in political economy, political sociology, and political science attempting to understand the origins of institutions and how they transfer to attitudes and norms. In political economy, it will add to a growing scholarship focusing on how historical colonial institutions affect the present (Acemoğlu and Robinson, 2012; Dell, 2010; Lowes and Montero, 2021). It goes beyond these studies, by exploiting rich quantitative and qualitative evidence to better understand the transmission mechanisms that create these historical legacies. The book is also in conversation with scholars in political sociology in the tradition of Mahoney (2010) and Lange (2009) who problematize the power configuration between the center and the periphery during historical times and how that influenced the subsequent evolution of bureaucracies and state institutions. The book departs from this tradition in two ways. First, in examining the concept of extractive institutions, I enrich their argument by focusing on concrete characteristics of imperial institutions, namely public investment in the periphery, physical violence, and protection/removal of property rights enacted by the imperial government, which could affect development directly. Second, from an empirical point of view, I combine rich historical data with modern analytical approaches to understand why extractive institutions are adopted, how they evolve over time, and how they continue to impact people's lives even after their legal forms have been abolished.

The book is also about historical processes of state formation and their impact on long-run development. As such, it speaks to a vast literature in New Institutional Economics, best known from the work of Acemoğlu and Robinson (2012), North and Weingast (1989), and North *et al.* (2009), as it examines the impact of "limited-access orders" and "extractive institutions" and explains why they persist. My approach improves our understanding of how different types of extractive institutions can affect development. It also demonstrates some conceptual similarity with Migdal (1988) in acknowledging the bifurcated structure

---

[2] Ostrom and Ostrom (1977) distinguish between exclusion and jointness of consumption as independent attributes of public goods. When it comes to jointness of consumption, public goods can be highly subtractible or nonsubtractible. Public goods can also be infeasible where no practical technique exists for either packaging a good or where the costs of exclusion are too high.

of the state's territory containing the "official" state and "web-like societies" in the periphery.

Military Colonialism: Between State-Making and Extractivism

Military colonialism is an institution which is arguably as old as the state. It was common in the ancient Near East, Egypt, the Greco-Roman world, Byzantine, Han China, Russian, and the Habsburg empires. Extended defense of a long border against an active enemy posed problems for historical states. In many cases, deploying full-time professional troops was demanding for the center in terms of material and human capacity. The peasant-soldier was an economical solution for the historical state to help protect its borders against external threats. Inhabitants of military colonies were self-sufficient (Rothenberg, 1960b): in exchange for their military services they would get a piece of land for their and their family's subsistence[3] (Pipes, 1950) and would be relieved of their usual manorial obligations.

Beyond the defense of the border, military colonies were also used as part of the imperial coercive apparatus to ensure the survival of the state. For this reason military colonies resemble other types of coercive apparatuses such as the police, the army, militias, paramilitary troops, etc.: they can support the state in case of threat and they can use violence (Carey et al., 2013; Staniland, 2015). The peasant-soldier was, however, a legal category – dedicating themselves to agriculture and manufacturing in times of peace and to war in times of war. Therefore, the peasant-soldier was neither an adequately trained military, nor an expert farmer (Rothenberg, 1966, p. 65). In the Habsburg case, the soldier was sent to various posts in towns and villages, doing patrol runs between them every eight days in times of peace (Perrot, 1869).

Military colonies differed from modern militias and paramilitaries in the amount of state regulation that governed every aspect of their inhabitants' life (from what type of agriculture they can be engaged in, to what uniforms to wear, and how to submit an official petition). The amount of regulation could very well be the result of the fact that military colonies were typically situated at the border of the historical state. In fact, scholarship on inter-state borders argues: "[b]orderland dwellers are frequently people that have suffered particular and discrete injustices as a result of the border" (Longo, 2018, p. 102). Scholarship in international relations argues that formerly disputed areas at the border have

---

[3] In the Habsburg case the basic allotment could not be sold, leased, mortgaged, or given away (Rothenberg, 1966, p. 27).

lagged in development (Schultz, 2017; Wolf, 2005; Wolf *et al.*, 2011) through discrimination and insecure property rights[4] (Simmons, 2005).

Conceptually, military colonialism is somewhere on a continuum between state-making and rent-extractivism. The military colony was part of the original *state infrastructure*,[5] a type of arrangement whereby people would become deferential to the capital (Mukhopadyay, 2014). This was likely achieved in a three-part process identified by Migdal (1988) and consisting of (1) compliance (control of means of coercion and punishment); (2) participation (organization of local populations for specialized tasks); (3) legitimation (accepting the state's rules and acknowledging that compliance is right). Migdal's (1988) account is also similar to what Tilly (1990) regards as fundamental for the construction of states: coercion, connection, and capital. People in the Habsburg military colony were expected to comply with the directives from Vienna, which essentially meant always being ready to defend the border. It also meant participating in the efforts of the higher military authorities to organize the military regiments effectively and observe the orders of the imperial authorities. Finally, legitimation was gradually achieved by the Habsburgs through a form of delegation of power. In a first instance, local authorities and indigenous leaders were given some recognition precisely to mediate or minimize the possibility of an outright rejection of the Habsburg imperial rule. Local military commanders were elements of state infrastructure whereby power was exerted onto local populations. When Habsburg authorities were considered legitimate enough, the local power holders would be replaced with Habsburg delegates.

Military colonialism is also an example of an extractive institution. As already mentioned, applied economists have investigated the notion of extractive institutions almost exclusively in the context of Western empires extracting resources from their overseas colonies. This is the case in the context of the Spanish extraction of silver from Peru and Mexico (Dell, 2010), extraction of crops such as rubber in the Belgian Congo (Lowes and Montero, 2021), or extraction of sugar cane in Dutch Indonesia (Dell and Olken, 2020). Because the extraction of resources

---

[4] The effect has to do with the fact that the settlement left nationals from both states on the "wrong" side of the new border, leaving them politically and economically disadvantaged in their new states. Similarly, disputed areas reduce international trade through the uncertainty over which state's rules and laws govern a given transaction, which reduces the movement of goods (Simmons, 2005).

[5] I use the term "state infrastructure" to refer to the establishment of an authority influencing the lives and the behavior of those within the state. This notion is inspired by what Mann (2008, p. 355) refers to as the "capacity of the state to penetrate civil society and implement its actions across its territories" or by what Soifer (2008, p. 235) means when he describes infrastructural power as "the set of relationships that link these institutions of control to the local communities they penetrate and to central state elites."

coincides with the notion of forced labor, this leads to what Sartori (1970) would call conceptual overstretching. The concept which appears most frequently, however, in the definitions provided by scholars is that of forced labor (Boone, 2014; Mamdani, 1996), the process by which some higher-order authorities coerce people to be involved in a project designated by the former. Military colonists in the Habsburg Empire were coerced into defending the empire. Hence, what is being extracted are the human resources which the empire deems necessary for the defense of the state. The vast "wild" periphery that constituted the eastern border with the Ottoman Empire was a vital resource in at least two respects. First, it was a buffer zone, padding the Habsburg territory from Ottoman attacks, giving the Habsburg center the time necessary for bringing additional troops to defend the state. Second, it constituted an important source of military human capital: the borderland dwellers in the military frontier constituted an additional military resource in other international Habsburg wars against Prussia or France. As a result, borderland dwellers formed the military capital of the Habsburg state.

Despite being located at the border, the military colonists were different from the state fugitives, as described by Scott (2010). Unlike other border areas such as the Zomia people in Southeast Asia, the military frontier was not home to the fugitive, mobile populations whose mode of existence was intractable to the state. Life in the military periphery was not an alternative to life within the state. Quite the contrary, every small move by borderland dwellers was carefully monitored and ruled by the Habsburg state with the help of the already existing structures of power and hierarchies in place. Living at the periphery meant therefore living within the state, rather than outside of it. While for some, running away from the Ottoman state might have been an option at some point in the early stages of the Ottoman conquest (1400 and 1500s), once they settled within the Habsburg realm, running was no longer an option. Leaving would be considered mutiny and would be severely punished. In other words, while originally military colonists might have had some ability to bargain, this changed when the military colony became institutionalized.

Argument at a Glance

I argue that there are three components or modus operandi of extractive institutions that help us understand their effect for long-term development. These go beyond the case of military colonialism, which is why I provide examples of colonial models from other times and geographies. The three components are imperial infrastructural investment, removal of property rights, and the use of violence. The three could also be considered components of extractivism, processes, or modes of operation for the purpose of achieving the ultimate imperial goal – hegemonic preservation and enrichment through extraction.

In the first case, the imperial center may invest in the "periphery" depending on whether such investment will facilitate even greater extraction. For example, the imperial center may invest in roads, factories, or local education in order to extract minerals or crops even more effectively. This is the case of sugar cane factories in Dutch Indonesia in the mid-nineteenth century, where locals were forced to be involved in the harvesting and processing of sugar cane (Dell and Olken, 2020). Despite coercive labor, locals also benefited from the construction of roads for the easy transportation of sugar cane, and increased literacy for more effective learning of the processing technology. Other types of resources, however, necessitated less investment on the part of the imperial powers. This was the case in the extraction of silver in Latin America between 1500 and 1650 (Brading and Cross, 1972; Dell, 2010) or the extraction of rubber in Belgian Congo (Lowes and Montero, 2021). In both cases, the extraction of such commodities required little investment in infrastructure. In the case of silver extraction, this was mostly done through amalgamation with mercury (Brading and Cross, 1972), which was achievable without much technology. Similarly, in the case of rubber, this was extracted from coagulated tree sap, which could be obtained with a sharp tool (Hochschild, 1999). As such, extractivism in the second case required little investment in roads or processing factories. Similarly, there was no need for an educated labor force beyond the very basic instruction directly relevant for the extraction of the minerals or crops.

The second component of extractive institutions which is relevant for long-term economic development has to do with property rights. In order to create obedient subjects who will take part in the imperial extractivist plans, many empires re-defined property rights completely or partially. In other words, some empires might have altered the ability of locals to access, manage, and/or alienate property, which are crucial elements for property rights, as identified by Schlager and Ostrom (1992). Property rights are important, as they change the incentives of individuals to invest their labor; in situations where there is limited ability to reap the fruit of one's own labor, there is little incentive to continue to invest, which results in lower levels of income in the long run (Acemoğlu et al., 2001). Silver extraction in Latin America is one case with restrictions on the ability of landowners to manage and alienate property. The Spanish colonists who were allocated lands in the New World had restrictions on how large their properties could get. An extreme case of removal of property rights is that of the military colony in Croatia, whereby all the landowners were expropriated. That land was subsequently given to individual family clans who would control the land under communal property rights for as long as they could support one soldier to defend the border.

The third component is the use of violence. There is no denying that all imperial projects entailed coercion through the simple act of imposing the empire's rule over another political entity. Yet, some empires went further in how extreme such violence was in their extractivist pursuits. Violence is one factor that is known to affect the developmental trajectory of the territory exposed to it. This is through the constant exposure to fear and social stress, which in turn affects the formation of social capital and the overall quality of institutions (Nunn and Wantchekon, 2011). Lowes and Montero (2021) explore how historical exposure to violence leads to more community cooperation in the case of historical forced labor in Belgian Congo. This, however, was still not enough to foster development because of the authoritarian local power structures which have been in place since colonial times (Lowes and Montero, 2021; Mamdani, 1996). In the case of slavery, historical violence led to less trust in community members because the latter were the ones who facilitated other members being sold into slavery (Nunn and Wantchekon, 2011).

All three elements, investment, removal of property rights, and exposure to violence, are part of the "historical treatment" that one should watch out for to investigate the root causes of long-term positive or negative outcomes. In order to trace out the effects of these elements, two additional conditions need to be met: *longevity* and *consistency* of the historical exposure. In other words, in order for a "treatment" to have long-term repercussions, it is important for it to have lasted for a long time and for it not to be mixed with periods where different treatments might have been applied. For example, a system of forced labor is much more likely to have repercussions in the long run if people were exposed to it for centuries as opposed to a decade. Similarly, in order to study long-term effects, it is also important that treatment is internally consistent. In other words, the treatment was not at any point interrupted or combined with other treatments.

It is equally relevant to evaluate what happens to the territory exposed to such historical institutions after the treatment is no longer applied or understanding the so-called "mechanisms of transmission." Simpser *et al.* (2018) discuss the distinction between path-dependent socio-economic processes, determined by some "critical junctures," and long-term individual behaviors. The first ones are "conjunctural causal processes," while the second category focuses on "micro-level persistent cognitions" (Simpser *et al.*, 2018, p. 421). Each one of these informed two different analytical traditions in social sciences that Simpser *et al.*

(2018) label as the Comparative Historical Analysis and the Modern Political Economy approaches respectively. For example, within the first tradition, Mahoney (2010) explores how the profit-focused aspirations of the Spanish Empire led to attempts to colonize regions which already had labor coercive systems in place. Given the hierarchical structures embedded within these systems, this in turn had a negative effect on development. By contrast, places which did not have indigenous labor already available ended up adopting more liberal economic principles in the eighteenth century which reversed their fortunes (Mahoney, 2010). Within the Modern Political Economy approach, Lowes and Montero (2021) explain how the historical forced labor for the extraction of rubber empowered some local elites who developed local power structures and contributed to under-development. In addition, historical violence helped solidify mutual insurance systems, helping locals cope with daily subsistence, which in turn led to greater inter-personal trust and pro-social attitudes.

In this book, I take a more unifying approach in exploring both possibilities: the specific experience with one extractive institution might have brought about both socio-economic processes and cognitions which might have been transmitted over time. Both of these could be visible in the short and long run. Given the experience of the Habsburg Empire with an institution which lasted more than three hundred years consistently and the rich availability of both quantitative and qualitative material, the case represents an excellent opportunity to investigate the transmission of both processes and cognitions in the long run. The empirical results indicate the persistence of under-provision of public goods over time, persistence of socio-economic aspects related to property rights which have to do with communal properties and lack of land inequality, and persistence of attitudes and norms. I test the extent to which different parts of the historical treatment might be correlated with specific norms. Empirical results on norms described in Chapter 6 indicate that having experienced communal properties in the past is associated with stronger family attachment, more distrust of outsiders, and lower willingness to take risks. Having experienced a highly extractive regime in the past is associated with lower involvement in politics including a lower likelihood of participating in demonstrations and a lower likelihood of signing petitions. Finally, cohort analyses indicate a waning effect, with cohorts who were born closer to the historical treatment having stronger feelings. The effect about lower political participation provides clues about the mechanism of transmission for under-provision of public goods: while historically, under-provision of public goods might have been a top-down process whereby the government would intentionally discriminate against borderland dwellers, after the abrogation of the military colony this turned into a bottom-up process whereby descendants of the borderland dwellers would fail to coordinate politically to signal to the government that they needed more provision of public goods. These effects are robust and cannot be explained by (1) temporal intermediary factors such as Word War II, communist collectivization and repression, and Yugoslav wars; (2) structural treatment factors (i.e. the extent to which the border as a physical space explaining the outcomes); or (3) alternative mechanisms including ethno-religious fractionalization and involvement in military affairs.

Why the Habsburg Military Colony?

The Habsburg military frontier is a well-known case within local historiographical literature, but it has remained largely unknown to Western audiences. Despite focusing on this particular example and bringing to light further historical evidence in a coherent framework, I also contribute to the more general question of where political institutions come from, how they develop, and how they get to impact the present. Therefore, I am both careful, on the one hand, with estimating causal effects and tracing them through time within the context of the Habsburg military frontier, and on the other hand, with making relevant analogies with other imperial spaces to gain more leverage on external validity. Therefore, the book offers both an in-depth analysis of center–periphery relations within the Habsburg Empire and more general insights about governance, delegation of power, and institutional legacies.

An important criterion for selecting the case was availability of both historical and modern data. The Croatian military colony was created in 1553 and it was abolished in 1881. A variety of primary and secondary sources exist to this day documenting its inner workings. In Chapter 3, I list some of the most representative primary and secondary works in Serbo-Croatian, German, English, or French. For the quantitative analyses, I also used a variety of censuses in German, Hungarian, and Serbo-Croatian. Most of these documents cover the Croatian part of the military frontier. This is indeed the oldest.

Additional sections were created in what is today Serbia after 1718 and Romania after 1760. Both of them lasted until around 1860, while the Croatian section lasted until 1881. The Croatian one therefore features one important characteristic which makes the study of its effects more likely to yield results – longevity of the "historical treatment." Additionally, both the Serbian and the Romanian sections of the border contained mixed civilian–military communities, which means that the historical treatment is not consistent: any results from an analysis of the Serbian and Romanian sections could be the effect of potential quirks of the civilian administration or the results could be attenuated or exacerbated because of the mixing between the military and the civilian communities. Despite the problems of longevity and consistency, I offer cursory descriptions of the circumstances under which the other two sections of the border were created, developed, and ended in Chapter 3.

The Croatian section of the border also contains additional features which make it appropriate for a quantitative analysis aimed at evaluating the causal effects of military colonialism. One of the crucial assumptions behind the regression discontinuity methodology which I describe at length in Chapter 4 is that all factors vary smoothly at the border apart from the treatment. This assumption is necessary in order for the observations across the Habsburg civilian side to be appropriate counterfactuals for the districts in the military region. I perform a variety of statistical tests to evaluate the plausibility of this assumption including examining differences in geographic features such as elevation, slope, annual precipitation, and temperature, suitability of land for particular crops, and length and density of rivers. Unlike the Serbian and Romanian sections of the border, these proved to be continuous in the Croatian one, which adds further credibility to the statistical results obtained using both historical and modern data. I include these statistical tests in Appendix A.

The institution under scrutiny in this book cannot be understood in isolation, but rather always in reference to the Habsburg civilian area. In other words, when statements are made in the empirical chapters that the military colony had lower road density, that people had more equal access to land, or that more violence was exerted onto the inhabitants, the point of comparison is always the civilian area. While historians of the Habsburg Empire such as Taylor (1948) or Judson (2016) have been very good at depicting the Habsburg Empire as very diverse, linguistically, ethnically, and confessionally, very few scholars have investigated the institutional diversity of the empire, indirectly introducing distortions into what constitutes "state space." In other words, the Habsburg state has been conveyed as institutionally homogenous. This is why the rigorous survey of the historiographical sources together with the quantitative analyses based on historical data that I conduct in this project shed light on the diversity of the institutional space within the empire.

Historical Parallels

An important question is that of the applicability of the insights from this book to other cases, or external validity: what do we learn from the Habsburg case which can be applied to other cases? First, there are multiple other military colonies throughout history. In fact, the notion of the "farmer-soldier" is an idea which is almost as old as the state. Historical records about farmer-soldiers date back to the third century BC and continue well into the twentieth century. Military colonists were typically local landless peasants, who were given land in exchange for military service. They were known for example in the Roman Empire as *limitanei* under Alexander Severus in the third century (Isaac, 1988). They were looked down upon by the professional troops who were paid regularly and were much better equipped. Under Diocletian and Constantine in the fourth century, the position of limitanei together with the farmsteads that pertained to them became hereditary. The *akritai* in the Byzantine Empire from the ninth until the eleventh century were another example of military colonists (Bartusis, 1997). They were the army units guarding the empire's eastern border and were recruited from Armenians and other native Byzantine populations. They acted as raiders, scouts, and border guards in the perennial border warfare between Byzantium and its eastern neighbors. In Han China from 202 BC to 220 AD, armies in the provinces and frontiers were often professional or semi-professional military colonists. Their main activity was the defense of the empire. They were placed in watchtowers, signaling information along the lines and "resisting intruders with bow and arrow, spear and shield" (Loewe, 1986, p. 481). Groups of conscripts were also assigned to work in farms to supply forces locally. In Transylvania, starting in the twelfth and thirteenth centuries, the *Szeklers* were used as frontier guards for the Kingdom of Hungary until the eighteenth century during the Habsburg Empire (McNeill, 1964). They were exempt from taxes and any kind of services in exchange for protecting the border. During peacetime, they simply supervised the border and, when necessary, they would block passages. Thus, they prevented the enemy's offensives in times of war by giving time to the hinterland to get the professional army ready. The *Cossacks* in Russia and Ukraine between the seventeenth and nineteenth centuries were another group similar to the military colonists in the Habsburg Empire. They were ethnically mixed, having settled on the southern Caucasian and Siberian borders of Russia (left bank Ukraine, north Caucasus, next to river Ural and throughout Siberia). The communities were economically self-sufficient with roughly equal number of soldiers and peasants. During peacetime, they would be involved in agriculture, trade, or industry, while in times of war, only peasants would continue such activities and care for dependents (Hartley, 2008, p. 191). They were used to protect Russia against the Tatars and Ottomans in the south, against Chechens in the north Caucasus, and against Siberian tribes in the east (Hartley, 2008, p. 19). In Chapter 7, I provide detailed descriptions of the military colonies in the Russian Empire.

Another question is how applicable are the insights in this project beyond the narrow institution of military colonialism and could they be applied to cases beyond Europe. As already mentioned, the theoretical framework proposed in this book applies to extractive institutions more generally including forced extraction of minerals, crops, or labor. Whether it is extraction of minerals or just labor force, what matters is the mode in which extraction operates. Therefore, the conceptualization of extractive institutions is more capacious than the one proposed by Acemoğlu and Robinson (2012, p. 76), according to whom such institutions "are designed to extract incomes and wealth from one subset of society to benefit a different subset." The conceptualization which I adopt in this book is closer to what Mamdani (1996) labels as "compulsions." Empires could exert different kinds of compulsions onto locals including "forced labor, forced crops, forced sales, forced contributions, and forced removals" (Mamdani, 1996, p. 23). It is also close to the process of extraction described by Boone (2014, p. 44), who contends that empires "extracted revenue, resources, and labor." What military colonialism and mineral or crop extraction have in common is the notion of recruitment of human resources. In order for the imperial authorities to extract silver, harvest rubber, defend the border, or build local roads, they need local human resources. The recruitment of local labor forces is what makes the extraction of minerals or construction of local infrastructure similar to defending the border. What makes them different is the project in which locals are involved.

When it comes to the first factor pertaining to the theoretical framework – imperial investment – there are some cases in which imperial authorities contributed to the construction of roads and transportation infrastructure. These in turn had an effect on reducing trade costs and removing inter-regional price gaps (Booth and Deng, 2017; Donaldson, 2018). Cases of underinvestment are much more common throughout history but are rarely reported by scholars due to survival bias.[6] In other words, scholars never or rarely discuss that imperial powers could ignore certain areas when it came to investment, while they actively invested in others. Typical examples of underinvestment are minerals and crops that did not necessitate extensive processing. Some well-documented examples are the extraction of silver from Latin America by the Spaniards (Brading and Cross, 1972; Dell, 2010) or the extraction of rubber from Belgian Congo (Hochschild, 1999). For changes in property rights regimes, the empirical social science literature provides

---

[6] Survival bias is a type of selection bias concentrating on things that made it past some selection process and overlooking those that did not, typically because of their lack of visibility.

abundant examples. For example, Dell (2010) explains how the Spanish imperial authorities applied caps on the maximum size of the property of landowners. Rothenberg (1966) also explains how landowners were completely eliminated in Croatia to make way for the construction of the military colonies. Finally, there are many studies about the effects of colonialism as a result of exposure to violence which conditioned locals' attitudes toward the perpetrators (Nunn and Wantchekon, 2011) and toward each other (Lowes and Montero, 2021; Nunn and Wantchekon, 2011), which in turn had repercussions for long-term development. Similarly, "lack of" violence is not reported due to survival bias, but one could hypothesize why not applying violence is better than applying violence for long-term development.

The applicability of the theoretical framework in this book beyond Europe is further justifiable given that the institution of military colonialism was in fact adopted by France in the early nineteenth century and applied to many of its colonies overseas including Algeria, Senegal, and Madagascar. The outright copying of the Habsburg model by the French also alleviates to some extent the additional concern that comparisons between sea-based and land-based empires are not warranted because political hierarchies between the *center* and *periphery* within sea-based empires might have been much stronger, often based on race (Kohli, 2020; Nedervene Pieterse, 1989; Rex, 2007). As some of the research in economic history indicates (Ogilvie and Carus, 2014), race is only one of the many characteristics which might create power asymmetries. Other characteristics which could create power asymmetries are gender, religion, parentage, social stratum, group membership, or possession of specific socio-political privileges. Therefore, political hierarchies existed in French Algeria as they did in the Habsburg military frontier. Austrian and French generals were at the top of the pyramid in the hierarchy of power while the indigenous populations in the Habsburg periphery (what is today part of Croatia, Serbia, and Romania) and the local Kabyle population in Algeria were at the bottom. Imperial subjectivities were created in highly analogous ways based on ethnic, religious, linguistic, and racial grounds which were meant to both solidify the political distance between the capital and the periphery and create a coherent imperial project at the same time. In Chapter 7, I describe some of the narratives that were circulating among the higher echelons of the French political and military bureaucracy in the nineteenth century, and I cite statements made in the French Chamber of Deputies in 1840 which stipulate the intention to adopt the Austrian or Russian military colonial models in the newly conquered territories in French Algeria.

Organization of the Book

The book is organized into eight chapters. Chapter 2 goes into detail about the notion of extractive institutions and proposes the theoretical framework that was briefly summarized in this chapter. This helps explain a conundrum in the literature according to which extractive institutions are sometimes beneficial and sometimes detrimental for economic development. I contend that the persistent effect of extractive colonial institutions depended on the extent of imperial infrastructural investment, the treatment of property rights, and the use of violence. The worst scenarios for long-run development demonstrate little public investment, the removal or weakening of individual property rights, and high levels of coercion through violence. In the second part of this chapter, I discuss the role of elites in the creation and perpetuation of such institutions. I argue that colonial subjects who had been deprived of public goods (because of under-investment from the center), had not enjoyed individual property rights for centuries, and had been exposed to imperial violence were likely to become alienated from the state. Such alienation persists over generations, outliving the formal institutions that created it.

Chapter 3 describes the historical context of the empirical investigations developed in the subsequent chapters. It discusses the emergence, development, and the end of military colonialism in the southern borderlands of the Habsburg Empire. The military frontier was a cost-effective institution to protect both the Habsburg state and Christian Europe against the expansion of the Ottoman Empire. After 1463, the Habsburg regions of Carniola, Carinthia, and Styria were subject to yearly Ottoman attacks with the local estates being hardest hit (Rothenberg, 1960a). The chapter outlines the main political tensions between the Habsburg emperors, local elites, and peasant communities that emerged in the early stages of the adoption of military colonialism through a rich documentation of historical conditions. Some of these tensions can be traced back to the extended negotiations between Ferdinand I (1503–1564) and the local landed estates, who became partially financially responsible for the maintenance of the military area (Fine, 2009). The people inhabiting the newly created colonies were freed from serfdom and given land in the form of communal properties in exchange for military service (Boppe, 1900). The chapter illustrates how military colonialism evolved over time (Koroknai, 1974; Völkl and Ernst, 1982; Wessely, 1973) and describes the types of policies that the imperial authorities adopted to ensure the longevity of this institution in different regional contexts.

Chapter 4 presents evidence for the key institutional properties of military colonialism that are evident in this historical context. The two striking socio-economic insights that emerge from the data reported in the censuses of Imperial Hungary before World War I are that lack of land inequality and communal property rights remained much more prevalent in the borderlands even decades after the abrogation of the military colony. The absence of large consolidated land holdings and of a landless rural working class, which were present in the rest of Hungary and Croatia, held back the modernization of agriculture and the growth of farm productivity, as well as the spread of manufacturing. Similarly, historical and modern data on access to public goods suggest that the asymmetry between regions formerly under civilian and military administrations persisted over time to the present day. These results are not attributable to (1) temporal intermediary treatment factors that could have affected the treatment and the control group differentially, (2) structural treatment factors that could have influenced the treatment group simply by being located in a border area, and (3) alternative mechanisms by which military colonialism affected the way the state behaved in the former military colony.

Chapter 5 adds a new empirical dimension to the quantitative findings on the historical persistence of under-development and under-provision of public goods reported in Chapter 4. The military family clan was the key demographic unit of the military colony and it defined its relationship to the imperial state. A certain level of collaboration and delegation of power to local chiefs is a well-known colonial practice, especially in the context of Sub-Saharan Africa (Lowes and Montero, 2021; Mamdani, 1996). Such forms of control were not alien to land empires in Eurasia. By collaborating with local clan heads in the military frontier, the Habsburg state achieved increased social control with modest resources, blurring the line between the local rules of social organization and the formal rules of the state. Family clans were highly effective in recruiting and managing men for defending the border. Nevertheless, exposure to the highly rigid hierarchical structures within family clans based on sex and age also entailed the development and persistence of specific norms and attitudes. I provide examples of norms conditioned by family clans using historical anthropological accounts. I explain how belonging to military family clans molded clan members' attitudes toward inner and outer groups in a way that prevented them from overcoming collective action problems. Specifically, being forced to live in family clans for over three centuries prevented people from liaising with others beyond their immediate family in a way that would allow them to be more engaged citizens and demand the state provide public goods.

Chapter 6 tests formally the legacies of military colonialism on attitudes and norms. Historical qualitative accounts suggest that centuries of restrictions on personal freedom, political rights, and economic opportunities alienated people from state institutions. Given the size of family clans, there were few opportunities for inter-clan interactions, which would have fostered horizontal solidarity in the form of reciprocity, cooperation, and equality. The longer existence of family clans in the former military colony made it very hard for the state to win the loyalty of the public, which in turn endogenously strengthened family networks and distanced them from the central state. Modern-day surveys indicate that people living in the former colony are more attached to their family, trust outsiders less, are less politically engaged, and have views that reflect stereotypical gender roles.

Chapter 7 discusses the scope conditions of the theory proposed in Chapter 2. It describes the specific characteristics of the Habsburg military frontier that make it a unique case, but also the lessons to be learned which are applicable to other historical cases. To illustrate the ways in which other states managed their peripheries, I examine the contemporaneous case of the Russian colonies which were created to defend the Russian empire against attacks by Poland-Lithuania and the Ottoman empires (Khodarkovsky, 2002). The oldest colonies are the Cossacks, who lived in their self-governing lands (Pipes, 1950; Romaniello, 2012). They had well-defined rights and duties and were known for their loyalty to the tsar and their brutality in battle. They continued to be part of the Russian army until 1917. Additional colonies with an administration very similar to the Habsburgs were created in the nineteenth century under Alexander I. The Habsburgs and the Russians constituted a model that the French Empire tried to emulate in its territories in Africa in the nineteenth century (Émerit, 1959; Rothenberg, 1966). Similar to the European colonies, the French also forced military colonists to live in designated areas, recruited additional indigenous forces, and created specific laws defining their obligations, their property, and the types of activities they could be involved in. The French military colonies consisted of both French and indigenous people and represented the main way of ensuring the security of their civilian settlements.

The final chapter concludes the book with a discussion of the theory's significance for broader scholarly and policy implications that result from the central argument. Uneven access to public goods throughout a state's territory can be reflective of historical exposure to institutions that alienated people from central state authority. Importantly, the argument and evidence presented in this book suggest that extractive institutions can affect modern access to public goods through both institutions and attitudes that get transmitted over generations. It also raises the point that while military colonialism is yet another example of the deleterious consequences of extractive institutions for development, it shows that what matters are the specific modes of operation of colonial extraction, including violence and the removal of private property, as well as under-investment in public infrastructure and under-provision of public goods.

2 Imperialism and Extractive Institutions: A Theoretical Framework

How do historical institutions affect long-term development? What explains the fact that sometimes such institutions have a positive effect on development, while at other times they do not? The theoretical framework proposed in this book aims to contribute to debates about the effects of imperial institutions on economic development. Empirically, it provides an in-depth analysis of one type of extractive institution – military colonialism – which provides further insights about how extractivism works and its long-term effects.

The notion of "extractive institutions" attracted extensive attention in literatures in social sciences and history to explain persistent economic underdevelopment, but without sufficient focus on the symbiotic relationship between the "colonizer" and the "colonized" and on what happens after the withdrawal of the "colonizer." Closer scrutiny over the workings of imperial institutions, including the utilization of direct and indirect rule (Gerring *et al.*, 2011), together with local population responses is crucial in order to better understand persistence. More generally, the study contributes to debates in political science on sovereignty, citizenship, and global justice.

The argument proceeds as follows: I first present the state of the literature on extractive institutions and economic development. I then propose three dimensions of extractive institutions that are crucial for understanding their impact on long-term economic development. The effect of extractive institutions depends on the imperial infrastructural investment, removal of property rights, and use of violence. The worst situations for development are the ones with little imperial investment, high transformation of local society where secure individual property rights are removed, and high coercion in the form of violence is exerted on the locals. The second part of this chapter examines the notion of indirect rule, which was aimed at extracting military labor, and the role of elites in the creation and perpetuation of such institutions. I conjecture that people who have been deprived of public goods (through under-investment from the center), have not enjoyed individual property rights for centuries, and have been exposed to imperial violence are likely to become alienated from the central state. Such alienation is likely to persist over generations, outliving the institutions that created it. Thus, I contend that in order to ascertain long-term legacies of such institutions, one also has to investigate grassroots norms, attitudes, and preferences that could be transmitted over generations through local elites.

The project makes three contributions. First, it solves a conundrum present in the literature: sometimes extractive institutions have negative economic consequences (Acemoğlu *et al.*, 2001, 2012; Dell, 2010; Guardado, 2018; Lowes and Montero, 2021; Nunn and Wantchekon, 2011) and sometimes they do not, or in fact are associated with positive economic outcomes (Dell and Olken, 2020; Kohli, 2004; Mattingly, 2017). As already mentioned, the answer has to do with the three-dimensional nature of extractive institutions, which has received little attention in the literature. Second, the project explores a new institution as an example of imperial extractivism which was widely used in human history – military colonialism, whose role was to ensure the state's territorial defense. Such an institution is an illustration of how the state can use human resources to achieve its goals, how it creates particular forms of subjectivity, and how such subjectivities create norms that transmit over generations. By focusing on one type of extractive institution in one particular place, the goal is to provide an account with high internal validity, establishing a reliable cause-and-effect relationship between a "treatment" (exposure to the institutions of military colonialism) and an outcome (historical and modern access to public goods and norms), while eliminating alternative explanations. The more specific historical goal is also to provide a well-rounded image of Habsburg military colonialism that does justice to the wealth of historical narratives and quantitative historical sources.

This study also emphasizes the importance of disaggregating the state, which is relevant for quantitative scholarship examining legacies of historical states and which assumes that states are monolithical entities with a homogeneous effect throughout their territory (Becker *et al.*, 2016; Dell *et al.*, 2018; Lee and Schultz, 2012). Borders, as implied by this research tradition, are understood as having the sole purpose of demarcating territories. In this project, I reconcile such views with perspectives from Migdal (1988), Scott (2010), and Mukhopadyay (2014) by exploring the forces that govern spaces that are far away from the capital and how such forces leave an imprint on people's attitudes and norms. Borders are distinct territories with separate political institutions that affect the provision of public goods and economic development long after the dissolution of the historical states that they were supposed to demarcate. They are more than thin lines that appear on the map delimiting two sovereign entities. They are in fact wide spaces, "projecting surveillance far from the demarcating line in both directions and creating thick webs of infrastructure and law-enforcement that extend many miles inland" (Longo, 2018, p. 2).

Finally, this chapter also problematizes the notion that colonial dynamics can only take place between a European sea-based empire and its colonies as is implied by the extensive social science literature. In fact, as this book shows, processes of rent-extraction and exploitation happened within Europe and their effects can be seen today. The imperial subject exposed to extractive institutions does not always have to "look" different from the people creating and using such institutions. The imperial authorities can create political differences among the imperial subjects by institutionalizing certain categories of citizens in a way that fosters new hierarchies of power and subjectivity (Ogilvie and Carus, 2014). As such, the book also contextualizes the institution of military colonialism within the broader practices of colonialism and compares to broader European contemporaneous practices such as serfdom.

Outcome(s) of Interest

I focus on a narrow aspect of development which is dictated by historical data availability. Overall, the data used in this study has to do with access to public goods, both historical and modern, and ranges from access to public roads, schools, and hospitals to access to water (in modern times). Nevertheless, scholars such as Sen (1999) propose a much broader conceptualization of development which he labels as "development as freedom," therefore defining development as the capacity of individuals to pursue their well-being. From this point of view, law and order together with education, democracy, health care, and productive economic opportunities all promote development. Therefore, I acknowledge that development and access to public goods are very general, capacious, and abstract terms. Access to public roads, schools, hospitals, and water are operational definitions for public goods which Ostrom and Ostrom (1977) would regard as meant for joint use where exclusion is feasible (e.g. toll roads, access to water) and potentially infeasible (e.g. hospitals and schools).

2.1   The Literature on Extractive Institutions

A variety of works address the question of long-term effects of extractive institutions. Following the framework proposed by Simpser *et al.* (2018), I divide them into two: the Comparative Historical Analysis (CHA) and the Modern Political Economy (MPE) literatures. The former is typically qualitative and focuses on "critical junctures" and path-dependent processes (Collier and Collier, 1991), while the latter concentrates on well-identified treatments, accounting for long-term individual behaviors, following the analytical framework proposed by

North (1990). I summarize first some of the key contributors to these research paradigms, followed by an outline of their shortcomings and proposed solutions.

The legacy of extractive institutions has been tangentially addressed in the CHA tradition. For example, James Mahoney examines how "mercantilist" and profit-focused ambitions of the Spanish Empire in the sixteenth century led to the targeting of regions where the Spanish could seize "state-led surplus extraction networks and employ already-developed coercive labor systems for the purpose of rapid *resource extraction*" (emphasis added) (Mahoney, 2010, p. 26). The structures that emerged from such actions were hierarchical and monopolistic, which in turn had a negative impact on development. By contrast, places in Latin America that did not have resources and readily available indigenous labor ended up reversing their fortunes after the eighteenth century, where liberalism became a more dominant doctrine both in Spain and Europe.

Extractive institutions are also present in accounts by Matthew Lange, Mahmood Mamdani, and Atul Kohli, who discuss the effect of British and Japanese colonialism, respectively. According to Lange (2009), there were occasional episodes in which the British used "development funds" in areas with mineral mining and they paid local chiefs to enforce "mining regulation through the customary courts" (Lange, 2009, p. 102). British direct rule had a positive effect for development in places like Singapore and Mauritius. This is because of a more extensive bureaucracy consisting of formalization of state duties, supervision of state agents, and recordkeeping. Similarly, direct rule also led to greater state infrastructural power, consisting of physically present legal-administrative institutions and greater state inclusiveness, which in turn, solidified the ties between the state and diverse societal communities. The three factors – bureaucratization, infrastructural power, and state inclusiveness – all contributed to greater subsequent development (Lange, 2009).

By contrast, indirect rule led to the empowerment of local despots or predatory "decentralized despotism" (Mamdani, 1996), with small and ineffective legal-adminstrative systems to collect taxes, register property, and enforce property rights. Local despots played a key role in entrenching extractive institutions, including "forced labor, forced crops, forced sales, forced contributions, and forced removals" (Mamdani, 1996, p. 23). Indirect rule, therefore, had a negative effect for development in places like Sierra Leone or Nigeria.

Extractive institutions are also an important component in the framework proposed by Catherine Boone distinguishing between neocustomary and statist regimes, which apply to land tenure questions in Africa. Colonizers opted for neocustomary regimes, as a solution to the problem of political control, while the colonizers "extracted revenue, resources, and labor" (Boone, 2014, p. 44). At the same time, colonizers chose a statist regime where they wanted to exploit the land themselves (for urban development, installations, or settlement), hence proceeding to allocate land access to users directly. This in turn led to postcolonial violence in places like Kenya, Zimbabwe, or Rwanda.

Kohli (2004) investigates the effect of Japanese direct rule in Korea, which aimed to achieve political control and resource extraction (Kohli, 2004, p. 67). Extractive institutions in Japanese Korea had a positive effect for long-term development (increased literacy and agricultural productivity), according to Kohli (2004). Japanese intervention was characterized by a series of policies whose aim was to discipline the labor force and keep society in check for the purpose of supporting the Japanese war effort.[1] This was achieved by strengthening the police force and education, which was possible through the collaboration between state institutions and local authority structures: "[s]o armed, the police used the knowledge and influence of the local elites to mold the behavior of average citizens in such diverse matters as birth control, types of crops grown, count and movement of people, prevention of spread of diseases, mobilization of forced labor and . . . report[ing] on transgressions" (Kohli, 2004, p. 37).

Within the MPE tradition, a variety of quantitative works investigates long-term legacies of extractive institutions with similarly mixed results: some works show that extractive institutions have a positive effect for development, while others find a negative effect. The canonical work by Acemoğlu and colleagues indicates that extractive institutions were adopted in places with high European settler mortality to extract the local natural and human resources (Acemoğlu et al., 2001). Such extractive institutions in turn caused subsequent long-term underdevelopment.

Work by Melissa Dell, Sara Lowes, and Eduardo Montero further strengthen the idea that extractive institutions have negative long-term effects for development by focusing on mechanisms of transmission. Dell (2010) suggests that historical rent-extraction in the form of labor conscription for mining in Spanish Peru contributed to lower levels of inequality, which in turn affected growth. Similarly, Lowes and Montero (2021) indicate that forced labor for the extraction of rubber in Belgian Congo caused lower underdevelopment through the empowerment of

---

[1] Historians have also investigated the role of state intervention and economic policy as a result of war. Vonyo (2018) argues that these were crucial to explain the German growth miracle after 1945.

local elites, who were less likely to provide public goods. Finally, slavery in Africa contributed to lower interpersonal trust in the places of origin, due to low-scale violence such as trickery and kidnapping by local communities (Nunn and Wantchekon, 2011); its effect on economic development in the place of origin is not explored.

More recent contributions provide causally identified estimates for the positive long-term effects of rent-extraction. Dell and Olken (2020) examine the case of Dutch colonialism in Indonesia and find that the construction of Dutch factories between 1830 and 1870 is associated with better infrastructure and a more educated and richer populace in Java. Such findings echo similar qualitative results that capture legacies of Japanese colonialism in Korea and Taiwan (Kohli, 2004) or quantitative results that capture the positive effects of British investments in railroads to facilitate imperial extraction (Donaldson, 2018).

The problem with the CHA and MPE traditions are the mixed results about the effect of extractive institutions: sometimes extractive institutions are good and sometimes they are bad. Therefore, it is unclear why and under what conditions extractive institutions could affect development. I discuss in the next section the three-dimensional structure of extractive institutions that has to do with investment in local infrastructure, removal of property rights, and violence. The second problem is that both the CHA and the MPE traditions focus almost exclusively on the supply side, where the state plays a key role in providing public goods and economic development. While the focus on the state during the time when such extractive institutions are in place is justifiable, it is much less clear why the state should still be the focus when such institutions are no longer in place. Such research traditions focus much less on how the population at the bottom of the political hierarchy was transformed as a result of the imposition of imperial institutions and how the norms and attitudes that were created during the time when extractive institutions were in place could perpetuate over time. Therefore, within the theoretical framework, I focus on the mechanisms that link extractive institutions to the ability of civic society and local elites to be involved politically. More generally, the argument is based on an in-depth analysis of the personnel, agencies, and other resources of the state that allow the latter to penetrate regions far away from the capital, reshaping political and social landscapes. It also captures the conditions under which peripheral political forces are able and willing to cooperate with the central government and the symbiotic relationship that emerges.

Besides the CHA and the MPE traditions, this book also speaks to the literature on the legacies of the Habsburg Empire. Modern political economy scholars have examined its legacies, holistically focusing on how effective institutions within the Habsburg Empire persisted over time (Vogler, 2019), how they contributed to long-term trust in them (Becker *et al.*, 2016), or how being under the Habsburg Empire contributed to more subsequent support for conservative and religious parties (Grosfeld and Zhuravskaya, 2015). Economic historians have studied extensively the economic disparities within the Habsburg Empire (Good, 1984; Pollard, 1986), emphasizing substantial differences between the "core" in the northwest and the "periphery" in the southeast. Klein *et al.* (2017, p. 66) attribute such disparities to structural factors such as "resource endowments" and "access to both domestic and foreign markets," which contributed to increased levels of urbanization and accumulation of social capital. The second set of factors, which may not be completely independent from the former, are the political factors. The economic differences within the Habsburg Empire stem from the asymmetric role of feudalism, which was weakened much earlier in the northwest than in the southeast. Feudal lords in the northwest were replaced by an entrepreneurial and manufacturing class (Good, 1984; Klein *et al.*, 2017), while in the southeast, they continued to exist, which contributed to the strengthening of agriculture and economic stagnation (Schulze, 2007). I contribute to such research about the regional economic disparities within the Habsburg Empire by focusing on the long-term effects of extractive institutions in the southeastern areas of the Empire.

2.2 The Argument: Empire, Extraction, and Society

I define extractive institutions as the transfer of economically valuable resources from indigenous groups to the imperial center. As such, they remove the majority of the population from participating in political and economic affairs (Acemoğlu and Robinson, 2012) and pull materials and opportunities from those under them. In other words, extraction refers both to an *outcome* and a *process* that entails the delivery of inadequate compensation to the locals. I argue that in order to understand long-term imperial legacies, one has to examine the interaction between the polices enacted by the imperial center, local policy practices, and indigenous responses. Examples of rent-extractive institutions include land alienation, corvée labor, excessive taxation, forced army service, and so on. Despite their differences, there are three criteria based on which the existence of a legacy can be evaluated. The three criteria can be thought of as ways or modus operandi of extraction. For example, in order to extract minerals or to ensure state security, the extractive state might have invested in local infrastructure (such as roads and railroads) to transport minerals quicker; similarly, the extractive state might redefine new property rights arrangements which might favor certain individuals over others in order to ensure obedience or to create an incentive structure so that locals or agents of the extractive state work to accomplish the goals of the extractive state; finally, the extractive state might also utilize violence against locals to further incentivize them to work in order to accomplish the extractive goals of the state.

Dimensions of Extractive Institutions

Intensity of imperial infrastructural investment, one of the three elements of extractive institutions, could set a territory exposed to it on a different economic trajectory. For example, investing in roads and factories, despite being built to facilitate extraction,[2] could decrease trade costs and interregional price gaps, and increase real income levels in the territory where the investment is made (Booth and Deng, 2017; Dell and Olken, 2020; Donaldson, 2018; Frankema and Buelens, 2013; Juif and Frankema, 2018; Van Waijenburg, 2018), in addition to bringing high return on investment to the colonial power (Buelens and Frankema, 2016; Buelens and Marysse, 2009). Investment in infrastructure projects was believed to have a considerable revenue potential, primarily in its ability to facilitate export production (Gardner, 2012). This was the case in India between 1853 and 1930, where the British invested in a vast network of railroads to facilitate the transportation of extracted resources such as coal, iron ore, cotton, and so on, to ports for the British to ship home to use in their factories. Before the construction of railroads, draft animals carried most of India's commodity trade on their backs, traveling no more than thirty km per day (Deloche, 1994; Donaldson, 2018). The construction of railroads reduced the costs associated with trade, diminished regional price differences, and contributed to higher income levels (Donaldson, 2018).

Another example is Dutch Indonesia between 1830 and 1870, where the Dutch invested heavily in large-scale sugar processing and transport infrastructure. The result of such investment was an improvement in the connection between sugar-producing regions and better market integration. In addition, Dutch investment resulted in increased access to electricity, more education for the locals, and higher household consumption (Bosma, 2007; Dell and Olken, 2020). Similar examples

---

[2] It is important to note that colonial investments can also happen outside of extractive goals, when the intent is to benefit the local population. Huillery (2009) for example finds that colonial investments in health, education, and infrastructure in West Africa had positive effects for long-run development. Similarly, colonial railroads affected the distribution and aggregate level of economic activity more generally in Africa (Jedwab and Moradi, 2016). Cagé and Rueda (2016) show that Christian missions lowered HIV prevalence where they made medical infrastructural investments and Gallego and Woodberry (2010) find that historical missionary activity in Africa had positive effects for education, but only in areas where Protestant and Catholic missions competed.

of colonial investments are the Japanese in Korea and Taiwan, who contributed to the development of transport infrastructure, productive activities, and education (Booth and Deng, 2017; Kohli, 2004). In the initial stages, this resulted in a high employment rate outside of agriculture and a high GDP, which translated into long-term development. All the economic progress, however, was made at the cost of high labor displacement and fatality as a result of poor working conditions (Kohli, 2004).

By contrast, if imperial authorities did not invest, that could have induced laggard economic trajectories or economic stagnation. This is the case of labor-intensive industries that did not require extensive processing such as the extraction of silver and mercury in Mexico and Peru under the Spanish between mid-1500s and early 1800s (Brading and Cross, 1972; Dell, 2010). The extraction of silver was done through a variety of methods throughout time. However, the method which yielded the largest amount of silver was through amalgamation with mercury (Brading and Cross, 1972). Overall, the extraction of silver required little processing infrastructure, hence little colonial investment. Locals who were conscripted to work were performing such procedures.[3]

Another example of colonial extraction with minimal investment is the extraction of rubber in the Congo Free State under the Belgians between 1880 and 1920. Collection of rubber was highly profitable because, apart from transportation costs, no cultivation, no fertilizers, and no capital investment on expensive equipment was necessary (Hochschild, 1999; Lowes and Montero, 2021). Rubber was historically obtained from coagulated tree sap, which could be extracted by slashing the vine with a knife while a container was placed under the vine to collect the sap (Hochschild, 1999, p. 161). Local labor was necessary for the collection of rubber. The colonial power simply recruited a number of local officials called *capitas* to organize local labor and to make sure that the rubber quotas were met. In addition, the areas where rubber was extracted were connected to rivers and therefore there was little need to invest in local infrastructure.

The partial or complete removal of property rights can affect long-run growth by removing the individual incentives to invest. At the most basic level, property rights define who can access, manage, and alienate property[4] (North, 1990; Schlager and Ostrom, 1992). Such rights are

---

[3] The labor system based on conscription was called *repartimiento* in Mexico and *mita* in Peru (Brading and Cross, 1972).

[4] More recent works also categorize property rights into security of ownership, security of use, and security of transfer (Ogilvie and Carus, 2014). In order for property rights to matter for development, all three have to be respected and they have to be generalized in the sense of being applied to all agents of the economy, not just a privileged subset.

at the intersection of the political, legal, and economic order (Abramson and Boix, 2019; Boone, 2014). Anyone who cannot exercise one or more of the three actions has incomplete or distortionary property rights, which translates into reduced incentives for individuals to invest their labor and to innovate. Property rights can provide incentives for assets to be allocated to their most productive uses because they motivate the transfer of assets to the people who value them most (Ogilvie and Carus, 2014). For example, secure property rights can contribute to more extensive agricultural activities, including more digging, ploughing, fertilizing, and weeding. These in turn have a positive effect on harvesting, threshing, butter-churning, and cheese-making (Caunce, 1997; Chambers, 1953; Ogilvie and Carus, 2014). These are only some examples of how more secure property rights translate into higher levels of income (Acemoğlu et al., 2001; Greif et al., 1994; North and Thomas, 1970, 1971, 1973). Property rights are insecure if there is expropriation risk, which means that individuals may fail to realize the fruits of their investments and efforts; for example, insecure property may raise the costs that individuals have to pay to defend their property, which renders their property unproductive (Besley and Ghatak, 2010). Similarly, property rights are insecure if there are no contracting institutions facilitating their secure transfer from one person to another (Ogilvie and Carus, 2014). Finally, property rights could also be distortionary if they are not private, by removing from the owners one of the following: ability to exclude and alienate their property (Schlager and Ostrom, 1992). Private property rights give individual owners incentives to use assets productively, to invest or increase their values, and to trade or lease them to others (Besley and Ghatak, 2010).

For example, in the case of silver mines in Peru that the Spanish used for 245 years (Brading and Cross, 1972), the imperial rulers restricted the size of the elite property in areas where mine workers were recruited from (called *mita*). This in turn precluded large landed elites from forming. According to Dell (2010), such restrictions prevented the emergence of agents who would have opposed the allocation of labor forces to the mines. These landed elites were Spanish colonists who were given pieces of land from which they could collect tribute and labor services. Over time, they could have turned into large landed elites had it not been for the Spanish policies restricting the size of their property. The absence of large landed elites turned over time into lower provision of public goods. It is probable that large landowners were benefiting economically from access to roads for which they were either lobbying the government or organizing local labor themselves (Dell, 2010, p. 1894). Following the categories proposed by Schlager and Ostrom (1992), preventing landlords from expanding and, more importantly, preventing others from selling their land (i.e. landowners would have likely been able to expand through the purchase of additional land) are examples of incomplete property rights, and a potential infringement on the rights to access and manage more property and on the right of others to alienate their land.

Similarly, in the Croatian military colony, which was in place for 332 years, the Habsburgs removed local landed elites precisely to ensure a constant supply of human capital for the defense of the border against intruders and for quelling internal dissent (Rothenberg, 1966).[5] The removal of landed elites had a dual purpose: on the one hand, it eliminated labor competition (working in agriculture for the landlord vs. working in the army for the Habsburg Empire to defend the border) and on the other, it provided incentives for the people at the bottom of the hierarchy to work for the Habsburg state (being a free peasant and working for the empire vs. being a serf and working for the landlord). The complete removal of landlords meant a complete infringement on all the types of rights outlined by Schlager and Ostrom (1992).

Finally, the use of violence to achieve the goals of the empire could also set the territory that is exposed to rent-extraction on a different developmental trajectory. Labor coercion has been a very common practice associated with colonial rule (Acemoğlu et al., 2001; Lowes and Montero, 2021; Van Waijenburg, 2018), whereby colonial states were able to extract additional income from the colonies. It existed in large parts of Asia, the Middle East, and the West Indies. Labor coercion can affect development in even more visible ways if it is violent.

Use of violence could set a territory on a different developmental trajectory through socializing individuals inhabiting those regions to fear and social stress.[6] If the source of stress is outside of their community, locals could develop an increased reliance on horizontal ties, community cooperation (Lowes and Montero, 2021), and disarticulation from the perpetrating state (Lupu and Peisakhin, 2017); if the source of stress is within their community, locals could avoid reliance on horizontal ties (Nunn and Wantchekon, 2011). In turn, such historical socialization could affect the formation of civic society, the empowerment of individuals to bring about change, and overall quality of institutions. Such

---

[5] As a result, the military colony has been an integral force of the empire, not only responsible for defending the southern borders but also being fully present in international wars (Perrot, 1869, p. 62).

[6] Note that the effects of physical violence have been extensively studied outside of rent-extractive imperialism. For example, some scholars find that violence fragments communities and damages social cohesion (Lupu and Peisakhin, 2017; Walter and Snyder, 1999), while others suggest that violence can force communities to overcome differences (Bauer et al., 2016; Bellows and Miguel, 2009; Gilligan et al., 2014).

empowerment could take the form of coordination to demand the local or central government for the provision of goods.

Historical violence, however, is difficult to trace. While violent perpetrators (the empires behind the infliction of violence) might have eliminated the episodes of violence from history on purpose to protect their own image (*false reports of nonviolence* or false negatives), they are likely to have come out subsequently either in the official sources of the successor states or in local written and oral histories of the colonized territories. At the same time, in some cases nationalist discourses, after the colonial rule ended, might have inspired the creation of narratives that portray past imperial governance as violent (*false reports of violence* or false positives). It is therefore difficult to adjudicate on the veracity of accounts of historical colonial violence. However, to exemplify such cases, I rely on more recent cases of colonialism due to more abundant historical evidence.

In the case of rubber extraction in the DRC under the Belgians, locals were exposed to *frequent* and *extreme* violence throughout the colonial period when they failed to meet their rubber quota, including imprisonment, torture, and killing[7] of villagers and their family members (Lowes and Montero, 2021). As a coping mechanism, individuals developed mutual insurance systems to help each other meet the demands of day-to-day subsistence, which overall contributed to greater interpersonal trust and prosocial attitudes. In principle, that should have had a positive effect on economic development had it not been for the despotic and incompetent village leaders (Lowes and Montero, 2021) who thwarted economic growth. In the case of slavery in Africa, locals were exposed to small-scale violence such as kidnapping and trickery, where people were sold into slavery in exchange for guns and iron weapons. To cope with the stress emerging from their own communities, people developed norms of mistrust, which were passed onto subsequent generations. In turn, such mistrust resulted in weaker institutions, which should be arguably associated with lower levels of development (Nunn and Wantchekon, 2011).

The collaboration between the local elites and the empire was crucial for the infliction of violence, given the limited administrative capacity of the colonial state. In addition, labor tribute systems had deep precolonial roots (Van Waijenburg, 2018, p. 48), which provided colonial governments with a rare opportunity to tap into pre-existing systems of surplus extraction (Lange, 2004; Mamdani, 1996). Similarly, placing the primary responsibility of labor recruitment in a local context meant that imperial officials were better able to exploit the nebulous distinction

---

[7] The violence in the DRC was carried out by private militias (Lowes and Montero, 2021).

between "free labor" and "slavery."[8] For example, in colonial Africa, local leaders would receive monetary incentives and political recognition for the recruitment of manpower; failure to do so would result in steep fines or even removal from power (Lange, 2009; Lange *et al.*, 2006; Van Waijenburg, 2018).

Episodes of small-scale violence are widespread throughout colonial history. Unlike the Belgian case, some violence might have been used, but it was not as *widespread* (how much of the local population it affected) and as systematic (how frequently it was used). While there may still be a possibility that historical accounts portrayed some rent-extractive episodes as less violent than they have been (false negatives), I rely on more recent cases of colonialism, following the logic that evidence from more recent history is more accurate (i.e. (1) many of the records are still intact; (2) if recent episodes of violence happened, they are more likely to still be present in collective memory; (3) definitions of what constitutes "violence" 150 years ago are closer to definitions of violence today than what constituted "violence" 500 years ago, for example). A well-documented example of "mild" rent-extraction is Dutch Indonesia (1830–1870). Both Dell and Olken (2020) and Elson (1994) contend that over the course of the rent-extractive colonial system, millions of Javanese worked in sugar processing and transport via both forced and free labor. There is no mentioning of imprisonment, torture, or systematic killing. This does not mean that they did not happen, but it is unlikely to have happened to the degree they did in Belgian Congo.

In a nutshell, I propose that the three most important components of rent-extraction that are discussed in the literature separately and that could affect development are imperial investment, removal of property rights, and violence. Empirically, the three dimensions may not be as clear-cut (i.e. historical examples suggest that the people exposed to violence also have their property removed from them). However, the three are distinct analytical concepts that provide good leverage to help unpack the effect of extractive institutions on economic development. They also help us understand why some literatures find a negative effect associated with extractive institutions, and others positive. The worst examples for development are places exposed to violence, removal of property, and little historical infrastructural investment. The best examples for development are the ones where the empire invested in local infrastructure and where locals were not exposed to violence or removal of property rights. Cases in-between that only have some elements of rent-extraction

---

[8] Slavery is considered the most extreme of "unfree labor" (Cooper, 1996; Hopkins, 1973), whereby individual workers are legally owned throughout their lives and may be bought or sold by owners, while never receiving any personal benefit from their labor. Less extreme forms of "unfree labor" would include short periods of unpaid labor.

will be somewhere on a negative–positive spectrum. Their effect will depend on what they are compared to. Ideally, to fully understand the effects of rent-extraction, one would develop a research design where neighboring regions that are very similar to one another on a variety of characteristics and that only differ in the exposure to one element of extractivism are compared to each other.

Table 2.1 summarizes these arguments. In order to illustrate how they matter, I turn to legacies of military rent-extraction in Croatia as a case displaying low intensity of imperial investment, high transformation of local society, and low use of coercion.[9]

The Role of Elites in Creating Institutions

In order to better explain the effect of extractive institutions, one has to understand how and why they came about. I therefore turn to the incentives of their creators and the incentives of those to whom they delegated power. In the end, the extraction of military labor was done through the co-optation of local power holders. A growing literature on the legacies of historical institutions explains that *elites* are important to understand institutional continuities. Specifically, what matters for the persistence of institutions is how elites form around them and how they reproduce over time (Robinson, 2012, p. 31). The logic is that those who hold power today determine the political institutions that they prefer, which cements their de jure power (Robinson, 2012, p. 34), creating institutional overhang.

Elites can be defined as "individuals who were highly placed in the distribution of wealth" (DiCaprio, 2012, p. 4), deriving their status from their relationship to property, whether physical or human capital. They enjoy a privileged status in society and exercise control over the organization of society, in addition to being "carriers of knowledge, capital, contacts, ideas, creativity and leadership" (Solimano and Avanzini, 2012, p. 53). All societies contain elites within them. Michels (1915, p. 1915) discusses that a "society cannot exist without a 'dominant' or 'political' class, and that the ruling class, while its elements are subject to partial renewal, nevertheless constitutes the only factor of sufficiently durable efficacy in the history of human development." The aim of the elite, according to Michels (1915, p. 1915), is to impose upon the rest of society a " 'legal order,' which is the outcome of the exigencies and of the exploitation of the mass... "

---

[9] Occasional killings or punishments in the form of impalement and death by hanging by the authorities were taking place in the military colony. Such forms of coercion were not as frequent and systematic as the killings of locals in the DRC under the Belgians for example. Their frequency in the DRC was compared to the Holocaust (Lowes and Montero, 2021). Therefore, I regard coercion as low in the military colony.

Table 2.1 *Components and intensity of extraction*

Component	High Intensity	Low Intensity
Imperial investment Examples	Construction of local infrastructure (e.g. roads, bridges, factories) Construction of sugar factories and roads in Dutch Indonesia (1830–1870) (Dell and Olken, 2020) Construction of bridges, railroads, factories in Japanese Indonesia to help Japanese war effort (1942–1945) (Shigheru, 1996)	Minimal on-site construction of infrastructure (e.g. construction of mineral processions plants, patrolling posts) Local mining infrastructure for extraction and processing of silver ore in Spanish Peru (1573–1818) (Brading and Cross, 1972; Dell, 2010) Military posts and fortresses by the Habsburgs in Croatia (1550–1881) (O'Reilly, 2006) Crop collection posts for the extraction of rubber by the Belgians in the DRC (1880–1920) (Frankema and Buelens, 2013; Lowes and Montero, 2021)
Removal of property rights Examples	Complete elimination of ability to access, manage, and alienate property Complete expropriation of landed elites (removal of ability to access, manage, and alienate property) in Habsburg Croatia (1550–1881)	Restrictions on the access, management, and/or ability to alienate property Removal of the ability of landed elites in Spanish Peru (1573–1818) to alienate (sell) their land (to prevent the emergence of large landed elites) (Brading and Cross, 1972; Dell, 2010)
Violence Examples	Widespread torture and killing Imprisonment, whipping and death of locals who failed to meet their rubber extraction quotas in the Belgian DRC (1880–1920) (Frankema and Buelens, 2013)	Limited torture and/or killing Indonesians working in sugar processing and transport – via both forced and free labor, under the Dutch (1830–1870). No mentioning of imprisonment, torture, or systematic killing.

Elites can have a positive or a negative effect for development depending on a mix of incentives and behavioral characteristics (DiCaprio, 2012). Their control over productive assets and institutions is what allows them to influence allocation of both resources and authority. Elites act in ways that are conducive to development when their own interests align with the interests of the masses. This means that they can choose political and economic institutions that are beneficial both to them and to the masses. For example, elites can opt for institutions that reduce income inequality or that increase employment when it is in their interest to do so. Alternatively, they can act in ways that are detrimental for economic development such as directing more resources toward favored and inefficient social groups.

More generally, however, the most important policy whereby elites can positively impact development is through the establishment of secure property rights (North, 1990; North and Thomas, 1973; Olson, 1965). This is a commitment mechanism that protects private property against expropriation and abuse. This means in turn that the integrity of economic contracts is guaranteed; investment in human and physical capital is expected to follow (Robinson, 2012). The absence of secure property rights means a less certain and fair environment for business activities.

The Role of Society in Perpetuating Institutions

The idea that elites are important for long-term growth outcomes is persuasive when the descendants of the same line of elites remain in power. This intuition has been well documented in Latin America (Dell, 2010; Paige, 1997; Robinson, 2012; Stone, 1990), where elite past actions solidify the persistence of elite families and identities. The persistence of the same line of elites is also documented in cases of indirect rule in Africa (Boone, 2014; Mamdani, 1996). It is less clear, however, what happens to development when new elites come to power along the lines described by Tawney (1941) and Waldner (1999), or in cases of direct rule in colonial Africa (Mamdani, 1996). Is it reasonable to assume that the preferences and behavior of the old elites align completely with the preferences of the new elites? While staying in power and maintaining their economic assets can be two preferences that make the old elites not that different from the new elites, more specific preferences such as insecurity of property rights or limiting access to education for the masses could be widely different among generations of elites, especially if the old and new elites are completely unrelated to one another.

Therefore, a more fruitful approach in order to understand continuity between the past and the present, in cases where the elite line was interrupted or where there has been regime change, is to investigate the social actors at the bottom of the imperial hierarchy. How do they change as a result of exposure to rent-extraction, how do they reach an equilibrium, how do they relate to the state authorities and to each other, and how does this relationship reproduce over time?

The agents at the bottom of this hierarchy are particularly important to examine, especially in view of the fact that they have been at the forefront of policy promotion activities conducted by the World Bank and other international developmental agencies since the 1990s in an attempt to return decision-making power to the people. Community-based projects, according to organizations such as the World Bank, can also result in good governance at the grassroots level by promoting decentralization and participation. The question remaining is how does society get to be involved and what is the effect of particular historical experiences in preventing people from participating. More specifically, how does historical exposure to insecure property rights, violence, or state discrimination (when it comes to the provision of public goods) affect nonelite preferences and behaviors and how do such preferences transmit over generations?

While not referring to any of the three specifically, Putnam *et al.* (1993, p. 7) provide a tentative answer to such a question by arguing that "the rules and the standard operating procedures that make up institutions [created by the elites] leave their imprint on political outcomes by structuring political behavior." As a result of exposure to specific historical institutions, people at the bottom of the hierarchy can develop attitudes and norms that prevent their political participation. Specifically, Putnam *et al.* (1993) argue that the institutions chosen by the elites can have an impact on grassroots participation in public affairs, horizontal relations of reciprocity, solidarity, and trust, and social structures and cooperation. These in turn affect the formation of social capital, which improves the efficiency of society by facilitating coordinated action (Putnam *et al.*, 1993, p. 167), which could in turn have an impact on the provision of public goods.

Networks of grassroots engagement which cover broad segments of society undergird collaboration at the community level. Both Putnam *et al.* (1993) and Granovetter (1973) argue that "strong" interpersonal ties like kinship and intimate friendship are less important than "weak" ties, such as acquaintances or shared membership in an association. The latter are relevant in supporting cooperation that crosses social cleavages, fostering wider cooperation within society, which will in turn improve the provision of public goods. Specifically, what matters for grassroots involvement is membership in horizontally ordered groups as opposed to hierarchical ones, which in turn affects practices of governance. The latter could form "weblike societies" competing with the state (Migdal, 1988) or collaborating with it in a "negotiated enterprise" (Mukhopadyay, 2014) through their structure and regularization. Grassroots engagement and norms of generalized reciprocity encourage social trust and they reduce incentives to defect.

In order to understand such preferences, one must first analyze historically the original events and conditions (Pierson, 2004; Tilly, 1984) but also the self-perpetuating processes that were triggered by these events. Mahoney (2000) calls these original events, together with their subsequent processes, path dependency. This consists of: (1) a critical juncture that initiates the causal process and (2) a series of mechanisms that help reinforce the process started during the critical juncture. Rubin (2017, p. 43) also explains path dependence as the situation in which "the initial impetus that triggers a series of events is far, far removed from the eventual outcome, and the initial *raison d'être* that sparked movement down a certain pathway." Imperial rent-extractive practices are path-dependent to the extent that they contain these two elements. An example of such initial conditions together with subsequent processes is Weber's (1905/1992) "Protestant Ethic and the Spirit of Capitalism." The Protestant Ethic is the initial condition that helped produce and reproduce capitalism (Weber, 1905/1992, pp. 181–182). This process was self-reinforcing and happened over a long period.

2.3   Theory Applied: The Military Colony in the Habsburg Empire

In this section, I discuss the notion of colonial extractive institutions within the context of the Habsburg military frontier, using the conceptual framework proposed in Section 2.2. The aim is to provide sufficient insights that patterns of colonialism and indirect rule had similar principles of governance both outside of Europe and also within Europe. Despite the narrow geographic focus, the case offers enough complexity and subtlety to allow the reader to rethink state–society relations and state formation. The narrow focus facilitates the understanding of the origins of military colonialism (the specific set of circumstances both in the center and in the periphery that led to the adoption of such institution), its evolution and de jure institutionalization, and finally, its consequences on the present. In Chapter 7, I provide explanations for how the practices of governance in the Habsburg Empire are applicable to other cases.

With the adoption of military colonialism, people in the imperial frontier became nonprofessional soldiers, "caught between two roles of 'free peasant' and lifetime soldier" (O'Reilly, 2006, p. 237). The military service, for example, was directly calculated by Vienna in 1700s to: 52

days annually on border watch, 49.5 days in regimental duty, 48 days on weapons training for a total of five months of military service. This was a total of 149 days or five months of military activities per year. The rest was spent in agriculture (O'Reilly, 2006, p. 238). As a result, inhabitants of the military frontier would always combine military and civilian responsibilities, contributing to the unity of the military border (Lesky, 1957, p. 89), under the leadership of a governor-general with civilian and military responsibilities. Out of the total military strength of the empire in 1799 of 823,950, 101,692 were soldiers from the military frontier (Pal, 1832).

Despite a high level of centralized decision-making, the imposition of military culture, and the more general adoption of collective properties, use of violence, and minimal investment in public goods would not have been possible without the utilization of some form of indirect rule, a "decentralized framework in which important decision-making powers are delegated to" the local authorities at the border (Gerring et al., 2011, p. 377). In the case of the Habsburg military colony, some decision-making powers and enforcement were relegated to indigenous community leaders, who were provided with carrots in return for their cooperation, and sometimes with sticks in case of disobedience. Such relegation facilitated the creation of a "friendly regime in the imperialized periphery" (Kohli, 2020, p. 5). Specifically, local family heads were responsible for maintaining order, providing manpower to the empire, and raising funds for the military equipment of the recruits from their family.

A variety of works about the nature of politics in Eastern Europe, sub-Saharan Africa, Latin America, Middle East and Asia reveal the informal power groups distinct from the formal state that, when woven together, are responsible for the development of the state (Centeno, 1997; Grzymala-Busse and Luong, 2002; Helmke and Levitsky, 2004; Lemarchand, 1972; Scott, 1972; Tsai, 2007; Wedeen, 2008). Such informal affiliations and power groups are different from the traditional Weberian state. Rather than competing with such groups, the state expands its power by encapsulating them within it. The power groups which regularize and define human interactions through sanctions, rewards and/or symbols (Migdal, 1988, p. 80) also happen to be effective for military organization and border defense.

Low Imperial Investment

Low cost was the main rationale behind military colonialism. This meant that investment in infrastructure was the lowest of priorities for the Habsburg central authorities. Despite multiple reforms to improve the lives of military colonists, the territory received few goods from the central government: little construction of schools, roads, and hospitals. In addition, except for the captain and a small number of non-commissioned officers, the grenzers received no pay, but were supported by their household (Rothenberg, 1966, p. 15). The official argument was that "with proper organization and leadership, the grenzers themselves could carry most of the expenses for the maintenance of such an establishment" (Rothenberg, 1966, p. 15). As a result, during the reign of Maria Theresa, the military colony was supplied with very little pay and rations (Rothenberg, 1966, p. 21).

Imperial authorities also used the argument that better provision of public goods could be antithetical to the military role of the colonists. According to Rothenberg (1966, p. 69), greater provision of public goods might have encouraged trade, which could have improved the livelihoods of locals, but in turn would have corrupted their "fighting spirit" and would have distracted the peasant-soldiers from their military duties (Blanc, 1957, p. 246). As a result, the Habsburg military colony exhibits the first component of extractive institutions that could negatively affect development: low investment in infrastructure.

An important question is what was happening to public goods in the civilian area. The Austrian government was interested in saving money by allowing the military colonists to be self-sufficient, but what was happening in the civilian area? Historical accounts suggest that the civilian areas controlled by local landlords had much more access to public goods compared to the military frontier. For example, Horvat (1939, p. 37) discusses how the areas ruled by the Frankopans and the Zrinjskis, two important trading families, had "the best roads in Croatia at that time."

Violence

Occasional state violence was present in the military colony. Historical accounts suggest that violence was the way to contain the "savage and wild Grenzer" (Rothenberg, 1966, p. 23) and that it was through "whips, clubs, shackles, and prison" that the military organization could be preserved (Valentić, 1984, p. 74). Thus, while likely present on the civilian side as well, especially during serfdom, violence seems to have been more intense in the military area. According to Valentić, it is "an understatement to say that the court proceedings against the grenzers were harsh" (Valentić, 1984, p. 74).

Many important Habsburg officials such as Duke Joseph of Sachsen-Hildburghausen were active supporters of the use of violence against the grenzers. In 1737, methods of physical violence included "the block and the gallows, impalement and quartering, mutilation, branding, the whip, hard labor, and exile." Slight changes were introduced with Title IV of the *Militär-Gränitz Rechten* of 1754, which limited punishment in peacetime to "flogging, running the gauntlet, prison with or without forced labor, and capital punishment by either hanging or firing squad." The use of torture, however, continued. Vaníček (1875c, pp. 314–315), for example, mentions the continuation of punishment by torture in 1820 such as caning. Grandits (2002, p. 219) further explains how in the mid nineteenth century every frontier regiment consisted of both a district and a disciplinary court where decisions were not necessarily "made according to law, but rather according to the officers' free judgement." In most cases, penalties handed down by the disciplinary court in 1850s included flogging. Grandits (2002, p. 219) indicates that "[t]his corporal punishment, from which in some cases even the elderly, women and even children were not spared, was carried out on a special studded bench on which the delinquent was bound so that they could hardly move. The convict was then beaten by a sergeant from the company." Even more cruelly, Valentić (1984, p. 74) describes how the "legs and arms were restrained with shackles, so that the person tied up could only scream. [. . .] After the beating ended, the Grenzer had to submissively thank the beater."

Another example that Valentić (1984) describes is "running the lines," which entailed a company of up to 300 soldiers lined up in two rows:

According to the free assessment of the bureaucrat or officer, the penalty was to run between the two lines from one to ten times. This means that the convicted would receive anything between 300 and 3000 blows, depending on how many times he had to go through the punishment company. It is difficult to say which was stronger in such a life of our Krajišniks: the cruelty of the penal system or the endurance of the people.[10] (Valentić, 1984, p. 74)

According to Valentić (1984), the smallest number of blows was 2.5 in 1840, received by an old man who had a doctor's certificate acknowledging that he would not be able to withstand a greater number of blows. Similarly, a 13-year-old boy only received 25 whips, as a result of his age.

Issues of "restraint" when it comes to the use of violence by authorities continued to be important topics of conversation among the higher echelons of the Habsburg military authorities until the late nineteenth century (Damianitsch, 1854, 1861; Heissenberger, 1872).

The second type of abuse for which there is some historical evidence is sexual violence against the women in the colony. For example, in 1841 a petition by a brigade in Petrinja mentioned that marriage

---

[10] Translation from Serbo-Croatian.

laws should be eased (i.e. to allow extra-marital affairs), because "celibate officers often lead an isolated and hard life without the solace of the family" (Rothenberg, 1966, p. 134). The abuses against women in the military colony are most vividly described by a Croatian intellectual, Imbro Tkalac, in the 1850s:

[...] the officer became the husband of all the women he wanted. If the [actual] husband did not want to face the most cruel persecution [...], he had to endure the ordeal in silence. [...] Even worse was the Colonel Knöhr of the Slunj Regiment in Karlstadt, who travelled through his regimental district, with a designated officer [...] to select the prettiest young wives of his soldiers for him. Colonel Knöhr had set up a real harem, which was always populated by five or six beauties. After a few weeks, they were sent home to make room for other successors. The whole city knew about this problem that lasted for years. But since Knöhr enjoyed a high level of protection from Vienna, the brigade and the division general did not dare to say anything; this stopped when Knöhr became a general and left Karlstadt. Some other officers did the same, but more discreetly, if at all.[11] (Tkalac, 1894, pp. 314–315)

Existence of violence or lack thereof is a relative statement. Did violence not exist under serfdom? There is limited evidence of violence provided by historians on the civilian side of the Habsburg Empire. On the contrary, Horvat (1939) mentions for example a certain benevolence that landlords had vis-à-vis their serfs. In addition, Horvat (1939, p. 40) discusses the level playing field that many serfs had toward their landlords. For example, starting at the end of the seventeenth century, some serfs got so rich that they were the ones lending money to the nobles, while the latter pledged additional land to the serfs.

Horvat (1939, p. 49) describes how throughout the territory which would become Yugoslavia in the twentieth century, the relationship between feudal lords and serfs was amicable. For example, Ante Radić, a Croatian intellectual from the early twentieth century, in his report about his visit to Bosnia and Herzegovina in 1899, mentions how impressed he was with the interaction between Jusuf-beg Resulbegovic-Kapetanovic, a classic Croatian feudal lord, and his farmer Puše Bokonjića. He describes the dialogue between them as a dialogue between equals (Radić, 1899).

Removal of Property Rights

Military colonialism entailed a high transformation of the local property rights regime. Serfdom and landed elites were eliminated. The

---

[11] Translation from German.

"winners" of this transformation were the colonists who received land grants. Their property rights were limited, however: these were communal properties with major restrictions on the owners' ability to manage and alienate them (i.e. constraints on the ability to sell, lease, mortgage, or give away land). Land belonged to family clans[12] or *zadrugas*.[13] Family clans were not a Habsburg invention and in fact existed in the civilian area as well. A legal textbook from 1840 on the basic laws of the military frontier explains that:

The house communions were not created by the Military Frontier Basic laws, but by the ancient nations [living there] [. . .] The legal charter of 1630 only laid down the principles according to which family divisions should take place [. . .] Similarly, the inhabitants of the houses in the neighboring [civilian] provincial districts of Croatia, Slavonia, and Banat are no less numerous than in the military zone districts, and there [in the civilian area], there is no law ordering the families to stay together.[14] (Stopfer, 1840, pp. 129–130)

Unlike the civilian area, the Habsburgs institutionalized communal properties and prevented them from splitting into individual properties (Erlich, 1966, p. 34) for economic and military reasons. Habsburg legal textbooks explain the economic reasons as follows: "[I]n order to continue with the economic activities of the border houses during the absence of the men who serve [in war], living together with many people in the same house, or in a commune of houses, is necessary" (Stopfer, 1840, p. 9).

The same legal textbook from 1840 emphasizes the importance of zadrugas for the recruitment of soldiers:

[T]his community system is the basis of the military border constitution. Without this system it would not be possible to set up seventeen regiments in a district which, according to its population, would only suffice for completing three regiments in the German-hereditary provinces. Consequently, this system must be maintained unaltered, and even the slightest modification would require the utmost caution. (Stopfer, 1840, p. 129)

---

[12] Examples of charters making the zadrugas legally binding for the military colonists are *Statuta Valachorum* issued by Ferdinand I in 1630 or Title IV of *Militär Gränitz Rechten* issued by Maria Theresa in 1754.

[13] The *zadrugas* define a category of residence, property, and kinship and could comprise anything between 10 and 60 members (Kaser, 1985, 1997). The typical structure included co-resident married siblings along with an articulated differentiation of agricultural tasks, household administration, and household work carried out by women (Halpern *et al.*, 1996, p. 426). The zadruga was called *Hauskommunion* in the 1600s or *Hauskommunität* in the 1700s in Habsburg documents.

[14] Translation from German.

By choosing to use zadrugas, which had strong social control over individuals (e.g. marriage rules, division of labor, and more importantly, social hierarchies), the Habsburg state did not have to incur the high costs of establishing a new system of recruitment, enforcement of rules, and battling a force that already existed and that made the rules. Therefore, the state never attempted to displace or transform deep-rooted social organizations in which people in the periphery lived out their lives. As such, it opted for a process of incorporation which resembled more a "negotiated enterprise" (Barkey, 2008, p. 1), an "informal brand of politics" (Mukhopadhyay, 2014, p. 11), or "political inertia" (Migdal, 1988, p. 31) than a competition about who makes the rules in society and who has social control (Migdal, 1988, p. 30). In the process of incorporation, the norms and institutions of the Habsburg formal state ended up mingling with the institutions of the informal "state." In doing so, the Habsburg state demonstrated its power to (1) *penetrate* society, (2) *regulate* social relationships, (3) *extract*, appropriate, and use resources in determined ways (Migdal, 1988, p. 4).

Migdal's (1988) theoretical framework applied to the Habsburg military colony invites us to acknowledge that the state is "only one organization in a mélange within the boundaries it seeks to rule" (Migdal, 1988, pp. 39–40). According to him, in order to understand the state, one needs to comprehend the wider social structure of power that states are part of. The image of the Habsburg state that I propose in this framework is different from the classic centralized, pyramidal structure offered by many historical European countries. The Habsburg state is an instance of a strong state that does not displace local power structures. Instead, it uses them as a kind of miniature "strongman governance" (Mukhopadhyay, 2014) whereby the Habsburg state's engagement with local leaders partially alters the nature of the state and local power politics. By utilizing local power structures, the Habsburg state ends up creating and consolidating its strength in the periphery. These are two modalities of governance that Charles Tilly calls "accumulation" and "concentration" (Tilly, 2003) by which the Habsburg state is able to create an institutional architecture that is cost-effective and politically expedient. Such institutional architecture is very similar also to the notion of indirect rule, which allows the empire to extract military conscripts.[15]

---

[15] Note again that following definitions and criteria provided by Doyle (1986); Gerring *et al.* (2011); Iyer (2010); Lange (2009); Mamdani (1996), the Habsburg military colony approaches a more direct style of rule, with centralized decision-making coming from Vienna and with many bureaucrats sent from Vienna and Budapest to rule over locals.

Military Colonialism vs. Feudalism

One potential unintended consequence of the extensive focus on military colonialism and emphasizing its negative aspects is that feudalism or serfdom would be a superior institutional set-up. But is feudalism less bad compared to military colonialism? Ultimately, both military colonialism and serfdom are examples of extractive institutions together with indentured service, peonage, and corvée (also called statute labor), which includes forced conscription for the extraction of minerals, crops, or for border defense, and even slavery. In all these examples, a higher political authority exerts pressure onto a weaker entity to utilize their labor in the interest of the former. As such, extractive institutions are not voluntary contracts, but rather a bundle of rent-seeking arrangements based on coercive power, aimed at redistributing resources from the weaker to the stronger entity (Acemoğlu and Wolitzky, 2011).

Serfdom is "an institutional system which obliged a peasant to provide forced labor services to his landlord in exchange for being allowed to occupy land" (Ogilvie and Carus, 2014, p. 473). The difference between slavery and serfdom is that slaves are considered forms of property owned by other people, while serfs are bound to the land that they occupy from one generation to the other. As such, slavery is the most extreme form of "unfree labor" (Cooper, 1996; Fall, 1993; Hopkins, 1973; Van Waijenburg, 2018).

There are a variety of elements that make serfdom extractive including an expectation that people had to work a fixed number of days per year, restrictions on movement, marriage, participation in factor and product markets, or more generally, an inability to leave such systems. The bigger difference between more "traditional" extractive institutions such as work in mines or crops and serfdom is the agent or entity for whom work is being enacted. In the case of serfdom, serfs typically work for a noble or for the church. In case of colonial work in mines or forced military conscription, the work is performed for the government.

The entity for whom the work is done has implications for the extensiveness and rigidity of the legal framework justifying its existence and explaining its respective mode of operation. Works for the state are much more complex, featuring entire legal frameworks and specific bureaucracies defined in the imperial capital for the "conduct of business" in the periphery. For example, traditional extractive institutions would entail the design of extensive legal codes stipulating the obligations of people exposed to them, means of appeal in case of injustice, the nomination of a bureaucracy with executive responsibilities in charge of implementing the legal framework on the ground, etc. By contrast, serfdom is a somewhat more parsimonious authority system consisting of delegating power to local nobles or churches. The latter are the ones deciding how people at the bottom of the hierarchy are treated. For much of the history of serfdom throughout the world, landowners had full control over their peasants including the right over their mobility, the future of their children (whether the children could become craftsmen or would rather remain in town working the land), and even the right to live or to die.

The question of whether serfdom or forced conscription is worse for development is an empirical question. Both serfdom and forced conscription are associated with under-development. For example, research on the second serfdom – the huge growth in landlord powers in the early modern central and eastern Europe (from the sixteenth to the nineteenth century) – suggests that it stifled economic development, which is why GDP per capita grew much more slowly in Eastern Europe compared to Western Europe (Brenner, 1976; Dennison, 2011; Ogilvie and Carus, 2014). This mostly had to do with the extreme rent-seeking behavior of noble landowners. Other mechanisms by which serfdom can affect growth include "restricting access to factor and product markets, preventing allocation of resources to the highest-productivity uses, and creating poor incentives for investment in human capital, land improvements, and technological innovations" (Ogilvie and Carus, 2014, p. 473). However, Ogilvie and Carus (2014) acknowledge some heterogeneity within the effects of serfdom on growth and that not all areas exposed to serfdom were equally bad. Whether serfs are fully prohibited from accessing product markets or whether they have poor incentives for investing their talents is highly dependent on the authority of the noble. This means that the effect of serfdom can be more idiosyncratic than one would predict: if people are "lucky" enough to have a benevolent landowner who does not use violence, who respects their property, and who allows them to keep part of their crops, then that should be better than a situation with an abusive landowner. For example, Ogilvie and Carus (2014, p. 475) explain that manorial courts operated by the landlord or his officials could refuse to provide justice or could "strip a serf of legal protection by outlawing him." As a result, there is considerable variation in how landlords treated serfs. For instance, Russian serfdom is regarded as one of the most coercive systems ever observed, frequently compared to slavery in nineteenth-century America. In a similar way, Tkalac (1894, p. 219) compared the position of the serfs in civilian Croatia to that of the indigenous manpower in the West Indies, while Blanc (1957), citing a report of a French bureaucrat, the Count of Chabrot, to the situation of the serfs in fifteenth-century France; this is because of the excessive taxes and the expectation of work for the feudal lord. Other historians, however, indicate that at times the relationship between the landlords and serfs was amicable in the Habsburg Empire (Horvat, 1939). Modern historians contend that serfdom in Habsburg Bohemia and Croatia was milder than in Russia (Dennison and Ogilvie, 2007).

Military Colonialism vs. Feudalism in the Habsburg Empire

An important question is how the property rights regimes are comparable in the military and civilian areas within the Habsburg Empire. Generally, there are substantial similarities when it comes to hierarchical structures and property types and sizes. Feudalism in the civilian area was originally a private-law contract which gradually turned into a public-law system because of landlord pressures on the crown. Feudal lords were in constant need of labor force and hence the adoption of such a legal framework was in their economic interest (Horvat, 1939). As a result of their pressures, local farmers became *adscripti glebae*, or tied to the land, and could be sold or transferred with the land. This was codified in law after the Tripartite Decree by Istvan Verboczy (1465?–1541), a legal codex documenting the responsibilities of nobles and serfs vis-à-vis one another which was issued at some point in the early 1500s under the rule of Vladislaus II of Hungary. Generally, the landlords dictated the amount and the type of work obligations.

Within the military area, "the feudal lord is the state, that is, its organs (emperor, general, officers)" (Adamček, 1984, p. 139). The colonists would be commanded by a captain who would have supreme authority over them while vice-captains would lead them to campaigns (Pavličević, 1984). As such, the entire society was subject to military discipline and command.

When it comes to *legal institutions*, Horvat (1939, p. 45) describes how within the civilian area, serfs had their own "peasant courts," which were the main pillars of the Croatian administrative state prior to 1848. The peasant courts consisted of several zadrugas. The elders of these zadrugas chose among themselves a senior judge who became an affairs administrator within the community. Before 1848, all elders would hold meetings twice a month "usually on the benches near the church on holidays" (Horvat, 1939, p. 45) to solve disputes between residents and only in rare, more difficult cases the landlords would get involved. Within the military area, each regiment was headed by a colonel – both a military commander and a judge. Thus, military authorities were much more involved in litigation and in the internal life of family clans.

With regards to *property*, lands within the civilian area belonged to feudal landlords who controlled both the land and the peasants associated with it. The serf or the *kmet* could use the land in exchange for offering a percentage of their crop and a specific number of days of work to the lord. Feudal landlords could dispose of their land together with the associated serfs as they pleased, including selling and leasing. Within the military area, the feudal system was abolished and the land turned into the personal property of the emperor with the colonists and their families having permanent and inalienable titles, in exchange for military obligations and corvée labor. Within the civilian area, serfs could acquire additional land (unlike the military frontier), but of course with the relevant additional obligations vis-à-vis the landlord. The acquisition could only be done with consent and knowledge from landowners. Nobody was allowed until 1848 to sell land without offering it first to blood relatives, and then to neighbors. When neither relatives nor neighbors would buy the land, it was could then be offered to other people.

Both the civilian and military area featured family clans living and working the land together. As explained by one of the prime historians of the Habsburg military frontier, "the house communions were not created by the Military Frontier Basic laws, but by the ancient nations [living there]" (Stopfer, 1831, pp. 129–130). In both the civilian and military areas, the key relationship was between the landlords/regimental officers, and the zadruga. In the latter case, the regimental officers were the state representatives. Both the landlords and the Austrian state recognized the benefits of kinship structures. For example, Horvat (1939, p. 32) explains that "peasant clans receive land according to their numerical strength, and it is according to this system that serfs are divided and the peasant strength of the landlord is also measured." Similarly, within the military colony, "the authorities believed that communal households permitted the mobilization of larger numbers, and also supported the Hauskommunionen as the basic unit of military control" (Rothenberg, 1966, p. 98). Thus, land was also allocated in the military area depending on the number of soldiers that family clans could produce.

However, an important difference emerges when it comes to the interference with zadruga authority structures. Within the civilian area, the feudal lord would typically respect the customs of the zadruga regime and would only sometimes intervene in the case of the nomination of a new family clan head and in the implementation of a clan division. Within the military area, however, the family heads would have to be confirmed by the military authorities – the captain or the colonel (Blanc, 1951, p. 48).

Additional differences between the military and the civilian area emerge when it comes to *inheritance*. In both cases, land would typically be bequeathed from one generation to the other following the principle of primogeniture (Blanc, 1951, p. 116). For example, in the nineteenth century, on the civilian side, it would be sufficient for one of the family's daughters to marry a man from outside of the family in order for the zadruga to be an independent community. On the military side, much stricter and more rigid rules about splitting and inheritance were in place. For instance, if there was no male in the family to take on the role of clan head, the woman inheriting the property would have to marry a soldier within two years (Desprez, 1847). Otherwise, the property would go to the state. Related to inheritance, Horvat (1939) describes how military colonists could not alienate lands in the way serfs could, while forests and pastures could only be used to the extent prescribed by king's rules and local administration.

Finally, the most important differences were about the type of *labor obligations* vis-à-vis the relevant authorities. Given its nature, the authorities strictly limited the type of activities that the inhabitants of the military colony could take on. Within the military colony, the inhabitants were first and foremost soldiers, having "their whole life dedicated to military duty, not to economic needs" (Horvat, 1939, p. 56). Cultivating land was a second priority to the military needs of the empire. The former would be the main responsibility of women, children, and the elderly.

The amount and type of military labor obligations changed over time. Inhabitants of the military colony had to guard the border and go to battle if so asked by the imperial authorities. For example, a document from 1635, *Modus et Constitutiones quibus Valachi resignandi per Regnicolas*, included responsibilities such as "maintaining guard, marching against the Turks, and carrying out individual and general military expeditions (*expeditiones tam partiulares quam generales*) in times of war" (Moačanin, 1984, p. 297). In addition, they would have to spend 10 days in occupied places, making trenches in the forests between the Habsburg Empire and the Ottomans. In times of peace, Horvat (1939, p. 63) explains that: "a certain number of farmers serve as cops in the territorial militia which monitors the border, take care of internal security, follow trade caravans coming from Bosnia and Herzegovina to the quarantine hospitals of Šibenik or Split."

In addition, the colonists had to be involved in unpaid state and municipal works. First, the "imperial" or "state" work consisted of building military constructions, cutting logs for the military barracks, bringing and lighting coal, building roads and bridges, building and repairing border fences, etc. According to Horvat (1939, p. 56), the municipal labor was determined according to the number of able-bodied men and the number of vehicles available to them. This included sowing barley and oats for the imperial shepherds, looking after the meadows for the imperial stallions, monitoring fences and hedges, building and repairing river embankments, constructing and maintaining wells, and constructing and repairing churches, apartments, and schools. This type of work put a lot of pressure on the population, and because of that it was a frequent cause of social tensions (Valentić, 1984, p. 75).

The Basic Laws of 1807 eased the obligations toward imperial and municipal authorities. Title V, "Concerning Governmental and Communal Labor on the Border," outlined the new responsibilities of the grenzers. They were liable for twelve days of paid labor each year and in addition had to provide relays (*Vorspann*) for certain enumerated classes of traffic at fixed rates. Valentić (1984, p. 76) estimates that in 1818, every inhabitant of the military colony had to provide corvée labor lasting 4.5 days, in addition to the usual military obligations. In 1848, the unpaid state work was abolished by the Croatian parliament.

Within the civilian area, the types of responsibilities were typical of other contemporaneous feudal structures in Europe. Generally, such obligations consisted of contributions in kind and days of labor for the landowner. In the sixteenth century, these were called *gospošćinom* or *rabotom* and they later became *robot* or *tlaka* in the upper Croatian regions (Horvat, 1939). Horvat explains that this all depended on the "arbitrariness of landowners," the type of crops produced, and the needs of the landowners, with limited intervention from the state. The number of days of labor was decided based on the size of the serf settlement and the number of family members. Serfs had to work the land of the landlord, the barren field, for the vineyard or cut and bring wood from the forest with or without burden beasts. Peasant serfs typically had one domestic draft animal – usually an ox, which was considered superior to horses for field work. The work lasted from sunrise to sunset with time to eat and to rest. In winter, work could cover forest work and preparing the tools for the summer including rakes, pitchforks, shovels, hoes, and brooms. If the serf refused to work, the landlord could hire another worker but at the expense of the family clan. Serfs who did not fulfill their work obligations could be fined. The landlord could ask for a payment in cash for which the family clan would be responsible; the amount could also include arrears payment for the work which had not been done. The serfs themselves had some legal power to fight their landlord in case of abuses, but such disputes rarely took place given the obvious power asymmetries between serfs and landlords.

Additional differences between the military and the civilian area emerged also when it came to *taxation*. In 1635, each household in the military colony had to pay 50 dinars. The magistrates would collect this amount from each household and hand it over to the vice-captain or captain. All the taxes that the colonists were paying were going to the state and constituted a tenth of their income. While not constituting taxes, a significant burden on the military colonists was the fact that they had to purchase their own uniforms or sometimes even produce and maintain their own equipment: for example, Rothenberg (1966, p. 29) explains that in 1752, "the introduction of new uniforms-tight, uncomfortable, expensive, and all too frequently changed to keep up with the fads of military fashion – was a grievous *vexation*" (emphasis added).

On the civilian side, it was common for the serfs to pay about a ninth of their agricultural production to the landlord until the nineteenth century. This could be grains, bundles of linen, hemp or yarn, wheat, or even wine if serfs were in charge of vineyards. In addition to the ninth, it was also typical for serfs to offer gifts to the landlord – *darova* – either in cash or in kind, including dried meat, bread, eggs. The payment to the landlord was in addition to the tithe which went to the church, and to the state taxes that had to be paid twice a year – in spring and in autumn (Horvat, 1939). The funds would go to fulfill the military and other needs of the empire (the hearth tax). Horvat (1939, p. 35) estimates that at the beginning of the eighteenth century, state taxes added to about one forint a year. Only after paying all these taxes was the serf allowed to sell his crop wholesale or retail (Horvat, 1939, p. 35).

Thus, there are similarities between the civilian and military areas in the Habsburg Empire. Both serfs and military colonists were at the bottom of some hierarchical authority structures. However, within the military colony, the life of the inhabitants was much more codified and rigid. The state had much more control over family clans through its military authorities, involvement in litigation, restrictions on inheritance, selling of property, and clan divisions. The rules were so strict that violence was used: sometimes in cases of disobedience and sometimes in cases of abuses by captains. The asymmetry in the utilization of violence between the civilian and military areas becomes apparent in qualitative historical accounts. For example, Vaníček (1875a, p. 314) mentions the hatred that military colonists felt for the imperial authorities as a result of excessive use of force while in the civilian area, while Horvat (1939, p. 49) depicts cordial interactions between locals and their landlords.

When it comes to fiscal and corvée obligations, it is difficult to make a comparison between the two areas given the changing legislation on both parts and the idiosyncrasies of individual landlords in the civilian area. The fiscal and labor obligations within the two regions likely had negative consequences for the lives of people exposed to them. For example, Blanc (1957, p. 225) mentions that a series of restrictions in the civilian area in Croatia in the second half of the nineteenth century had deleterious effects on the local economic life. Such restrictions had to do with prohibition on the ability to cut wood from the forest and breed goats, and limitations on grazing. At the same time, in the military area, the largest burden was the military service together with the obligation of family clans to help support the troops that were stationed permanently in their communities. Colonists were so dissatisfied with such obligations that this led to the popular motto: "God, deliver us from pestilence, from famine, and from the army!" (Blanc, 1957, p. 225).

Given the high rigidity of state institutions within the military colony, it is likely that it is associated with worse economic outcomes. In Chapter 4, I demonstrate empirically using quantitative data how the military colony had a lower provision of public goods both during its existence and afterwards.

Military Colonial Elites

Elites were crucial for the creation and development of the Habsburg military colony as an institution. These were located along a thick hierarchical structure. I include them in three categories: high-, intermediary-, and low-level elites, depending on their level of influence and control over people. Such elites played an important role in the exploitation of the people at the bottom of the hierarchy, alienating them from state authorities. Elites were often perceived as "foreign," were frequently violent toward their subalterns, and were corrupt in seeking opportunities for rent and treating the areas where they were assigned as private property.

At the highest level of authority and control, there was the king or queen, who made the ultimate decision about whether the colony existed or was abolished. From this point of view, the style of rule could be regarded as a direct type of rule with highly centralized decision making (Gerring et al., 2011, p. 377). For example, Archduke Ferdinand I of Austria (1503–1564) is the first king who approved the creation of the military frontier. This was in the year 1522 at a time when the once powerful Hungarian kingdom was faced with increased Ottoman attacks. Following advice from the estates worst affected by the Ottoman incursions, Ferdinand I moved mercenary troops to prevent further advances by the enemy (Amstadt, 1969; O'Reilly, 2006; Rothenberg, 1966). The Ottoman attacks and the subsequent measures taken by the Hasbsburgs to counteract them are compatible with the classical idea of war making states (Tilly, 1990).

Over time, the decision about the management of the colony became much more bureaucratized. It was for this purpose and additional military affairs that the Viennese Aulic War Council (Hofkriegsrat) was created in 1556. This was the central military administrative authority of the Habsburg monarchy responsible for decisions about the construction of fortresses, army equipment, and the planning of wars. Its functions were transferred to the Military Directory (Militär Direktorium) by Maria Theresa in 1743, which was directed by an army general.

After 1848, the management of the colony was transferred to the Hungarian War Ministry. Over time, many subsidiary offices were created such as the position of the "Inspector General" under Maria Theresa and Joseph II, whose role was to make recommendations about improving the military border. Despite the increased bureaucratization of the military colony, either the king or queen still had to make the final decisions. For example, in 1746, in order to remove the ability of the Inner Austrian estates from making patronage appointments to the military colony, Maria Theresa sent a letter to the estates proclaiming that "[i]t is our exclusive right to appoint all officers from ensign to commanding general" (Rothenberg, 1966, p. 23).

At intermediary levels, there were a variety of offices and positions over time, nominated by the king or queen, that were in charge of the military colonial administration. For example, around 1630, *Capitanate* and *Dörfer* were created for the better management of the border. These were sub-divisions of Border, each commanded by appropriate officials, appointed by the Crown. By the close of the eighteenth century, the leading figures of the military frontier were border fortress captain-generals (originally, *Obrister Feldhauptmann der niederösterreichischen Lande,* who later became officers of the captaincy), who were Austrian appointees and/or Hungarian nobles. O'Reilly (2006, p. 240) explains that the "Captains, or regional military rulers [. . .] played an extremely important role in the development of the military frontier, by creating a cohesive area, a genuine region, out of a few military posts [and] constituted the military elite." As such, each captain was responsible for the maintenance of a border fortification (*Grenzfestung*/*Grenzort, confinium*) which was subordinate to a larger fortress that functioned as headquarters for a section of the border (*Grenze*/*Grenzgebiet*). Similar to these were captain-generals (*Kreisobrist*/*Kreisoberst, supresum capitaneus partium regni Hungariae, prorex, banus*), who were in charge of military affairs in the districts (*Kreise*/*partes*). These were what Rubin (2017, p. 33) would call *coercive agents,* imposing the Habsburg ruler's will by force.

Without adequate monitoring, however, these captains acted less in the imperial interests and followed their personal ambitions more, ending up behaving like "big landowners," entrepreneurs, and stock breeders, treating lands allocated to them from the Treasury administration as their own property (O'Reilly, 2006, p. 241). Their position was further solidified by receiving income from activities such as: levying fines, selling wine, operating butcher shops, managing inns, selling exemptions from guard duty, and appointing sub-officers. In addition, the captain-generals ignored the rules of the Frontier Organization Commission (*Grenzeinrichtungkommission*) from 1702, according to which frontier lands could never be sold or inherited. They sublet the lands on favorable terms to their preferred subtenants. Finally, some of the corvée work that privates had to do was in fact done on the property of the captain-generals, who were also in charge of promotions.

In 1787, with the adoption of the canton system,[16] the civil, economic, and judicial aspects of the military frontier came under the direction of a separate administration. Every canton was looked after by officers selected for their interest and experience in directing the agricultural economy, fluency in the local language, and administrative ability (Vaníček, 1875c, pp. 17–30). At the head of each canton stood a major in a hierarchical structure imitating that of a regiment, with battalions and company districts being administered by subalterns, while the villages were supervised by so-called village heads (*Dorf-Ober*) and deputy inspectors (*Unterinspectoren*) selected from senior non-commissioned officers (Amstadt, 1969; Rothenberg, 1966). Similarly, all these cantons had a number of secondary offices, including military judges, one engineer, a bookkeeper, and a surgeon. The whole system was highly paternalistic, attempting to exercise as much control as possible over the grenzer population (Rothenberg, 1966).

The positions at the lowest level of authority also changed with time. Until 1754, colonists were authorized, subject to the ultimate control of the appointed Habsburg officials, to elect their own leaders, specifically, their own captains (*vojevode*) and magistrates (*knezovi*) (Seton-Watson, 1911, p. 23). The vojevode and the knezovi were the only ones who stood out from a homogenous border guard society, as they enjoyed some privileges, but received no payment (Grandits, 2002). Such leaders performed important roles as legitimizing agents (Rubin, 2017), further solidifying the perceived authority of the Habsburgs in the borderlands. The ability of colonists to select their own leaders could be regarded as a form of indirect rule, whereby the Habsburg authorities could rule over the military colony only with their help. The goal of having such positions could be interpreted as what Mamdani (1996, p. 865) would regard as recognizing the "historicity of the colony and the agency of the colonized." Grandits (2002, p. 79) describes that the knezovi were in charge of both civilian and military matters for several villages. They were also responsible for collecting taxes, determining the number of guard families and those fit for duty, and passing on requests and complaints for the residents. The knezovi could sometimes be direct commanders of their unpaid companies in their area, which is why they would also hold

---

[16] Joseph II (1741–1790) was an admirer of the Prussian monarchy, where the military was divided in five thousand hearths for military regiments, or fifteen hundred for cavalry regiments (Rothenberg, 1966). The canton system was seen as a panacea to the lack of uniformity in the training and discipline of the Habsburg military colony.

the title of vojevode. The situation changed with the regulations of 1754, which ended the ancient office of the knezovi and concentrated all the powers in the hand of the military officers, who were replaced by other regimental officers, among whom the Austrian state found its most loyal supporters (Rothenberg, 1966, p. 38).

At the very bottom of the hierarchy, there were the family heads or *starješina*, who were in charge of transmitting orders from above and who were responsible for the actions of their households (Schwicker, 1883, pp. 230–234). Blanc (1957, p. 119) regards the family head as the military chief, transmitting orders and being responsible in front of the authorities for actions of his family. Family heads would be elected by the family – an competent elderly person, regarded as a good father, and reasonably competent at administering the property. They would have to be subsequently confirmed by the military authorities (the captain or the colonel) (Blanc, 1951, p. 124). As such, the clan leader would have the role of mitigating and softening the orders coming from the top, overall making them seem less despotic (Blanc, 1957, p. 119).

The relationship between the family heads and the military authorities became even clearer with the variety of legal documents that were issued over time. One of the documents that clearly lists the responsibilities of the family heads is the Basic Laws of 1807 or "Grundgesetze für die Carlstädter-Warasdiner, Banal, und Banatische Militär-Gränze (Vienna, 1807)." Articles 57–58, for example, indicate that the oldest and most capable man in the group (the housefather) assumes responsibility for the members of the communion and for the management of family finances. The elderly woman on the other hand is responsible for the other women of the household together with internal housekeeping (Stopfer, 1840, p. 190). Together they have to over see to "the good order, religion, and morality in the Communion" (*Religion und Sittlichkeit gute Ordnung, Fleiß und Einigkeit in der Communnion zu sehen*).

Despite some representation and the existence of some local power structures, which would indicate an indirect style of rule, the kind of governance arrangement within the military colony is compatible with Doyle's (1986) and Lange's (2009) definition of direct rule. A governance arrangement, according to them, can be labeled as "direct rule" if the local governors are appointed by the center and are not born in the areas where they are appointed. Despite the fact that at the very bottom of the hierarchy there can be locals in charge, if above them there are imperial authorities, then it would still be called direct rule. Similarly, the type of rule in the military colony is also compatible with the definition of indirect rule provided by Gerring *et al.* (2011) entailing a highly centralized decision-making whereby the king or queen and the subordinating military bureaucracies would have the ultimate say in matters related to the present or the future of the military colony.

Colonial Elites' Abuses and Alienation from the Central State

Because of red tape, limited accountability, and inadequate supervision, there were many opportunities for authorities to abuse the people at the bottom of hierarchy. Some social science works warn about the long-term effects of such historical abuses. As already mentioned, historical exposure to violence can lead to subsequent distrust or aversion toward political authorities (Lowes and Montero, 2021; Lupu and Peisakhin, 2017) while corruption can indeed lead to less trust in institutions (Ares and Hernández, 2017; Bowler and Karp, 2004; Chanley *et al.*, 2000). The Habsburg military colonial institutions also created a highly hier-archical society that caused people at the bottom of the hierarchy to distrust the state. In O'Reilly's (2006, p. 243) words, the colony became a space where the relationship between the individual and the state was equivalent to the relationship between slave, master or *Unterthan*, and sovereign. I argue that the distrust in state authorities stems from three types of disarticulation: (1) Imposition of "foreign" power; (2) Abuse of power by highly positioned military officers; and (3) Forced religious conversions.

Imposition of "Foreign" Power
The first source of disarticulation is the perception of lack of legitimacy of the officers sent by Vienna. This has to do with the lack of knowledge of the nominated officers about local customs and habits, and the reli-gion of their subordinates (Rothenberg, 1966, p. 29), which contributed to an overall perception of detachment of the military officials from the daily lives of the peasants in the periphery. The perceptions of foreign-ness of the military authorities became much more of a problem with the abolition of the positions of *vojevode* and *knezovi* in 1754, whom the soldiers at the very bottom of the hierarchy could choose. After 1754, these two positions were replaced by other regimental officers, among whom the Austrian state found its most loyal supporters (Rothenberg, 1966, p. 38). These were mostly German, and as such exponents of the Habsburg "alien" rule (Hitchins, 1985; O'Reilly, 2006; Tinta, 1972).

Corruption
The second type of disarticulation stems from the corruption of the military generals and captains who transformed themselves from rep-resentatives of the empire in the periphery into entrepreneurs, stock

breeders, and ultimately large landowners (O'Reilly, 2006, p. 240). As already mentioned, they allocated land to soldiers that they favored (Wessely, 1973, p. 78). In addition, every soldier had to perform six days of corvée labor in the spring and in the summer, from which the captains benefited directly. The transformation in the power of generals and captains has to do with the gradual accumulation of power without adequate accountability structures in place. This process is also emphasized by some historical observers: "[. . .] in a country of soldiers, all power is concentrated in one hand. In all the rest of civilian Europe, the administration is divided into civil, legislative, police and military administration, where one is accountable to the other. Only in a military state [. . .] is all power concentrated in one person, the military commander" (Von Pidoll zu Quintenbach, 1847, p. 74).

Historical qualitative sources indicate an additional cause for the alienation of the soldiers at the bottom of the hierarchy: the lack of just promotions. Many captains used their power as patronage to nominate their own people for other positions of power. Similarly, they could also promote people who were paying for their own promotions (O'Reilly, 2006, p. 241). Additionally, many soldiers were forced to work many more days as corvée laborers for their captains than the amount and the type of work prescribed by law.[17] For example, corvée labor should have been mostly focused on things like the "erection and repair of government buildings and churches" and the "rebuilding of houses which had burned out without negligence on the part of the inhabitants" (Stopfer, 1831, pp. 275–276). In practice, corvée labor was used for the personal benefit of the captains.

Complaints about these latter unjust promotions and excessive corvée labor were ubiquitous during the time of Maria Theresa. In 1746, there was even a "serious" revolt in the Karlstadt generalcy in relation to career promotions and low payment (Rothenberg, 1966, p. 31). Similar revolts also happened in the Lika regiment in 1751 having the "usual causes: government corruption, heavy burdens, and failure to give just rewards and punishments" (Rothenberg, 1966, p. 32). The heavy burdens inflicted on border guards, according to historians, created "mutual" hatred and bitterness (*gegenseitigen Hass und Verbitterung*) between colonists and the state, and led to the demoralization of border people (Vaníček, 1875c, pp. 314–315). Additionally, Vaníček (1875c) suggests that the grenzers were in the habit of retaliating against their captains by complaining about fictitious or distorted facts.

---

[17] In mid-1800, each acre of arable land or meadow required from the owner a day of manual labor or half-day for a man bringing equipment with him (Desprez, 1847, p. 727).

Forced Conversions

A final type of distress inflicted on some of the military colonists was the practice of forced conversions. Despite the fact that the many charters guaranteed freedom of religion within the military colony, the Catholic Church was opposed to the Orthodox having their rights recognized. Many times, it tried to convert Christian Orthodox to Catholicism. This was particularly the case, according to Rothenberg (1966, p. 13), in the Warasdin generalcy around 1690, when practices of conversion were accompanied by brute force. Generally, Vienna turned a blind eye to all the different kinds of abuses that the grenzers were suffering from. Because of these abuses, there were frequent rebellions in the military colony. Duke Joseph of Sachsen-Hildurghausen was nominated in 1735 to examine the cause of the military colonists' complaints. His conclusion was that the flawed administration in the colony caused the inhabitants of the military colony to complain and not the practices of forced conversion. Rather than addressing the problem of forced conversions, the duke suggested a series of organizational reforms such as the abandonment of the old generalcies and the adoption of smaller, equally sized administrative units, called regiments, with an equal share of inhabitants.

The Habsburg military colony offered extensive opportunities for abuses by the colonial elites in a way that alienated the people at the bottom of the hierarchy. In addition, the central government invested less in local public goods and was strict about the maintenance of communal properties to protect the military organization of the border. Thus, the region displays the three elements that I argue should have negative consequences for long-term development: limited investment in infrastructure, removal of individual property rights, and exposure to violence. These are also the three elements that are relevant to evaluate the impact of extractive institutions. Depending on their presence and their intensity, we could see differential consequences for economic development.

While these processes can sometimes overlap in reality, they constitute also an analytical framework for evaluating the effects of historical institutions. The best cases for subsequent economic development after an episode of imperial extractivism are those where the empire invests in infrastructure and protects individual property rights. By contrast, the worst cases are the ones in which the empire underinvests, removes private property, and exerts violence. The Habsburg military colony is an example of an extractive institution with low investment in infrastructure, distortionary property rights (initially expropriating landowners), and implementation of communal properties with restrictions on the ability to alienate property. Finally, the military colony also displays some violence exerted against locals, but never as frequent and as systematic as other known colonial cases.

The next empirical chapter offers more detailed historical insights into how the Habsburg state adopted military colonialism, how such institution allowed the state to protect its territory, and how the military colony changed over time. The subsequent empirical chapter offers evidence about how the alienation caused by military institutions persisted over time and what the long-term effects of exposure to military colonialism are.

3   The Habsburg Military Frontier

In this chapter, I present an overview of the Habsburg military frontier, including its territorial expansion, the military and sanitary role that it performed for the empire, and the major reforms that were made to the administration to improve the economic welfare of its inhabitants. The empirical evidence is based on a variety of modern and historical primary and secondary sources.

The historiography of the military colony is extensive in French, German, and Serbo-Croatian. The seminal historians of the military frontier are: Boppe (1900); Damianitsch (1854, 1861); Demian (1806); Heissenberger (1872); Lopašić (1884a); Milleker (1925, 1926); Pal (1832); Von Pidoll zu Quintenbach (1847); Schwicker (1883); Stopfer (1831, 1840); Vaníček (1875a). Some of these works focus on very small portions of the frontier such as Milleker (1925, 1926), covering the period between 1764 and 1872. Others provide geographic and socio-economic details on the military frontier in the early 1800s (Demian, 1806; Pal, 1832). Many works also delve into the characteristics of the military administration and infrastructure in the region in the early 1800s (Boppe, 1900), while some provide invaluable details about the military legislation including marriage (Damianitsch, 1854) or the circumstances under which disciplinary action could be taken against soldiers in the mid-1850s (Damianitsch, 1861; Heissenberger, 1872). Similarly, important compendia presenting the broader military legal frameworks have also been published: see for example Stopfer (1831, 1840). Finally, some military historians try to compare the Habsburg military frontier to others such as the Russian one (Von Pidoll zu Quintenbach, 1847), while other scholars provide comprehensive overviews of the development and the end of the military frontier (Lopašić, 1884a; Schwicker, 1883; Vaníček, 1875a).

The modern contributors to the historiography of the military frontier include: Blanc (1951); Ferguson (1954); Kaser (1997); Lesky (1957); Heeresgeschichtliches Museum (1973); Horel (2009); Roth (1988); Probszt-Ohstorff (1967); Rothenberg (1960b, 1966); Sokol (1940); Völkl and Ernst (1982); Wessely (1954). Some of these modern works resemble the style of focus of the earlier historians. For example, some scholars revisit specific sections of the border (e.g. Banat in the case of Roth (1988) or the Slavonian, Croatian part of the border in the case of Probszt-Ohstorff (1967)). Others focus on both the geography and history of Croatia (Blanc, 1951). In a similar way to Schwicker (1883) and Vaníček (1875a), there are also comprehensive overviews of the history of the institution of military colonialism in German (Kaser, 1997; Sokol, 1940; Völkl and Ernst, 1982; Wessely, 1954), in English (Rothenberg, 1960b, 1966), or comparative studies concentrating on different frontiers (see the Russian-Habsburg comparison by Ferguson (1954)). Finally, Lesky (1957) discusses extensively the sanitary role of the military colony during the 1700s and early 1800s.

The international political context in the fifteenth and sixteenth centuries was conducive to the creation of the military colony. In 1519 Charles V (1500–1558) inherited the vast possessions of the House of Habsburg, which included the original Habsburg duchies in the eastern Alpine region, Spain and its dependent territories, Sardinia, Sicily, and Naples (Judson, 2016). However, in addition to the extensive dominions – truly an "empire on which the sun never set" (Jászi, 1929, pp. 31–34) – Charles V also inherited extensive social and political problems. The most important problem was the resistance of the local landowners against the attempts of the monarchs to reform and centralize authority. According to Jászi (1929, p. 41), "the largest strata of the nobility hated the dynasty as the destroyer of the ancient privileges." Another problem on an international level was the Ottoman Empire, whose powers Charles V had to contend with (Ingrao, 2000; Judson, 2016). In the end, the struggle against the Turks, which was felt by the nobles too, led to a consolidation of Habsburg power. Jászi (1929) describes for example how the masses felt more and more clearly the growing power of the dynasty in the face of which feudal forces became increasingly weak.

Between 1400 and 1500 the Ottomans expanded their territory at a greater speed than in the 1300s.[1] Historians argue that prior to the creation of the military colony in 1521,[2] Turkish attacks had been a common

---

[1] The Ottoman Empire had a hierarchical structure, with the Ottoman sultan at the top and the peasants, at the bottom, seen as the protected people of the sultan (*reaya*), who were drafted Christian children, prisoners of war, and kidnapped slaves who could become Ottoman civil servants. Between the sultan and the peasants, there were the soldiers or *sipahi*s, who in exchange for land would receive plots of land to collect taxes from.

[2] There is some debate about the exact year when military efforts to defend the Habsburg Empire commenced, with the options being 1521, 1522, and 1526. Pálffy (2012), based on Thallóczy (1903), makes the case that sending 2,000 infantrymen by the Archduke in 1521 represented the first attempt by the Austrian provinces to help in the assistance of the defense of the Hungarian border with the Ottoman Empire.

occurrence (Blanc, 1951; Rothenberg, 1966). The Ottomans conquered much of the Balkans in the fifteenth century, establishing their rule over the north shores of the Black Sea, while in the sixteenth century, they established their rule in what is today Hungary. Ottoman raiders first appeared before Mottling (Mettika) in Carniola in 1408 and made occasional incursions into Carniola, Carinthia, and Styria. After 1463 they practically became yearly occurrences (Rothenberg, 1960a, p. 494). An important part of the population relocated, was captured, or was killed as a result. Blanc (1957, p. 75) cites sources that estimate a few thousand inhabitants (much of the population in the region) were massacred. The population that was captured was typically relocated and transformed into tax-paying Ottoman peasantry. A part of the population also managed to escape at the news of Ottoman raids. Prior to leaving, they destroyed everything to prevent any indirect help (e.g. the crops, wells, or goods left behind) to the Ottomans. The very few areas that still remained populated to some extent were the areas very close to the Croatian fortresses that became "no man's land"[3] (Blanc, 1957, p. 71). By and large, by the end of the sixteenth century, the entire territory between the rivers Kupa and Una, which coincides with the subsequent military colony, was a huge desert (Blanc, 1957, p. 51).

The local elites were unable to withstand the Ottoman attacks, which is why they abandoned their lands and sought refuge with other noblemen especially further north in Carniola, where noble refugees were welcomed. It was in 1518 that the estates of Inner Austria – Carniola, Carinthia and Styria, which were most exposed to the raids – demanded the establishment of an outer defensive zone in Croatia (Rothenberg, 1960b, p. 15). As a result, King Ferdinand I (1503–1564) undertook extensive military preparations and in June 1522 moved the Austrian military forces into Croatia (O'Reilly, 2006, p. 229). The recently settled men were able to meet Ottoman raids with ambush, counter-raids, and reprisals. Ferdinand I issued specific "privileges" (*Privilegien*) in the years 1524–1545 as gratitude for their courage (Szántó, 1980). Despite some success in holding the enemy back, the Ottomans defeated the Hungarian armies at Mohács, captured Buda in 1541, and almost destroyed the Croatian lands. The ineffectiveness of their efforts together with the high military expenditures became a considerable concern for the Habsburg crown. A commentator wrote to the king in 1577 and suggested that a "system of fortresses is the only means by which Your Majesty will be able to contain the power and the advance of the enemy, and behind which Your countries and peoples will be secure" (Szegő, 1911, p. 52). A variety of historiographical works

---

[3] These are fortresses like Ogulin, Slunj, Karlovac, Petrinija, etc.

discuss the system of fortresses in Hungary including Agoston (1998) and Pálffy (2008, 2009, 2012).

King Ferdinand embraced such suggestions and organized the Congress of the Inner Austrian Lands in 1578. During this congress, he signed the *Brucker Libell* document, which stipulated the financial obligations of every land to help cover the military costs (Fine, 2009). The only concession that the estates received was the ability to nominate their own people for some administrative positions in the border establishment, but not highly ranked positions such as military generals. The king still reserved the prerogative to confirm these appointments. The military officials would lead the mercenaries and the peasants in the area to serve "not only as a protective wall against the Turks, but also in case of rebellion, against Hungary" (Lopašić, 1889, p. 351). They would also act against other enemies of the empire (Von Hietzinger, 1817, p. 29). The commanding general, nominated by the king, would act both as a regimental commander and a civilian governor, exercising the role of a district captain, company commander, and mayor (Lesky, 1957, p. 89). Soldiers would go on patrol along the border and they would ring the alarm bells when necessary (Kaser, 1997).

3.1 The Slavonian and the Croatian Frontier

During the same Congress of the Inner Austrian Lands in 1578, the imperial authorities decided to split the military area into two administrative regions. One region was the *Krabatiche Gränitz* or the Croatian border and consisted of the area between the Dalmatian coast and the Sava river. This region was subsequently called the Karlstadt (German name) or Karlovac (Serbo-Croatian name) border after the name of its main fortress Karlovac, which was built in 1578. The second region was called the *Windische Gränitz* – the Slavonian border – and extended between Sava and Drava. It would later be called the Warasdin (Varaždin) border. Lower Austria, Upper Austria, Carniola, Carinthia, and Salzburg contributed to the reinforcement of the Croatian frontier, while the Styrian nobility supported the Upper Slavonian border. As an example of the costs that the estates had to cover, the Archduke Charles, the general in charge of the Croatian and Slavonian border, would receive 500,000 florins for the army at the border, which was composed of the two military bodies, one in Karlovac and the other in Varaždin. The armies included 1,250 hussars, 500 arquebusiers, 682 sergeants at arms, and 4,282 infantry men for a total of more than 7,000 men. The soldiers were distributed along fortified posts, which were most at risk of being attacked (Perrot, 1869, p. 42). Beyond the inhabitants' military activities, the area also started to feature fortified villages, blockhouses, and watchtowers, becoming a strong line of defense against Ottoman incursions (Wagner, 1973).

The map in Figure 3.1 shows the Croatian and Slavonian regions overlapping with modern international borders, together with the main territories in the regions controlled by the Habsburgs and the Ottomans around the 1550s. In addition, the map highlights every major border fortress in the Ottoman and Habsburg lands. To avoid label overcrowding, I include the names of only the most important ones. Between 1521 and 1566 only thirteen castles were able to resist the Ottoman siege for more than ten days and only nine for more than twenty days (Agoston, 1998). As a result, Vienna made the decision to modernize the key strongpoints in Hungary, with the help of Italian military engineers and technicians. Thus, the process resulted in the development of the ideal city type, the fortified town, or *Festungstadt*, well known in Italy, France, and the Netherlands (Agoston, 1998, p. 133).

Despite the construction of such military infrastructure, being in a border area created a lot of insecurity for the local population. To incentivize people at the very bottom of the military hierarchy to stay, King Ferdinand issued his first charter about the "Uscocs" (Serbian term meaning escapees to refer to the escapees from the Ottoman lands[4]), according to which escapees were granted land as hereditary fiefs[5] (Blanc, 1951, p. 117) in exchange for military service.[6] Unlike other people in the civilian area, these were free men, organizing themselves in companies of 200 under their elected captains, called *vojvode*. The captains received an annual income, while the other soldiers would get booty from the Turks.[7]

The signing of *Brucker Libell* and the creation of the Croatian and Slavonian military frontiers also meant a clear separation between the civilian and the military administrations of the Habsburg Empire. While on the civilian side, the Habsburgs continued to share power with the landowning nobility and the Church, who had their interests represented in the Croatian diet (*Sabor*) and who had a chief executive in the person of the *Ban*, on the military side, the entire administration was fully

---

[4] The term "Uscocs" is in many documents used interchangeably with terms such as "Rascians" or "Vlachs." Rothenberg (1960b) argues all these interchangeable terms refer to the escapees from the Ottoman lands.

[5] A few historical works examined the image of the Vlach as the representative of the newly arrived colonists in the military frontier, among others, Lazanin (2003) and Völkl (1982).

[6] For the first twenty years, they would be free of taxes, while afterwards, they would only pay a quitrent (Lopašić, 1884b, pp. 388–389). A charter from 1538 about the same group (now called "Rascians" (Lopašić, 1884a, pp. 5–6)) indicates that they received free land in the vicinity of the town of Warasdin and a special military status.

[7] A third of the booty, however, was to be retained by the paymaster and for the purpose of ransoming captive frontiersmen.

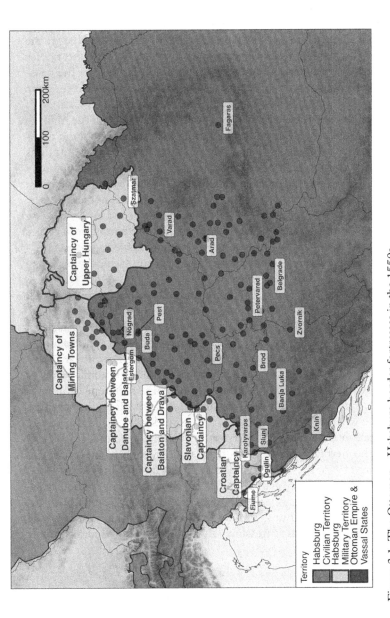

Figure 3.1 The Ottoman – Habsburg border fortresses in the 1550s

Notes: Redrawn based on Magas (2015); Pálffy (2009). Modern country boundaries and elevation in the background. All the dots represent border fortresses. To avoid label overcrowding, I include labels for only the most important ones.

appointed by either nobles or the king. The separation of power between the two regions caused tensions between the state and nobles, given that the estates wanted to regain their power over the military area (Rothenberg, 1966). In other words, the nobles viewed the land in the military colony as a continuation of their territory. Similarly, given that in the middle of the sixteenth century most peasants were serfs, the nobles feared that the freedom of the military colonists would inspire the peasants on the civilian side to demand similar freedoms and refuse the "respect and labor that are due to feudal lords" (Lopašić, 1884c, p. 293). Another cause of tension was that some of the inhabitants of the military colony were Christian Orthodox while the Croatian nobility was Catholic. Having their right to maintain their religion and religious institutions officially recognized, the Orthodox inhabitants of the military colony were seen as schismatics (Rothenberg, 1960b, p. 69). Military colonists, on the other hand, never wanted to be controlled by the nobles. In fact, an account by the Duke of Sachsen-Hildburghausen cited in Rothenberg (1966, p. 10) reveals that colonists would rather "be hacked into pieces than be separated from their officers and become subjects of the Croatian nobility." Nevertheless, the border was kept in place despite strong pressures.

While in the 1500s and 1600s, the military colony only consisted of the Karlstadt and the Warasdin generalcies, the Habsburg military frontier expanded with time. Following the second Ottoman attack on Vienna in 1683, the Austrian emperor amassed a large international army to push the Ottomans back and moved the border southward, capturing parts of Croatia-Slavonia that had been under Ottoman control for over two hundred years. As a result, the third regiment came into place – the *Banal Gränitz* or the First and Second Banal regiments. This is the place where Ottoman refugees came from Serbia in the late 1600s. The migration from Serbian lands into the military colony is what reinforced the Serbian component of the military colony. According to Rothenberg (1966, pp. 12–13), in the Banal regiments, they constituted more than half of the population and were only a minority in the Warasdin regiment. Other Christian Orthodox and Catholics also fled Bosnia, Dalmatia, and Central Europe to become frontier guards.[8] Some of the refugees feared Ottoman repression, while others migrated for economic reasons.[9]

---

[8] Blanc (1951) argues that it was enough for the Habsburgs to offer similar advantages to the Bosniacs to want to move to the military colony.

[9] Blanc (1957, p. 84) also argues that many families changed their minds about whether to live within the Habsburg military colony confines or the Ottoman Empire, depending on who was offering more benefits.

Land was one of the main methods for the Habsburgs to attract fiscal/economic migrants, given the fact that it was abundantly available in the military area. Boppe (1900, p. 44) explains how the inhabitants of the military colony obtained official land titles at the end of the seventeenth century in exchange for their military services: "the division of land is done according to the family size and their needs. When a family grows bigger, they acquire new land; they receive land titles on condition that they always perform their military obligations." The families consisted of several households, sometimes of up to 60 individuals, owning property together. The land was still owned by the Habsburg crown but it was assigned to military colonists who were considered an ever-ready military force (Perrot, 1869, p. 50). The second important way of attracting colonists was to provide relief from the usual manorial obligations that most peasants in the empire had. Colonists no longer had the condition of debt bondage and indentured servitude toward a feudal lord. Feudal lords in the military colony had been completely abolished. Finally, other kinds of privileges included retaining a share of booty from the enemy, the ability to choose their own leaders: captains (*vojvode*) and magistrates (*knezovi*), and freedom of religious worship. Such freedoms can be interpreted as what Barkey (2008, pp. 12–13) calls a "negotiate[d] and willingly relinquish[ed] [. . .] degree of autonomy" for the purpose of maintaining compliance, resources, political coherence, and durability. Hence, in the original stages, there was a certain degree of bargaining and negotiation when it came to the process of becoming a military colonist. This is why the institutionalization of military colonialism may be somewhat different from other forms of forced labor. However, once it was agreed upon, leaving was no longer an option and mutiny was severely punished. This was done with the help of other military colonists who were faithful to the crown or in the worst case with the help of soldiers coming from outside the military colony. Severe punishments could be implemented on behalf of the empire through them and they took the form of executions and long-term hard labor (Vaníček, 1875a, pp. 505–506).

The early abolition of feudalism in the early 1500s is different from the abolition of feudalism in 1848. In the initial stages of the Ottoman attacks, many feudal lords tried to create local militias and personal armies of peasants. The small armies were no match for the Ottomans. Local nobles abandoned their lands and saw themselves in a position of asking for protection from other great noble families in the regions of Zagorje, Turopolje, and Carniola (which correspond to regions close to Zagreb and south Slovenia) (Blanc, 1957). For example, Lopašić (1895, p. 56) describes how the local noble Franjo Blagaj guarded his own castle located on the Korana river, while in 1572 a permanent guard was approved for his lands. Despite all his efforts to keep his lands, Franjo fled to Kranj, a place in modern-day Slovenia. His brother, Stijepan Blagaj, received the castle Kočevje. Croatian nobles who lost their land during the sixteenth century due to Ottoman attacks tried to get their land back. The monarchy, however, was very firm in keeping the military colony free from nobles and free from serfdom. Rothenberg (1966, p. 52) for example describes how in 1769 a noble would face a very heavy fine if they encroached on the lands of the military colonists.

In 1556, a separate political organization was established in Graz, the Austrian *Hofkriegsrat*, which was responsible for the military operations and the colonization of the abandoned areas of the military colony. This was supposed to replace the king's direct supervision of military affairs in the colony. Through the Hofkriegsrat,[10] the military colony also developed a separate system for the administration of justice, different from the civilian area. Within the colony, people were subject to the immediate authority of their superiors, which was determined by their military rank. In criminal cases, the prosecution went to the colonel and in some cases it was brought to the War Council. For grave crimes potentially punishable by death, the judgment was passed on to the governor-general, who could exonerate the accused. In cases of revolts or crimes against the state, justice would be conducted quickly without appeal.[11]

Additional significant changes were introduced in the last decade of the seventeenth century to the composition and the administration of the defensive frontier (Koroknai, 1974; Wessely, 1973). The large territories re-conquered by Austria during the Great Turkish War of 1683–1699, which ended with the Treaty of Karlowitz in 1699, resulted in extensive alterations to the southeastern border (Völkl and Ernst, 1982). The new territories[12] included the marchlands of Transylvania, the Szekler frontier being inaugurated in 1764, and the Wallachian frontier in 1766 (Pecinjacki, 1985). A special Danubian frontier was also established in the Syrmia region, which extended all the way to the Transylvanian border, east of the Tisza and south of Maros rivers. With its expansion, the

---

[10] The Hofkriegsrat (or Aulic War Council, sometimes Imperial War Council) established in 1556 was the central military administrative authority of the Habsburg monarchy, the predecessor of the Austro-Hungarian Ministry of War. The agency was directly subordinated to the Habsburg emperors with its seat in Vienna.

[11] The members of a tribunal would get together in the city center together with the suspect. The judicial procedures would be publicly explained, the suspect interrogated, judged, and, if found guilty, executed in front of the other troops (Boppe, 1900, p. 46).

[12] A few historiographers examined specific sections of the frontier, which contribute to a better understanding of the military frontier as a whole: Krajasich (1974) and Turković (1936).

military frontier experienced ethnic transformations in the east. While Bulgarians, Greeks, and Germans were already present in the region, the long war with the Ottomans attracted Serbian families (Nedeljković, 1936; Pavličević, 1984) seeking refuge in the Austrian lands.[13] Romanian families were also attracted to the Transylvanian section of the border. From a political standpoint, after the Treaty of Karlowitz in 1699, Croatia gained autonomy over justice and home affairs, but it was closely connected to Hungary. The assembly or the *sabor* elected and delegated three representatives to the Hungarian parliament, whose laws also prevailed in Croatia. Unlike in Transylvania with independent government agency, the highest Hungarian government body (the Hungarian Chamber and the Hungarian Court Chancellery) had jurisdiction over Croatia as well (Borbála, 1997, pp. 64–68).

After the Treaty of Karlowitz, concerns arose about the rights and obligations of the border inhabitants (Wessely, 1954) given that they had lost some of their original function once the Ottomans no longer posed a threat. The emperor allowed the grenzers to keep their rights and titles, gave them partial relief from military services, and asked the locals in the Danube, Tisza, and Maros frontiers to pay taxes. A fixed contribution was calculated based on the amount of personal service and the size of their landholdings (Wessely, 1973, p. 72). They remained under the command of their captains, who also collected taxes from them. The grenzers, especially the ones in the Maros frontier, continued to complain about the tax burdens (Wessely, 1973). After their repeated complaints, in around 1740 the court decided to reduce taxes for the grenzers who were fighting in war alongside the professional army.[14]

After the Treaty of Passarowitz of 1718, Syrmia and the city of Belgrade were added to the Habsburg territory. The Slavonian grenzers were sent to Syrmia to aid in the construction of border fortifications, particularly the main fortress of Peterwardein (Wessely, 1973, p. 81), contributing to the territorial extension of the military colony. In addition, the authorities decided to tax all the inhabitants of the Slavonian

---

[13] According to some estimates, at least 40,000 families fled to the north at the end of the seventeenth century under the leadership of Patriarch Arsenius Cernojevic (Gavrilović and Krestic, 1997; Gavrilović and Samardžić, 1989).

[14] The military services rendered by the grenzers were of little significance: their loose organization and lack of sufficient equipment led to them not being involved in major battles. The grenzers considered particularly burdensome the demand that they observe military discipline and the requirement that they provide equipment out of their personal funds. At times of war, they received some public funds but they were at best, "inadequately nourished and equipped out of public funds" (Wessely, 1973, p. 75). As a result, mutinies were relatively frequent.

frontier with the captains in charge of tax collection.[15] In 1721, the peacetime strength of the grenzers in the Slavonian and Danube frontiers was fixed at 5,844 infantry and cavalry men. On February 8, 1735, a new plan to reform that military frontier was created and implemented to deal with the fact that the number of soldiers recruited was not enough to fulfill wartime needs. The plan consisted of dividing all able-bodied grenzers above the age of 18 into three groups. The first group would consist of soldiers in active service, who could be ordered to perform service outside the country. A second group would be made up of soldiers occupying the fortified lookout posts. The third group would consist of soldiers involved in farming. All three groups would be exempt from taxation and the payment of customs duties. Remuneration for the latter two groups consisted of farmland. The grenzers who performed military service outside of their frontier region were the only group that was paid by the treasury. Therefore, with the new plan, the frontier areas were split along territorial and administrative lines, based on the type of service performed (Wessely, 1973, p. 85). These reforms were subsequently extended along the Croatian frontier.

3.2   Frontier Institutions in the Banat, Uskok District, and Serbia

The Banat became the northernmost province of the military colony under Habsburg rule after the Treaty of Passarowitz, located south of the river Maros, east of the Tisza, and north of the Danube. Because it had not had any military institutions before, Banat stayed under the imperial government administration in Vienna, while the government focused on re-colonizing the territory (Wessely, 1973, p. 89) after the Ottoman withdrawal. It was in 1743, after the dissolution of the Tisza–Maros frontier, that the military institutions were extended into Banat.

Between the Treaties of Passarowitz (1718) and Belgrade (1739), another strip of land on the right bank of the Sava river became part of the military colony. The Uskok district witnessed continuous flows of in- and out-migration, exemplifying the competition between the Habsburg and the Ottoman empires in attracting people to populate the border areas. Wessely (1973, p. 91) notes that the Ottomans were promising tax exemptions for five years, while the Habsburgs only for three. Despite the somewhat more convenient fiscal conditions, the former Habsburg

---

[15] Wessely (1973, p. 82) estimates that in 1725, the grenzers paid a total of 10,000 florins in taxes together with the corvée labor in the construction of the Peterwardein fortress. The grenzers also had to provide 25,000 florins in special contributions, together with the daily provisions for 634 men and 53 wagons for the construction of the Brod fortress.

soldiers would end up "robbing the country they had left" (Wessely, 1973, p. 91) because of dire economic conditions in the Ottoman lands. Some soldiers preferred to stay in the Habsburg lands and enjoy the prestigious status of "grenzer" than being reduced to the status of peasant in the Ottoman lands. The map in Figure 3.2 displays the changes made to the border after the Treaty of Karlowitz of 1699. The Danube, Tisza, and Maros frontiers were inhabited by Serbs, Romanians, and Bulgarians.

After the Treaty of Passarowitz, the citadel of Belgrade (previously in Ottoman hands) became one of the main points of defense against Ottoman forces. The citadel itself was enlarged and many regular troops were stationed there. The area of Belgrade and northern Serbia that was Habsburg after 1718 also became inhabited by German speakers who were mostly Catholic. They had been encouraged by Vienna to serve as reserve troops for the protection of the citadel against surprise attacks. These were veterans who wanted to settle in Serbia with their wives and children, after receiving housing allowances and military duty exemptions for several years. Other people also received an income for their military service while the captains made sure that the land was cultivated and no fertile soil went to waste (Wessely, 1973, p. 97). These measures, however, were short-lived. The Treaty of Belgrade (1739) terminated Austrian rule in Serbia. The militia was transferred to Slavonia and Syrmia. This increased the need for the Habsburgs to strengthen the Slavonian frontier by extending it into Syrmia.

3.3 Frontier Institutions in Transylvania

The first military settlements in Transylvania were established around 1690. However, the organization of the entire Transylvanian military frontier (extending along the Carpathian mountains) was conducted between 1760 and 1780, during the Habsburg war against Prussia (the Seven Years War, 1756–1763) (Göllner, 1973). In 1763, the frontier militia of the Banat of Temesvar was created, with two infantries made up of German settlers, Orthodox, and Vlach populations. General Buccow proposed the creation of two Romanian infantry regiments between 1762 and 1765, each composed of 3,000 soldiers, two additional Szekler regiments, and two Hussar regiments (Vaníček 1875b, p.75). Many peasants were happy to enroll because it would give them an opportunity to escape from feudal obligations. The Szekler were less supportive of the extension of the border, which is why it took until 1780 to be fully extended into Transylvania.

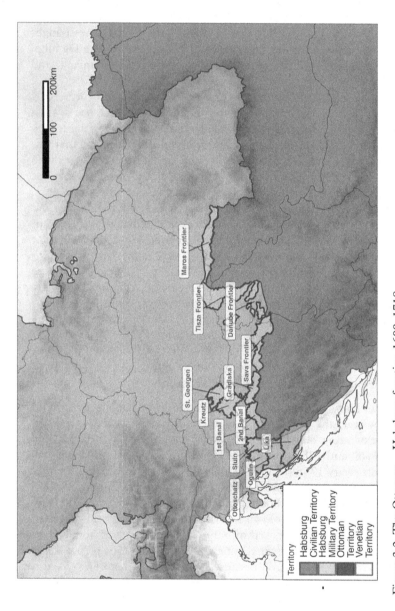

Figure 3.2 The Ottoman – Habsburg frontier, 1699–1718

Notes: Redrawn based on Birken (1981); Lesky (1957); Wessely (1954). Modern country boundaries and elevation in the background.

Göllner (1973) estimates that the number of soldiers in Transylvania went up to around 17,000 in 1790. Similar to the other areas of the military frontier, soldiers were allocated a plot of land in exchange for their services and had to pay minimal taxes. In a similar way to the other colonies, peasants were willing to become soldiers because that entailed freedom from the shackles of serfdom, despite pressures from nobles who wanted to keep their land and the serfs under their control. The following regiments were established in 1773: the first Romanian infantry regiment, the second Romanian infantry regiment, the second Romanian Dragons regiment, the first Szekler infantry regiment, the second Szekler infantry regiment, and the Szekler Hussar regiment (see Figure 3.3). Every regiment was made up of two battalions and every battalion of two companies. Similarly, in 1776 the Šajkaš Battalion of Titel, which originally coincided with the Theiss district, was attached to the frontier (Szabó, 2000).

Soldiers in Transylvania enjoyed usufructuary rights over the land without being able to sell or bequeath it to multiple sons: the land could only be given to the first-born son, while his brothers would work under his supervision (Göllner, 1973, p. 70). The land plot size could vary between half a hectare and 20–30 hectares. Together with the land, the peasants would form a family community. In a similar way to the other sections of the military colony, desertion would be punished by death (Göllner, 1973, p. 89). If entire families left, their goods and lands would be confiscated and given to the military administration. Protests against the state and mutinies would be tried and convicted according to the military code. Despite such punishments, many grenzers revolted against the authorities (most famously around the 1790s) and ran to Wallachia or Moldova in the second half of the eighteenth century. The reason had to do with abuses by local nobles who ignored their status as grenzers, continued to consider them as serfs, and forced them to work longer than the four days that Maria Theresa established as corvée. In addition, they had excessive military obligations (Göllner, 1973, p. 114). Habsburg authorities attempted a variety of reforms but did not have much success.

The Transylvanian regiments were abolished around 1859. The very first ones to be disbanded were the Szekler regiments after the Hungarian War of Independence ended in 1848/9 with Russian intervention and in which the Szeklers supported the Hungarian revolutionary army. In 1867, Transylvania became part of the reformed constitutional monarchy of Austria-Hungary.

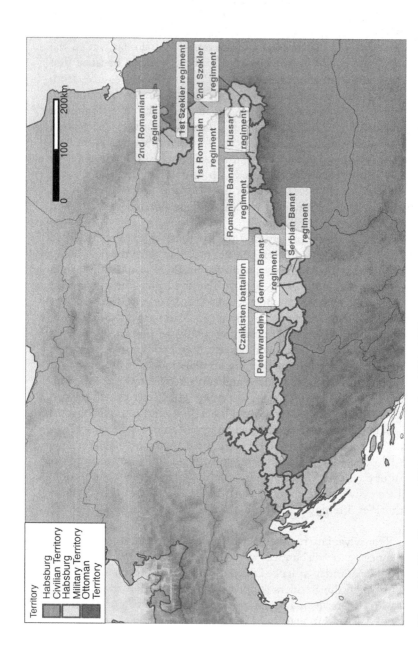

Figure 3.3 The Ottoman – Habsburg frontier, 1762–1873

Notes: Redrawn based on Birken (1981); Lesky (1957); Wessely (1954). Modern country boundaries and elevation in the background.

3.4   The Military Colony: Persistence and Change

In the previous sections, I provided details of the geopolitical context surrounding the creation of the military colony: what the original reasons behind its creation were, how it first appeared in what is today Croatia, how it expanded into Serbia and Romania. In this section, I outline some of the key reforms and political changes that affected the military institutions or allowed them to continue to exist.

The Military Colony under Maria Theresa

Under Maria Theresa's rule (1745–1780), the Habsburg Empire became more centralized. The military colonists of the Croatian and Slavonian generalcies contributed substantially to the Habsburg military defenses against Prussia, reinforcing the queen's armies. According to Vaníček (1875d, p. 403), they constituted more than a quarter of the Austrian army of about 88,000 soldiers participating in the various war campaigns of the Austrian Empire. They played a key role in the anti-Prussian campaigns at Lobositz (1756) (Delbrük, 1900) and Kolin (1757) (Fuller, 1925, p. 41). The colonists from the Szluin and Gradiska regiments also represented more than fifty percent of the army of 3,500 men in the raid against Berlin of 1757. The colonists proved to be very competent, serving as a "light infantry," protecting the main Austrian army against surprise attacks. In addition, the grenzers fought for the Habsburgs against the French and Bavarians in southern Germany, Alsace, and Italy.

Despite their successes, only a few of the grenzer units had uniforms and few were equipped to meet the standards of western armies. For example, most in Karlstadt and the Slavonian generalcies wore "white linen trousers tied at the ankles, sashes bristling with daggers and pistols, long Turkish muskets, and hooded red cloaks as worn by Karlstadters and Slavonians" (Rothenberg, 1966, p. 19). Figure 3.4 displays examples of uniforms that these soldiers were wearing in 1762.

Such uniforms seem to have persisted well into the 1800s. For example, Perrot (1869, p. 66) comments on the soldiers' clothing:

In summer, they have no other clothing than their pants and their shirt of big white fabric, and sometimes a kind of brown jacket with red frogs [type of coat fastener], which they also wear for work in the fields. In winter, they are seen wrapped in their large hooded red coats, which are lifted from behind the end of the rifle thrown over their shoulders. As for the uniform, blue pants tightened with the calf and a jacket of black or white wool are used only for parade days and in days of war.[16]

---

[16] Translation from French.

Lika

Otocac

Glina / 1. Banal

St. George / Gjurgjevac

Figure 3.4 Officer uniforms from the frontier zone, 1762
Source: Bautzen Museum (1762). Die Bautzener Bilderhandschrift.
Folios: 108, 109, 121, 112.

As already indicated in the previous chapter, the grenzers lived for many years in an obsolete system of administration and command both before Maria Theresa and for some portion of her reign. For many years, such arrangements were unsatisfactory for the colonists: the pay and the rations were usually in arrears (Rothenberg, 1966, p. 21), causing mutiny and desertions. In an effort to deal with the grenzers' lack of discipline stemming from dissatisfaction with the imperial authorities, to prepare them more effectively for modern war, and to reform the colony overall, Maria Theresa transferred the functions of the *Hofkriegsrat* (1556–1848) to a Military Directory or *Militär-Direktorium* in 1742. This was a staffing agency of the military authorities in Vienna (Rothenberg, 1960b, 1970). Maria Theresa also nominated Duke Joseph of Sachsen-Hildburghausen (of the many minor German princes seeking fame and fortune under the Habsburg banners (Rothenberg, 1966, p. 16)) for the control of this office. In doing so, she abolished the Inner-Austrian military administration and dissolved the functions of the Court War Council at Graz. Rothenberg (1960b) considers the changes that Maria Theresa made as the end of an epoch in the history of the border. While for nearly three centuries prior to the time of Maria Theresa, diminishing the Turkish threat was the heart of Habsburg preoccupations, the colony became more of a valuable instrument against repeated attempts of local nobles and privileged estates to dispute the rule of the Habsburgs.

During his time in office, Duke Hildburghausen abolished the obsolete captaincies and organized the two generalcies into new administrative districts, called regiments (Wessely, 1973, p. 57). These regiments took the names of their home stations and districts in 1753. Consequently, the old Warasdin generalcy turned into the Gjurgjevac and Kreutz (Križevci) regiments after that year. The former Karlstadt generalcy transformed into Lika, Ottoschatz (Otočac), Ogulin, and Szluin (Slunj) regiments. Similarly, an edict from 1747 transformed the Slavonian border into three regiments: Brod, Gradiska, and Peterwardein. Duke Hildburghausen also attempted to achieve some uniformity when it came to the costs incurred by the colonists. Despite such attempts, there were still some differences among the regiments: for example, the soldiers in the former Warasdin regions had to purchase their uniforms and equipment, while the soldiers in the former Karlstadt and Banal regions received free uniforms (although they had to pay out of pocket for maintaining them).

Beyond changes to the territorial administration, Maria Theresa also passed additional legislation to further regulate the rights and obligations of the grenzers, reflecting new concepts of statehood and rights in the era of Enlightenment.[17] The most important piece of legislation affecting the colonists was Maria Theresa's *Militär-Gränitz-Rechten* of 1754, whose role was to re-iterate that all activities in the border region would be subordinated to military considerations. New stipulations were put in place about a new system of military courts, with judicial proceedings being handled by military judges. Title IV of the *Militär-Gränitz-Rechten* also indicated that the communal households – the *Hauskommunitäten* – would be preserved. Each household would get a plot of land as long as it fulfilled its military obligations and with the stipulation that the land was crown property. The size and the quality of land would depend on the type of military service performed.[18] Finally, according to the allocation rules, the land could not be sold, leased, or given away. According to Art. 77 in Chapter IV of the *Militär-Gränitz-Rechten*, it was not possible to inherit land, as was the case with the Dalmatian borderlands under Venetian rule or the northern Bosnian frontier under Ottoman rule. All transactions regarding land had to be approved by the relevant military authorities. Overall, all these measures were aimed at preserving the exclusive military character of the border population.

While the original *Militär-Gränitz-Rechten* were intended for the Karlstadt and Warasdin regiments, they gradually extended into the Banal and other border regiments, with the exception of Transylvania. Generally, the legal code reinforced the Austrian authority in the periphery. Some of the measures adopted caused dissatisfaction among the grenzers leading to riots, mutinies, and rebellions. Colonists deplored that their native leaders (the *knezovi*) were terminated and were replaced with "foreigners" (Rothenberg, 1966). In addition, the grenzers were hostile to the Habsburg counter-reformation efforts of the eighteenth century, which meant that the Catholic clergy was coercing locals to convert to Catholicism. Finally, the grenzers were dissatisfied with government corruption, heavy burdens, and failure to give just rewards and punishments, which they overall interpreted as a plan to potentially eliminate their special status.

To appease discontent, in 1755 Maria Theresa promulgated a new set of laws to supplement the code of 1754 and which prohibited the use of grenzers for private labor; all transgressions would be punished. Similarly, illicit punishments against the grenzers were prohibited. The

---

[17] Enlightenment thought was deeply influential in the politics of European rulers such as Catherine II of Russia, Joseph II of Austria, and Frederick II of Prussia. Their conduct and policies became known as enlightened absolutism (Black, 1992).

[18] Rothenberg (1966, p. 27) explains how in the Karlstadt regiments, the basic land allocation was about eight yokes of good land, ten of mediocre, and twelve of poor land.

new set of codes also made some concessions concerning the acquisition of uniforms, arms, and equipment. While there was continued pressure for the grenzers to convert to Catholicism, the number and intensity of revolts decreased over time. Despite some of these minor changes, "the problem of providing a sound economic base and a modest degree of prosperity for the grenzers remained unsolved" (Rothenberg, 1966, p. 39).

At the end of the Seven Years' War (1756–1763), the Habsburg lands were burdened with an increasing public debt, which is why the military colony proved to serve its original purpose: providing cheap manpower for war. The war years, however, affected the well-being of the colonists: according to Rothenberg (1966, p. 42), the grenzers were nearly destitute as a result of the war: it had ruined the agriculture that the regiments were so heavily dependent on. According to Vaníček (1875b, p. 611), the Karlstadt, Ogulin, and Lika regiments were particularly affected by the war and in 1765 locals were starving. To improve the conditions of the grenzers, the authorities permitted the establishment of grain markets in Karlstadt, Gospic, Ottoschatz, Bjelovar, and Koprivnica, which were the main urban centers in these regiments. Kaser (1997, p. 476) further discusses the economic problems in some regiments in the late eighteenth century that were exacerbated by the discrepancy between population growth, insufficient agricultural expansion, and the occasional weather shocks which prevented good harvests. According to Kaser (1997, p. 477), it was only in 1814 that imperial intervention together with an intensification of agriculture led to "the stabilization of the relationship between production output and food demand."

The Military Frontier Zone as a Sanitary Cordon

One important role that the military colony played, particularly during the reign of Maria Theresa, is that of a sanitary cordon or *Sanitäts Kordon*, which was meant to prevent the transmission of the Levantine plague which spread in the Ottoman Empire by 1750 (Lesky, 1957, p. 103). The imperial edict from December 24, 1737 reflects the view that "the military organization is the best and only remedy against the evil propagation of the plague." The sanitary role became functional in 1765 after pressure from border administration officials including the Duke of Saxe-Hildburghausen and barons Beck, Engelshofen, Siskovich, and Khevenhüller (Lesky, 1957, p. 88). To combat potential plague outbreaks, contingency stations (*Kontumazstationen*) were created to prescribe both people and property quarantine limits (Lesky, 1957, p. 84). Such stations had to issue health passes, report cases of plague, and provide medical intelligence service under the authority of the Health Commission in Vienna – the *Sanitäts-Hofkommission*. The exact process by which people and goods were treated is described by Lesky (1957, p. 87):

In every contingency station, there was a lieutenant, commanding a cavalry of 30 men. Three of them had to be on guard at all times. Three men had to stand on the crossing side, stopping all the people who came into the contingency station as soon as they arrived. Thereafter, they would visit the contagion surgeon (*contagions-chyrurgum*), their goods would be recorded, and they would be accompanied into the hospital or contingency house. Two men would patrol the contingency house for 20 hours, from which nobody would be let out until the contingency order had expired. Afterwards, they would go along with the servants and the contingency staff mentioned above to get their pass. Two men from the lieutenants group escort the people to the toll booth after confirmation from the contingency team.[19]

The institution called *Sanitäts-Hofdeputation* was in charge of all health agendas related to plague control, determining quarantine times, establishing and repairing of contingency stations, employing contingency personnel, and dealing with a variety of contingency complaints. More generally, the central authority was constantly trying to improve and redesign methods for disinfecting and isolating humans, animals, and goods. The regional pillars of the sanitary cordon were the regimental commanders and the medical commissions at the seat of each regimental district: Karlstadt or later Zagreb, Esseg or Petrovaradin, Timişoara, and Sibiu. The original personnel against the plague consisted of about 4,000 men. When cases of plague were reported in Constantinople, the number of soldiers would increase to 7,000. The border soldiers were not allowed to bring dogs or other animals to the border patrol stations and if they noticed them on the border, they had to shoot them immediately to prevent a potential spread of plague.

Many times there were fake rumors about plague outbreaks. For example, Lesky (1957, p. 91) explains how Greek merchants in Transylvania tried to sell their goods at higher prices by spreading rumors of outbreaks in the Ottoman Empire. Similarly, Wallachian monasteries would do the same to prevent official visits from the church hierarchy, while Wallachian peasants would do so in order to avoid taxation.[20] In order to verify such rumors and to anticipate diseases, "medical spies" or emissaries would be sent out to foreign territories, being paid about two florins a day (Lesky, 1957, p. 91).

---

[19] Translation from German.

[20] If a village was affected by plague, it would be exempt from taxes for a short period.

Lesky (1957) describes the process of human border crossing in the Habsburg lands from the Ottoman side during times when there were serious plague threats: the first experience was a conversation with the contingency station leader and then, a conversation with the contingency doctor. This would take place in a room on the side of the border crossing. If the contingency doctor ended up touching the subject, he himself would be subsequently exposed to the same procedures. Kinglake (1996, p. 2) also mentions how in times of plague, the regulations were strictly enforced:

If you dare to break the laws of the quarantine, you will be tried with military haste; the court will scream out your sentence to you from a tribunal some fifty yards away; the priest, instead of gently whispering to you the sweet hopes of afterlife, will console you at dueling distance; and after that you will find yourself carefully shot, and carelessly buried in the ground of the lazaretto.[21]

Soldiers on the border were allowed to shoot anyone crossing the border illegally (Lesky, 1957, p. 89). In cases of death during times of plague, there were specific funeral rituals prescribed: "Four men . . . take the corpse with a touch and put it in a four-ringed coffin. Then in the place where the deceased is supposed to be buried . . . the corpse is taken from the coffin, placed beside the grave and the clothing is disposed of" (Schopf, 1846, p. 189). When it came to the transportation of merchandize across the border, products such as cotton and sheep wool (commonly imported from Turkey) would be subject to a process of disinfection, which included being fumed with sulfuric or nitric acid vapors or heating up to 50 or 60 degrees Celsius. Prior to 1762, cotton would be kept in the contingency stations for up to 84 days. The number of days was reduced to 42 days after 1770, when it became clear that the process of ventilating materials was futile (Chenot, 1798, p. 83).

Lesky (1957, p. 97) discusses the negative consequences that all the anti-plague sanitary measures had for the economy. In Transylvania, the wool, cloth, and hat makers were severely affected by the quarantine measures. Before the establishment of the contingency stations, they could travel easily to the Turkish lands and obtain their primary materials from Turkish producers, but also sell their goods on Ottoman markets. The long time (sometimes weeks and months) that people had to wait at the contingency stations heavily affected the profit that they could make. Table 3.1 lists the number of days that people had to wait at the border in the second half of the eighteenth century.

---

[21] Translation from German.

Table 3.1 *Number of days at the contingency stations*

Time	Times of Plague	Times of Suspected Plague	Times of No Plague
1760s	84 Days	42 Days	21 Days
The Sanitary Norms of 1770	42 Days	28 Days	21 Days
The Chenot Rules of 1785	21 Days	10 Days	–

Source: Lesky (1957, p. 99).

Lesky (1957) discusses how the length of the quarantine changed with time because of two factors. The first has to do with the increased reliability of the health news service. After 1779, there were permanent military medical officers in the Ottoman Empire and it was no longer necessary for the Habsburgs to send medical officers to ascertain the medical situation in the Ottoman lands (Lesky, 1957, p. 99). The second factor relates to changes in the scientific knowledge about the transmission of plague.[22] In the early 1700s, the conventional wisdom was that the plague was transmitted through fabrics and clothes (as opposed to flea bites only discovered in 1898): "The plague enters the shaggy commodity with the air and attaches itself to the delicate, much bent and intewoven fibers, persisting much longer and more frequently than in the air itself" (Chenot, 1798, p. 83). This is why travellers had to first take their clothes and linen off and wash them with vinegar. Chenot's introduction of new methods of dealing with contagion of plague reduced the number of days people had to stay in quarantine at the border.

The role of the military border as a sanitary cordon ended in 1857 with the Danube Shipping Act between Austria, Bavaria, and Turkey, when quarantining was no longer necessary. The contingency stations, after having lost their *raison d'être*, became contingency stations for livestock, being the sole reminder of the once-powerful cordon sanitaire against the plague in the eighteenth and nineteenth centuries (Lesky, 1957, p. 102). According to Rothenberg (1966), the additional sanitary responsibility imposed excessive pressures on the grenzers, who also had various regimental responsibilities and regular training, which disrupted the agricultural economy in the region. Rothenberg (1966, p. 127) argues that in times of peace, the cordon guard was the most burdensome obligation of the grenzers: duty was for a week every six or seven weeks (Von Hietzinger, 1817, pp. 362–364).

[22] The cause of the plague and its means of transmission was only discovered in 1894 by Alexander Yersin. Despite lacking this knowledge, the sanitary cordon was effective in preventing the spread of the plague, especially through the isolation of the people in the contingency stations. For example, according to Lesky (1957, p. 104), the further geographic spread of the plague was prevented in 1765 and 1767 in Semlin (Zemun), but also in the context of the Russian-Turkish War (1768–1774).

The Frontier after Maria Theresa and Joseph II

After the death of Maria Theresa and her son, Joseph II, the military colony underwent a long crisis stemming from the pressures of the Hungarian and Croatian diets to dissolve the military colony, coupled with extended wars against the French, Ottoman, and Prussian empires. The fundamental problem remained the incompatibility between the maintenance of a large military colony at little or no expense to the Habsburg state and the existence of autonomous, self-sufficient communities. The constant warfare led to further deterioration of the economy in the military colony. A petition from the "sharpshooters of the Karlstadt generalcy from 1793" asked the emperor for immediate relief and the abolition of zadrugas – the institution of the village community that tied the military colonists to the communally owned land. In response to such requests, Leopold II (the successor of Joseph II) only provided a few fiscal concessions and allocated some army horses for agricultural use.

The improvements were limited and thus poverty remained widespread in the colony. Authorities were never too eager to provide aid to the military frontier. They believed that prosperity was antithetical to the society made up of house communities that formed the social basis of the border. Specifically, military authorities were opposed to greater encouragement of trade and development because this was perceived to be corrupting the fighting spirit of the grenzers. Blanc (1951, pp. 247–248) describes how it was forbidden in the military confines to run an inn or open a shop or for outsiders to invest any kind of capital. Doing so would be detrimental to the patriarchal communities that constituted the social basis of the military border. Engaging in economic activities would have distracted the colonists from their military responsibilities, would have weakened their "submissive" spirit, and would have led to further requests for redistribution of resources from the government.

The same preoccupation with the deteriorating obedience of the grenzers also was apparent in the lack of access to education for the locals. King Joseph II, for example, mentioned in 1779 in a lengthy memorandum to Count Hadik (president of the Hofkriegsrat between 1774 and 1790) that it was imperative for the empire to retain the services of the military colonists and, therefore, state support for education in the military colony should be limited. Too much education could be harmful to soldiers. In his own words:

The schools which already exist are not to be neglected for some education of the people, but this should not be carried too far as this could be rather harmful than useful for the circumstances of the natives because too much education would make the usefulness of these people [for the state] dangerous; also when selecting Staff Sergeants, one should look mainly at their virtuousness, good conduct in war and their ability, than at [their] writing or German language; which can also be observed with the officers; as there the art of writing will not be so necessary as with regular infantry regiments. That is why they will have to be relieved from unnecessary submissions and protocols.[23]

Figure 3.5 displays a portion of the original memorandum sent by Joseph II to Marshall Hadick together with a transliteration in German. The authorities' perception that too much knowledge might cause harm to the natural aptitudes of the population is also acknowledged by Vaníček (1875b, p. 580), who argues that for the "development of Greek Oriental schools, the state did nothing. [The little education that existed] was the effort of aristocracy, the metropolitan, and the clergy."[24]

Despite the apprehension about expanding the access to education, Joseph II wanted to improve the economic condition of the locals. He admitted that different regiments required different levels of support. In his view, the Karlstadt generalcy was the most impoverished, followed by the Banal regiments, and the Slavonian regiments. The king continued to evaluate the economic well-being of his subjects in the military colony. According to state officials who conducted the research for the king, there was a fundamental incompatibility between the shackles of military colonialism and economic freedom. Field Marshal Lacy reported that the soldiers in the military colony could not be both prosperous peasants and cheap regular soldiers at the same time (Rothenberg, 1966, p. 66).

Despite such warnings and recommendations, Joseph II and the military authorities did their best to maintain an almost exclusively agricultural economy in the regiments (Blanc, 1951, pp. 198–233). Overall, the maintenance of the military colony was cost-effective for the Habsburg state: General Klein argued in 1803 that the cost of a border regiment is about one-fifth that of a regular military unit (Vaníček, 1875c, pp. 120–122). In addition, the entire military frontier could provide over one hundred thousand trained soldiers in times of need.

The Frontier during the French Occupation: 1804–1814

Local rebellions in the early 1800s in Serbia and Bosnia posed a serious threat to the traditional loyalties of the grenzers in Slavonia and Croatia. These events reached a peak with the Serbian uprising of 1804. Napoleon had invaded Egypt and the Ottoman sultan used his Balkan troops to defend Egypt against Napoleon. As a result, local Ottoman bureaucrats ended up developing their own fiscal apparatus without adequate

---

[23] Translation from German.

[24] "Greek-Oriental" was the historical label of what today is called Eastern Orthodox.

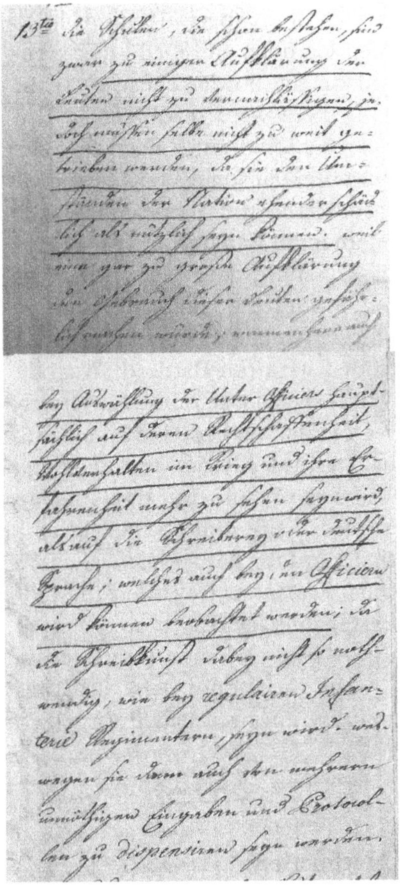

Die Schulen, die schon bestehen, sind zwar zu einiger Aufklärung der Leuten nicht zu vernachlässigen, jedoch müssen selbe nicht zu weit getrieben werden, da sie den Umständen der Native eherder schädlich als nützlich seyn können. weil eine gar zu große Aufklärung den Gebrauch dieser Leuten gefährlich machen würde; [?] auch

bey Auswählung der Unter Officier hauptsächlich auf deren Rechtschaffenheit, Wohlverhalten im Krieg und ihre Erfahrenheit mehr zu sehen seyn wird, als auf die Schreibung oder deutsche Sprache; welches auch bey den Officiern wird können beobachtet werden; da die Schreibkunst dabey nicht so nothwendig, wie bey regulairen Infanterie Regimentern, seyn wird. weswegen sie dann auch von mehreren unnöthigen Eingaben und Protocollen zu dispensiren seyn werden.

Figure 3.5 Memorandum excerpt by Joseph II to Marshall Hadick
Source: Kriegs Archiv Memoirs (1779), Folios 57-58.

supervision from the sultan. Peasants had to pay taxes to both the sultan and the local Ottoman bureaucrats. The dissatisfaction of the peasants culminated in the First Serbian Uprising (1804–1813), with the aim of gaining independence from the Ottoman Empire. The leader of the uprising, Karadjordje, approached Austria and promised Serbia's submission to the Habsburg Empire in exchange for support against the Ottoman Empire; Austria declined the offer. Despite differences between the grenzers and the Serbs and despite the absence of a common South Slav identity, there was a sense of empathy among the grenzers for their neighbors in Serbia. The grenzers therefore accepted the imperial decree not to help Serbia with resentment (Rothenberg, 1966, p. 102). Despite fundamental differences between Catholic and Orthodox grenzers, the common fate that they shared on the border constituted the linking bond. Between 1806 and 1809, there were rebellions in Peloponnesus, Bosnia, Western Bulgaria, Macedonia, and Thessaly. The Austrian War Council was worried about potential spillovers. These concerns were justified: in 1808, an Orthodox priest and a series of enlisted men mutinied in the Wallach-Illyrian regiment in Banat (Vaníček, 1875c, pp. 296–298). In 1806, the Treaty of Pressburg gave Napoleon Venice, Istria, Dalmatia, and Ragusa together with the ability to maintain a military road through civil and military Croatia. The war between Napoleonic France and Austria concluded with the Battle of Wagram of 1809, in which the part of Croatia on the right side of the Sava river, including the six Karlstadt and Banal regiments, was ceded to Napoleon. These regions together with Carniola, Carinthia, Istria, and Dalmatia constituted the French Illyrian provinces. French rule over the Croatian frontier lasted four years. Napoleon regarded the military border as a bastion to defend his empire and a springboard for potential advances in the Balkans. One of Napoleon's generals, Marmont, regarded the military border as an example of a successful military society and argued that it should be preserved. According to General Clarke (reprinted in Boppe (1900, pp. 41–53)), military Croatia should not be regarded as just another province, but as a vast military encampment from which cheap manpower could be recruited.

The Frontier in the Era of Metternich: 1815–1847

After the fall of Napoleon, the Austrian military policy was mostly directed at maintaining internal security. Rather than fighting the Ottomans, the grenzers were systematically mobilized to reinforce the imperial forces in Italy and to prevent revolts in Hungary. Despite efforts to keep the grenzers "uncontaminated," new nationalist sentiments permeated military Croatia, where locals were more receptive due to economic hardship. Despite some disloyal military officials, only a few officers were suspended during the French rule (Rothenberg, 1966, p. 123). While extended periods of peace and improvements in public security led to population growth, land allocations and the number of livestock did not increase proportional to the population. As a result, even in the era of Metternich, the grenzers remained poor and agricultural methods remained primitive (Rothenberg, 1966, p. 132). An English traveler in the mid-1800s suggested that zadrugas were to blame for the dire conditions: "the younger and more active laborers have become further and further removed from each other in relationship and in sympathy; and this has developed all the evils of Communism [...] which takes away all stimulus to exertion" (Paton, 1849, p. 176). The problem with shirking that the traveler mentioned was also reflected in locals' views: "My second cousin has ten children, and therefore ought to work ten times as much as I do" or "My third cousin is a drunkard, or a spendthrift; what avails my individual toil, when we share the results [of our work]?" (Paton, 1849, p. 176). Such perceptions of injustice caused by shirking also materialized in the many petitions that the grenzers submitted to the authorities requesting the abolition of the zadrugas. The Hofkriegsrat, however, denied such petitions, making the argument that zadrugas were the foundation of the military regiments. The view of the Hofkriegsrat is again described by Paton (1849, pp. 177–178):

Ninety-nine officers out of a hundred think that Communism ought to be abolished; but the greatest caution ought to be used in dealing carelessly with the other parts of *an institution that is of such value to the state*. The young soldiers presently work both at home and in military service, from twenty to twenty-three years of age and *the communities, from their number, have no difficulty in furnishing soldiers, who are fed by the house, and not by the state*; but if the lands were re-divided, a small family would, in many instances, have difficulty in either sparing him from work in the field, or nourishing him out of the house (emphases added).

The Hofkriegsrat continued to oppose the expansion of trade and industry, which would have jeopardized the existence of zadrugas. A French traveler explained how, on the military frontiers, there were "no factories, no machines, no industry. There is hardly any noise but the occasional discharge of firearms" (De Beaujour, 1829, p. 427). In order to further illustrate the evolution of the local economy within the military colony, I digitized the Habsburg censuses between 1830 and 1842. Figure 3.6 depicts the evolution of commercial enterprises, number of factories, number of commercial shops, and special commercial occupations. To ensure comparability, the y-axis is presented in logarithmic scale. While there is a slight increase in the number of commercial enterprises from 6,300 in 1830 to over 8,000 in 1839, the other variables that capture the size of the private industry seem to remain very stable and low. There are around 800 commercial occupations and 600 shops in 1830 and they gradually decrease to around 750 and 490 respectively in 1842. Similar to the qualitative accounts presented by de Beaujour (1829), the number of factories stays indeed close to zero. Unfortunately, no similar figures are presented in the censuses for the civilian area, so it is difficult to make a comparison between the civilian and military zones.

However, in order to show to some extent the stark asymmetry in the presence of private industry in the military colony, I divide the

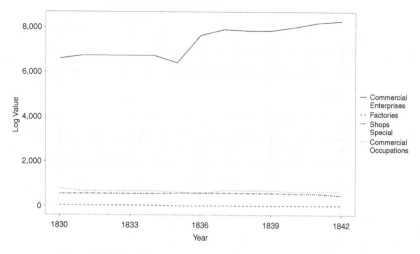

Figure 3.6 The size of the private industry within the military
colony, 1830–1842
Source: K. K. Statistischen Central-Commission (1830–42).

number of commercial markets by the population size and multiply by
10,000. The final variable captures the number of commercial markets
for every 10,000 inhabitants. The stark differences between the military
and the civilian areas are presented in Figure 3.7. There is some vol-
atility in the markets to population ratio for the civilian area, but on
average, it stays above 0.3. In the military colony, however, the markets
to.population ratio stays almost always around zero.

The absence of private industries had implications for the lives of the
families within the military colony. De Beaujour (1829) further describes
the poor conditions in which inhabitants lived:

Nothing seems so sad and miserable as the dwellings of these isolated families:
they are simple earth or wicker huts, open to all sides to the winds, having as
furniture only a copper pot and a rush mat, often covered with lice. In the middle
of the hut there is a hearth whose smoke escapes through an opening made on
the roof, where a bad loaf of corn or barley is baked. The ones who are better off
make their meals from a kind of bread with milk; the others live off of grass or
roots: never meat, not even dried vegetables.[25] (De Beaujour, 1829, p. 427)

The revolutions of 1848 changed the civilian territory: serfdom was
completely abolished and the peasants who were land tenants were given
ownership rights for the land that they were in fact using. Parts of the

[25] Translation from French.

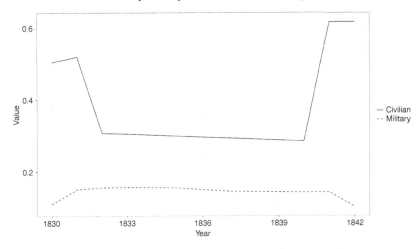

Figure 3.7 The market to population ratio within the military
colony, 1830–1842
Source: K. K. Statistischen Central-Commission (1830–42).

military colony such as the Szekler regiments in Transylvania were abolished (Göllner, 1973, p. 173). New economic concessions were made to
the grenzers with the Basic Rights of May 7, 1850, or the new *Grundgesetz*. The same stipulations aimed to preserve the military character
of the military colony. Properties of the grenzers, according to these
rights, were now inheritable and the occupational restrictions were lifted
(Rothenberg, 1966, p. 158). The military colonists were now "in full
possession of the land" (*als wahres, beständiges Eigenthum*), as indicated in
sections 10 and 11 of the *Grundgesetz*. They reinforced the principle that
each family had to have enough land to provide enough men and ensure
their subsistence for military service. To this end, the real estate assets of
every family community were divided into "community" (*Communitat*),
"foundation goods" (*Stammgut*), and "surplus goods" (*Ueberland*). The
foundation goods represented the patrimonial assets of every family and
consisted of a yoke of land for the house and garden and multiple yokes
of arable land. The foundation goods were not alienable and could not
be shared unless the family died out or lost enough members so it was
no longer possible for the family to exploit the land. In the first instance,
the military officers would intervene to force other people in the village
to lend a helping hand to the family in need. If a family still could not
support itself, the family was authorized to alienate its foundation goods.
The surplus goods on the other hand could indeed be alienated and sold
with permission from the regimental captain. Transforming a field into
a meadow and the meadow into plowed land also required permission

from regimental authorities. Disregarding such formalities could lead to a fine. If a plot of land remained uncultivated for longer than three years, the owner would receive a warning and the land would be given to another family (Perrot, 1869, p. 53).

Despite attempts to improve the economic situation of the grenzers, agricultural production lagged behind civilian Croatia. Blanc (1951) notes that the government was aware of the economic problems in the military colony, but wanted at the same time to preserve the military constitution of the colony; the two were seen as fundamentally incompatible. The families were protected for the ultimate goal of ensuring the longevity of the military institution. In many ways, the military frontier, according to Blanc (1951), was very similar to the military colonies under Constantin and Alexander Severus in the Roman Empire, where a man was both a soldier and a farmer. The family leader served as an intermediary between the Habsburg military commanders and the rest of the population, ensuring the transmission of orders from top down and providing legitimacy to the central state.

The Abolition of the Military Colony: 1859–1881

Serb nationalism among the grenzers became more and more evident in 1848, especially in the regiments with a majority Orthodox population. The revolution created considerable South Slav cooperation in civilian Croatia and Serbia, which cut across divisive religious loyalties (Rothenberg, 1966, p. 166). The last episode in which the grenzers were mobilized was the wars against Piedmont and France in 1859 and against Prussia in 1866. In 1868, after the Hungarian–Croatian subcompromise,[26] the military frontier had become obsolete and ineffective and put a strain on Vienna and Hungary (Szabó, 2000). Croatia-Slavonia became part of Imperial Hungary but autonomous from the Kingdom of Hungary; according to the agreement, Hungary would work for a closer integration of the military frontier into the civilian area (Kolossa, 1987). Despite requests for the abolition of the military frontier, which in Transylvania had already taken place,[27] both the Habsburg military and Emperor Franz Joseph continued to oppose it.

---

[26] The Croatian–Hungarian sub-compromise was a pact signed in 1868 that governed Croatia's political status in the Hungarian-ruled part of Austria-Hungary. It lasted until the end of World War I. The pact confirmed the existing territorial distinction between Croatia-Slavonia and the remainder of the Kingdom of Hungary.

[27] Szabó (2000) discusses how the Szörény County was established by Article 27 of 1873 as a part of the process of turning the military frontier into a civilian administrative unit. Before that, it belonged to Temes County, which together with the territories of Temes, Torontál, and Krassó was part of the Banat military frontier.

Grandits (2002) explains that the introduction of compulsory military service put a strain on the military budget. A joint meeting of the Austro-Hungarian government took place in August 1869 to deal with the "profound crisis that seemed to be emerging more and more," because of the high military budget (Grandits, 2002, p. 226). The threat to the joint army budget and the fear of South Slav nationalism forced the emperor's hand in 1869 to approve a plan to gradually abolish the military colony (Rothenberg, 1966, p. 173). On June 9, 1872, the emperor issued an edict placing the territory under Hungarian rule, transforming the frontier's military government into a civilian government, and establishing civil jurisdictions and districts (Szabó, 2000). The frontier was no longer considered effective against the plague and hence the sanitary establishments were discontinued. The military company districts were abolished, as the competences of the rural communities were expanded by a new rural community order. The "Law on the Organization of Jurisdiction" of June 19, 1872 removed judicial power from the regimental authorities, while new district and district courts were being established in civil Croatia. In 1873, the civilian and the military administration were separated while all educational, judicial, and religious matters were handed to the Sabor (parliament) of Croatia. Gradually, all military counties were included within the civilian structure and started acquiring civilian public institutions (Dénes, 1928; Hajdú, 2005).

An additional separate task for the Croatian parliament was to eliminate the economic disparities between civilian and military Croatia. Education was maintained at a low level by local authorities on the grounds that education could have aroused the ambitions of the military colonists and triggered them to abandon their posts. Perrot (1869, p. 67) noted that "ignorance is deep in the confines; the regimental schools there are insufficient, both in number and equipment; in some districts, especially in Southern Croatia, there is low population density; the villages are far from one another so that children do not live in the village where the school is located and cannot easily get there in any season." Rothenberg (1966, p. 187) estimated, based on the figures by other historians of the late nineteenth century, that in 1870 only 33 percent of boys and 25 percent of girls attended any kind of school and over 75 percent of the population was illiterate. The situation changed with the integration of the military frontier within the civilian area. Grandits (2002, p. 299) explains how in the first decades after the termination of the military frontier, the education system was standardized to match the conditions in civilian Croatia. Specifically, the teachers' position changed fundamentally: teachers received better training and the state provided higher wages.

Another reason for the economic disparities between the two regions has to do with the low development of the railroad network in the south. The Hungarian kingdom (in charge of the military colony after 1868) did not see the development of the railroad network favorably in the south because of fears of increased Slavic nationalism (Mollinary, 1905). The first railroad that touched the Croatian civilian area was in 1860 and it connected Vienna and Budapest to the outskirts of the empire. Originally, all the railroad network in Hungary was owned and planned by the state. However, in 1880 it was made possible by the Hungarian parliament for individuals, cities, or companies to build rail lines for their own needs. As such, the first private rail lines were inaugurated in 1886 but only covered the civilian area. Rothenberg (1966) mentions that the Hungarian authorities were suspicions of the Serbs in Novi Sad, Belgrade, the military frontier, and Bosnia after minor insurrections, fearing that together would create a large South Slav state.[28]

Before the demilitarization decision was made in Vienna, the first changes to the land tenure system took place in March 1868. The law of 5 March, 1868 suspended the previous restrictions on the ability of locals to sell their property and the military service obligations of landowners. Property could be freely sold from that moment on without major restrictions. The reform allowed for the first time non-border residents to acquire large properties in the military frontier (Grandits, 2002). According to the reform, the division of the households was also much easier to implement. With the abolition of military service and replacement of military administration and jurisdiction with civil institutions, there were important changes to the life of border guards: no more men deployed for sanitary cordon services, no more military exercises, no more village and household inspections, which were common during the military regime (Grandits, 2002, p. 229). Grandits (2002, p. 229) explains how the carrying of weapons, which was "of great importance for the pride of the border guards," was taxed very heavily. This led to local dissatisfaction and to an identity conflict but contributed to the spread of civilian norms.

On 8 August, 1873, the Banat frontier was abolished and incorporated into the Kingdom of Hungary, while part of the Croatian frontier had already been incorporated into Croatia-Slavonia on 1 August, 1871. In 1873, Emperor Franz Joseph issued a statement arguing that all the steps had been taken in order to place the military colonists on equal status with all the inhabitants of the Dual Monarchy, including the introduction of a complete civil administration and universal military service.

---

[28] These fears led to the invasion of Bosnia-Herzegovina in 1878 by the Dual Monarchy, after an international mandate.

The former frontier inhabitants started being on equal footing with their civilian counterparts when it came to taxation. Grandits (2002, p. 234) estimates that property tax increased in the military colony from 1873 to 1877 by more than 250 percent, which contributed to local dissatisfaction. By the time of its dissolution in 1881, the military frontier comprised approximatively 33,422 square kilometers of land with over 1.2 million inhabitants, stretching over 1,900 kilometers as a narrow strip of land from near Fiume/Rijeka, close to the border with Italy, to Transylvania in Romania (O'Reilly, 2006, p. 231). It was on August 1, 1881 that the last vestiges of military colonialism in the Habsburg Empire were removed.

There are two overarching reasons why the military colonies ceased to exist around the nineteenth century according to Rothenberg (1966). First, the emergence of liberalism was incompatible with the notion of the existence of military colonists as a separate social caste. Some Habsburg officials themselves admitted around the mid-nineteenth century that the system was "not well suited for highly developed countries" (Pidoll zu Quintenbach, Carl Frhr. v., 1844, quoted in Rothenberg (1966, p. 196)). Second, the emergence of universal conscription and more advanced war technology rendered the existence of a military establishment obsolete. In the following chapter, I investigate the effect of military colonialism on short-term socio-economic outcomes and how these helped reinforce particular individual cognitions which are visible to this day.

The military colony was a concept that the Habsburg Empire adopted in the sixteenth century to defend the Habsburg territory against inimical incursions. While originally there were only a handful of soldiers placed in the border region, with time entire border districts were created with locals having a different status compared to the neighboring serf populations. Inhabitants of the border became free but with heavy military responsibilities and with tight restrictions on property and employment. Given its original success in the part of the Habsburg Empire that coincides today with Croatia, it gradually expanded in other areas that bordered the Ottoman Empire and which today coincide with Serbia and Romania. A variety of laws were passed throughout the colonies' existence, regulating both the obligations of the colonists and their entitlements and solving principal–agent problems that emerged from the Habsburg Empire delegating state bureaucrats to govern in the military colony. The Habsburg frontier was disbanded officially in 1881. Both some of its institutions and consequences outlived it, as I show in the next chapter.

4 Military Colonialism and Economic Development

Poverty and under-development were constant characteristics of the military colony. In this chapter, I present a panoply of historical and modern statistics to demonstrate that they persisted even after its abrogation. I connect these developmental outcomes to the institutional legacies of military colonialism, such as relatively low levels of inequality and the continued prevalence of communal property rights. The evidence in this chapter comes from the digitization of a variety of maps and historical censuses from the Habsburg and Hungarian empires, Yugoslavia, and modern-day Croatia.

4.1 Dimensions of Military Colonialism

The maps in the following figures exemplify the key characteristics that pertained to "military colonialism": involvement in military affairs, communal property rights, and under-provision of public goods. Figure 4.1 shows the distribution of military personnel in 1856 based on the Austrian Ministry of Internal Affairs (1859). The first panel depicts modern-day Croatia according to county-level administrative units in Imperial Austria (Kreis) and Imperial Hungary (county), and the military administrations on the frontier lands. The second panel shows regions (Land) in Austria-Hungary. Darker tones indicate a much stronger presence of soldiers in the military colony than outside of it. As I will show later in the section on occupational structure, the average percentage of soldiers for the entire country in 1857 is about one percent. The military area contains about four percentage points more soldiers compared to the civilian area.

The second important characteristic of the frontier is strict collective property rights that were much more prevalent in the military colony than outside of it. While there is limited data on the prevalence of communal properties during the existence of the military colony, one possible proxy is the number of family members: it is plausible that in areas with communal properties there should be families with more members. I created such a variable by dividing the total population

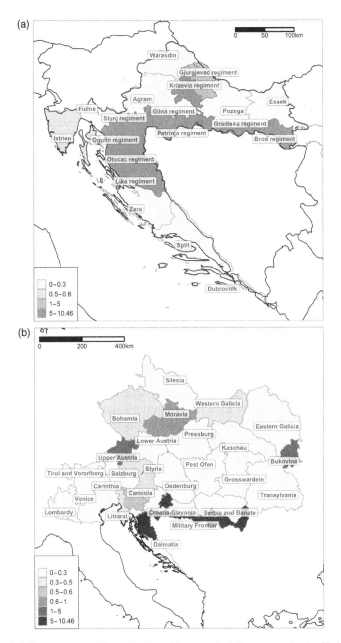

Figure 4.1 Percentage soldiers in the military and civilian areas in the Habsburg Empire, 1857

Notes: Redrawn based on Liechtenstern and Amon (1795); Von Czoernig (1855); Lesky (1957). Data is from the Austrian Ministry of Internal Affairs (1859). The first panel displays modern-day Croatia according to county-level administrative units in Imperial Austria (Kreis) and Imperial Hungary (county), and the military administrations on the frontier lands. The second panel shows regions (Land) in Austria-Hungary.

size by the number of families based on data from K. K. Statistischen Central-Commission (1849–51). In the section on communal property rights, I present analyses based on official data from 1895 which contain more precise measures of the extent of communal properties. In 1895, 14 years after the abrogation of the military colony, the area covered by zadrugas or communal properties is almost 13 percentage points larger than the civilian area (about 14 percent of the area of a settlement is covered by zadrugas in 1895, on a country level). Figure 4.2 displays the ratio between population and families in both what is today Croatia and the entire Habsburg Empire in 1851. In a similar style to the previous figure, darker tones signify greater intensities. The military colony seems to have much greater ratios – population/families compared to the civilian area that is now in Croatia – but also compared to all other regions of the Habsburg Empire, as shown in the second panel of Figure 4.2. Specifically, the military colony seems to have around 9 members per family as opposed to 4–5, which seems to be the norm in the civilian area in 1851.

Finally, the third characteristic of the frontier is under-provision of public goods. For a long time, the Habsburg government under-invested. This was precisely because the military colony represented an easy, affordable way to draft soldiers. Having soldiers supported by their families was much cheaper for the empire than assigning dedicated funds from the imperial coffers. In addition, imperial authorities associated the provision of public goods with an opportunity for the colonists to pursue other professional careers, which would have distracted them from the main roles envisioned by the imperial authorities. I operationalize the term "public goods" as access to railroads. The maps in Figure 4.3 illustrate the railroad network in 1879 based on Unknown Author (1879). The first panel shows the distribution of railroads in what is today Croatia while the second panel map displays the railroads throughout the empire. Overall, railroads are much more sparse in the military area compared with the civilian area.

4.2   Measuring the Legacies of Military Colonialism

To examine the consequences of the establishment of the military colony for long-term development in Croatia, I use the geographic border as a natural experiment. This approach allows the isolation of the effects of the military colony by comparing municipalities in the former military colony to municipalities from the civilian Habsburg Empire right next to the dividing line. The boundary forms a multi-dimensional discontinuity in longitude-latitude space, and regressions take the form:

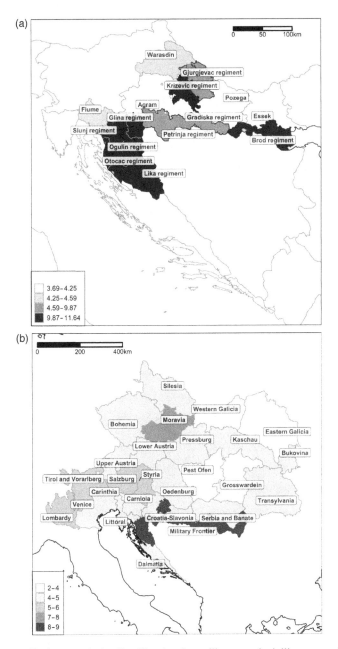

Figure 4.2 Ratio population/families in the military and civilian areas in the Habsburg Empire, 1880

Notes: Original map showing, in the first panel, the boundaries of modern-day Croatia and the settlements in the military and civilian areas in 1880. The second panel shows the regions in Austria-Hungary. Data is from the Royal Statistical Office in Zagreb (1898).

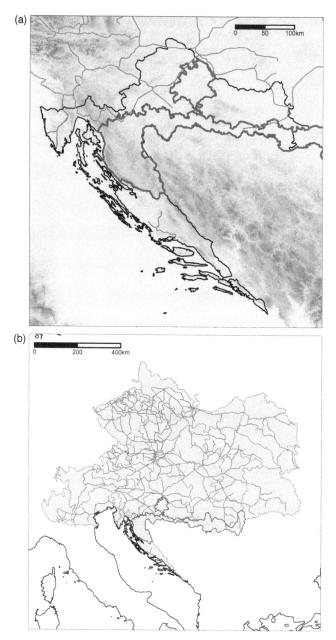

Figure 4.3 Railroad distribution in the military and civilian areas in the Habsburg Empire, 1879
Notes: Redrawn based on Unknown Author (1879). The grey lines are
railroads *(befahrene Eisenbahnen)* in 1879. Elevation in the background.

$$Outcome_v = \alpha + \gamma_{Mil.Frontier} + f(\text{geographic location}_v)$$
$$+ \sum_{i=1}^{n} seg_v^i + \beta dist.Zagreb_v + x_v + \epsilon_v \qquad (4.1)$$

where $Outcome_v$ is the dependent variable of interest in municipality v, and *Mil. Frontier* is an indicator equal to 1 if municipality v was in the Habsburg military colony and equal to zero otherwise. The term - $f(\text{geographic location}_v)$ is the RD polynomial, which controls for smooth functions of geographic location. Therefore, I show results for different degrees of polynomials, as well as for different sizes of bandwidth around the border (from 10 to 70 km). In the RDD specifications, these samples are defined in terms of GIS-computed distance to the Habsburg civilian border. In order to ensure that the specification is comparing municipalities across the same segment of the boundary, I use boundary segment fixed effects: I split the boundary in to eight different segments of 127km each. Therefore, seg_v^i equals 1 if municipality v is closest to segment i and zero otherwise. The term *dist. Zagreb* is the distance of municipality v from Zagreb and is included to explicitly control for proximity to the region's largest urban area. As a robustness check, I also replace the distance to Zagreb with distances to other important centers including Vienna, Pecs, Karlovac, Belgrade, or Osijek. For the sake of brevity, I do not include those results here.

I also consider the possibility that the results might be affected by spatial autocorrelation in the residuals, as suggested by Kelly (2019). Following the method used by Dray *et al.* (2006) and Rozenas *et al.* (2018), I first conduct Moran's I tests for spatial autocorrelation and then include Moran eigenvectors and synthetic covariates capturing residual autocorrelation on the right-hand side. As such, x_v is a vector of synthetic covariates capturing residual autocorrelation (Dray *et al.*, 2006).[1] Finally, ϵ_v are error terms clustered at relevant geographic units.

Similarly to Dell (2010) and Gelman and Imbens (2017), I use a local linear RD polynomial and border fixed effects for the baseline specifications. There are a variety of assumptions surrounding the utilization of regression discontinuity designs. The first one is that all relevant factors besides the "treatment" vary smoothly at the boundary (Keele and Titiunik, 2015, p. 130). The physical border between the civilian and military area was finalized during the regency of Joseph II. The decision to create a border mostly had to do with putting an end to the increasing

---

[1] The Moran eigenvector method diagonalizes the $N \times N$ connectivity matrix $\mathbf{C}$ (where $c_{ij} = 1$ if districts i and j share a border) to select the set of m eigenvectors with the largest achievable Moran's I coefficient of autocorrelation. To prevent multicolinearity, the algorithm extracts eigenfunctions of $[\mathbf{I} - \mathbf{X}(\mathbf{X}'\mathbf{X})^{-1}\mathbf{X}']\mathbf{C}[\mathbf{I} - \mathbf{X}(\mathbf{X}'\mathbf{X})^{-1}\mathbf{X}']$, where $\mathbf{X} = [\iota_n XL]$ is the $N \times (k+1)$ matrix of covariates.

animosities between the grenzers and the feudal lords who were trying to encroach on the land of the grenzers. Therefore, a mixed civil-military commission was formed in 1767 in charge of tracing a demarcation line between the civilian and military area.

The important question to justify the usage of the regression discontinuity framework is why did the Habsburg authorities require that specific territory to become part of the military colony and how did they determine which regions to include. The *outer line* of demarcation to the military colony has always been the adjacency to the Ottoman Empire (O'Reilly, 2006; Rothenberg, 1966). The military colony would act as a buffer zone, slowing Ottoman advances and providing the Habsburg professional army enough time to counteract the Ottoman attacks (Rothenberg, 1966, 1970).

Similarly, a second important question is how was the drawing of the *inner line* of demarcation between the civilian and the military area made. Historians indicate two factors determining where the line was drawn. The first has to do with natural features such as rivers. For example, the river Glogovina in the west constituted the natural line dividing the Križevci regiment from the civilian area, while the Zdela creek to the west divided the Gjurgjevac regiment from the civilian side (Altić, 2005). The second factor has to do with socio-economic interests. Many individual nobles in the civilian area were fighting not to have the villages under their control taken away from them. In such places special civilian-military commissions were created to decide on the line of demarcation (Altić, 2005; Rothenberg, 1966). The socio-economic interests could therefore raise endogeneity concerns: richer landlords could be more resistant and oppose the central state much more than poorer landlords. As such, any differences between the civilian and the military area could be the result of pre-existing differences in elite power. In the final analyses, I examine differences between the civilian and the military area in portions of the border that coincide with rivers and portions that do not. Anticipating the results, differences between the two regions remain significant when isolating the effect to segments of the border that coincide with rivers. In order to have enough statistical power, I include all the observations in the main analyses.

The shape of the military colony also changed with time, as indicated in the previous chapter, until it reached a somewhat stable shape in 1699 after the Treaty of Karlowitz. The unusual "mushroom"-like shape visible after 1699 is a remnant of the border configuration from previous centuries. Therefore, the northern section of the border (head of the "mushroom") was adjacent to the Ottoman territories prior to 1699. Within the border itself the lines of demarcation among regiments were drawn in such a way that Ottoman settlers are evenly distributed throughout the military colony to prevent rebellions (Altić, 2005).

While historical documents do not mention additional criteria, concerns remain that other underlying characteristics may have influenced the assignment to the military colony. Such concerns are fundamentally about the RD assumption that all factors besides being the military frontier vary smoothly at the boundary. Such assumption is necessary for observations located just across the Habsburg civilian side of the boundary to be an appropriate counterfactual for observations located just across the Habsburg military colony. To assess the plausibility of this assumption, I investigate differences in important geographic characteristics such as elevation, slope, annual average temperature, annual average level of precipitation, maize suitability (as an example of a crop relevant for the area), kilometers of river, and density of rivers (length of river divided by the area of the municipality). Examining continuity in geography is particularly important in order to investigate the effect of military colonialism: if the two areas are not balanced, then the results would reflect the differences in geography, as opposed to the historical exposure to military colonialism.

I obtained elevation data by overlaying a map of modern Croatian municipalities on 30 arc second (1 km) resolution elevation raster included in the National Elevation Dataset by USGS. I created a similar raster for slope using GIS software. For average temperature and precipitation, I collected data from the Center for Environmental Data Analysis.[2] When it comes to maize suitability, I utilized the raster from the Caloric Suitability for Individual Crops dataset, for rain-fed agriculture under medium input (Galor and Özak, 2016). The final outcomes for all these variables are zonal statistics. For density of rivers, I downloaded the river data (in vector shape file format) from the European Environment Agency, calculated river length in kilometers, and divided the result by the area of the municipality. The unit of analysis is 2011 municipality or *općina*. The results are displayed in Figure 4.4. The same coefficients (unstandardized) are presented in Table A.1 in section A of the technical appendix. The unstandardized coefficients in Table A.1 do not indicate significant differences when it comes to elevation, slope, precipitation, river length, and river density. The unstandardized coefficients indicate a slight difference in temperature and river density, but such differences are small compared to the mean. The evaluation of these factors mitigates the possibility that these two regions might have been different

---

[2] The specific data on temperature and precipitation can be found at: http://data .ceda.ac.uk/badc/cru/data/cru_ts/cru_ts_3.21/data/tmp/ – temperature and http://data.ceda.ac.uk/badc/cru/data/cru_ts/cru_ts_3.21/ data/pre/ – precipitation. Last checked: May 15, 2018.

from the very beginning in such a way that what explains the differences between the north and the south is geography, as opposed to political institutions directed by the center.

In addition to geographic factors, one would ideally also investigate differences in socio-economic factors prior to the establishment of the military colony in 1553. Such data unfortunately is not available. To make up for that and to provide further evidence that there are no pre-existing differences between the two areas prior to the establishment of the military colony, I use cartographic data on the length of trade routes and the presence of trade centers from Magocsi (2002, p. 11). Such variables are supposed to capture potential differences in economic activity between the two regions. All the results use regressions of the form described in equation 4.1. The results for historical trade routes and trade centers also do not indicate a statistically significant difference as indicated in the two rows of Figure 4.4. Therefore, such analyses suggest that neither geography nor socio-economic processes were different prior to the establishment of the military colony.

An additional assumption that is made in RD designs is no selective sorting along the treatment threshold (along the border between the civilian area and the military frontier). This would be violated if individuals with particular traits that are conducive to the provision of public goods and prosperity were more likely to move to one side of the border, leading to a larger indirect effect on public goods. In other words, military colonists might have migrated precisely because of poverty and low provision of public goods. The qualitative evidence suggests otherwise. During Habsburg times, there were both positive and negative incentives in place that prevented migration. The desirability of freedom[3] and freedom of religion are some of the positive incentives that motivated people to stay in the military colony. Some of the negative incentives included: "Deserters were to be executed by hanging, but defectors to the Turks were to be impaled. In such cases too, the principle of collective responsibility made the families of all culprits liable for punishment" (Rothenberg, 1960b, p. 117). Therefore, during the Habsburg Empire, restrictions on mobility and the threat of losing one's status (freedom and land) is what prevented the movement of the grenzers to the Habsburg civilian side.

In order to provide additional supporting evidence for the assumption of no selective sorting, I collected data on the percentage of out-migrants in 1857 (based on the Austrian Ministry of Internal Affairs

---

[3] For example, in 1627, the Warasdiner grenzers declared that they "they would rather be hacked into pieces than be separated from their officers and be subjects of the Croatian nobility" (Rothenberg, 1966, p. 10).

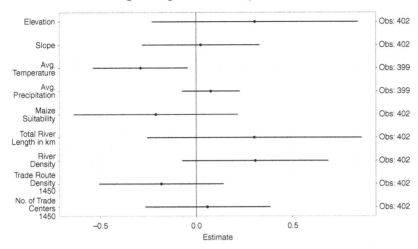

Figure 4.4 Balance of geographic variables
Notes: The unit of analysis is the 2011 municipality. Elevation and slope are obtained by overlaying a map of modern Croatia districts on 30 arc second (1 km) resolution elevation data included in the National Elevation Dataset by USGS. Temperature and precipitation are the average values for 2010, based on data from the Center for Environmental Data Analysis. Maize suitability is from the Caloric Suitability for Individual Crops dataset (Galor and Özak, 2016). River density is calculated based on data from the European Environment Agency. Trade route density and trade center counts (1450) are calculated based on maps from Magocsi (2002). Every regression includes the following covariates: a linear polynomial in latitude and longitude, distance to Zagreb, and boundary segment FE.

(1859)), 1944 (based on a 1944 Catholic parish census, Draganović (1939)), and the net migration rate in 2011 (based on the Croatian Bureau of Statistics (2017)). The results do not indicate any statistically significant difference in migration patterns. The results are presented in tabular format in Table A.2, section A of the technical appendix.

Migration caused by sorting along ethnic lines is also unlikely. Historical sources indicate that in the civilian area and in the military colony, people "profess the same beliefs, they speak the same language [...] only the population density is higher there [in the military area] and people are more superstitious there, because ignorance is more widespread there" (Perrot, 1869, p. 65). More generally, according to Perrot (1869), the slight differences between the military confines and the civilian area have nothing to do with geography or with people's "races and ethnicities," but rather with the particular institutional conditions that made the military colony different. In order to further check potential sorting along ethnic lines, I digitized and geolocated a variety of historical and modern censuses: 1921 (Yugoslavia Opšta Državna Statistika, 1932), 1931 (Kraljevina Jugoslavija Opsta Državna Statistika, 1940), 1991 (Republika Hrvatska Republicki Zavod Za Statistiku, 1992), 2001, and 2011 (Croatian Bureau of Statistics censuses for 2001 and 2011). While ethnic identity is still important today (being a Serb or being a Croat), the difference in concentration of Serbs and Croats is not statistically different. The percentage of Croats and Serbs in 1921, 1931, 1991, 2001, and 2011 is balanced on the two sides, as illustrated in Tables A.3 and A.4 in the appendix.

Similarly, I also investigate the possibility that certain historical events might have affected only of one of the two areas causing people to migrate. Such events include attacks by the Ottoman Empire, destruction during WW2, and the Yugoslav Wars. These are likely to only have minor effects on the historical and modern outcomes that I examine in the subsequent sections. For the possibility that Ottoman attacks might be driving the results, I geolocated all the places that historians such as Blanc (1957) indicate as having been pillaged or attacked by the Ottomans. Once I eliminate those places from the statistical analyses, the main results still hold. For WW2 and the Yugoslav Wars, I collected extensive data on destruction, presence of concentration camps, and massacres, and investigated whether the two areas that I compare, might have been affected by them asymmetrically. The results presented in the alternative explanation section of this chapter do not indicate that such factors should be of concern.

An equally important question is what I am comparing the treatment group to or, in other words, what did the non-frontier area look like. As already explained in Chapter 2, communal properties existed in both the civilian and military area. Within the civilian area, the feudal regime recognized and protected the zadruga (Blanc, 1957, p. 115). In a similar way to the military colonies, the noble communicated directly with the community leader when it came to the lease of land, granting of privileges and administration of corvée labor that peasants had to do for the noble. For example, an important Croatian historian of the early twentieth century explains that:

[...] the relationship between serfs and the feudal lord is not established between individuals, but rather within the framework of the family (*rod*). The land owned by the *kmet* (peasant serf) is a collective property. The chief of the zadruga is responsible for the entirety of the property, and hence is a true owner. The families of serfs receive a quantity of land proportional to the number of their members.[4] (Horvat, 1939, p. 32)

---

[4] Translation from Serbo-Croatian.

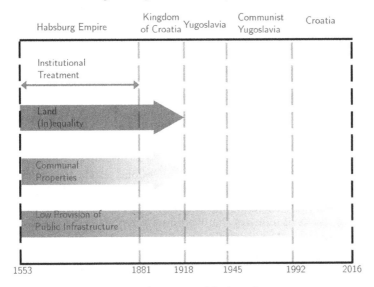

Figure 4.5 Road map for the empirical results

This is the system which functioned until 1848. Most of the land was given by nobles to serfs. The part that was kept by nobles, was fully at the discretion of the noble. That land was typically still cultivated with the help of locals. The rights and duties of the peasant serf, as well as the rights and duties of the noble – the landowner–were different depending on the local circumstances and time, as explained in Chapter 2.

In the following sections, I present historical and modern-day evidence for the socio-economic consequences that resulted from 328 years of military colonialism. I first show how under-provision of public goods is a process that outlived the military colony, being visible to the present day. I then move on to present two key short-lived phenomena that were visible in the immediate aftermath of the military colony: low land inequality and communal properties. In the next chapter, I investigate the long-term persistence of norms. Figure 4.5 displays the short-and long-term effects of military colonialism. Gradient arrows indicate a fading effect while solid arrows indicate a process that ended sharply, as a result of some policy intervention. For example, the difference in land inequality between the civilian and former military area (i.e. more land inequality in the north compared to the south) ended in 1918 with the creation of the Kingdom of Yugoslavia (Blanc, 1957; Tomasevich, 2001). The lands of large owners that were present in the north were confiscated, divided, and redistributed. There was no direct policy intervention against communal properties, which were the very essence of military colonialism, which is why they continue to exist until around 1944. This is the year that many historical anthropologists mention as the end-point for communal properties, given the economic shock induced by the war which rendered communal living obsolete. Finally, low provision of public infrastructure in the historical area lasts to the present day although the difference seems to be fading over time.

Access to Public Goods: Historical and Modern

As already indicated, under-provision of public goods was a characteristic of military colonialism: the area designated for the drafting of soldiers received fewer public goods than the civilian area to prevent the development of industry that would have rendered the job of a soldier less attractive. The immediate follow-up question is to what extent such under-provision persisted historically. In order to answer that, I use access to roads and railroads as a proxy for access to public goods. I digitized a series of historical maps depicting public roads and railroads. I then calculated the length of these roads and divided them by the area of the district to get a measure for road and railroad density respectively. A lower density[5] would mean lower access to public goods. The results in Figure 4.6 display the estimates for the *Mil. Frontier* term in equation 4.1 for eight different outcomes of interest: actual and planned railroad density in 1869 and 1884, thoroughfares (main roads) in 1940, asphalt roads and "good" roads in 1957, and residential and road track density in 2017. The results are based on maps such as Kiepert (1869); Unknown Author (1884); Generalstab des Heeres, Abt. für Kriegskarten und Vermessungswesen (1940); and Bohinec and Planina (1957), and data from Open Street Maps. The same results are also presented in tabular format in Table A.5 in the technical appendix. The results point very strongly in the direction of lower road and railroad density in the former military colony. Such differences were present before the end of the military colony, were present during the brief existence of the Kingdom of Croatia, continued to exist under communism, and were still visible in 2017.

Access to roads is one type of public good. A natural question to ask is: to what extent are such differences visible when it comes to other kinds of public goods? Can we see the same differences when it comes to hospitals and healthcare for example? Historical censuses from the communist period under Tito contain data on maternal care and the extent to which women were giving birth in hospitals (Socijalistička Federativna Republika Jugoslavija Savezni Zavod Za Statistiku, 1967, 1973).

---

[5] Note again that geographic characteristics in the two regions are balanced on average.

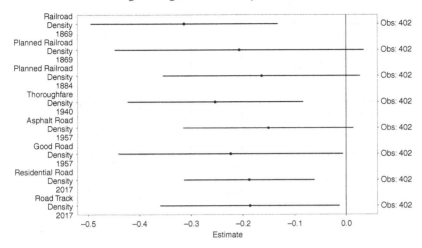

Figure 4.6 Effect of military colonialism on historical roads and railroads, 1869–2017
Notes: The unit of analysis is the 2011 municipality. Data is based on Unknown Author (1869, 1884), Generalstab des Heeres, Abt. für Kriegskarten und Vermessungswesen (1940), Bohinec and Planina (1957), and Open Street Maps. Every regression includes the following covariates: a linear polynomial in latitude and longitude, distance to Zagreb, and boundary segment FE.

Conventional wisdom would indicate that communism with its egalitarian ideology should have eliminated historical economic differences between the two regions. In other words, communism should have acted as an equalizer, eliminating all historical regional disparities. The empirical evidence suggests otherwise, however: the asymmetry in access to public°goods persisted. Children are less likely to be born in hospitals and pregnancies are less likely to benefit from professional help both in 1964 and later in 1970.

Such differences are statistically and economically significant. For example, in 1964 the average percentage of children born in hospitals in Croatia was about 66% and almost 80% in 1970. The cantons in the former military colony seem to have fewer babies born in hospitals by about 10 percentage points. The difference seems to go up in 1970 to 11 percentage points. When it comes to the percentage of children born without professional help, the average for Croatia in 1964 is 14% and in 1970, 7%. The cantons in the former military colony have more children born without professional help by about 3.1% in 1964 and by 3.2% in 1970. Such results are indicative of the long-lasting effect of military colonialism, an effect that was still visible after 19 years of communism in 1964 and 25 years, in 1970. These results are presented in a graphical format in Figure 4.7. The same results are presented in tabular format in Table A.6 in the appendix.

Lower access to public goods can be traced up to the modern - day in 2011 when it comes to access to water and sewers – two types of goods that are administered by the local commune governments with both local and central government financial support (Ott and Bajo, 2001). I use data from the statistical report issued by the Croatian Bureau of Statistics based on the "Census of Population, Households and Dwellings 2011" (Croatian Bureau of Statistics, 2017, pp. 157–211). I calculate the percentage of dwellings that do not have access to water supply. Overall, the results are highly statistically significant: there are around five percentage points of dwellings, which do not have access to water in the former military colony. The coefficient represents approximately half of a standard deviation. The results are similar irrespective of specification, sample selection, and inclusion and exclusion of variables. The graphs in Figure 4.8 show the main discontinuity in access to public goods in 2011. The unit of analysis is 2011 municipality. The lighter dots represent municipalities in the former military colony. The higher the jump at the border, the greater the discontinuity. The difference is about five percentage points in access to water and six percentage points in access to sewers. This is a substantial difference given the country mean in Croatia in 2011 of nine percent.

The sample in the analysis for the 2011 census does not contain the municipalities that bordered the Ottoman Empire directly or that have bordered Bosnia since 1991. This allows me to alleviate the concern that regions adjacent the Ottoman Empire were more vulnerable to attacks. In addition, it also reduces the worry that low access to public goods may be because of spillover effects as a result of proximity to Bosnia, one of the countries with lowest GDPs in Europe.[6] In order to further alleviate the concern about border effects – being attacked by the Ottomans – I am eliminating from the analysis all the municipalities that according to Blanc (1951) were attacked by the Ottomans at some point in time. Despite the creation of the military colony, Ottomans kept attacking certain parts of the military colony during the sixteenth and seventeenth centuries. During those times, "many locals ran away, entire villages were deserted and numerous localities were destroyed and burned"

---

[6] Alternatively, eliminating such districts alleviates the possibility that proximity to the Ottoman Empire and, proximity to Ottoman institutions might have shaped the norms of people living in the area, which subsequently led to lower levels of trust and a culture of lower political involvement. If the uncertainty of living on the border persisted or if there is a contagion effect of Ottoman institutions, those should be the highest in this area. By eliminating these districts, I am ruling out such alternative explanations.

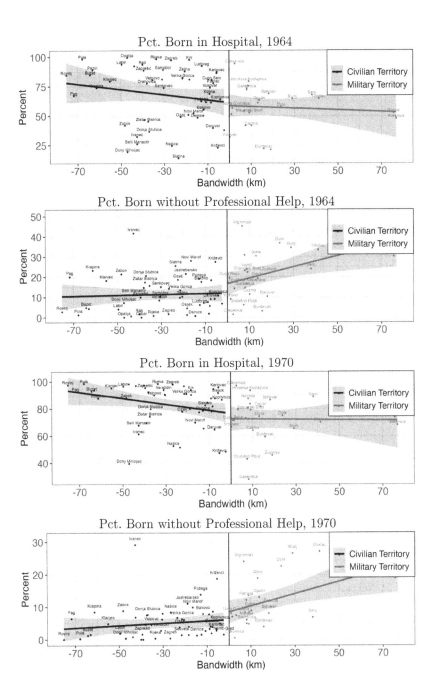

Figure 4.7 Effect of military colonialism on births and access
to hospitals for women, 1964–1970
Notes: The unit of analysis is canton. Distance from border (marked
with 0) is displayed on the x-axis. The y-axis displays the main
dependent variable

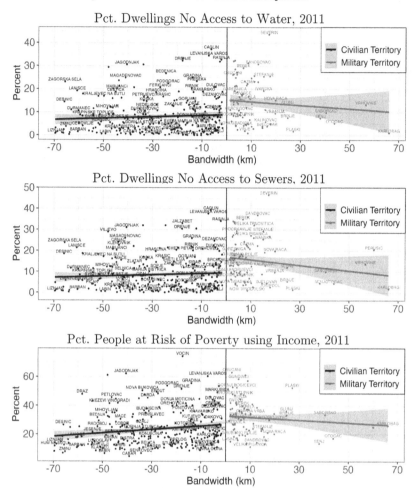

Figure 4.8 Effect of military colonialism on access to water, sewers, and income, 2011
Notes: The unit of analysis is municipality. Distance from border (marked with 0) is displayed on the x-axis. The y-axis displays the main dependent variable

(Blanc, 1957, p. 65). The settlements that were attacked are: Gorski Kotar, Lič, Lokve, Plaski, Lička Jesenica, Modruš, Ogulin, Gomirje, Vrbovsko, Ostarije, Delnice, Dreznica, Ravna Gora, Gvozd, Karlovac, Banija, Glina, Topusko, Jesenica, Mrkopalj, Dreznik, Bosiljevo, Kostajnica, and Sisak. Nevertheless, Blanc (1957) suggests that settlements outside of the main roads remained intact: "Nothing is more stable than a rural population, which, in the face of all the misfortunes, all the threats, remains attached to the ancestral land and, despite the past danger, persists in cultivating the land" (Blanc, 1957, p. 69). Even after eliminating the municipalities which were attacked by the Ottomans, the coefficient for the military colony is still around five percentage points.

In order to further mitigate concerns having to do with the proximity to the Ottoman Empire/Bosnia, I am also including distance to Ottoman Empire/Bosnia as an independent variable. The coefficient for the distance variable does not reach statistical significance (see subsection A of the appendix). Finally, it could also be the case that particular types of people self-selected to move to the border area. Historical accounts indicate that the military frontier was partly repopulated after Ottoman attacks with Christian Orthodox who fled out of Bosnia, Dalmatia, Serbia, and Central Europe (Blanc, 1951). In order to account for the fact that Christian Orthodox areas may be different, I eliminate from the sample the districts that were once in the Lika regiment and that in 1857 featured the highest number of Christian Orthodox inhabitants. The results still remain highly significant and around five percentage points.

The effects of the military colony are also visible when it comes to economic prosperity but the results are not as robust. I measure economic development using data from the Croatian Bureau of Statistics in collaboration with the World Bank. The two institutions created maps and calculated the geographic distribution of the risk of poverty and social exclusion for small areas of the Republic of Croatia based on standard surveys of local households, the European Union Statistics on Income and Living Conditions (EU-SILC Statistics) and the Household Budget Survey conducted by the Central Bureau of Statistics. The unit of measurement is percent and the unit of analysis is municipality. The third row in Figure 4.8 suggests that the population is at higher risk of poverty (using income method) by more than three percentage points in the former military colony (which is approximately a fourth of a standard deviation), but these differences are not always significant and are sensitive to model selection. These results are also presented in Table A.7 in the appendix.

4.3   Socioeconomic Processes: Land Inequality and Communal Properties

In the previous section, I provided evidence that districts which were formerlly in the military colony have lower access to public goods both historically and to the present day. Overall, roads and railroads are less dense, women are less likely to give birth in hospitals, and there is on average lower access to public infrastructure such as water and sewers. In this section, I delve into mechanisms: why has this area had lower access to public goods? The literature in social sciences including political science, economics, and sociology generally provides two kinds of explanations: *top-down* and *bottom-up* accounts. The *top-down* explanations mostly have to do with the role of the state in providing access to public goods. For example, Acemoğlu *et al.* (2001); Boix and Rosenbluth (2013); Dell (2010); Dell *et al.* (2018); Engerman and Sokoloff (2000); Mattingly (2017); North and Thomas (1973) and Tilly (1990) suggest that historical institutions matter for the provision of public goods. Specifically, factors such as the enforcement of property rights, ability to collect taxes and to wage wars, or socio-economic processes caused by state (in)action such as inequality or ethnic fractionalization could be consequential for the long-term provision of public goods. State action (such as forced population movements) could also be responsible for the creation of heterogeneous communities, which could result in some communities being more dependent on the state provision of goods (Charnysh, 2019).

The second set of theories focuses on the characteristics of groups and the ability of their members to act collectively and to promote group interests. Approaches in this area explain the under-provision of public goods in terms of individual incentives to free-ride in collective endeavors (Besley, 1995; Clague *et al.*, 1999; Muller and Opp, 1986; Olson, 1965; Schlager and Ostrom, 1992). Fewer works, however, try to connect the two types of theories. It could be the case that historical state (in)action could in fact condition individual incentives and attitudes. I argue for an integrated approach and show how the institutional "residuals" of military colonialism get to condition individual preferences. First, I explore the institutional legacies of military colonialism in the immediate aftermath of its abolition: land inequality and collective property rights. Previewing the results, the former military area has much less land inequality and collective properties. This is consistent with the very logic of military colonialism (abolition of landed elites and institutionalization of communal properties). Habsburg land tenure policy removed landowners in the military colony in 1553 and prevented their return or the emergence of a new class of landed elites until 1881 (Rothenberg, 1966). In the subsequent chapters, I explore how these institutions got to condition individual preferences, including lack of political involvement and risk aversion.

4.3.1 Land Inequality

Land tenure patterns have been studied extensively in the context of colonial institutions. They could be an important mediator for long-term outcomes including democracy (Acemoğlu and Robinson, 2000, 2006; Boix, 2003; Fukuyama, 2011; Mares, 2017; Moore, 1966; Scheve and Stasavage, 2017) and economic growth (Alesina and Rodrik, 1994; Engerman and Sokoloff, 2000; Persson and Tabellini, 1994). For example, Dell (2010) contends that in the case of Latin America, *haciendas* (large lands in the hands of a few elites) secluded peasants from the effects of extractive institutions of the colonial society. According to her, large landed elites received higher returns from investing in public goods because they enjoyed more secure property titles. It is also likely that they were better able to lobby the government to obtain engineering expertise and equipment and to organize local labor to facilitate the creation of public goods (Dell, 2010, p. 1866). This is also compatible with the notion that in communities where landlords control the public sector, public goods will be provided, although the kinds of public goods may be incorrect (Stiglitz, 1983). The same logic could apply to modern-day Croatia. Given that landed elites were never disbanded in the civilian area, they could potentially explain the historical and modern differences in the density of roads and railroads. The property rights of large landed elites remained largely intact until the formation of the Kingdom of Yugoslavia in 1918, when the newly formed government implemented comprehensive land reforms which aimed to provide a solution to the problem of peasant poverty and lack of land (Hrstic, 2017).

Before the creation of the military border in 1551, the area that would become the colony under Ferdinand I was highly similar to the civilian one. Both regions were part of the Croatian Kingdom and were ruled by a deputy governor on behalf of the Hungarian king, called a *ban* (Van Antwerp Fine, 1994). They were divided in to counties or *županije*, led by a count or *župan*, which was a hereditary position. Similarly, within these countries, there were three kinds of territories: "family holdings of the local Croatian nobles," ecclesiastical estates, which were separate from the authority of the count, and free towns, which stood directly under the king (Van Antwerp Fine, 1994, p. 205). Overall, the nobles had a lot of power within the Kingdom of Croatia. They were collecting taxes from peasants and could mobilize them on their behalf to go to war.

The abolition of landed elites upon the creation of the military colony was precisely aimed at creating a set of incentives that would allow peasants to want to stay in the designated area. Unlike peasants in the rest of the empire, who were serfs, these were free people. Through the institutionalization of communal properties, the Habsburg crown promoted the ability of indigenous communities to subsidize military conscripts who would help fight the Ottomans and defend the empire's territorial integrity. Therefore, land inequality in the military area should have been much lower compared to the civilian area during the existence of the military colony. The question that emerges is to what extent did low land inequality persist in the aftermath of this historical institution. In order to answer this question, I digitized and geolocated data from the Royal Statistical Office in Zagreb (1898), Royal Statistical Central Office in Budapest (1902, 1913), and Hungarian Statistical Office (1915). The Royal Statistical Office in Zagreb (1898) census was commissioned by the parliament of the Kingdom of Croatia, Slavonia, and Dalmatia, or the "Triune Kingdom," which was a nominally autonomous political entity within the Austro-Hungarian Empire between 1868 and 1918. The census measured agricultural potential, including the presence of fertile areas and orchards, and the extensiveness of communal properties. The censuses from the Royal Statistical Central Office in Budapest (1902, 1913) were organized by the Hungarian Empire after the Austro-Hungarian compromise of 1867 (called *Ausgleich* in German), which attributed Croatia-Slavonia to the Hungarian Empire.

The results in Figure 4.9 display the discontinuity in land (in)equality between the military and civilian areas based on data from the Royal Statistical Central Office in Budapest (1902). The most relevant measure is the number of people who own large properties (more than 100 acres), which is a direct measure for the presence of large landholders. The other two proxies that indirectly capture land inequality are the presence of domestic servants and agricultural smallholders. A high percentage of domestic servants indicates employment in manor houses and, hence, the presence of landlords, while a large number of smallholders provides some indication about the distribution of smaller property owners. The first and second row in Figure 4.9 show that there are many more agricultural landowners with more than 100 acres of land and many more domestic servants in the north compared to the south. Results in the first three rows of Figure 4.10 and Table A.8 in the appendix confirm that the results in Figure 4.9 are also statistically significant: on average, there are three percentage points fewer domestic servants in the military colony, which is substantial given that the average mean for the country in 1900 is seven percent. Similarly, the former military colony has fewer large landowners and more agricultural smallholders. Not surprisingly, land inequality was much larger in the civilian area. This area was principally ruled by land rulers who controlled vast territories.

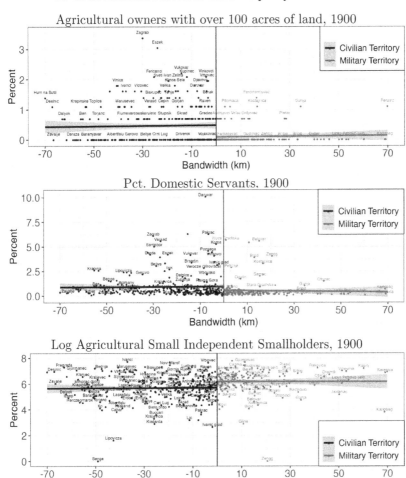

Figure 4.9 Effect of military colonialism on land inequality, 1900

Notes: The unit of analysis is settlement. Distance from border (marked with 0) is displayed on the x-axis. The y-axis displays the main dependent variable.

To what extent did the presence of landed elites impact economic growth through agricultural productivity? Increases in agricultural productivity are known to contribute to economic growth in two ways. First, agricultural productivity constitutes economic surplus, which can be used either for further production in agriculture or transferred out, providing capital for economic growth. Second, agricultural productivity can increase the purchasing power of rural residents and expand the market for industrial products (Christensen and Yee, 1964). When it comes to the relationship between inequality and economic growth, the literature (Alesina and Rodrik, 1994; Engerman and Sokoloff, 2000; Persson and Tabellini, 1994) contends that its effect depends on the conditions that generated the existing income distribution to start with, such as geography, technology, and wars (Boix, 2009, 2015). More recent work suggests that land inequality is associated with more investment in public goods (Dell, 2010) through the incentives that it creates for large landed elites to invest. Some other studies suggest no relationship whatsoever (Boix, 2010; Forbes, 2000; Voitchovsky, 2005). Only a handful of scholars have investigated the relationship between land inequality and agricultural productivity in particular. Johnston and Kilby (1970); Johnston and Clark (1982); Johnston et al. (1995); and Vollrath (2007) argue that land inequality should be associated with low agricultural yield because of labor misallocation, labor supervision costs, and potential policy distortions. As such, land inequality could create a bad incentive structure. On the one hand, inequality could positively impact productivity through the fact that large landed elites could own many more means of production which could result in higher agricultural yields. Therefore, the effect of land inequality for agricultural productivity could go both ways.

Unfortunately, there is no reliable data for agricultural yield around the time when the military colony was abolished and shortly thereafter. One proxy that could be correlated with agricultural productivity is the presence of agricultural means of production such as horses and cattle or mobile assets such as carriages. The presence of carriages denotes increased capacity to transport water, produce, materials, traded goods, people, etc. Similarly, horses and cattle indicate a potential increased ability to work the land through plowing, mowing hay, drilling grain, and disking fields. To investigate the effect of large landowners on productivity, I use the data from the Royal Statistical Office in Zagreb (1898) and compute three variables: ratios of carriages to inhabitants, cattle to inhabitants, and horses to inhabitants. The results in Figure 4.10 – fourth, fifth, and sixth line – indicate only a slight statistically significant difference between the military and the civilian area when it comes to the ratio of carriages to people. Specifically, there are more carriages per person in the military colony than outside of it. At the same time, there are no significant differences when it comes to the ratio of cattle or horses to people. Hence, the statistical results do not provide much support for the connection between land inequality and agricultural productivity.

There are similar patterns of land inequality in 1910, which is almost thirty years after the end of the military colony. While the regression coefficients decrease in magnitude slightly compared to Figure 4.10,

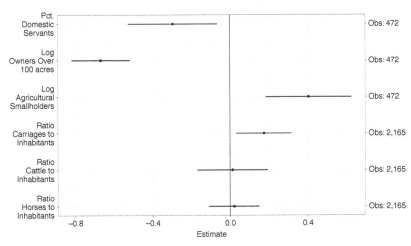

Figure 4.10 Effect of military colonialism on land inequality, 1900 – coefficient plot
Notes: The unit of analysis is county-level administrative unit in Imperial Hungary (jaras) for 1900 and settlement in 1895. Data is based on the Royal Statistical Central Office in Budapest (1902); Royal Statistical Office in Zagreb (1898). Every regression includes the following covariates: a linear polynomial in latitude and longitude, distance to Zagreb, and boundary segment FE.

the effects are still statistically and economically significant. The discontinuity in the presence of large landed elites for 1910 is depicted in Figure 4.11. The relationship between land inequality and agricultural productivity can be better tested with 1910 data, given the existence of measures that better describe the latter concept. I use tax municipality cadastral income in crowns that derives from agricultural yield (from arable land, garden, orchard, vineyards, pastures, and reed) from the Hungarian Statistical Office (1915). The results in Figure 4.12 do not indicate any statistically significant difference in taxed income. This finding for 1910 together with the lack of statistically significant results for 1900 indicate that the effect of land inequality on productivity is inconclusive. There is little evidence that military colonialism left an imprint on agricultural productivity. Similar to other cases of imperial institutions (Dell, 2010), growth in the form of access to public goods in the civilian area occurred through the elites who likely lobbied the central government to invest in roads and railroads for example or who invested in transportation themselves. The results do not indicate that access to public goods was achieved by higher productivity in the civilian area.

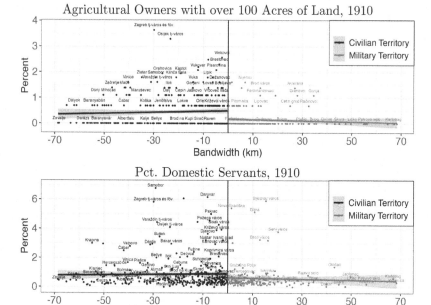

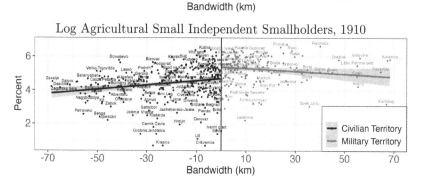

Figure 4.11 Effect of military colonialism on land inequality,
1910
Notes: The unit of analysis is settlement. Distance from border
(marked with 0) is displayed on the x-axis. The y-axis displays the
main dependent variable

The fact that the northern part had both higher inequality and
more historical and modern public goods is consistent with classical and neoclassical approaches (Kaldor, 1955; Keynes, 1920) to
the relationship between inequality and economic development. Such
approaches suggest that the marginal propensity of the rich to save
increases with wealth, which in turn affects aggregate savings, the

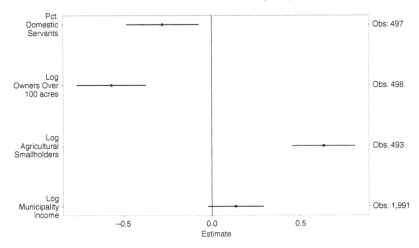

Figure 4.12 Effect of military colonialism on land inequality, 1910 – coefficient plot
Notes: The unit of analysis is county-level administrative unit in Imperial Hungary (jaras) for 1910 and settlement in 1909. Data is based on the Royal Statistical Central Office in Budapest (1913); Hungarian Statistical Office (1915). Every regression includes the following covariates: a linear polynomial in latitude and longitude, distance to Zagreb, and boundary segment FE.

accumulation of capital, and economic growth. These results are antithetical to modern theories about the negative effects of inequality for economic development. Such theories contend that the distributional conflict biases political decisions in favor of appropriation, which diminishes the individual effort of the masses to economic growth (Engerman and Sokoloff, 2000). Large landowners in the civilian side of Croatia were able to protect the peasants from the highly exploitative conscriptive institutions in the military colony. In addition, they were able to force serfs to adopt new agricultural methods and adapt to the market (Kaser, 1997).

4.3.2 Communal Property Rights

Communal land tenure patterns existed before the establishment of the military colony. As already indicated, in the Serbo-Croatian vernacular, these were called "zadruga." With the creation of the military colony, communal land tenure was institutionalized. This meant the peasants could no longer split their property as they wanted and the empire could utilize the family hierarchical structures in place to recruit obedient soldiers. As already shown in the previous chapters, a variety of legal documents were issued over time to stipulate that the zadruga or the house community was the key socio-economic unit of the military colony. Historical scholarship on family clans in Croatia began to split around 1848 in the civilian area as a result of the variety of political and economic movements that were happening throughout Eastern Europe (Erlich, 1966; Mead, 1976). To what extent did communal land tenure patterns persist potentially longer in the former military colony? To answer this question, I digitized and geocoded the census published by the Royal Statistical Office in Zagreb (1898). In order to obtain a more fine-grained measure for communal properties, I created three different variables: first, I took the log of the area covered by communal properties; second, I calculated the percentage of the area taken by communal properties from the total area of the settlement, and third, I calculated the proportion of people living under communal properties (population size multiplied by the size of the communal properties, divided by the area of the municipality). The graphs in Figure 4.13 show the sharp discontinuity between the military and the civilian area for the three continuous variables – log area covered by zadruga, percent area convered by zadruga, and population size living in zadruga. The results are highly significant for all three cases as indicated in Table A.10 in the appendix: zadrugas take much more space from the municipality area, and many more people live on communal properties. In addition, the differences are highly economically significant. For example, communal properties are larger by about 107 yokes in the military area compared to the civilian area (note that the average communal property size is 436 yokes).

Both Habsburg and Croatian authorities acknowledged zadrugas as a key institutional characteristic providing locals the means of subsistence. In order to maintain them, a variety of laws were passed to prevent the impoverishment of people and the subsequent potential consequences including riots, banditry, and emigration. At the same time, there was also an awareness that such institutions contribute to economic stagnation. Between 1868 and 1881, during the Unionist parliament under the leadership of Ban Levin Rauch and Ivan Mažuranić, a variety of laws were passed that aimed at dividing zadrugas. Yet, the criteria for division were not fully clear. For example some were in favor of dividing them according to the wishes of household heads, while others were in favor of divisions by family lineage. In addition, discrepancies emerged between the laws created by state authorities versus customary law with regards to landownership, inheritance and legal rights, and women's rights (Pavličević, 1989). As a result, many zadrugas were split in secret. For example, Pavličević (1989, p. 335) explains that in both civilian

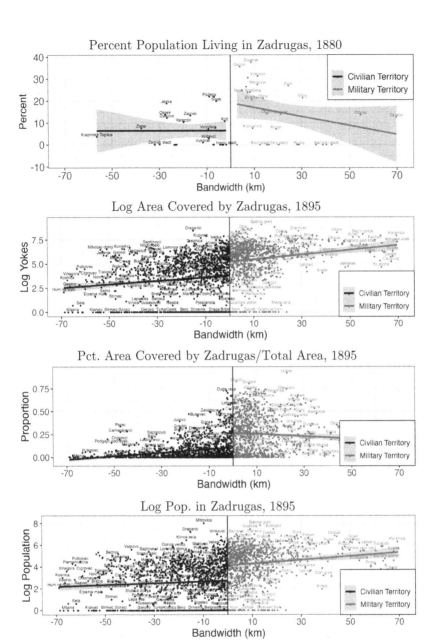

Figure 4.13 Effect of military colonialism on communal properties, 1880–1895

Notes: In the left column, distance from border (marked with 0) is displayed on the x-axis. The y-axis displays the main dependent variable.

and military Croatia, many more people lived in secretly split zadrugas that were only formally still managed as cooperatives. Secretly split zadrugas "lived in a kind of wild marriage with the state, tax, and judicial authorities and were the cause of many disturbances and protests of the peasants" (Pavličević, 1989, p. 335). In order to show empirically the prevalence of secretly split zadrugas, I use data from Zoričič (1883) and Royal Statistical Office in Zagreb (1898). The results visible in Table A.10 (columns 5–7) indicate that secretly split zadrugas were indeed more prevalent on military colony territory in 1880, but that was no longer the case in 1895. This suggests that people who were dissatisfied with the zadruga regime likely decided to split in secret just around the time of the abrogation of the military frontier. The empirical evidence no longer indicates differences in secretly split zadrugas after that.

Communal property rights continued to exist in the territory of the military colony for about 40 years after its abolition until World War I (Erlich, 1966; Mosely, 1976b). Erlich (1966) contends that the disappearance of communal properties is associated with two factors. One is the economic shock caused by the agrarian world crisis that lasted from 1873 until 1895, which resulted in a drop of the price of grain and put an end to communal living(Erlich, 1966, p. 48). The second factor is the emergence of the modern state which was increasingly reliant on taxes in cash. In order to pay such taxes, the peasant had to sell more and more of his products, which put him in touch with the cash economy and which rendered the self-sufficient zadruga economy obsolete (Erlich, 1966, p. 49).

4.3.3 Historical Occupational Structure

Another relevant question is: what happened to the inhabitants after exposure to military colonialism? What kinds of jobs did people have during the existence of the military colony and what kinds of jobs did they pursue after its end? Answering these questions is important to evaluate potential additional dimensions of the historical institution. In order to address these, I used data from the Austrian Ministry of Internal Affairs (1859), a census that was ordered in an era of increased centralization and need for collection of data on the entire population in the Habsburg Empire. This census started in 1849, 32 years prior to the abolition of the military colony, and so it illustrates how military colonialism functioned toward the end of its life.

The census presents data on many kinds of jobs, including priests, writers and artists, lawyers, doctors, manufacturers, farmers, and craft workers. Such jobs are not covered in subsequent censuses. Because one cannot examine how these evolved over time, I do not present them. In 1857, there seem to be some key occupations for which there is a statistically significant difference between the military colony and the civilian areas. These jobs are military personnel, civil servants, and day laborers. About one percent of people in every district (*Bezirke*) in 1857 is a military official. In the military colony, there are almost four percentage points more people involved in the military compared to the civilian area, which represents almost two standard deviations away from the mean. Additionally, there are also fewer civil servants (*Beamte*) by about 0.1 percent, given that the average number of civil servants per district is 0.9 percent. The difference in civil servants is reflective of the idea that the state is much more present in the civilian area than in the military part. The soldiers and the family clans in the military area are likely the substitute for the "official state" represented by civil servants. Finally, there seem to be fewer day laborers (*Tagelöhner*) in the military area by 0.5 percentage points, while the mean for all districts is approximately one percent. This probably indicates that the military jobs are much more stable compared to the jobs in the civilian area where people need to offer their work to a new employer much more frequently.

In order to investigate how the occupational structure might have changed in the immediate aftermath of the abolition of the military colony, I use data from the Royal Statistical Central Office in Budapest (1902, 1913) for 1900 and 1910. The results are graphically depicted in Figure 4.14 and presented in a tabular format in Table A.11 in the appendix. It is worth noting that there is still a somewhat higher percentage of military officials in the former military colony but this difference is no longer statistically significant. While the difference between the military and the civilian area is higher by about five percentage points in 1857, this difference goes down to 0.05 percentage points in 1900 and to 0.1 percentage points in 1910. Similarly, while in 1857 there are few civil servants in the military area, this difference ceases to be statistically significant in 1900 and 1910. It could be the case that people who were once soldiers are now taking on positions as civil servants. The percentage of day workers[7] seems to always be much lower in the military area: in 1857, the difference is about eight percentage points and highly statistically significant; this difference goes down to six and seven percentage points in 1900 and in 1910, respectively. The number of traders is lower in 1857 (note that the confidence intervals are very small) and evens out in 1900 and 1910. The results therefore point in the direction of convergence between the two regions. Within 19 years,

---

[7] Day labor is the work performed by one individual where the worker is hired and remunerated one day at a time, without the promise of any additional labor in the future.

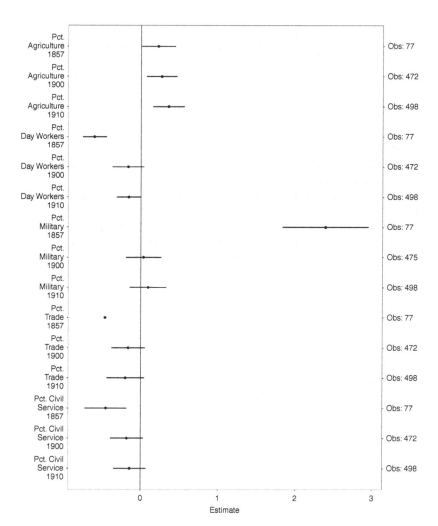

Figure 4.14 Effect of military colonialism on occupational structure, 1857–1910

Notes: The unit of analysis is county-level administrative unit in Imperial Austria-Hungary (kreis) for 1857, and (jaras) for 1900 and 1910. Data is based on the Austrian Ministry of Internal Affairs (1859); Royal Statistical Central Office in Budapest (1902, 1913). Every regression includes the following covariates: a linear polynomial in latitude and longitude, distance to Zagreb, and boundary segment FE.

people pick up occupations that are similar to the civilian area when it comes to trade and agriculture. However, it is also worth noting that there are many more people involved in agriculture in the former military colony both in 1900 and in 1910 by about five and seven percentage points.

Alternative Theoretical Mechanisms

As I showed in the previous subsections, the elements that have to do with property rights only lasted for a very short time while under-provision of public goods is visible to the present day. A relevant question is how did under-provision of public goods last. Is it the case that people at the bottom of society failed to engage collectively in the provision of public goods or could it be that the government continued to discriminate against descendants of military colonists?

For example, it could be the case that low involvement in public affairs was caused by ethnic heterogeneity rather than the lack of horizontal ties beyond extended family communities (caused by institutionalized zadrugas). As already indicated, the military colony was inhabited mostly by Serbs, Croats, Hungarians, and Germans (O'Reilly, 2006; Rothenberg, 1966). Previous research shows that heterogeneous communities tend to cooperate less, which is why they need the state for the provision of public goods. Specifically, heterogeneity could impede informal cooperation and also increase demand for third-party enforcement provided by the state (Charnysh, 2019). The results in Table A.18 in the appendix do not indicate significant differences between the military colony and the civilian area when it comes to ethnic/religious fractionalization in 1921, 1931, 1991, 2001, and 2011. This renders little plausibility to the hypothesis that ethnic fractionalization is the confounding factor explaining why the historical area of the military colony has lower access to public goods.

The second important alternative theoretical mechanism for the under-provision of public goods may have to do with the substitution effect caused by involvement in military affairs. In other words, it could be the case that people might have continued to work as soldiers, preventing them from getting involved in lucrative activities conducive to economic development or from signaling to the government the need to invest more. In other words, the military profession might have distracted the attention of locals from lobbying the government for public goods and from being involved in public affairs. As I have shown previously, the difference in percentage of soldiers is only statistically significant in 1857. Such difference is no longer visible in 1900, the closest census to

1881 – the year of the termination of the military colony. The difference between the military and the civilian area remains insignificant in 1910, 1931, and 1991, as indicated in Table A.19.

The third important alternative theoretical mechanism has to do with the supply side of the story. If it is mostly people at the bottom of the hierarchy who fail to coordinate politically, then there should be limited evidence for local governments or elites acting differently on the two sides of the border. Previous research on colonial extraction found that local elites become less accountable, more authoritarian, and less likely to provide public goods through the delegation of power by the imperial elites to local authorities (Lowes and Montero, 2021; Mamdani, 1996; Nathan, 2019). As already indicated in the section on socio-economic processes, local elites are much more visible in the area with public goods – the civilian area – and less so in the military colony. In addition, there were many fewer civil servants active in the area as late as 1910.

While there is no data available that captures perfectly the performance of local bureaucrats, data on local government transparency could be used as a proxy for local government performance. It could be the case that local governments prevent "active citizens' participation in taking decisions on the collection and spending of local funds" (Ott *et al.*, 2018, p. 2). As such, local governments could hide from the public the way they allocated public monies. The data on government budget transparency is from Ott *et al.* (2018) and covers 2017. One variable in their data captures the quantity of budget documents published on the local government units' official websites ranging from 1 – very low – to 5 – very good. The results in Table A.18 in the appendix do not indicate that local governments in the military colony are any more or any less transparent than those in the civilian area.

4.4   Alternative Explanations

Given the longue durée nature of access to public goods, it is worth considering alternative explanations for the difference in access to public goods between the two areas which have nothing to do with the Habsburg historical institutions. A variety of factors could impact access to public goods directly which are unrelated to the institution of military colonialism. In this section, I evaluate the effect of such factors. I group them in two categories: (1) temporal intermediary factors or historical shocks that could have affected the military and the civilian area differentially; (2) structural factors that could (have) impact(ed) the observations in the military area simply by being in a border region.

Historical Shocks

First, there have been many important historical events that could confound the effect of military colonialism on access to public goods. Such events include Ottoman attacks. This should be of limited concern, given that the main analyses for modern outcomes do not include municipalities that are contiguous with the Ottoman Empire and, subsequently, Bosnia. The logic is that regions closer to the border with the Ottomans are more likely to be attacked. In addition, to further alleviate this concern, I have already eliminated settlements that were attacked by the Ottomans between the fifteenth and the eighteenth centuries and the results for access to public goods still hold. I do not include them here to save space.

Effect of World War II
Other kinds of intermediary factors include the Ustaša regime being in power (1930–1945) – a Croatian ultranationalist and ultra-fascist organization, whose members organized massacres and built concentration camps to exterminate thousands of Serbs, Jews, and Roma (Tomasevich, 2001). Charnysh and Finkel (2017) suggest that the presence of concentration camps could lead to a real estate boom in the surrounding communities, which in turn might affect development. In order to evaluate this possibility, I compiled a list of all concentration camps that were built by the Ustaša regime, prisoners of concentration camps, and massacre death counts based on historical accounts. The sources include: Hoare (2006); Israeli (2013); Paris (1961); Pavlović and Pavlowitch (2008); Tomasevich (2001) and Yeomans (2015). Results in Table A.12 indicate no differences when it comes to the number of concentration camps being built, the number of prisoners, and the number of massacres in the two regions. Similarly, it is not the case that Allied powers (US and Britain) bombed one area more than the other (see the same table).

Effect of Yugoslav Wars
The Yugoslav Wars were a series of ethnic conflicts, wars of independence fought in the former Yugoslavia between 1991 to 2001 (Pavković, 2011). One concern for the validity of the modern results is that they are driven by the wars in Yugoslavia in the early 1990s. Beyond many finer nuances, it was the unification of the territories inhabited by Serbs in Bosnia and Croatia that was at stake in the conflict. In 1992 the Republic of Serbian Krajina declared independence from Croatia and had de facto control over central parts of the territory. This land was legally protected by the United Nations Protection Force. The question that emerges is:

to what extent are the modern results on access to public goods a result of the events and processes during the period 1991 to 1998?

Despite some overlap between the historical and modern Krajina, there is still substantial territory that is distinct between the two regions. The map in Figure A.1 in the appendix shows the spread of the Habsburg military border (historical Krajina) and the area of the Republic of Serbian Krajina (Modern Krajina). The intersection of the two represents approximately 44 percent of the total area of the Habsburg military frontier zone. In addition, the map also depicts the number of absolute deaths in the Yugoslav Wars based on UCDP data (Sundberg and Melander, 2013), which shows that they were likely to happen both inside and outside of the historical Habsburg military zone and the Serbian-occupied area.

Beyond human fatalities, there was also material destruction as a result of the war. To evaluate that, I used the number of damaged buildings and the extent to which they were damaged. The data is available in a document published by the International Court of Justice (2001). A total of 2,323 historical buildings classified as cultural monuments were damaged or destroyed in Croatia in the period 1991–1995 as a direct result of Serbia's campaign against Croats. The list of damaged and destroyed cultural monuments in the area comprises the following types of buildings: historic-memorial, civil, military/defense, ecclesiastical, sepulchral/cemeteries, sculpture/street furniture. The results in Table A.13 in the appendix indicate in fact that the Yugoslav wars affected the former military colony to a lesser extent, as reflected in the number of deaths based on data from Sundberg and Melander (2013), the number of buildings destroyed based on the gravity of the damage, or the number of buildings depending on their type (columns (8)–(11)).

To further alleviate concern about the differential effects of exposure to war, I also use perception data from EBRD's Life in Transition Survey (LITS) (2016) to analyze whether descendants of the military colonists are more likely to respond that they or their ancestors were targeted as a result of these events – see Table A.14 in the appendix. The results indicate that the respondents or their families were not more likely to report injury or having had to move because of WW2. There is also no systematic difference in perception about injury as a result of the conflict in Yugoslavia.

Finally, another concern related to the effect of the Yugoslav Wars is whether the differences in public goods are driven by the fact that many Serbs had to leave during the war, leading to shortages in human capital. In order to deal with this concern, I used data from the censuses from 1991 (before the conflict) and 2001 (after the conflict) and restricted the analysis to municipalities where the absolute value of the percentage change in Serbs is less than 5 percent, in other words, where there is a minimal change in the Serbian ethnic composition. The main results for access to public goods remain largely unchanged.

Effect of Communist Collectivization and Repression
Communism was in place in Croatia between 1945 and 1992. An important part of the communist program was the collectivization of agriculture (Pop-Eleches and Tucker, 2017). Given that zadrugas persisted much longer in the military colony, one could argue that municipalities in the military area might have been collectivized more extensively. In order to evaluate this hypothesis, I collected data on the number of cooperatives or "Broj opštih zemljorad-ničkih zadruga" and the number of households with no cooperative members or "Broj domaćinstava iz kojih nijedan član nije zadrugar" from the Federal People's Republic of Yugoslavia – Federal Statistical Office (1952a, pp. 10–40). In addition, I collected data on the number of cooperative plows or "Poljoprivredne sprave - plugovi svih vrsta (sem ralica)" from the Federal People's Republic of Yugoslavia – Federal Statistical Office (1952b, pp. 15–48). The results displayed in Table A.15 in the appendix do not indicate any difference in the level of collectivization between the former military colony and the civilian area.

Communist regimes could also be repressive toward their citizens, despite the fact they may not be as repressive as personalist or military regimes (Davenport, 2007). Results in Table A.16 in the appendix do not indicate that the communist authorities violently repressed the inhabitants living in the territory of the former colony. The results are based on data from LITS - EBDR (2016).

Structural Factors: Military Colonialism as a Physical Border

The second set of alternative explanations focuses on structural factors. The link between military colonialism and economic development could simply be the result of the military colony being placed at the border (initially with the Ottoman Empire and, subsequently, Bosnia). A large literature suggests that borders could be spaces for fugitives and state runaways (Scott, 2010), or spaces co-administered by contiguous nations, blurring the space of sovereignty (Carter and Goemans, 2014; Lee, 2020; Longo, 2018), nationality (Sahlins, 1989), and ethnicity (Cederman *et al.*, 2009; Gleditsch, 2007; Michalopoulos and Papaioannou, 2016). In addition, contested borders are typically associated with lower economic output, due to the higher economic transaction costs (Simmons, 2005; Wolf *et al.*, 2011).

As already mentioned, in the analyses where the dependent variable is based on modern data, the municipalities that are directly adjacent to the Ottoman/Bosnian border are not included. However, to further mitigate the concern about the effect of the border as a physical space that could be directly correlated with economic output (e.g. borders are often contested and see military action, or illegal crossings or trade), I pursue two strategies. The first one is to include in the main model a variable that captures the distance to the Ottoman Empire/Bosnia. If the border was indeed connected with economic outcomes, one would expect to see a positive coefficient for the distance to the Ottoman Empire/Bosnia variable. The effect for military colonialism remains positive and significant while the distance to Bosnia variable is negative and not always significant, as indicated by the results in Table A.17 in the appendix.

The second strategy is to run placebo tests to ascertain the extent to which running any line (that has the same shape as the line that divided the Habsburg civilian area from the military colony) in a north–south direction would generate a similar effect. To assess this, I re-estimated the models for the main outcomes of interest at 1-kilometer intervals from the actual military colony. The tests suggest that similar results could only be obtained if one moves the border line up to 10–15km. This re-enforces the idea that the results are driven by the line dividing the civilian area from the military colony, located in the middle of the country, as opposed to proximity to the border with Ottoman Empire/Bosnia. Thus overall, the results obtained for access to public goods are robust to a variety of alternative explanations.

In previous chapters, I explained how the military colony was different using qualitative accounts based on a variety of historians. In this chapter I included quantitative evidence after digitizing a variety of historical censuses and maps, confirming the types of policies that were present within the military colony: a much higher percentage of soldiers, many more dense family units (i.e. many more family clans), and a lower level of access to public goods in the form of access to transportation infrastructure. After the abrogation of the military colony in 1881, the restrictions on employment were removed. Thus, in 1900 and 1910, the differences in soldiers between the civilian and military areas were no longer significant. However, the analysis of historical data reveals the presence of institutional overhang: the much greater land equality (limited presence of large landed elites) and communal properties in the few decades in the aftermath of the elimination of the military colony. These differences between the former military and civilian areas are likely to have lasted until 1918. Similarly, quantitative analyses suggest that low access to public goods can be traced to the modern day. Such results cannot be attributed to (1) temporal intermediary factors that could have affected the military and the civilian area differentially; (2) structural factors that could (have) impact(ed) the frontier area simply by being in a border area; and (3) alternative mechanisms by which military colonialism affected the way the state behaves in the former military colony. In the next chapter, I investigate the relationship between military family clans and the state, unraveling why ruling through family clans was an attractive option for the Habsburg Empire. In doing so, I also discuss the norms and social customs embedded in the clans that might have allowed the transmission of particular kinds of attitudes which could be visible to the present day. I provide empirical evidence for the transmission of the latter to the modern day in Chapter 6.

5   Colonial Institutions and Social Norms

The military frontier was abrogated in 1881. Yet, despite its disappearance, certain elements that pertained to the institutional "treatment" persisted. As shown in the previous chapter, low land inequality and communal properties continued to exist at least for another forty years until around World War I. Access to public goods continued to be lower both in the short and long run on the territory of the former military frontier. As already argued, the socio-economic unit of the military colony was the zadruga, which was strategically adopted by the Habsburgs precisely because it ensured the survival of the locals and because it was conducive to obedience. But how did such structures facilitate that? Equally important, how did such structures mold the norms and customs of the people living within them? In this chapter, I focus on micro-mechanisms of transmission. I provide an answer to the question about norms and attitudes by presenting an in-depth case study on the life within a zadruga, based on anthropological and sociological accounts from 1930s. In the subsequent chapter, I show how certain norms and attitudes such as trust vis-à-vis in-groups and out-groups, risk aversion, and political participation were affected by life within family clans using both qualitative and quantitative evidence.

5.1   Family Governance: Family Clans and the State

The idea that states can govern through family clans is not new. In fact, Olson (1993); Weingast *et al.* (2012) contend that the local elites or representatives of family clans can be involved in a process of state-making. As such, local elites in the periphery do not compete with the state, as Migdal (1988) would argue. Rather, local elites end up becoming a constitutive participant in the "state-building project" (Mukhopadyay, 2014, p. 5). They reflect local power structures, deep-rooted social organizations that were captured by the imperial government to create the institution of the "border," while at the same time, being part of the larger, dynamic process of state formation. Communal families continued their existence not in opposition to the state, but rather, as micro-instantiations of state authority asserting itself in the periphery and filling the gulf between the ruler and individual imperial subjects. The presence of family clans in the periphery is not indicative of a weak state, which would be Migdal's (1988) interpretation, but rather, their presence indicates a partnership of convenience or "a 'negotiated' enterprise" (Barkey, 2008, p. 1).

A large literature contends that communal families are in fact "prior to the state in both historical and analytical senses" (Ahram and King, 2012, p. 173). At some point, all societies were built on family ties and well-defined interpersonal relationships, where each clan jointly owned land and shared responsibility for each other's actions. People got together because safety was in numbers: larger communities were more secure offering a safety net against starvation and exposure to violence. In order to continue to survive and maintain internal coherence, such clans also developed norms related to inheritance, family responsibility, arranged marriages, command and control, etc. The main purpose of such norms was to build emotional attachment among clan members, foster internal harmony, and overall, nurture solidarity, which in turn, would have had an important role in reducing internal conflicts.

The Habsburg Empire followed principles of governance for the military colony different from the principles of governance in Vienna or Budapest. Local elites played a key role in legitimizing the power of the empire in the periphery, as predicted by Olson (1993); Weingast *et al.* (2012). The social hierarchies pertaining to such clans made them an attractive option for the Habsburg Empire in order to maintain control. For example, Mosely (1976c, p. 29) specifically mentions the importance of family clan leaders who were also the elders and who were universally respected and obeyed by family clan members. With their help, the Habsburg "king was [perceived as] a kind of zadruga elder on a national scale." As such, there was a certain kind of "mythology surrounding village elders" as keepers of legitimate politics and justice, as Mukhopadyay (2014, p. 14) would argue.

By collaborating with local heads, the Habsburg Empire managed to have increased social control over the locals, blurring the line between the local rules of social organization and the rules of the state. In doing so, the Habsburg Empire incorporated the formal and informal organizations within which people lived, dictating how they related to their families and to the wider members of their community. Boppe (1900, p. 44) explains how the power exercised by family heads simplifies internal administration. Migdal (1988, p. 26) refers to such organizations as the symbolic configurations that are intimately tied to rewards and sanctions and whose role is to integrate a "transcendental purpose into otherwise mundane behavior needed for survival." In other words, given the high costs associated with imposing new imperial rules onto the periphery, it was more effective for the Habsburg Empire to utilize local organizations that helped consolidate imperial rule further.

From the very beginning, the Habsburg authorities believed that the zadruga (the family clan) – an ancient Slavic arrangement, was the key to the good functioning of the military colony. Perrot (1869) notes how hierarchies of power embedded within local family clans were crucial for the creation of the institution of military colonialism and how, in their absence, the empire would have had to create them:

This [zadruga] is what will make him [the soldier] a more docile and obedient subject. Accustomed to receiving his task in the community from the patriarch, he will obey like a man who feels born to always obey, the sergeant and the captain. Thus, if collective property had not existed, the border commanders should have invented it before establishing their colonies. It was much more convenient for them to find it all organized there, to set up their buildings on these foundations which seemed prepared expressly to receive them![1] (Perrot, 1869, p. 57)

Several family clans would form a village, which could elect their own magistrates (*knezovi*)[2] and their own military captains (*voïvode*) (Sišić, 1918, pp. 479–490). It is the magistrates that had to ensure that each patriarch provided adequate food and care for all male members of his house community above the age of seventeen (Sišić, 1918, p. 481, Article 5). Perrot (1869, p. 64) argues that around mid-nineteenth century, in times of war, the regular army regiments of the Austrian army comprised 128,900 men, who cost 20,823,000 florins. The 60,000 men in the military colony cost the empire 3,980,000 florins. It would use this latter sum for the construction and maintenance of barracks (Perrot, 1869). Only a tiny fraction of this amount was used as payment for soldiers in the colony.

As such, the authorities adopted laws meant to solidify the link between the patriarchal regime and the imperial institutions. Rules were created to define how communities were administered and dissolved, how property was distributed and transmitted, together with the rights and duties of each community member. One of the first legal documents

---

[1] Translation from French.
[2] The position was abolished in 1754.

that the imperial authorities issued was *Statuta Valachorum* (the Statute of the Vlachs),[3] a charter issued in 1630. This charter confirmed that all men between the ages of sixteen and sixty were subject to military service both against the Turks and against all the enemies of the emperor. The charter also made the family clan, which pre-dated the Habsburg Empire (Stopfer, 1840, pp. 129–130), the basic unit of the border's social and economic organization. Subsequent documents such as the Military Rights of 1754, the Basic Laws of 1807 and 1850 indicate that living within a zadruga was an obligation, with no individual being allowed to separate from their zadruga or to divide the communal property.

An individual could move from one family clan to another only in exceptional cases, following authorization from the patriarch and the regimental authorities. Transgressing such rules and leaving without permission could in a first instance result in apprehension and return to the family, while a second transgression could result in imprisonment and physical disciplining. Sometimes, the family clan could become too numerous for life under communal living to be possible. The laws in the military confines allowed for the property to be split into two or more parts, provided that each one of them was large enough for the new family to be able to survive and provided that the newly formed family could provide soldiers for military service. For example, the Basic Laws of 1807 indicate that families could be split in two situations: (1) all men had to agree on the division; (2) at least three men "fit for duty" had to remain for each of the divided branches so that one of them could be available for military service. If three men were not available, the division was not allowed to take place. Beyond such legal requirements, regimental commanders possessed extensive discretion to judge whether a family was allowed to split or not; military necessities were almost always a priority for the commanders who would supervise all the steps of the division process (Grandits, 2002, p. 148).

The state also prescribed laws prohibiting the inhabitants of the military colony from taking on jobs of their choice. In times of peace, they would have to allocate a hundred days of military service a year and spend the rest of the time working the land. In times of war, inhabitants would have to abandon agricultural work and be ready to defend the state. Beyond agriculture, grenzers were also allowed to become

---

[3] The term *Vlach* or *Wallach* was used to identify the refugees from the Turkish territories, but it had no religious or ethnic connotation (Rothenberg, 1966; Seton-Watson, 1911; Von Czoernig, 1855).

carpenters and blacksmiths, provided that the interest of the community was not affected. When it came to trade, only sons of soldiers who were unfit for military service could take on those roles (Perrot, 1869, p. 59). The grenzers could sell/buy cattle and tinder only upon receiving authorization from the higher authorities of the regiment. In the border passage points and in close vicinity to military fortresses, the inhabitants could exchange with the Turks some limited raw products for manufactured goods. Overall, however trade was severely limited (Perrot, 1869).

Despite working to defend the state, the inhabitants of the military colony were not paid. With the exception of the captain and a small number of non-commissioned officers who were receiving outside payment, the military colonists or the grenzers received no pay but were supported by their zadruga (Rothenberg, 1966, p. 15). Each zadruga, regardless of size, had to provide one armed man,[4] a person between the ages of 16 and 60 in service to defend the Habsburgs against the Ottomans and other enemies of the empire (Von Hietzinger, 1817, p. 29). In times of peace, they would simply guard the border line. The government would bear the cost of arms, ammunition, and would offer a pair of shoes every year (Desprez, 1847, p. 727). The family clans had to provide the uniforms for their soldiers (Boppe, 1900, p. 45) in addition to food when they were going on patrols. The law of the military colony guaranteed that a solider would have access to the fruits of the harvest and part of the money of the zadruga, irrespective of whether he participated in the community work or not. In addition, his family and children would be fed in his absence. The additional provisions that the state was making for the military colonists were exemptions on property tax, which were proportional to the number of soldiers coming from those families (Perrot, 1869, p. 62).

Military colonists lived in communal households under the leadership of an elected patriarch (*starješina*) (Rothenberg, 1966, p. 98). The homes, the land, the cattle, and the major tools were held as common property and individual members had equal rights over them. The only personal possessions that individual members could have, were personal money and some agricultural tools. Later in the early nineteenth century, individual members could also have more clothes, jewelry, and

---

[4] Normally, the grenzers had to work their land and would be called for training and guard duty on a rotating basis. In the event of mobilization, the entire force would be divided into three groups. The first group would be the active service battalions and join the field army; the second group would be in charge of the frontier defenses; the remainder would continue with their normal occupations and act as a general reserve (Rothenberg, 1966, p. 16).

linen, despite the fact that they might have been purchased with communal money.[5] Filipović (1976) argues that individual property became increasingly important in the South-Slav space with the introduction of the cash economy. This also coincided with more and more zadruga members living in different sleeping quarters - usually buildings lacking a hearth (Filipović, 1976, p. 273).

House fathers were generally unconditionally obeyed throughout the history of the military colony. As a result, they would be able to call to arms all the soldiers within their zadrugas within minutes, if the Habsburg center ordered them to do so. According to the *Statuta Valachorum* charter of 1630, if the alarm bell rang, between 5,000 and 7,000 people had to be available[6] within a few hours (Sišić, 1918, p. 488, Article 11). Similarly, zadrugas could also raise about fifty thousand fighting men in the mid-1700s for planned battles (Rothenberg, 1966, p. 15).

The patriarch was usually someone over the age of fifty, who passed the age of active military service, someone in charge of transmitting and enforcing imperial rules, maintaining the "necessary calm and order" (Von Hietzinger, 1817, p. 30), and taking responsibility for the actions of his house members (see for example, art. 55–90 of the Basic Laws - *Grundgesetze* of 1807 in Stopfer (1831, pp. 185–242)). The presence of house fathers simplified internal colonial administration. Military generals or captains were in direct contact with the house fathers. The former had to keep an up-to-date property booklet on which the land cultivated by the family clan was recorded including the area, class of land, and its value. The land recorded in these booklets could be of three types: the land dedicated to the harvest, the one dedicated to pay taxes, fees, and duties, and the land dedicated to the military posts (*chardaken*). Additional information in these booklets included the number of florins and the number of days of work which are owed to the state. A prototype of these booklets corresponding to 1606 is reproduced in Table 5.1 based on Blanc (1957, p. 443).

Every booklet was completed by each family clan head. Habsburg inspectors would be in contact with each one of them and would make copies of the booklets on behalf of the regimental captains. In this manner, Habsburg authorities would keep track of the number of days and the amount of money that military colonists owed. The frequent interaction between the Habsburg inspectors and family heads led to such

---

[5] Such possession were usually referred to as *osobina, osobac,* or *osebunjak* in the South-Slav space.

[6] An English traveler also explains that "[b]y signals from hill to hill, the whole population, from Dalmatia to Moldavia, can be alarmed in a few hours, and at each head quarters an effective force placed at the disposition of the commanding officer" (Paton, 1849, p. 174).

Table 5.1 *Military colonial booklet prototype from 1606*

Type of Harvest	Funds	Class	Area		Of which Exempt		Taxable		Other Charges		Corvée Labor		Work for the Community		
			morgen	klafter	fl.	cr.	fl.	cr.	fl.	cr.	Hand	Horse	Ordered and Paid	For every Individual	For Head of Cattle
Fields															
Meadows															
Gardens															
Vines															
Total															

Notes: Family booklet model pertaining to a military colonist based on *Archives Historique de Guerre from 1606*, reproduced in Blanc (1957, p. 443). Abbreviations: fl. = florins; cr. = crowns.

a degree of state control that, according to historical accounts, "a single inspector can in a day check the situation of a company, by bringing together in a meeting place all the heads of families and by comparing their booklets to the general register" (Boppe, 1900, p. 46). The high level of state penetration is also vividly depicted by a French general to Napoleon, during the short French rule over the military colony:

Croatia should not be considered like a regular province, but rather like a large military encampment; its population is an army which carries its means of subsistence within its bosom and which, still half-barbaric, differs from nomadic peoples only by this organization, the results of which are perhaps without example in the history of nations... The officers of economy, far from harming the progress of agriculture, serve primarily to make it prosper; in this respect they provide the greatest details of administration, determining the kind of grain which is to be sown, the portion of the harvest which is to be paid by each family into the vast granary of the company; finally, an economic officer is a factory manager who sets in motion with method and foresight to obtain these products. Without it, half of the land will be fallow. *Twice a month, he visits all the families of the company and reports on their situation and their needs... Each year, the colonel visits the families of the regiment.* Laws and discipline, applied in such an immediate way to the cultivation of the land, are the best way to bring a barbarous and lazy people into existence and to help civilize them. (Blanc, 1957, p. 120) (*emphasis added*)

Sometimes, the family leader would do more than maintain the "necessary calm and order." An English traveler to the military colony from 1880 was mentioning how sometimes family heads could become abusive: "and when the family or cluster of families grew numerous, the patriarch was often a tyrant, or, by some defect in the head or heart, incapable of managing his descendants or collaterals to their satisfaction" (Paton, 1849, p. 175). The money was seldom used for supporting individual members of the family (Radosavljevich, 1919, p. 146). Nevertheless, the sense of family life is what allowed individual members to put up with the many inconveniences (Radosavljevich, 1919, p. 144).

The elderly figure was also in charge of managing the family economy (including purchases and sales) and needed to give his consent in order for someone to work outside the zadruga property; in addition, a portion of the income obtained outside of the family property needed to be given to the family fund. A zadruga member who disobeyed the patriarch or who did not contribute their fair share of labor, could be deprived of the benefits that could otherwise accrue to them (Perrot, 1869, p. 58). Upon the death of the patriarch, the property would be inherited by the eldest son. In case of no son, property could also be inherited by a daughter, who would have to marry a grenzer within two years (Desprez, 1847, p. 727). If the daughter cannot get married to a grenzer, she would have to sell the buildings to one within two years, to avoid expropriation by the state. If an entire community died out, the lands and the buildings would go to the male relatives of the last owner (Perrot, 1869, p. 60). Finally, if none of these conditions could be met, the property would return to the state and be used to better endow existing communities or to create new ones.

The wife of the family leader (the matron) was responsible for assigning different tasks to the women in the household which would be in the form of days of service for the care of the house and kitchen (Perrot, 1869, pp. 54–55). Both the father and the mother of the zadrugas were elected and subsequently confirmed by the military authorities. In cases where there was no male left within the zadruga to fill the role of head, the right would be passed on to a leading female house member. She would subsequently have to marry a man who was already a grenzer or who had the capability of becoming a grenzer.

But how did family life in a zadruga actually work? Many of the historical materials from the nineteenth and early twentieth century focus on legal aspects pertaining to life in a military colony including rules and regulations that people had to follow and the punitive measures associated with disobedience. While such rules and regulations are examples of technocratic language that the empire used in order to make its presence known, the ways in which the state penetrated the very core of family life are much more difficult to tease out without first-hand information. Only a few historical accounts by French and British travelers or by military officials provide some clues about the far-reaching influence of the state onto family life in the military colony (Boppe, 1900; De Beaujour, 1829; De Saint-Aymour, 1883; Paton, 1849; Perrot, 1869). As already indicated, the two main ways whereby the Habsburg state controlled the locals were through the inspectors who were keeping track of the land and the size of taxes in kind, cash, or in the form of days of labor, and through the economic officers, who were charged with ensuring the agricultural success in the colony. The latter would decide on the type of grain that must be planted and the amount of harvest which must be poured by each family in the vast granary reserve of the company. Without economic officers,

the land would be fallow: he visits all the families in the company twice a month and reports on their situation and their needs. The captain, accompanied by his officers, sees them for himself once a month; in the same spirit, each senior officer visits six companies every three months; and each colonel travels to see all the families of the regiment. (Boppe, 1900, p. 48)

The extent of state penetration in the periphery is likely to have had repercussions beyond the immediate relationship between imperial agents and family heads. A few anthropological and sociological accounts from around the second half of the twentieth century offer us important indications about such ramifications which went all the way to the individual level (Erlich, 1966; Kaser, 1985, 1994; Mosely, 1976b). The family system created "obedient" Habsburg subjects who would be willing to sacrifice themselves for the welfare of the empire. Understanding this system is crucial for appreciating how military colonialism might have affected the attitudes and norms of the colony inhabitants and how these might have persisted over generations. I argue that exposure to this family clan system can be traced on two levels: norms that have to do with family clan socialization and norms which have to do with family hierarchy.

Attitudes about Family Clan Socialization

The fact that people were so dependent on their peers is likely to have deepened their connections with family members. Anthropologists such as Voorhees *et al.* (2020, p. 12) describe how an individual becomes a person within a family collective by developing a capacity for "self-triggered thought and an integrated worldview that becomes aligned with the point of view of the kin." As such, individuals get to be recognized as units and members of a social collective. They develop a capacity to tell that the other members of the collective are individuals like oneself (similar), yet simultaneously different. Such cognitive ability allows them to grasp a categorical concept that binds a collection of similar objects into an abstracted unity. This in turn allows members of the collective to conceptualize the "I" or "me" in reference to the group. Therefore, the family clan constitutes a system that connects individuals and enables the perspective of one person to be transformed into that of another. One's biological birth becomes a position within a cultural kinship system. A child becomes "one of us" after being born, which entails a series of behavioral and affective conditions that mold a child's identity.

Being part of a social collective entails cooperation on a variety of levels. One example of cooperation is the idea of helping a relative in need, which is a clan moral imperative. In cases of upward social mobility, descendants are expected never to forget their family roots. For example, children consider it to be their duty to care for their parents in old age and infirmity. Cooperative behavior in this case is part of a culturally defined identity, which is related to the larger process of reflective self-consciousness. This in turn gives individuals the capacity for conceptual abstraction of the self and of the group that they belong to.

The strength of the ties among clan members is reflected in the bias toward inner-group and out-group members. This is the tendency to evaluate one's own group or its members (the in-group) more favorably than groups to which one does not belong (the out-group). Such tendency stems from a desire to protect one's own group. Any perceptions that the group is threatened become so visceral that they trigger physiological reactions that could be as strong as if they are directed at the individual (Voorhees *et al.*, 2020). This is because the individual is no longer able to distinguish their own identity from that of the group to which they belong; hence, any threat to the group becomes a threat to the individual.

The literature in psychology analyzes the problem of the in-group-out-group bias extensively (Hewstone *et al.*, 2002; Rabbie and Horwitz, 1969; Tajfel *et al.*, 1971), demonstrating its presence within different cultures and societies and providing motivational and cognitive explanations for its existence. Previous literatures also show that the outer-group bias has implications for negotiations, conflict resolution, competition between groups, international trade agreements, hiring decisions, and many aspects related to fairness and cooperation (Ruffle and Sosis, 2006). Work on the kibbutz system in Israel (Ruffle and Sosis, 2006) indicates that when paired with people who share a common fate, the level of cooperation of individuals is higher than when paired with outsiders. Older sociological and anthropological scholars such as Banfield (1958) or Coleman (1990) contend that societies based on strong family ties have a positive role in promoting good conduct among related family members; selfish behavior is only considered acceptable outside of the family ties. Todd (1983, 1990) creates a typology of family structures and discusses how different types are responsible for the diffusion of political ideologies. According to him, there can be liberal family types where children become independent and leave the nuclear family at an early age or there can be authoritarian family types where children continue to be dependent on their families through adulthood and still live with their parents after they get married. Liberal family types are associated with the spread of liberalism, while authoritarian types are more likely associated with the transmission of communism and social-democracy. The relationship between family ties and social capital and economic outcomes is empirically tested using modern methodology by Alesina and Giuliano (2010) who find that societies that rely extensively on family structures have less generalized trust and a lower civic sense. Greif and Tabellini (2007) also show how the presence of nuclear family in Europe, as opposed to the family clan, is the key to explaining levels of urbanization in Europe (more nuclear families) and China (more family clans).

Attitudes about Family Hierarchy

Another group of norms which are related to exposure to extended family clans, has to do with compliance with and deference to authority structures. Being part of dense familial connections regulates people's behavior in subtle and powerful ways, creating the "organizational or conceptual universe of a community and the principles that govern it, that make it coherent and thereby make it objective for its adherents" (Leaf and Read, 2012, p. 48). Such universe frames the organization of social interactions in the form of structured patterns of prescriptions, prohibitions, and interpretations that are affectively salient. In addition, it also frames stories, myths, and narratives that become worldviews of family clan members (Voorhees et al., 2020). These worldviews are ultimately self-sustaining, internalized webs of knowledge, beliefs, attitudes that arise through the concatenation of individual experience and incorporation within a system of ideas. These in turn constitute the criteria for evaluating one's own behavior and the behavior of others.

Gabora and Steel (2017) discuss the notion of *reflective self-consciousness* to distinguish between the ability of the individual to have feelings and sensations and the ability to reflect on the self in the past and the self in the future by making analogies, taking perspective, and engaging in self-triggered recall.[7] This is what further enables individuals to contribute to that worldview which allows them on the one hand, to have a consciously recognized social identity, which is defined by group membership and social roles within that group, and on the other hand, to have the ability to identify deviations from the rules of the group. Individuals

---

[7] In the psychology literature, *self-triggered recall* enables individuals to process information recursively with respect to different contexts and perspectives. This is what allows individuals to access their memory voluntarily and act out events that occurred in the past and might occur in the future.

are enculturated from birth with behavioral, institutional, and norma-tive instantiations of such worldview. This is also what allows mutual understanding among members of the social collective.

These instantiations motivate individuals to monitor themselves and members of their own group to make sure that everyone acquiesces. Given the hierarchical structure of family clans in the military colony, conformity was further strengthened by the elders, who were historically, the liaison between young men who were supposed to defend the impe-rial borders and the Habsburg state. Respect for the elders likely began in early infancy through a process of *indoctrination*, which established the psychological mechanisms facilitating respect for authority and the potential punitive measures for deviance.

Therefore, the first criterion based on which hierarchy was created was age. Every zadruga had a *starešina* at the top of family hierarchy. Other names to define the same position were *gospodar, domaćin,* or *kut-njik*. This was typically the oldest member of the family clan, presiding a council of all adult male members of the zadruga,[8] where decisions were made based on consensus. The elderly figure had executive power being in charge of implementing the decisions of the family council.[9] In addition, he was also responsible for creating work schedules for zadruga members and making sure that the work was completed on time. Beyond the familial responsibilities, he also represented the household in village assemblies and in dealings with the government, including ensuring that the right number of men are recruited to defend the border. The women within the zadruga were also following the additional authority of the elderly female (who could be the family clan leader's wife but not nec-essarily). She was typically called *domaćinca, gazdarica* or *maja* and she was considered an advisor and mediator for the elderly man, supervising the daughters-in-law and the production of dairy products.

Second, zadrugas also had a clear structure based on sex. Men were in charge of the livestock and agriculture, while the women were responsible for raising children, preparing food, making clothes, and occasionally some agriculture.[10] Women could take turns preparing the food on a weekly basis, elderly women being excepted completely, and young brides being excused from this task in their first year of marriage.

---

[8] Because of the presence of this council for decision-making, some sociologists and anthropologists have looked at zadrugas as early forms of democratic institutions (e.g. Filipović (1976)).

[9] The prestige was the only reward for the elderly figure.

[10] Filipović (1976, p. 277) mentions that women could help with some tasks in the field, including weeding, digging, harvesting and even grazing cattle. Plowing was probably the only exception of work in which women were not involved.

Every zadruga member had an equal right to food and clothing while the elderly and the disabled enjoyed full security.

In order to capture the norms about socialization and attitudes of deference to authority structures more systematically, I analyze and re-present the anthropological insights offered by Mosely (1976b) who conducted fieldwork in the area close to the military colony in the 1930s, about fifty years after the abrogation of the military frontier. Mosely (1976b) is in fact one of the scholars who coined the term "zadruga" in Western anthropology. Such a term was adopted in the anthropological and sociological literature to refer to an "an extended family consisting of two or more small or biological families (father, mother, minor children) owning land, livestock, and tools in common and sharing the same livelihood" (Mosely, 1976c, p. 59). While it was very common to use the term "zadruga" in the entire Croatian territory, due to its legal institutionalization on the military side, Filipović (1976) suggests that in other regions of the Balkans, including countries like Bosnia and Herzegovina, Serbia, Montenegro, and Macedonia, it was more customary to refer to zadrugas as *kuća* - house, *čeljad* - people, group,[11] *zajednica* - community, or in the military frontier, *Hauskommunion* or *Familiengemainscaft* (Utješenović-Ostrožinski, 1859). Beyond the terminology itself, the notion of family clans was not unique to the Slavs or South-Slavic people; family clans also existed among Germanic people, in the Caucasus, India, Africa, and indigenous communities in North America and was typically associated with livestock herding and agricultural communities.

While the earliest mentioning of zadrugas in the South-Slav space is around 1390, they continued to be mentioned in the Middle Ages in the lands controlled by Venetians, Austrians, Hungarians, and Ottomans (Filipović, 1976, p. 270). At the very core of zadrugas was the notion of kinship, with male members being related in the male line and with women entering the zadruga through marriage. As such, all family members lived in one place, although individual families could have had separate cabins for sleeping. Some members could also spend time away from home in order to cultivate land or to graze the livestock in areas away from home, but they would never work for themselves. As such, land, livestock, and agricultural tools were used communally.

Before the emergence of cash economy, only large zadrugas could maintain themselves successfully being able to carry out the necessary division of labor. For example, an old wooden plow would require several oxen and multiple people to guide them. Therefore, a large zadruga would have ensured easier and quicker cultivation of land (Filipović,

[11] Filipović (1976, p. 269) indicates that the term *kuća* - house could be traced as far back as 1349, in Dušan's Code, where the term was used with the same meaning.

1976, p. 273). Similarly, while some members of the zadruga could look after the family livestock in the mountains, the others would be responsible for agriculture. After the emergence of cash economy together with changes in social and economic life, the working procedures changed. This meant that many more people could work and earn money outside of the zadrugas.

5.2   Empire and Clan Politics: The Varžić Family Clan

Showing how people lived within such communities is crucial to understand why it was cost-effective for the state to utilize such social structures and the long-term implications for the day-to-day interactions of people. Such communities do not exist anymore, so an attempt to depict life in a zadruga can only be done by examining historical primary and secondary works. Erlich (1966) and Mosely (1976a) are two examples of Western anthropologists who have done extensive fieldwork in villages in the Balkans in the 1930s. Erlich (1966) conducted a medium-n study of family cultural changes in the South-Slav region (including former Yugoslavia, Albania, and Bulgaria), focusing on the patriarchal family system, how it changed, the causes for such changes, and how people felt about them (e.g. introduction of cash economy, the impact of World War I and World War II, etc.). Erlich (1966) used thick brush-strokes to depict such communities, attempting to find commonalities and regional cultural patterns. Mosely (1976a) on the other hand, was much more focused on depicting particularities of individual zadrugas including their integration within village life, members' behavior within the family clan, tracing the history of individual zadugas, growth of female inheritance, and rationales for zadruga divisions.

In one of his studies, Mosely (1976a) examines one family clan - the Varžić zadruga, "under the impact of changing custom and of an increasingly capitalistic and individualistic outlook on life" (Mosely, 1976a, p. 32). In this section, I utilize some of the insights captured by Mosely, focusing on the cultural norms and attitudes, which allowed the Habsburg Empire to recruit soldiers for the purpose of defending the border and which might have persisted to the present day. Ideally, one would focus on a zadruga that was within the military colony. No historical secondary ethnographic, anthropological or sociological source however focused specifically on the family clan within the former military colony. However, elements that have to do with family socialization and with family hierarchy should be visible on both sides. What makes a difference is that zadrugas on the military side lasted longer, which is why such norms should be stronger on the military side. Therefore, in order to capture the elements that have to do with family socialization and family hierarchy, I focus on Mosley's ethnographic study, being aware of the differences and similarities between zadrugas in the military colony and the civilian area. The family clan that Mosely (1976a) investigates was located in the village of Zelčín, the region of Slavonia, very close to the border between the military and civilian area, in what is today Croatia.

In his study, he provides a variety of anthropological insights ranging from division of labor, mobile and immobile assets (e.g. land, livestock, clothes, etc.), the special role of the zadruga head within the clan (*starješina*), the emergence of individual property, etc. Therefore, in the following sections, I present key aspects of the Varžić zadruga that have to do with family socialization and attitudes toward authority. When it comes to family socialization, I focus on in- and out-group trust and collectivist outlook. When it comes to family hierarchy, I focus on age and sex as the two criteria that allowed the Habsburgs to control local populations. In Chapter 6, I evaluate empirically the extent to which such norms still exist to the present day.

The History of the Varžić Family Clan

The village of Zelčín is located in an area with rich black soil, sometimes inundated, where many locals in the 1930s were involved in the raising of cattle and swine and the production of wheat and maize. At the time when Mosely (1976a) did his ethnographic study (in the 1930s), the Varžić zadruga consisted of twenty-six members, two brothers with their wives, four married sons together with their spouses, and fourteen children – all descendants of Ivan Varžić, who died in 1915. In order to better trace the position of the different members within the family structure, I created a genealogical tree based on the information provided by Mosely, which is visible in Figure 5.1. The earliest members that were still present in family collective memory could be dated back to 1820. Ivan Varžić's (III-11) position within the family tree can be seen in the third row. The youngest members are visible in the sixth row – sixth generation in the 1930s.

The Varžić zadruga emerged after the emancipation of serfs in 1848, at the time when Pavao (I-1) (the earliest ancestor about whom members had any recollection in 1928) was the head of the household (see first row in Figure 5.1). The first partition of the zadruga took place in 1900 when the household counted seven couples and six children. The partition occurred as a result of peer effects. One family member (Marko (III-1)) explained: "Everyone was dividing up throughout Croatia; well, he too wanted to separate out" (Mosely, 1976a, p. 45). However, after more interviews, Mosely contends that the decision to divide the land came after Marko's wife, Eva (III-3), ended up inheriting eighteen yokes of land from her uncle and three yokes from her own father, becoming the

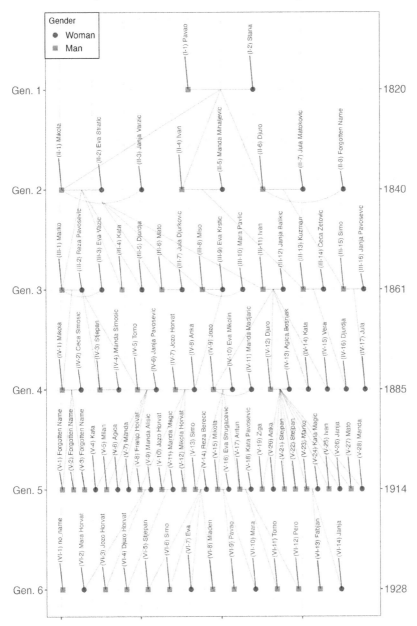

Figure 5.1 The Varžić family tree
Notes: The family tree is created based on the family member
information provided by Mosely (1976a).

first wife to have property of her own. Marko and Eva had twenty-one yokes of their own land while the entire zadruga possessed about forty yokes of land. The zadruga ended up splitting in 1900 in to three: (1) Marko, his wife, three sons, and two daughters-in-law; (2) Mišo (III-8), his wife, and daughter; and (3) the other ten members remained in the old zadruga with Šimo (III-5) at the head.

As such, Mosely (1976a) considers female inheritance as the beginning of the end for zadrugas.[12] More and more unitary families wanted to split from the larger household. A daughter who married out of the large household could have no claim to the property before 1900. The situation started to change after that date. Land inheritance is potentially one of the factors empowering women and contributing to the deterioration of patriarchy: now, "women are allowed 'to boss'" (Mosely, 1976a, p. 47).

The Social Roles in the Family Clan

Unlike other zadrugas, the Varžić household was made up of two leaders at the time Mosely conducted his ethnographic study in 1928, Jozo (IV-9) and Djuro (IV-12), who together were called *kućni gospodar*. The two figures also had an important role in internal conflict resolution, especially as the zadruga expanded. Despite having two leaders, what kept everyone together was the focus on a shared ancestor and the idea that everyone had the same set of relatives. The adult married men were the ones deciding on the external affairs of the family clan, usually after dinner.

All zadruga members had a clear division of labor. The three younger men, Šimo (V-13), Antun (V-17), and Marko (V-23), looked after the horses; Mikola (V-15) looked after the swines and was occasionally helped by Žiga (V-19), while during school holidays he was helped by the younger members of the zadruga, Pavao (VI-9) and Torno (VI-11). Finally, Stjepan (VI-5) and Šimo (VI-6) were the cattle herders (*govedar*). See rows 5 and 6 of Figure 5.1 to identify their position in the genealogical tree.

The work of the women was headed by Agica (IV-13), who was the wife of one of the zadruga leaders, Djuro (IV-12). Zadruga members referred to her as the "cook." Jozo (IV-9), the other co-leader, was first married to Eva Mikolin (IV-10) and then a second time to Manda (IV-11). His second wife entered the zadruga after Agica, Stjepan's

---

[12] Mosely (1976a) also admits that social factors such as women's empowerment are part of the range of factors that contributed to the dissolution of zadrugas. Divisions would not have been able to occur so easily had it not been for the series of laws in the 1870s which enabled divisions even at the request of a single household member.

wife. Despite being older, Manda was not the matron of the zadruga. Agica performed this role, in charge of preparing meals for the entire household, and was assisted by Anka (V-20), who was fourteen at the time Mosely was conducting his ethnographic study and who was an apprentice when it came to zadruga household duties. Some of her responsibilities included fetching firewood and washing dishes. The other wives, Ceca (IV-2), Manda (IV-4), Janja (IV-6), and Anka (IV-8), took over the cooking for the entire family every week, under Agica's supervision. The cooking duties would start on Sunday morning and end on Saturday evening.

Despite consisting of 26 members, the Varžić household also used workforce outside of their zadruga for their dairy farm, where they owned twenty-five cows. The clan hired a person to look after the cattle in exchange for payment in kind in the form of cheese and thirty-six bushels of wheat. In his original ethnographic study, Mosely (1976a, p. 34) commented that other zadrugas with equally numerous members would normally delegate one married couple from within their clan to work on the dairy farm. However, the Varžić clan preferred to "incur the additional expense of hiring an outside worker rather than have one of their small-families 'exiled' to the isolated salaš" (Mosely, 1976a, p. 34). The Varžić clan was also in the habit of hiring day laborers for mowing the lawns and harvesting potatoes.

Property: Mobile and Immobile Assets

Mosely (1976a, p. 35) describes the entrance to the zadruga garden as "through a large double-gate (*kapija*) and through two man-sized gates (*vrata*)," one of which led to the porch of the old house and which served both as a kitchen and a place for eating and gathering. The living and the dining room featured wooden tables, benches, and a great hearth in one corner nearest to the street. There were seven rooms, six of which were inhabited by the married couples and children, while the seventh was used as a storage room until one of the sons got married. Most of them were built in 1925, according to Mosley's estimates, and were located on the other side of the garden. All the grains and firewood were stored in a brick barn, located halfway between the sleeping rooms and the "old house." The family clan was in possession of a dug well, a large stove for baking bread over the summer, a chicken coop and a large pigpen, a corn-crib on stilts, a large haymow, a horse barn, a manure pit, and a wooden kitchen for making plum brandy and sausages during summers. When it comes to land, the Varžić family clan was also in possession of a large garden used for grazing cattle and an orchard with plums, apples, and pears, a smaller garden at the village periphery used only for housing some of its livestock, and a dairy-farm, one kilometer away.

Mosely contends that the Varžić family clan was one of the more well-off families in the village, possessing over 138 acres (56 ha) of land in 1928. Approximately 43 acres of the family land came from the division of an older family clan in 1900. About 85 acres came from a neighboring Hungarian noble and approximately 14 acres came from a neighboring villager. The family clan also enjoyed usufructuary rights over communal village pastures that were commonly owned by the "Zelčin Land Association."[13] Another thirty-three families from the village could use these lands mostly for grazing and breeding cattle.

Figure 5.2 displays the family lands in the Zelčin village. I identified the zadruga lands in the Austrian Third Military Survey (1869) based on the names of the many plots of lands that are listed by Mosely (1976a). I created white polygons to better depict the family's immobile assets on the historical Austrian maps. I also included modern satellite images of those lands on the right in Figure 5.2. The closest land to the family hearth was Markov laz, which was one minute away. According to the family division in 1900, the area of Markov Laz was 4,207 "spans."[14] About a third of that belonged to Marko, and the rest was enjoyed communally. Staro Selo was another plot of land which was about 3 minutes away from the hearth; it was about 5,000 spans; most of the land was enjoyed communally and slightly more than a fifth belonged to Mišo. Other plots of land could be between 15 and 30 minutes away from the hearth. The largest part of these plots of land was controlled by the family clan, while about a quarter of each plot belonged to either Mišo (III-8, born in 1858) or Marko (III-1, born in 1848).

The family clan also possessed a substantial amount of livestock. In 1928, there were eight horses, two foals, eighty-two cows, 111 pigs and one boar, sixty geese, one hundred chickens, four dogs, and eight cats (Mosely, 1976a, p. 39). The Varžić family clan was eighty percent self-sufficient. In 1928, it was trying to keep costs at a minimum, covering its own wheat, maize, oats, potatoes, and cabbage, but also meat, dairy products, and plum-brandy. In addition, it was even trying to keep the production of clothes within the family and take part in the construction of buildings. On some occasions, the clan would hire external workforce

---

[13] Mosely (1976a, p. 37) explains that the "Zelčin Land Association" was created in 1860 after the abolition of serfdom of 1848, when the communal pasture was passed from the nobles to the peasants. In order to provide forage for members of the village, the "Zelčin Land Association" ended up owning 270 acres of land.

[14] A "span" in vernacular is a *hvati*, a historical unit of length that was common in Croatia and Serbia analogous to a fathom. 1 *hvat* is equivalent to 1.896 meters. 2,000 spans represent one yoke, which is equivalent to 0.57 ha or 1.422 acres.

(a)   (b)

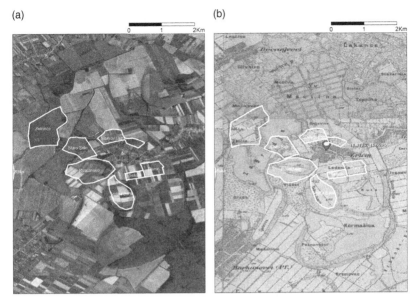

Figure 5.2 The Varžić land
Notes: The names of the plots of land are identified based on information from Mosely (1976a). The first panel displays the plots of land as identified in the Third Military Survey (1869), while the second panel depicts satellite image with the land in 2021.

for the making of bricks and masonry. Finally, the other twenty percent of "non-self-sufficiency" would go toward the purchase of goods for internal consumption: sugar, salt, coffee, salt, some farm equipment, etc. According to family members' accounts, the clan's annual expenditure was about 11,000 Croatian dinars, while both local and national taxes would have been about 20,000 dinars. About 3,350 dinars was dedicated for hired labor. Finally, Mosely estimates that in 1928, the per capita zadruga annual spending was about 1,433 Croatian dinars, which was equivalent to $28.66 in 1928 or $531.70 in 2021. The cash income would have come from the sale of pigs, cattle, and wheat in the city that was closest to their village, Osijek. The full distribution of purchases is presented in Figure 5.3. The figure shows the amount of spending in Croatian dinars in 1928 for the household. The largest amount of money went toward purchasing women's clothing or fabrics that would later be used to make dresses or clothes. Less than half of the amount going toward clothing was to purchase clothes or fabric for men (2,000 dinars). The budget also included an amount for the purchase of shoes for both men and women (three pairs of sandals for person per year).

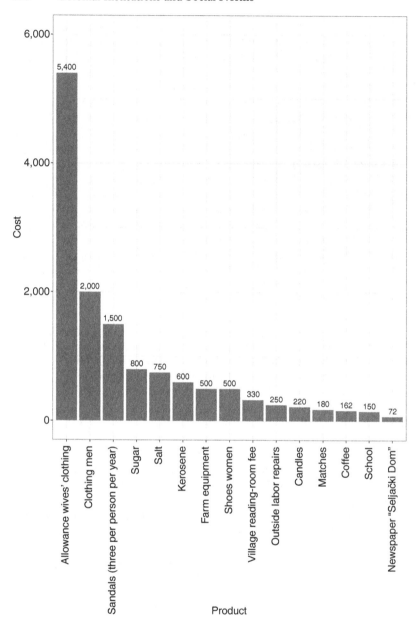

Figure 5.3 The Varžić annual spending

Finally, the budget for school was relatively low (even lower than the annual expenses for coffee or for the purchase of candles and matches), which may not be that surprising, given that literacy rates were relatively low in 1928.

Historically, individual members of the zadruga were not supposed to have any individual property. However, as Mosely (1976a) notes, the situation started to change at the end of the nineteenth century. Such changes were reflected in the dowries and gifts that wives received after getting married. The old custom of the dowry only consisted of a marriage outfit or two wooden chests containing clothing for the wife, shirts for the husband, and household linen; in more well-off families, the wife could also have a cow or a sow added to her dowry. After getting married, the newlywed woman would lose any claim to the zadruga household to which she belonged prior to marriage. All the inheritance claims would go to her brothers. However, starting in 1890, it became customary for newly married women to also receive land as a form of dowry.

For example, in the Varžić clan, Agica (IV-13 – fourth row in Figure 5.1), who in 1928 was the oldest surviving wife, received one yoke of land from her step-father. By contrast, Eva (IV-10), Jozo's first wife, only received her marriage outfit, while all her father's lands went to her brother. Subsequently, her brother made her a gift of 10,000 dinars ($200 in 1928 or about $ 3,700 in 2021), which she subsequently used to buy two yokes of land in the village. According to Mosely (1976a), those two yokes of land yielded wheat in 1937 that was sold for a substantial amount. This was divided afterwards among Eva's children, Šimo (V-13), Mikola (V-15) and Antun (V-17) – see the fifth row in Figure 5.1 – each one receiving 605 dinars. This amount represented the "individual property" (*osobac*), which was separate from the zadruga income.

Jozo's second wife, Manda (IV-11 – fourth row in Figure 5.1), received one cow, when she got married. She sold it and bought two sows instead which had many shoats that she subsequently sold. According to Mosely, in 1928 she was saving money to buy fabric to knit her daughter's wedding outfit. Many other women in the family clan only brought their marriage outfit when they got married: Reza (V-14), Šimo's wife; Eva (V-16), Mikola's wife; Kata (V-18), Antun's wife; Kata (V-24), Marko's wife. All of them, however, had male relatives (e.g. fathers and grandfathers) who ended up bequeathing them some land. Mosely (1976a, p. 43) suggests that the inherited land was a "temptation," constituting reasons for them to want to break away from the zadruga and develop nuclear families with individual properties. Nevertheless, at the time when Mosely conducted his ethnographic study, individual members were not permitted to spend time working their own land or looking after their own livestock. At the same time, their income was never mingled with that of the entire family clan, and they were allowed to spend it as they saw fit.

Division of Family Clans

Despite the formal end of the military colony in 1881, zadrugas continued to exist, also exemplified by the Varžić zadruga. An important question to be answered is what led to the end of these types of institutions and why did locals not get rid of them right away. Mosely mentions a variety of factors that contributed both to the maintenance (despite the formal abrogation of the military colony) and dissolution of family clans. On the one hand, the strong household leadership, together with a focus on preserving and enlarging the economic basis of the family clan, solidified the zadruga as an institution. Similarly, some zadruga members were very fond of the type of services and "public goods" that zadruga members benefited from, and hence wanted to keep the institution alive. For example, a former zadruga member who was interviewed by Erlich (1966) in the 1940s provides a nostalgic account of the services that members (no longer) benefited from:

Among us five sisters-in-law each had to take care of the cooking once every five weeks. For four weeks I was without any cares, only working in the fields, and rather light work too. And now? the wife has to take care of everything by herself, the children, the livestock, the heavy work in the fields, the cooking, the making of clothes... and along with all that there are worries and troubles. (Erlich, 1966, p. 58)

The natural tendency for a zadruga was to gradually grow larger, reaching a point where it had to divide. Part of the reason why zadrugas kept getting larger has to do with the exclusion of women from the inheritance of property[15] and agricultural equipment (Mosely, 1976c, p. 23), as already illustrated in the case of female members in the Varžić clan. The lack of female inheritance is, according to Hudson et al. (2015), one of the key ways whereby family clans in general were able to subordinate female reproductive interests to those of men, which allowed the preservation of resources within the patriline. Things started to change at the end of the nineteenth century when more and more women would inherit property.

---

[15] Once the law changed to allow women to inherit land, it would become much easier for the zadrugas to split: "When several wives bring different quantities of land, strong pressure arises for the division of zadruga into its component small-families" (Mosely, 1976c, pp. 25–26). Every newly formed family would create a new unit combining the shares of the husband's and wife's inheritance.

A variety of macro socio-political events are cited by the literature as contributing to the end of zadrugas. Such events include the agrarian world crisis that lasted from 1873 until 1895, which resulted in a drop of the price of grain and which put an end to communal living (Erlich, 1966, p. 48). Another factor is the Croatian state, which wanted to create a modern government administration for which taxes in cash were needed. In order to pay such taxes, the peasant had to sell more and more of his products, which put him in touch with the cash economy and which rendered the self-sufficient zadruga economy obsolete (Erlich, 1966, p. 49). These factors external to the family clans likely contributed to the gradual development of individual property rights and the growing demand for what Mosely (1976a, p. 52) calls "luxury." Finally, World War I is another example of an exogenous factor that contributed to the disappearance of the family clan. There is, however, consensus that family clans were much more persistent in the military colony simply because the laws there would prevent all these factors from taking effect before 1881: "[w]here the zadruga had been the foundation of the military colonies of the frontiersmen (*graničari*), as in the regimental villages of Croatia, Slavonia and the Banat, its disappearance was less sudden" (Skendi, 1976, p. 14).

All these factors likely contributed to demands for dissolution. Filipović (1976) contends that the frequent disagreements between zadruga members (likely caused by these exogenous factors) sealed the fate of the extended family. In large communities, the likelihood of such disagreements would be much higher. Sometimes, such disagreements would be so heated that a village arbitrator or government official would have to intervene. The inheritance would be divided by family, where every family would be defined by the presence of a male, while the elderly figure would receive a valuable asset such as a saddle or a horse in recognition of his special status. In different regions, there could be variations on inheritance. For example, certain mobile assets such as dough troughs and weighing scales, or immobile assets like water wells or meadows would remain communal property, while the others would be distributed.

5.3   Associations, Social Capital, and Public Goods

An important question that remains to be answered is how can family clans co-exist with under-provision of public goods. As shown in Chapter 1, the area of the military colony had family clans that were larger and which persisted longer. At the same time, that area also had lower access to public goods both during and after the termination of the military colony: lower road and railroad density, lower access to hospitals, and lower access to sanitation. In the end, extended family clans are what Putnam *et al.* (1993) would call a "rich associational life," which would in principle promote (1) *civic engagement* or active participation in public affairs; (2) *political equality* or horizontal relations of reciprocity; (3) *solidarity, trust, and tolerance.* A variety of scholars have shown that such associational life is conducive to economic development (Algan and Cahuc, 2010; Knack and Keefer, 1997; Zak and Knack, 2001). So, how is it possible that associations in fact coexist with lower developmental outcomes?

The answer has to do with the *type* of associational life within the military communities. In order for such communities to be effective in the style proposed by Putnam *et al.* (1993), such communities need to have individuals who are independent, connected to one another, and equal (i.e. with limited hierarchies and featuring horizontal relations of reciprocity). Such characteristics are supposed to instill a spirit of cooperation, solve collective action problems, and enhance a community spirit. For example, according to Putnam *et al.* (1993), these characteristics are much more present in the north of Italy than they are in the south. Their presence in the north has to do with the "rich network of associational life" which gave "the medieval Italian commune [in the North] a unique character precisely analogous to [...] a 'civic community' " (Putnam *et al.*, 1993, p. 126). Putnam *et al.* (1993) trace the characteristics of civil society to medieval times.

Zadrugas did not meet such criteria. These were associations based on blood bonds with limited inter-familial exchanges, constructed on vertical solidarity. Putnam *et al.* (1993, pp. 15, 136) indicate that such forms of vertical solidarity are synonymous with "a social life of fragmentation and isolation, and a culture of distrust" or "power asymmetries, exploitation and dependence." For example, unlike the north of Italy, where historically, during long winter evenings families "would gather in the stables or kitchens of the farmhouses, to play cards and games, to knit and to mend, to listen and to tell stories" (Putnam *et al.*, 1993, p. 143) or where "one farmer got his hay baled by another and where farm tools [were] extensively borrowed and lent" (Putnam *et al.*, 1993, p. 167), in southern Croatia, in the area of the former military colony, such inter-familial activities rarely took place. Rather, such activities would be segregated by clan. The circle of trust would decline at the edge of the family clan. As such, families would become suspicious of people outside of their circle.

This limited inter-familial exchange is compatible with what Henrich (2020) calls "segmentary lineages," which allow clans that are more closely related and who control adjacent territories to create more powerful alliances. In other parts of the world, according to recent social science research, populations featuring segmentary lineages are associated with lower trust in outsiders and an "honor psychology" (Moscona *et al.*, 2020) in addition to a higher propensity to be involved in conflict. As already discussed, the fact that family clans were institutionalized in the south until 1881 meant that familial cleavages lasted much longer in the south of Croatia, which in turn prevented the emergence of generalized reciprocity and social trust. Limited horizontal solidarity developed and with it limited opportunities for reciprocity, cooperation, and equality. The limited opportunities for reciprocity and cooperation together with the higher outer group distrust transmitted over generations resulting in a lower propensity to coordinate in order to demand more access to public goods. Examples of public goods include access to water, access to sanitation, public broadcasting, etc. Public goods require that citizens experience a short-term loss (their contribution) in order to realize a long-term gain (of the public goods). The tension that arises is between what is best for oneself and what is best for the group. The other major tension is a common-pool resource problem (e.g. drinking water and cutting down trees). Common-pool resources allow people to experience short-term gain (by getting what they want in the early life of the source) but also present the possibility of long-term loss; as such, there is a conflict between acting in one's interest and taking as much as possible the first time, and taking a lesser amount so that the common pool gets restored. Conflicts emerging from common-pool resources are widespread during the history of the military colony.

Low social capital stemming from limited community interaction affected the provision of public goods. In order to have access to the latter, clan members needed to cross clan boundaries and think that their effort benefited everyone, including themselves, their clan, and the wider society. In other words, community members needed to develop trust in one another in order to improve public goods (Lo Iacono and Sonmez, 2021). The likely mechanism underlying the relationship between trust and public goods is largely driven by a learning effect: subjects transfer what they assimilate during sequences of dyadic exchanges to their decision to act for the collectivity. Historically, there is evidence in the military colony that clan members were even fed up with the work for the clan, let alone the work for the wider society. The problem of shirking is most vividly depicted by a French traveler in the early nineteenth century who was told: "My second cousin has ten children, and therefore ought to work ten times as much as I do" or "My third cousin is a drunkard, or a spendthrift; what avails my individual toil, when we share the results [of our work]?" (Paton, 1849, p. 176). Collective action problems are likely to have lasted to the modern day, triggering public policy specialists to argue that citizens also need to get involved in the process of providing public goods and not simply rely on local governments to initiate and complete public goods projects (Ott and Bajo, 2001, p. 7).

In order to sustain community cohesion and cooperation, it is crucial to cross familial cleavages and encompass broader segments of society. Because community cohesion was allowed to develop much earlier, citizens of northern Croatia were prepared to act collectively to achieve their shared goals, and hence, were better able to demand more effective public service. In the next chapter, I test the relationship between the longer existence of family clans and in- and out-group trust in a more systematic fashion.

The institution of military colonialism in the south of Croatia ensured a longer duration of communal family clans. Their leaders were deeply involved in the process of state-making, as opposed to competing with state forces. While such family clans existed prior to the formation of the military colony, the Habsburg Empire was strategic in incorporating such social structures that would facilitate minimal economic investment and ensure military obedience by blurring the lines between the rules of the state and the rules of family clans. As such, the empire was always able to recruit soldiers from the family clans who would subsequently be able to go out and defend the border. To ensure their persistence and prevent changes to local power dynamics, the Habsburg Empire created strict rules preventing the dissolution of zadrugas focusing on mobility within the frontier zone, the number of men recruited for duty being proportional to the size of the property, employment in non-military industries, property inheritance etc. In order to better show the relationship between the central state and individuals in the periphery, I presented an in-depth analysis of a zadruga – the Varžić family, an extended family clan consisting of 26 family members, which still existed in 1928. The family clans still displayed characteristics of zadrugas within the military colony including preferences for bequest on the patriline, self-sufficiency, obedience toward authority structures, and communal control over the family's mobile and immobile assets. Nevertheless, there were changes that indicated the transition to individualism: more and more women could inherit property and laxer rules about the division of land. In the next chapter, I investigate whether the longer persistence of family clans within the military colony coincides with the longer persistence of attitudes, including in- and out-group attitudes, collectivism, respect for authority structures, risk avoidance, attitudes toward women, and attitudes toward the state.

6   Lasting Legacies Political Attitudes and Social Capital

Family clans were in place in the territory of the military colony for centuries. As shown, Croatian censuses suggest that family clans were still present around 1900, twenty years after the abrogation of the military frontier. Qualitative evidence indicates that these survived until World War I or shortly thereafter. In the previous chapter, I illustrated how particular kinds of social norms, including respect for authority figures, attitudes toward marriage, and attitudes toward women, persisted by providing an in-depth examination of the Varžić family, a zadruga that was still in existence around 1930. In this chapter I investigate the extent to which social norms which are closely associated with family clans might have outlived them. In cases where they did, I also investigate the mechanisms which ensured their survival.

The Habsburg military frontier is particularly relevant for studying persistent effects on attitudes and norms because they can be demonstrated without "compressing history." The plethora of different sources, from contemporaneous traveler accounts and older anthropological surveys to modern-day statistical data, provides an opportunity to demonstrate the persistent transmission of these norms throughout the last century and a half between the end of military colonialism and today. I present evidence for how family clans impacted the transmission of specific types of attitudes, which stem from specific institutional treatments. For example, I investigate the extent to which communal properties might have caused the transmission of specific norms which have to do with family socialization and family hierarchy. I use the more capacious term "family socialization" to include trust in inner/outer groups, collectivist attitudes, and patience and risk avoidance. I utilize the term "family hierarchy" to refer to conformity and respect for authority, and attitudes toward women. Similarly, I explore how the historical provision of infrastructure might have evolved hand-in-hand with lower trust in institutions or might have triggered people to participate in politics less. These norms stemming from exposure to communal properties and from under-provision of public goods are graphically depicted in Figure 6.1.

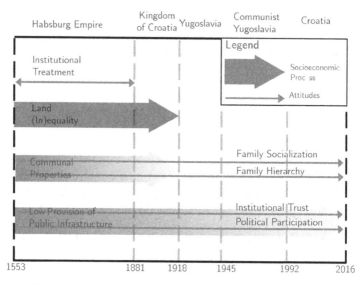

Figure 6.1 Guidelines for cultural attitudes

In the final part of this chapter, I explain how these attitudes and norms persisted over generations through family horizontal (intragenerational) and vertical (intergenerational) transmission. The findings in this chapter speak to a burgeoning literature in comparative historical analysis and modern political economy which discusses how historical events and institutions impact norms, attitudes, or, more generally, "cognitions"[1] in the longrun. The terminology used by some scholars especially in reference to negative historical institutions is "cultural baggage" (Kuran, 2012).

Showing that historical institutions have an impact on the present is compatible with the definitions of historical legacies provided by Beissinger and Kotkin (2014) and Wittenberg (2015), who argue that a legacy is not an outcome per se, but rather a durable causal relationship between an antecedent cause and a subsequent outcome which continues to have an effect, despite the disappearance of the original cause. This logic applies to the historical context in the following way: the institution of military colonialism (*cause*) was in place between 1553 and 1881; family clans, which are part of the institutional treatment, continued to exist until around World War I (*residual, short-term cause*); finally, the attitudes that were conditioned by family clans outlived the latter

---

[1] Simpser *et al.* (2018) use the term "cognitions" instead of "culture" because of the broad range of meanings which are ascribed to culture and which can cause confusion.

(*effect*). Therefore, both institutions and attitudes can be interpreted as transmission mechanisms, which also dominate the field of imperial, authoritarian, or communist legacies (Simpser *et al.*, 2018).

Therefore, this chapter is in conversation with an abundance of works within the political economy tradition. Political scientists have investigated the long-term impact of negative historical shocks. For example, Lupu and Peisakhin (2017) examine how communist deportation affected stronger identification with one's ethnic group, having more hostile attitudes toward the perceived perpetrator, and more political participation. Rozenas *et al.* (2018) investigate how large-scale violence can have an intergenerational impact on political preferences. Specifically, they find that communities more exposed to indiscriminate violence in the past will – in the future – oppose political forces they associate with the perpetrators of that violence. Within the same tradition, Rozenas and Zhukov (2019) study the impact of Stalin's coercive agricultural policy and collective punishment campaign in Ukraine in the 1930s. Their findings indicate that this policy is associated with more loyalty for the regime when there is a credible threat of retaliation in response to opposition and with more adversity toward the perceived perpetrator when the threat subsides.

Within economics, historical experience of violence such as slavery is associated with lower interpersonal trust today (Nunn and Wantchekon, 2011). This line of research highlights the antagonism against the perpetrator: in many cases community members in Africa were trying to protect themselves and gain economic advantages from colonial powers by selling their neighbors into slavery (through local kidnappings and other forms of small-scale violence). This created norms of community mistrust which persisted over time. Similarly, historical experiences of violent forced labor in the case of Belgian Congo are related to lower trust in local authorities and higher trust in community members (Lowes and Montero, 2021). According to the authors, present local authorities are the descendants of the chiefs who historically were the perpetrators of violence on behalf of the colonial powers. As a coping mechanism, victims of violence resorted to local informal systems of risk-sharing and insurance, which contributed to more trust in local communities and social cohesion. The examples of slavery and forced labor indicate that the identity of the perpetrator is important for the way in which violence is exerted. This has implications for the creation of trust. Antisemitism is also a type of perception that might have persisted over time in places in Germany where historical pogroms existed almost half a millennium ago. The persistence of such ideas is caused by a lack of population mobility (Voigtländer and Voth, 2012).

Other scholars examined legacies of positive historical experiences. For example, work by Becker *et al.* (2016) indicates that Habsburg rule is associated with greater levels of trust and lower corruption, compared to the neighboring empires through the perpetuation of positive beliefs about an efficient historical state bureaucracy. Similarly, Guiso *et al.* (2016) discuss how Italian cities which achieved self-government in the Middle Ages have a higher level of civic capital in modern times than similar cities in the same area that did not.

6.1   Attitudes Stemming from Communal Properties

Living in family clans for over three centuries is likely to have affected people's cognitions in a direct way. People's survival, identity, security, marriages, and success depended extensively on the prosperity of family clans. As already explained, family clan members were endowed with an extensive array of inherited obligations, responsibilities, and some privileges in relation to one another.

The relationship between clan membership and culture is not new. In his book, Henrich (2020) focuses on how longer persistence of clan membership in certain parts of the world impacted norms and attitudes which have to do with (1) affinity toward family and distrust in non-family members; (2) deference to rules and authority; (3) zero-sum thinking; (4) risk avoidance. The military colony is a good setting to trace and evaluate the transmission of such norms and attitudes by comparing the northern regions where family clans were allowed to split earlier, to southern regions where family clans were strictly enforced until 1881. Following the structure of the previous chapter, I group the types of norms stemming from living in family clans into two categories: norms which have to do with family socialization, and norms which have to do with family hierarchy.

Norms about Family Socialization

The focus on the "next of kin" is likely to have transformed the social interdependence into emotional interdependence, which led people to strongly identify with their in-groups and make sharp inner and outer group differentiations. As already mentioned in the previous chapter, being born within a family clan automatically came with a placement within a cultural kinship system, which allowed individuals to conceptualize the "I" or "me" in reference to the group. This notion of belonging also came with a variety of prerogatives and responsibilities. The fact that family clans persisted much longer in the military colony provides a unique possibility to investigate these norms and attitudes and compare them to places where such norms likely dissolved much earlier.

Affinity toward family members is at the very core of the notion of family clans. Scholars of the Balkans and of the South-Slav nations of Europe discuss the concept of "familial collectivism" and define it as "sentiments of common membership in a particular lineage" (Burić, 1976, p. 131). This lineage could encompass close relatives and distant kin who are related to one another both on patri- and matrilineality. The kinship relations link group members into a coherent whole, and provide the vocabulary for group members to communicate with each other in everyday life (Voorhees *et al.*, 2020, p. 22).

Family clans within the Habsburg military frontier are likely to be associated with many of the outcomes analyzed in relevant economics literature: greater reliance on internal family members is likely to come at the expense of greater social distancing from out-groups. Unlike individuals under civilian administration before 1881, who were entirely freed from serfdom after 1848 and who had much more freedom to split or bequeath their property, people in the military colony could not fully enjoy such privileges until the twentieth century. Former military colonists were, therefore, heavily dependent on the mutual cooperation of extended family members and self-restraint to avoid the tragedy of the commons (which could include depletion of common-pool resources such as food, water, and other goods).

The family clan was a micro-Leviathan within the borderlands of the Habsburg Empire. The historically limited reliance on the central government for the provision of goods and welfare is what determined the strengthening of the zadruga communities, which ensured their members' subsistence through a primitive form of welfare such as care for the elderly, pregnant women, and widows. Family clans became *substitutes* for the central state, which likely facilitated trust among clan members and an expectation that others would cooperate. The comparison between zadrugas and states is also articulated by first-hand accounts. For example, a person who lived in the family clan system and who grew up in the 1930s mentions that "the zadruga system resembled a miniature state in which [...] the executive power was vested in the head of the house, chosen by older members of the family" (Vucinich, 1976, p. 171).

Attitudes toward inner and outer groups seem to have outlived the military colony. Historical anthropologists discuss the persistence of such attitudes in the 1930s and 1940s and examine them in close connection with the individualism/collectivism dichotomy. I treat the latter separately in the next section. Erlich (1966) for example notes that despite the emergence of "individualistic trends" during the inter-war period which are connected to the disintegration of the zadruga regime, characteristics of the "collectivist period" were not completely lost. Erlich (1966, p. 401) contends that such characteristics have to do with a "certain generosity" which continued to be expressed more strongly vis-à-vis family members and less for outer groups: "family relations were so strong that they dwarfed all others." Such attitudes continued to exist. For example, "by every gesture, the peasants' son showed how important it was for them to support their poorer relative." More generally, "one's greatest pride was to play the protector and the sponsor" (Erlich, 1966, p. 407). Erlich (1966) also describes how such inner-group biases sometimes turned into nepotism, where a recommendation over the phone along the lines of "try to do what you can for him, he's a relative of mine, from my village" would go a long way. Given that such attitudes existed in the 1930s and 1940s, it could very well be the case that some of these might still be visible today. Therefore, I hypothesize the following:

H1a: People in the former military colony trust their families more.
H1b: People in the former military colony trust non-family members less.

Given the fine line between support for one's family and nepotism, it is likely that the areas where family clans were more prevalent because of historical institutions are also areas where corruption might have persisted longer. Supporting one's family could also have meant hiring relatives or close friends regardless of their merits and abilities, which according to previous literature could play a vital role in the development of pervasive corruption (Stinchfield, 2013). Given that nepotism and corruption are secret phenomena by their very nature, social scientists have been using perceptions about them as proxies for actual corruption (Knack, 2007; La Porta *et al.*, 1999; Mauro, 1995; Rose-Ackerman, 1999). While bribery and nepotism are conceptually distinct, the two can go hand-in-hand, with places with high corruption also being places with high nepotism (Stinchfield, 2013). Given the much longer persistence of family clans in the south compared to the north, I hypothesize the following:

H1c: There should be higher perceived incidence of corruption within the former military colony.

In order to test these hypotheses, I use surveys from the Life in Transition Survey (LITS), conducted in three waves in 2006, 2010, and 2016, commissioned by the European Bank for Reconstruction and Development. The goal of these surveys was to understand how the transition to an open market-oriented economy might have affected the lives of the people in more than 30 countries including most of Central and Eastern Europe. The samples chosen were nationally representative. The sampling method followed a two-stage sampling method, with census enumeration areas as primary sampling units according to the most recent census and households as secondary sampling units. Fifty sampling units were selected from the sample frame, with probability proportional to size, using as a measure of size either the population or the number of households.

The surveys contain a variety of questions that enable us to examine quantitatively whether the attitudes and norms mentioned by travelers to the military colony in the late 1800s and by historical anthropologists in the 1930s and 1940s can still be observed today. There are 1,000 respondents in the 2006 survey, 1,000 in the 2010, and 1,500 in the 2016. While most questions were asked in all three surveys, there are some questions which were only asked in certain waves, which is why there is some heterogeneity in the number of observations in the empirical analyses. The respondents in every wave are clustered within 50 nationally representative primary sampling units (PSU). The location of the respondents is visible in Figure 6.2.

In order to estimate the effects of military colonialism on in-outgroup bias and nepotism, I utilize the geographic regression discontinuity framework that I used previously. The unit of analysis is different from previous empirical exercises. While in Chapter 4 the unit of analysis was an administrative unit (e.g. municipality, settlement, or canton, depending on the level of aggregation of the data from the different modern and historical censuses), the unit of analysis in this chapter is the individual or the survey respondent. Similar to the analysis discussed in Chapter 4, the estimations include an indicator equal to one if the unit is located in the former Habsburg military colony and zero otherwise and controls for geographic location, distance to Zagreb, and border fixed effects to ensure that the specification is comparing units across the same side of the border. In contrast to the estimations on socio-economic outcomes, the estimations in this chapter where the unit of analysis is the individual also include controls for age, income, and education. In order to evaluate heterogenous treatment effects, I examine the effect of military colonialism on three different samples: people who live in urban or rural areas, and urban and rural areas combined. Given that urban areas are more dynamic and more likely exposed to shocks (e.g. population

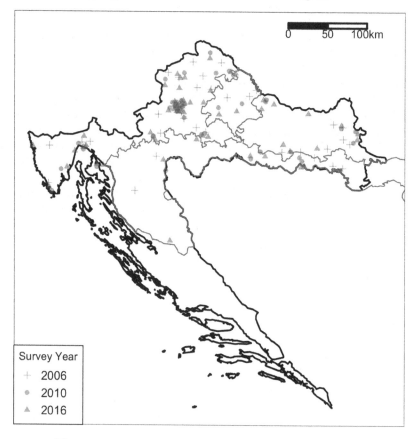

Figure 6.2 Location of LITS survey respondents, 2006–2016

movements, trade), it could be the case that such areas were more likely to have changed and escaped the shackles of historical determinism.[2]

The results in Figure 6.3 display the standardized effect of military colonialism on in-out-group biases. The first three rows indicate the effect of military colonialism on the respondents' answers to the following question: "To what extent do you trust people from the following groups? Family living with you." Answers range from 1 (complete distrust) to 5 (complete trust). The first line is the effect of military colonialism for trust in family for the entire sample, the second, for the urban sample, and the third, for the rural sample. The next three rows are the

---

[2] The rural/urban distinction is consistent with research on the persistence of antisemitism in Germany by Voigtländer and Voth (2012), whereby local continuities between plague-era pogroms in medieval times and violence against Jews in the 1920s, votes for the Nazi Party and deportations after 1933 are the strongest in rural areas.

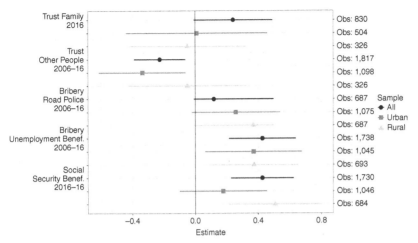

Figure 6.3 Effect of military colonialism on in-out-group trust and corruption

Notes: The unit of analysis is the individual. Data is based on EBRD LITS 2006, 2010, and 2016. Every regression includes the following covariates: a linear polynomial in latitude and longitude, distance to Zagreb, border-segment fixed effects, age, perception of income, and education. The trust variables range from 1 (complete distrust) to 5 (complete trust). The bribery variables range from 1 (never) to 5 (always).

coefficients corresponding to the three samples and which reflect people's answers to the question "Generally speaking, would you say that most people can be trusted, or that you can't be too careful in dealing with people? Please answer on a scale of 1 to 5, where 1 means that you have complete distrust and 5 means that you have complete trust." The results show a surprising amount of consistency with the historical ethnographic insights. People in the former military colony have slightly higher trust in their families and less trust in people outside of their families. When splitting the sample by category of residence (urban vs. rural), the results are no longer statistically significant for trust in family, but continue to be strong for non-family members. Thus, there is a kind of continuity in the idea that family relations dwarf all the other types of relations (Erlich, 1966).

The last three groups of results reflect differences between the civilian and military area when it comes to perceptions about the incidence of corruption at the level of road police, in order to get unemployment benefits, and to get social security benefits.[3] Similar to the first two questions, there are three types of coefficients for the entire sample, urban, and rural residents respectively. The precise wording of the question is: "In your opinion, how often do people like you have to make unofficial payments or gifts in these situations? 1) Interact with road police; 2) Request unemployment benefits; 3) Request other social security benefits." The answers range from 1, which means never, to 5, which means always. The results indicate that respondents in the historical military colony are likely to say that they have to bribe the road police and the relevant authorities to get unemployment and social security benefits more frequently than their counterparts in the former civilian area. The effect is not large: the average for the entire country is between 1 – never and 2 – seldom. The coefficient also represents about a third of a standard deviation. The difference between the two areas, however, is statistically significant. Table B.1 in the appendix displays the coefficients for these outcome variables together with their mean and standard deviation. Such results therefore confirm some of the intuition of the historical anthropologists: while family clans do not exist anymore, there are some traces of norms and attitudes which could be linked to the Habsburg military colony.

Another important dimension which has to do with socialization within family clans and which is closely connected with in- and out-group bias is collectivism. The duality individualism–collectivism that many economists and social psychologists utilize today was coined earlier by scholars such as Tönnies (1887/1957), who distinguishes between the notions of *Gemeinschaft* (community) and *Gesellschaft* (society), or by Weber (1864/1947), who categorizes social relations as either *communal* or *associative*. The closest to the individualism–collectivism dichotomy is the difference between *collectivity* and *self-emphasis* proposed by Parsons (1937/1949). Triandis (2018) discusses this dichotomy and contends that collectivism reflects a social pattern of closely linked individuals who see themselves as part of a collective including family, co-workers, or tribe, and who are primarily motivated by rules imposed by those collectives. People who are members of such organizations prioritize the goals of the collective over their own goals. By contrast, individualism is a pattern whereby individuals see themselves independent from the different groups of which they are members. They are motivated by their own

---

[3] Note that due to its illicit and hidden nature, the true extent of corruption is difficult to measure. I therefore use perception about the incidence of corruption as a proxy for the actual level of corruption, which is also standard in the literature on corruption (Knack, 2007; Kunicova and Rose-Ackerman, 2005).

desires, preferences, and personal goals and potentially conduct cost–benefit analyses of associating themselves with others (Triandis, 2018, p. 2).

Triandis (2018) acknowledges that all people have both individualist and collectivist traits. He exemplifies that a collectivist would donate to charity because their families would expect them to be kind. Similarly, a collectivist would want their in-group to be homogenous, with all members acting and feeling in a similar way. An individualist, on the other hand, would donate to charity because they personally think that this means being kind. They also emphasize group harmony more and prioritize expressing their own opinion less. History is more important to a collectivist than to an individualist. A collectivist would trace their lineage many generations back, while an individualist would be the center of their own life, with the past or the future being less relevant (Triandis, 2018, p. 8).

The example of donating to charity provides a few dimensions based on which individualism and collectivism can be recognized. First, within collectivism there is extensive interdependence between the identity of the self and the identity of the group, whereas within individualism, there is much more independence. Furthermore, within collectivism it is possible for group members to share resources and a set of norms to which everyone adheres. Second, individual and communal goals are closely aligned within collectivism, with group goals having priority over individual aspirations. Third, duties and obligations are the elements that guide the behavior of individuals who are part of a collective. As such, what matters for collectivists is human relationships even when they have no obvious advantage.

Recent empirical work in economics suggests that individualism is correlated with economic growth and even the adoption of democracy. By emphasizing personal freedom, individualists get to appreciate innovation and get to regard it as a personal accomplishment (Alesina and Giuliano, 2015; Gorodnichenko and Roland, 2021; Heine, 2008). When it comes to economic development, Greif (1994, p. 942) explains that the collectivist system is more efficient in "supporting intraeconomy agency relations and requires less costly formal organizations (such as law courts), but it restricts efficient intereconomy agency relations" which are crucial for long-term, sustainable growth. According to Greif (1994), both formal enforcement institutions such as courts and "intereconomy," anonymous exchange are important for growth. As far as democracy is concerned, Gorodnichenko and Roland (2021) find that despite facing potentially more challenging collective action problems, countries with individualistic cultures are more likely to end up adopting democracy earlier than countries with collectivist cultures.

Family clans within the Habsburg Empire are the prime example of collectivism. Erlich (1966, p. 399) discusses exactly how within zadrugas an individual "shows a tendency to sacrifice himself for the community." Such a person turns to their group for "security, esteem, acknowledgment, and glory" (Erlich, 1966, p. 399). Collectivism is a cultural feature of the military colony which was visible even to historical outside observers. A French traveler around 1860 noted the prevalence of collectivist attitudes in the military area and its negative impacts on individual incentives to invest in one's property and work. According to him, living in a family clan must "singularly dampen the ardor and ambition, weaken the spring, diminish the person" (Perrot, 1869, p. 56). He was probably referring to the erosion of individual incentives to invest in innovation, given that the output would have had to be shared equally among clan members. He further describes the negative effects of collectivism on individual incentives as "indolent apathy":

[. . .]what characterizes them [military colonists] is a certain carefree and narrow-minded laziness. Who are they working for? With the family clan in place, their children are more or less sheltered from need [. . .] Besides, their property, which they can neither invest in as they see fit, nor sell and bequeath to whomever they want, does it belong to them enough for there to be pleasure and profit in improving it? So they have these maxims, which describe them very well: "go late to the fields, come back early to avoid the dew; what is more important than work is that God helps me." Being used to counting on God and the (Austrian) emperor, they refuse to accept that modern agricultural tools and modern equipment can make their work easier.[4] (Perrot, 1869, p. 67)

The negative effects of collectivism on individual incentives to invest in private property are also noted by another French traveler about 15 years after Perrot. This traveler does precisely mention the residual legacies of the institution of military colonialism that can be seen in the immediate aftermath of its termination.

In order to maintain this strange organization [i.e. the military colony], the government is using this Slavic old communist system [i.e. zadruga]; the property is common among all the members of the family under the authority of a father and the mother of the family elected from among the elders by all the members of the group and assisted by a kind of council. This patriarchal life should make the ones living under it happy and carefree; however, it actually prevents the birth and development of the working class and of the domestic service, it

---

[4] Translation from French.

has the effect of destroying any initiative and consequently any responsibility. Austria has abolished the military frontiers, but it has not been able, from day to day, to change the social attitude and manners of its former defenders.[5] (De Saint-Aymour, 1883, pp. 39–40)

There is extensive qualitative evidence for the persistence of collectivist attitudes toward the end of the nineteenth century. Some of these social norms were also visible in the early twentieth century. Erlich (1966, p. 341) emphasizes how being part of a collective translates into an incessant need to receive validation from one's group: "the yearning for respect and glory for the tribe, the family, and the individual as hero, overshadowed all other human aims and completely absorbed men's interest. Only these aims were recognized as legitimate. In such an environment, it was collective aims that dominated, and men remained completely subordinated to the demands of their environment." Erlich's historical observations on the zadrugas confirm Triandis' (2008) psychological insights according to which people who are part of collectives end up prioritizing the needs of the group over their own needs.

The persistence of collectivism through the 1930s and 1940s is confirmed by Erlich (1966). While she acknowledges that individualism was rising during the interwar period coinciding with the end of the zadruga regime, "the characteristics of the collectivistic period have not been completely lost" (Erlich, 1966, p. 401). According to her, such characteristics are visible in "a certain generosity, as in the lack of interest in minute details of work" (Erlich, 1966, pp. 401–402). When it comes to families living together, Grandits (2002, p. 435) explains how the regions with old-style zadrugas featured transitional forms of collectivism around the year 1948. This means that several married men ran the household together with their fathers until the latter passed away. Given that certain norms associated with zadrugas outlived them, it is worth testing whether in modern times:

H2: People in the former military colony have a more collectivist outlook.

The typical ways in which economists measure collectivism is through questions that demonstrate one's emphasis on personal achievements and individual rights (Hofstede, 2001; Schwartz, 1992). People who are individualistic are people who stand up for themselves, choose their own affiliations, and believe that they can be successful through hard work. In order to evaluate the persistence of collectivist attitudes,

[5] Translation from French.

I use the same survey and some of the questions that have been used in economics previously to measure levels of collectivism. These are in disagreement with statements like "Effort, hard work, intelligence, and skills are important in order to succeed in life," or "the reason why there are people in need in your country is because of laziness and lack of willpower." A negative answer to these questions has been used in previous research (Greif, 1994; Gorodnichenko and Roland, 2021) as a proxy for collectivist attitudes: in other words, someone who disagrees with the idea that intelligence and skills are important to succeed or someone who disagrees that people are poor because they are lazy should have a more collectivist outlook on life.

While anthropological literature suggests that collectivism was relevant in the aftermath of the abrogation of the military colony, the modern quantitative evidence is somewhat difficult to interpret. The results in Table B.2 in the appendix only provide some suggestive evidence that collectivism might still be present today. There is no difference between the respondents in the former military colony and those located outside of it when it comes to disagreement with the idea that one needs effort, hard work, intelligence, and skill in order to succeed in life. However, individuals in the former military colony are substantially more likely to disagree with the idea that people are poor because they do not work hard enough. The coefficient represents about a third of a standard deviation and it is very large compared to the mean, as indicated by the basic summary statistics at the end of Table B.2 in the appendix.

Risk and competition avoidance are two additional features that are likely to be associated with family clan socialization. Risk is a notion that has been widely examined in a variety of social science disciplines, including economics, sociology, anthropology, psychology, and neurology. Most studies conceptualize *risk as analysis*, bringing logic, reason, and scientific reason to hazard management. For example, economists developed the theory of expected utility and theories of decision-making under uncertainty (Von Neumann and Morgenstern, 1947). Subsequent works also regarded risk as having to do with probability of loss, the size of credible loss, the expected loss, and variance of the probability distribution over the probability of all possible outcomes (Trimpop, 1994; Vlek and Stallen, 1981). Such outcomes could include but may not be limited to possible benefits or costs for the physical, economic, or psycho-social well-being of oneself or others. Therefore, risk as analysis is a rational, deliberative, analytical system that functions by way of established rules of logic and evidence.

More recent studies investigate *risk as feelings*, focusing on the association between non-material aspects and risk-taking, including emotional experience (Slovic *et al.*, 2004; Trimpop, 1994) and fast, instinctive human reactions to danger. Slovic *et al.* (2004) discuss fear as an important emotion which is uniquely tied to risk, especially in situations where decisions need to be made quickly: "reliance on affect and emotion is a quicker, easier, and more efficient way to navigate in a complex, uncertain, and sometimes dangerous world" (Slovic *et al.*, 2004, p. 313). Such emotion is often subconscious. Epstein (1994, p. 716) describes the process by which external events can trigger such emotion:

When a person responds to an emotionally significant event... the experiential system automatically searches its memory banks for related events, including their emotional accompaniments... If the activated feelings are pleasant, they motivate actions and thoughts anticipated to reproduce the feelings. If the feelings are unpleasant, they motivate actions and thoughts anticipated to avoid the feelings.

Therefore, risk is an experiential system encoding reality in visual representations, metaphors, or narratives where affect becomes attached that individuals utilize to make decisions.

Both the notion of risk as analysis and the notion of risk as emotions contain elements of rationality. It is likely that people base their judgment not only on what they think but also on how they feel. Both appear to form the psychological dimension of utility maximizing. Risk as emotions is the likely mechanism which allowed human society to survive for millennia, long before the emergence of any theory about expected utility and assessment of risk. As human society evolved, the reliance on instincts and emotions for the evaluation of risk was replaced with the more complex ways of analyzing risk and decision-making.

Family clans should in principle be associated with less risk-taking. One mechanism connecting family clans and risk-taking that Henrich (2020, p. 273) postulates is the idea of monogamous marriage, which is the basis of family clans and which "suppresses men's competitiveness, risk-taking, and revenge seeking." Family clans within the military colony are also likely to have instilled risk aversion within their members through a reliance on traditions and enculturating them with a variety of prescriptions which tell clan members how to act. As such, situations of uncertainty are rare. When danger is involved, family clan members are likely to want to avoid it. Therefore, having lived in a military colony in the south for much longer is likely to have stifled risk-taking and competition. In other words, people would have preferred stability and predictability. These traits in turn are likely to have transmitted over generations.

There is little direct historical evidence on the extent to which members of zadrugas were more risk-acceptant or risk-averse. One can intuit risk aversion based on the variety of rules and norms in place, precisely to avoid any situation of uncertainty or a situation that would entail individuals engaging in risky behavior. Beyond rules, however, there are hints in the historical anthropological literature that allude to more risk aversion: compliance and reliance on "destiny." For example, Erlich (1966, p. 405) contends that in the areas where family clans were common, "one's attitude toward fate was such that one seemed neither to want luck nor to strive for happiness. On the contrary, one was always prepared for tragic turns or death." As already mentioned, engagement in risky behavior presupposes an awareness of danger either as a result of an analytical process or as a result of emotions. Subjection to destiny provides some indications that people in family clans were more averse to risk.

In order to investigate the extent to which aversion to risk might have persisted over time, I use data from LITS. The data also contains questions which measure specifically whether people are willing to take risks and whether they would choose a secure job over a high-paying job, if given the choice. For aversion to risk, the question is formulated as: "Please, rate your willingness to take risks, in general, on a scale from 1 to 10, where 1 means that you are not willing to take risks at all, and 10 and means that you are very much willing to take risks." For job preference, the question reads as follows: "Imagine you could choose between two jobs, Job A and Job B. Job A offers an average salary, and not much chance for promotion, but it is a safe long-term job. Job B offers a high salary, and a lot of chance for promotion, but significantly less job security. Which job would you choose?"

To summarize, I hypothesize the following:

H3a: People in the former military colony are less likely to take risks.
H3b: People in the former military colony prefer higher job security over higher payment.

The results in Figure 6.4 provide suggestive support for the two hypotheses. Note that the mean for both the 2010 and 2016 surveys, is around 5 (exactly half way between total willingness to take risks – 10 and no willingness whatsoever to take risks – 1) – also see Table B.3 in the appendix. While the effect is not statistically significant, people in the former military colony are less willing to take risks both when examining the entire sample, and when examining the urban and rural samples separately. The coefficient represents about a fifth of a standard deviation. When it comes to risk aversion measured as preference for job security, the effects are clearer. People in the former military colony are much more likely to prefer the job that pays average salary and has long-term security, as opposed to the job that pays more, but is not as secure.

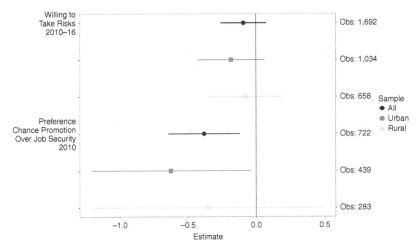

Figure 6.4 Effect of military colonialism on risk-taking
Notes: The unit of analysis is the individual. Data is based on EBRD
LITS 2006, 2010, and 2016. Every regression includes the following
covariates: a linear polynomial in latitude and longitude, distance to
Zagreb, border-segment fixed effects, age, perception of income, and
education. The risk variable ranges from 1 – not willing to take risks to
10 – very willing. The job security variable asks the respondent to
choose between a high-security job with low chance of promotion (1)
and a low-security job with high chance of promotion (2).

This effect is statistically significant for the urban areas, but not for the
rural ones.

Norms about Family Hierarchy

Another potential cultural trait which could be a direct result of having lived in family clans for much longer and which is discussed by the
literature (Henrich, 2020) as a potential legacy of extended families is
conformity and deference to authorities, which was at the very core of
military colonialism. Pertaining to family clans is likely to have molded
people's attitudes toward power structures in a visible way, structuring
patterns of prescriptions about family clan members behavior toward
authority structures. This likely happened through a process of mythol-
ogizing the clan authority figures (Voorhees *et al.*, 2020) which might
have persisted over generations. Deference to authorities is likely to have
deepened with the rigid enforcement of communal properties through a
process of continuous reflection of one's position within the family clan
and one's relationship with the family clan leader, where approval from
and obedience toward the family clan leader was a confirmation of one's
sense of belonging.

Similar to in-out-group bias and collectivism, Erlich (1966) also traces the persistence of conformity and obedience through to the interwar period. At the head of the zadruga, it was the father who was obeyed and shown respect unconditionally. According to Erlich (1966, p. 61), right around World War I in some areas:

> [...] the authority of the father was unimpaired. A younger son, even if married, never dared sit down in his presence or speak without being asked something. Nor did a married son dare smoke or drink in his father's presence, which holds to this day, nor dare he talk to his wife much before him.

She also explains that people were conforming to authority "naturally," almost as if they had a natural inclination to obey. Conformity to family values was further strengthened by rules that have to do with public morality. Costs related to public shaming would render an individual to act in ways that are compatible with those.

While respect for paternal authority (in the authoritarian style described by Erlich) might have been lost with the disappearance of family clans, it could be the case that the more general respect and subservience to authoritarian structures might have persisted. In order to measure conformity, I again utilize data from LITS. While there are no direct measures for deference to authorities, I use alternative proxies that are likely highly correlated with conformity: whether people prefer authoritarian political structures and whether they believe that they should be questioning the authorities. I specifically investigate whether people in the former military colony are more likely to say that democracy or a market economy is preferable to any other type of system. For respect for the authorities, I investigate people's agreement with the statement that one should be more active in questioning the (institutional) authorities (as opposed to showing more respect for authorities). Similar to the previous results, I split my sample into three groups: all individuals, respondents located in urban areas, and respondents in rural areas. A negative answer means more questioning, while a positive answer means showing more respect.

I hypothesize the following:

H4a: People in the former military colony are more likely to prefer authoritarian political structures.
H4b: People in the former military colony are less likely to support the questioning of the actions of authorities.

The results in Figure 6.5 indicate no support for authoritarian structures. There is no difference between the two regions as far as popular preferences for democracy, preferences for a planned economy, or the

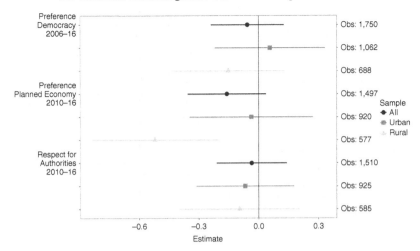

Figure 6.5 Effect of military colonialism on preference for authoritarian structures

Notes: The unit of analysis is the individual. Data is based on EBRD LITS 2006, 2010, and 2016. Every regression includes the following covariates: a linear polynomial in latitude and longitude, distance to Zagreb, border-segment fixed effects, age, perception of income, and education. The preference for democracy variable is an ordered variable ranging from 1 (an authoritarian government may be preferable) to 3 (democracy is preferable). The preference for a planned economy is also an ordered variable ranging from 1 (a planned economy may be preferable) to 3 (a market economy is preferable). The respect for authorities variable records respondents' answers to the question about whether citizens should question the actions of authorities – 1 or whether citizens should show more respect to them – 10.

extent to which authorities are questioned are concerned. There is only a negative effect for people in rural areas not preferring a planned economy, which is difficult to interpret, given the lack of consistency with the other results.

Attitudes toward women are at the very core of the institution of the family clan. For a long time, women remained under the control of their fathers and under the control of their husbands after getting married. Hudson *et al.* (2015) contend that women should arguably be the most vulnerable in clan societies, with their main role being to reproduce the patriline. The clan patriarch must define the parameters of marriage choice in order to strengthen the male kinship bond for his own clan and in order to avoid the loss of the clan (Hudson *et al.*, 2015, p. 540). This is also the view shared by Fukuyama (2011, p. 233), who contends that "in agnatic societies, women achieve legal personhood only by virtue of their marriage to and mothering of a male in the lineage." Given that women can be a source of rupture in the "web uniting the men in the patrilineage" (Fukuyama, 2011, p. 55), the fierceness and sensitivity with which men guard the subordinate status of women is no longer surprising. Fukuyama's observations about modern clan societies also apply to the family clans institutionalized by the Habsburg military colony: the reason why many women including widows and unmarried daughters have limited inheritance rights has to do with a need to keep the property within the clan line (Fukuyama, 2011, p. 540).

There are five important ways whereby clan societies can control female interests. The first is arranged marriages, which allow the family patriarch to strengthen the clan's alliances with outer groups by strategically marrying off daughters to other clans with whom they want to create alliances. The second is patrilocality, which means that women leave their parental home upon marriage and live with their husband and their families. As such, clans are formed based on patrilineality. Within the clan itself, all men are typically related to one another, which is what allows the formation of male alliances in patrilineal clans (Hudson *et al.*, 2015). Additionally, the children resulting from the couple's marriage grow up residing among patrilineal relatives such as the children of the father's brothers. Co-residence and interaction among them likely further contributes to strengthening of interpersonal trust and bonds within the family clans. The third way of controlling female interests is by creating complete economic dependence for women, further reinforcing the subordination of female reproductive interests to male ones. This is achieved through property rights and inheritance laws which favor men over women and which allow the maintenance of resources within the patriline. The fourth way is early marriage for women. Raising young girls is costly for the family of origin in terms of investing in their health and welfare. Raising girls also poses additional difficulties once they reach puberty where protecting their "honor" can become a tough responsibility (Hudson *et al.*, 2015, p. 542). Therefore, early marriage solves a variety of problems for the girl's family of origin. The fifth way by which clan societies control female interests is through outright violence. If women challenge male domination in decision-making, men in the patriline can use physical force to enforce the predominance of their interests over those of women.

Attitudes toward women that persisted after the termination of the military border are discussed at length by Erlich (1966) and Mosely (1976a). For example, when it comes to inheritance and dowry, the bequest of immobile assets such as land was through someone's father. Inheritance typically involved equal division of a father's land holdings among his sons; this could have happened before or after the father's death. At least until 1870, it was only men who were allowed to inherit land (Mosely, 1976b). When women got married, they were only entitled to a marriage outfit, which constituted "a suitable contribution toward the establishment of the household" (Erlich, 1966, p. 209). In fact, the inability of women to inherit land was one of the key factors "keeping the zadruga holdings intact and adjacent" (Mead, 1976, p. xxii). The Croatian law of 1870, however, changed that. Prior to that law, zadrugal land could be divided among the daughters when there was no son, and in any division of a zadruga, a female member had the right to only half of the amount a man would get. During the existence of the zadruga as an institution, it was much more common for women to inherit mobile assets. Women had dowries that consisted of a marriage outfit, additional outfits for herself and for her husband, bedding, and towels together with a chest to keep them in. Occasionally, livestock such as a cow or a sow were added as part of the dowry (Mosely, 1976a, p. 42).

Similarly, both Erlich (1966) and Mosely (1976a) discuss the importance of arranged marriages as a key factor in maintaining family clans. In rare instances, the parents of the person getting married together with other relatives could also have played a role in choosing a spouse (Erlich, 1966, p. 183). Sometimes, additional rules were developed to specify what happened if the husband died. In those cases, "custom" dictated that the surviving wife was to marry one of the husband's brothers or cousins. Such custom permitted that strategic alliances be maintained. For a long time, people to be married almost had no say in the matter: "The children never discuss the marriage. It often happens that the son is forced, and in the majority of cases he obeys because of his shyness and his customary obedience" (Erlich, 1966, p. 188).

In her anthropological study, Erlich (1966) also provides slight hints suggesting that raising young girls may be less beneficial for the family of origin. For example, she notes the different behavior of parents toward their sons and daughters, especially as girls get closer to marriage age:

Different treatment of sons and daughters is not noticeable at first, but the nearer the girls get to marriage, the less care the parents take of them, they seem unreliable to them, for at any time they may leave them and run off to their young man. (Erlich, 1966, pp. 124–125)

This account provides some evidence for the theoretical insights outlined by Hudson *et al.* (2015), according to whom raising girls is costly for the family, which is why family clans are in favor of early marriages for girls.

These customs which are so closely intertwined with the very notion of family clans do not exist anymore. However, the norms that controlled female interests for such a long time might still be reflected in people's attitudes about the role of women in society. I use again data from LITS to investigate the extent to which attitudes toward women might have persisted to the modern era. LITS 2016 specifically contains questions that gauge people's agreement with statements that reflect gender stereotypes that might be reminiscent of the zadrugal patriarchal regime. Given the likely legacy of stereotypes about women's roles and the available data from LITS 2016, I hypothesize the following:

H5a: People in the former military colony are more likely to think that men make better political leaders.
H5b: People in the former military colony are more likely to think that women should do the household chores.

The results in Figure 6.6 provide some support for these hypotheses. While the coefficients are small (note that the mean for the variable that captures agreement that men make better leaders than women is 4.23 for the entire country, while the mean for the agreement that women should do the household chores is 2.34; the minimum for both questions is 1 – total disagreement and the maximum is 5 – total agreement), there are some slight indications that people in the former military colony are more likely to agree with the statement that men make better leaders than women and that women should do the household chores. This difference is less visible in rural areas (likely because of small sample size). Hence, there is some evidence that the patriarchal regime embodied by family clans persisted to the present day in the form of attitudes toward women.

6.2   Attitudes Stemming from Historical Under-provision of Public Goods

A final set of norms which I explore in this chapter, and which derive not so much from family clans but rather from being discriminated against when it comes to the provision of public goods and services and from living under an abusive authoritarian empire for over 300 years, are attitudes toward the state and people's political participation. Exposure to historical violence and discrimination is known to have an impact on political development (Blattman, 2009; Kalyvas, 2006).

Norms about Institutional Trust

The Habsburg Empire is the political entity that exerted particular forms of violence against locals. This is different from the type of violence

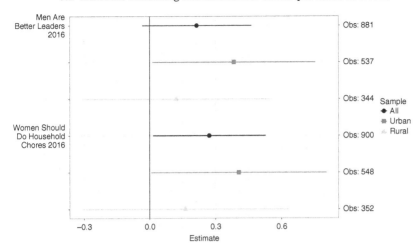

Figure 6.6 Effect of military colonialism on women's roles
Notes: The unit of analysis is the individual. Data is based on EBRD
LITS 2006, 2010, and 2016. Every regression includes the following
covariates: a linear polynomial in latitude and longitude, distance to
Zagreb, border-segment fixed effects, age, perception of income, and
education. The variables capture agreements with the following
statements: (1) Men make better political leaders than women. (2) A
woman should do most of the household chores. Answers range from
1 – disagree to 5 – agree.

exerted by locals onto members of their own community, such as in
the case of slavery in Africa where family and community members were
more likely to turn against each other (Nunn and Wantchekon, 2011).
The fact that the perpetrator of violence was external to the group,
makes this case more similar to the episodes of violence that the Con-
golese were exposed to under the Belgians (Lowes and Montero, 2021),
the forced movements of Tatars in Stalin's Russia (Lupu and Peisakhin,
2017), or the forced deportation of nationalist insurgents from western
Ukraine to Siberia, also under Stalin (Rozenas *et al.*, 2018). The long-
term effects of historical violence in this region of the Habsburg Empire
are likely to be consistent with broader research focusing on the formative role of violence in political development (Balcells, 2012; Blattman,
2009; Kalyvas, 2006; Lyall, 2009), and also consistent with the decay-
ing impact of violence over time (Costalli and Ruggeri, 2019; Lupu and
Peisakhin, 2017). Historians of the military colony do mention that corporal punishments prevailed in the military colony and that feelings of
pain and fear "undoubtedly influenced the mentality of that small world
in Krajina" (Valentić, 1984, p. 75).

In addition, as already mentioned in Chapter 2, any long-term attitudes toward the state could stem from the perception that the Habsburg rule in the military colony was a "foreign" power, and that the delegates of the center to the periphery were abusive, exerting unjust treatments over their subjects when it came to their freedom, bodily integrity, or payments for their labor. Thus, the peasant in the military colony would refuse anything which comes from outside and in particular "anything which is of Austrian origin" (Blanc, 1957, p. 223); therefore, they would not trust "the (agricultural) innovations, not only because they do not know the new methods for cultivating the land, and because they never practiced them, but rather because they are frequently imposed by the feudal lord or the military authority" (Blanc, 1957, p. 223). While such perceptions were against the Habsburg leaders during the time of the empire's existence, they likely transferred over onto subsequent states. As explained by Putnam *et al.* (1993), distrust, the unpredictability of sanctions stemming from the state, and, potentially, fear of government authorities percolated through the social ladder, resulting in a general apprehension toward governmental authorities. While such reluctance was originally toward the Habsburg state in Vienna, it likely carried over through to the subsequent states that had the former military colony under their jurisdiction, including Hungary, Yugoslavia, and subsequently Croatia.

During the existence of the military colony, the asymmetry of power between the center in Vienna and the military colonists was so stark that it made some historians compare it with the relationship between a "master and slaves" (O'Reilly, 2006, p. 243). The first way in which such asymmetry was visible was through the use of violence. Despite the fact that violence was not as widespread and systematic as in other cases of colonialism such as Belgian Congo (Lowes and Montero, 2021), violence did exist. As discussed by Rothenberg (1966, p. 23), medieval methods of torture such as "the block and the gallows, impalement and quartering" were widely used against the colonists until the end of eighteenth century. Mentions of physical violence exerted by the imperial authorities were still depicted in historical accounts of the mid-nineteenth century (Vaníček, 1875c). Violence against women was also prevalent until the end of nineteenth century, as discussed in Chapter 2. The asymmetry between the center in Vienna and the military colonists in the periphery was further strengthened through non-physical violence, including encroachments on the property rights of the colonists, and forcing them to work on the lands of the imperial delegates.

Social science research suggests that such historical experiences profoundly shape how victims interact with the state and how they think about politics. Scholars discuss three types of attitudinal effects that

· can be elicited onto the victims of physical and non-physical violence stemming from the state: some could withdraw from political activity (Benard, 1994; Wood, 2006); others could mobilize and coordinate politically (Bellows and Miguel, 2009); some could also develop feelings of victimization that emerge as a result of such experiences (Canetti-Nisim *et al.*, 2009). Given that military colonialism ceased to exist in 1881, this allows the examination of how these effects could potentially be transmitted through family socialization, which is an important mechanism of transmission, as shown by the previous literature (Bisin and Verdier, 2000). Historical exposure to violence can shape the identity of the victims and such identities could be transmitted from parents to children (Lupu and Peisakhin, 2017).

The kind of alienation produced by the state is depicted by historians. For example, Vaníček (1875c, pp. 314–315) uses the terms *Hass und Verbitterung* or hatred and bitterness to describe such alienation, while Rothenberg (1966, pp. 14, 20) discusses the "deterioration of the morale" of the border establishment or a certain "predilection towards mutiny and desertion" as a result of the abuses committed by the delegates of the Habsburg Empire in the colony in the late seventeenth and eighteenth centuries. Rothenberg summarizes the reasons behind one (typical) revolt from 1755 as "labor service, often for private gain, exacted by certain officers [. . .], beatings, and other brutalities inflicted on the enlisted men" (Rothenberg, 1966, p. 36). The same author quotes a military representative and makes the argument that the "obsolete system of administration and command" in the military colony contributed to a profound distrust in governmental authorities (Colonel Vlasic cited in Rothenberg (1966, p. 136)). Such discontent sometimes flared into violence. Rothenberg (1966) mentions the revolts that broke out in the Warasdin generalcy and the Theiss-Maros districts at the end of seventeenth and early eighteenth centuries. These were subsequently quelled by the professional military authorities.

Historical anthropologists of the 1930s and 1940s offer few insights about people's attitudes toward the state or about how exposure to military colonialism for so many centuries might have impacted people's trust in state authorities. This is likely because they were much more interested in the social norms and attitudes that were directly derived from family clans and much less in the attitudes toward the central state that might have been transmitted over generations. Yet, even in the absence of intermediary qualitative evidence for the persistence of distrust in government, could it be that historical exposure to violence and abuse might have impacted attitudes in the present day? As already indicated, the literature provides contradictory conclusions: people might be politically less active or, quite the contrary, they may be more involved.

In addition, it is likely that trust in state authorities might be lower in areas exposed to violence than in other areas. As such, I hypothesize the following:

H6: People in the former military colony trust government institutions less.
H7a: People in the former military colony vote less.
H7b: People in the former military colony are less likely to engage in forms of contentious politics such as protests and demonstrations.

To test these hypotheses I use data from the same source that captures trust in a variety of institutions including the government, parliament, courts, parties, armed forces, and the police. The exact wording of these questions is: "To what extent do you trust the following institutions?" The options are: the government, parliament, courts, parties, armed forces, and police. Answers range from complete distrust – 1 to complete trust – 5. The results in Figure 6.7 display the effect of military colonialism on trust in institutions. They indicate no statistically significant difference in the level of trust in institutions between the two areas and no consistent statistically significant results when it comes to whether respondents come from urban or rural areas. Based on the signs of the coefficients, there are some interesting slight differences, where urban respondents trust authorities less while rural respondents more (yet the differences do not reach conventional statistical levels consistently). When looking at the entire sample, people in the former military colony seem to trust armed forces more, but the results are no longer statistically significant when examining the rural and urban samples separately. The limited evidence for the persistence of distrust may not be that surprising given the amount of time between the end of the "treatment" (1881) and the time when the public opinion survey was conducted, and the different political regimes that have been in place since the fall of the Habsburg Empire.

Norms about Political Participation

When it comes to political participation, I use the respondents' answers to the question: "Did you vote in the most recent local-level/ parliamentary/ presidential elections?" Answer can be either yes or no. Finally, I also investigate whether military colonialism might also be connected to other forms of political participation such as signing of petitions and participation in demonstrations. The precise question is: "How likely are you to attend a lawful demonstration/ sign petitions?" The potential answers are: "have done," "might do," and "would never do." In order to facilitate ease of interpretation, I code the first option with 1 and the

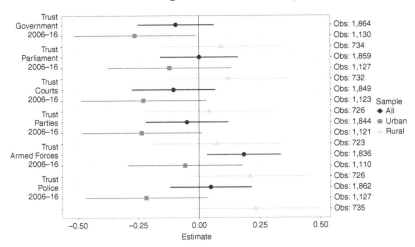

Figure 6.7 Effect of military colonialism on trust in institutions

Notes: The unit of analysis is the individual. Data is based on EBRD LITS 2006, 2010, and 2016. Every regression includes the following covariates: a linear polynomial in latitude and longitude, distance to Zagreb, border-segment fixed effects, age, perception of income, and education. The trust variables range from 1 (complete distrust) to 5 (complete trust).

other two with 0 (although the results remain virtually unchanged if the original answer scheme is kept). The results displayed in Figure 6.11 indicate that there is no difference between the former civilian and the military areas when it comes to voting, but there is a difference in terms of how likely people are to participate in demonstrations and to sign petitions, with people in the former military colony being much less likely to do so. The results are particularly strong for signing of petitions, where the coefficient represents a quarter of a standard deviation, as reported in Table B.7 in the appendix. The coefficients are similar in size for both urban and rural areas.

So, overall the results do provide some indications about a potential withdrawal from the political arena of the descendants of the people who had been historically exposed to institutional violence and different kinds of abuses. This is consistent with scholars such as Benard (1994) and Wood (2006). These results are also compatible with economic views according to which, alienation from the historical state can cause people to be less willing to coordinate. Because of the latter, "uncoordinated private actions will lead to under-provision of public goods" (Besley and Ghatak, 2006, p. 286). Interestingly enough, Croatian specialists in local government spending also emphasize that citizens can elect politicians

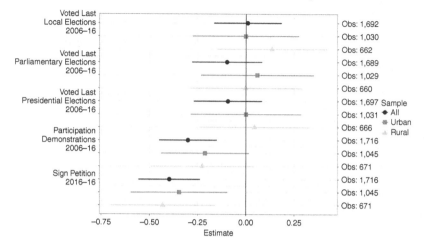

Figure 6.8 Effect of military colonialism on political participation
Notes: The unit of analysis is the individual. Data is based on EBRD
LITS 2006, 2010, and 2016. Every regression includes the following
covariates: a linear polynomial in latitude and longitude, distance to
Zagreb, border-segment fixed effects, age, perception of income, and
education. The trust variables range from 1 (complete distrust) to 5
(complete trust).

who can subsequently provide public goods but can also initiate pro-
grams themselves for the provision of water mains, local roads, and
others (Ott and Bajo, 2001, p. 7). The challenge, however, is getting
citizens to get involved: people "*should show interest* in the budget [for
public goods], get informed about it and *participate in the budget process*"
(Ott *et al.*, 2018, p. 12) (*emphasis added*). Therefore, the lack of political
participation is likely to go hand in hand with the results about the lower
provision of public goods in modern times presented in Chapter 4: the
reason why people in the former military frontier have lower access to
public goods such as water and sewers has to do with their inability to
coordinate and participate in the local budget process.

6.3   Transmission of Norms and Attitudes Over Time

The correlation between historical experiences and modern-day norms
and attitudes is not surprising, given the panoply of works that examine
how institutional practices persist long after the institutions themselves
disappeared (Dardena and Grzymala-Busse, 2006; Lupu and Peisakhin,
2017; Nunn and Wantchekon, 2011; Wittenberg, 2006). The in-out-
group attitudes, perceptions about the incidence of corruption, risk

aversion, and political participation are examples of norms that seem to be correlated with historical military colonialism. Historical travelers, anthropologists, and modern survey data indicate that these continue to exist up to the modern day. The equally important question is how these attitudes were transmitted over time. Theories about intergenerational transmission suggest three factors which are relevant for the persistence of norms: family (Lupu and Peisakhin, 2017; Nunn and Wantchekon, 2011; Voigtländer and Voth, 2012), social groups (Putnam, 2000; Putnam *et al.*, 1993), and formal education (Bisin and Verdier, 2000; Dardena and Grzymala-Busse, 2006). Given that these norms are highly personal and that they are different from views on nationalism, for example, which could be taught in school (Dardena and Grzymala-Busse, 2006), these attitudes are more likely to have been transmitted from parent to child or through teaching by family members. In other words, trusting one's family or trust in people for example is unlikely to have been reproduced over time by means other than family transmission.

Family clan culture and individual psychology are closely connected in a process of enculturation within patterns of prescribed and proscribed behavior, beliefs, and attitudes that come to be experienced as natural and unquestionable. As such, individuals develop worldviews which combine elements of personal identity, group identity, and purpose. Voorhees *et al.* (2020, p. 30) discuss how the formation of worldviews is accompanied by "a linkage between social identity and survival related circuits in the brain," which are necessary for defending both the social identity and the group upon which this identity depends. Such linkage occurs through emotions which are related to biological survival instincts and which allow individuals to value their group membership and role performance.

It is likely that parents transmitted these psychological and social behaviors to their children. Children are not only taught the skills for immediate survival, but also how to think symbolically about the world, together with rites, practices, and attitudes that sustain both personal and cultural identities (Voorhees *et al.*, 2020, p. 16). What allows these attitudes to persist is an ability of individuals to explore possibilities and revise interpretations to establish or restore consistency. The same logic also exists in the economics literature. Guiso *et al.* (2008) describe how individual beliefs are initially acquired through cultural transmission and are subsequently slowly updated through experience, from one generation to the next. Tabellini (2008) goes further and connects the intergenerational transmission of attitudes (specifically, trust) with the choice of institutions: if there is an internal shock to institutional trust, then the next generation will be less trusting and will choose institutions with weaker enforcement, which will result in poor behavior and low levels of trust among future generations. This therefore creates a self-enforcing outcome by which low levels of institutional trust persist among future generations (Nunn and Wantchekon, 2011).

Life in family clans in the former military colony enabled individuals to interact in ways that were culturally appropriate. The clan system of beliefs is what permitted enculturated individuals to interpret the experiences of everyday life according to a jointly shared cultural reality. Successful adherence to clan values was likely associated with feelings of personal validation, while deviations were likely accompanied by feelings of guilt and shame, which were further exacerbated by the indignation and anger of other clan members. The latter could react with condemnation, and an impulse to punish as a result of potential deviation from the expected behavior of those being part of the group. The feelings of indignation are what connected the social to the biological body. Therefore, both the positive and negative constraints allowed individuals to teach and learn a certain set of norms and attitudes that persisted over time.

In order to gauge the transmission or the transformation of norms over time, I split my sample into three different groups, corresponding to the three different age cohorts based on the year when they were born. Thus, the three main cohorts are people who were born before 1945, people who were born between 1945 and 1990, and finally, respondents who were born after 1990. I chose these year thresholds as these capture the exposure to different political regimes. The grouping of respondents is similar to the procedure described by Pop-Eleches and Tucker (2017). People who were born before 1945 are likely to be the carriers of reminiscent attitudes from the time of the Habsburg military colony. The regime prior to communism, which is the Kingdom of Yugoslavia, was in place between 1918 and 1941. The Axis occupation of Yugoslavia in 1941 allowed the radical right Ustaše group to come to power forming the Independent State of Croatia between 1941 and 1945. The cohort born after 1945 is the cohort which was socialized under communism. Between 1945 and 1990, Croatia was a socialist republic, part of the six-part Socialist Federative Republic of Yugoslavia. The group born after 1990 is the group born under a democratic regime in the Republic of Croatia. The youngest respondent was born in 1998, which means that they were 18 years old in 2016 when they took part in the survey.

Given the amount of time that has passed since the treatment stopped, the results obtained are very likely attenuated for two reasons. First, none of the survey respondents were exposed to the treatment. The oldest respondent in the sample was born in 1917, which means that they were 89 in 2006 when they answered the survey questions. However, there is a chance that the parent or definitely the grand parent of this respondent was exposed to the military colonial regime. Second, the old respondents were also exposed to additional political historical shocks and events including communism and the Yugoslav Wars which likely altered their norms and attitudes.[6] Along the same lines, younger cohorts would be very far away from the historical treatment. Therefore, their responses would be unlikely to be reflective of the legacies of military colonialism but rather a combination of exposure to newer political regimes together with some norms and attitudes inherited from their parents. Nevertheless, a cohort analysis where respondents are grouped based on the year of birth and compared to one another would be reflective of the (dis)continuities of the norms inculcated by the Habsburg military colony and more importantly of the rate of change of these norms.

As in the previous analyses, the regressions on which the figures are based include the same control variables which I used before. These include a dummy for whether a respondent is located in the former Habsburg military zone, location of the primary sampling unit from which the respondent is drawn, border-segment fixed effects, age, income, education, and survey fixed effects. The results presented only reflect the coefficient for whether the respondent is in the historical military frontier zone or not. In this section, I only present the variables which in the previous section proved to be statistically significant. I also ran analyses for the other variables which proved to be statistically insignificant. They continue to be insignificant in the cohort analyses. In order to save space, I do not include them.

The first set of results which proved to be significant has to do with family socialization, which includes trust vis-à-vis inner and outer group members and perceptions about the incidence of corruption. Results in Figure 6.9 show standardized coefficients for a variety of outcomes of interest. Given the considerably smaller sample size for both the older and younger cohorts, the coefficients for these groups rarely achieve statistical significance. However, their size relative to the coefficients for the other groups reveal to some extent the degree to which the norms created by the military colony wane over time. For example, the coefficients in Figure 6.9 reveal that trust in family members is higher among generations born before 1945 within the former military colony, although it never reaches statistical significance. Trust in other people is highly statistically significant and reveals some interesting patterns: older people have the lowest amount of trust in other people; the effect decreases for the generation exposed to communism (born between 1945 and 1990). Younger cohorts, however, do have more trust in other people compared to older cohorts. These two results together point to a predictable waning of the effect of military colonialism: the effect is highest

---

[6] For example, the generation exposed to the Independent State of Croatia between 1941 and 1945 might have received a distinct historical shock, which would make them respond in a way which does not have any relationship to the Habsburg military colony.

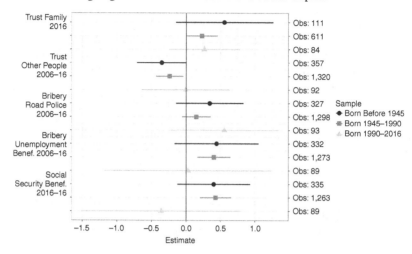

Figure 6.9 Effect of military colonialism on in-out-group trust and nepotism cohort analysis
Notes: The unit of analysis is the individual. Data is based on EBRD LITS 2006, 2010, and 2016. Every regression includes the following covariates: a linear polynomial in latitude and longitude, distance to Zagreb, border-segment fixed effects, age, perception of income, and education. The trust variables range from 1 (complete distrust) to 5 (complete trust). The bribery variables range from 1 (never) to 5 (always).

for the generations that are temporally closest to the historical treatment and it becomes less visible for younger generations. When it comes to perceptions about corruption, similar patterns hold: older generations tend to think that they frequently need to bribe the road police, to get unemployment benefits, and to get social security benefits, while younger people less so.

Risk-taking is a variable which was negative when looking at the entire sample. People in the former military colony were less willing to take risks. The results for the cohort analysis do not indicate any easily interpretable results. Most of the results are statistically insignificant. The generation born between 1945 and 1990 seems less inclined to accept a job with high chance of promotion with limited job security. For the generation born after 1990, there are not enough observations to compute confidence intervals for the variable which captures preference for secure jobs.

The cohort analysis of political participation reveals some interesting patterns. While many coefficients are still not statistically significant, older generations seem to be less likely to have voted in the last

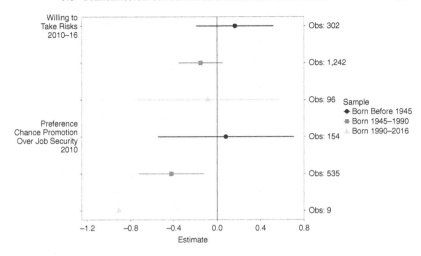

Figure 6.10 Effect of military colonialism on risk-taking cohort analysis

Notes: The unit of analysis is the individual. Data is based on EBRD LITS 2006, 2010, and 2016. Every regression includes the following covariates: a linear polynomial in latitude and longitude, distance to Zagreb, border-segment fixed effects, age, perception of income, and education. The risk variable ranges from 1 – not willing to take risks to 10 – very willing. The job security variable asks the respondent to choose between a high-security job with low chance of promotion (1) and a low-security job with high chance of promotion (2). The setting up of a business variable reflects people's responses to the question of whether they set up a business (1) or not (0).

elections: local, parliamentary, and presidential. The difference is not visible for subsequent generations. Older generations are also less likely to sign petitions but equally likely to participate in demonstrations compared with their counterparts in the former civilian area. The limited willingness to sign petitions seems to be exacerbated over generations with younger cohorts being much less willing to do so.

One important question is why do some norms persist but not others. As already argued, the likely mechanisms by which norms persisted is family intergenerational transmission. Descendants of people who were originally exposed to the institutions of military colonialism, get to acquire some of the norms and attitudes about the world from their parents. For example, they learn from their parents that they should trust their families, that they should trust outsiders less, and that in order to get government benefits, they need to make unofficial payments, etc. The offspring of these parents get to transmit these attitudes later to their

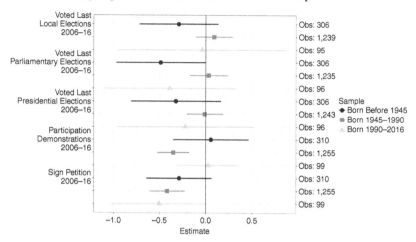

Figure 6.11 Effect of military colonialism on political participation cohort analysis

Notes: The unit of analysis is the individual. Data is based on EBRD LITS 2006, 2010, and 2016. Every regression includes the following covariates: a linear polynomial in latitude and longitude, distance to Zagreb, border-segment fixed effects, age, perception of income, and education. The voting questions record whether the respondent voted in the last elections. Answers range from 0 (No) to 1 (Yes). The question on participation in demonstrations or signing of petitions records whether the respondent did any of the two actions in the past – 1 or not – 0.

own children. The new attitudes will have two components: one component which is inherited from parents and another one which is acquired through lived experience. If the lived experience is incompatible with the inherited knowledge, the belief system will be updated. As shown in the main findings, preference for authoritarian structures and trust in government are not statistically significant. The qualitative historical evidence suggests that such norms persisted at least in the immediate aftermath of the historical treatment. Yet, the modern data indicates that they did not survive to the modern day. The lack of statistical significance when it comes to the distrust in government authorities as a result of the heavy historical abuses by the Habsburg state is not surprising. Much research indicates that distrust in the authorities as a result of historical experiences comes with a perception about the new government being related to the government who perpetrated the violence (Lupu and Peisakhin, 2017). Given that the democratic government after the 2000s has no relation to the Habsburg state, it is therefore no surprise that trust in the government is not different on the two sides of the border. When it comes to preference for authoritarian structures, it is more difficult to explain why they have not persisted. The most likely explanation is that the questions in the survey do not necessarily capture the hierarchies that were present within the family clan communities. Asking whether people prefer democracy or a planned economy, or whether they question the actions of the authorities does not necessarily capture the family clan obedience.

Attitudinal Legacies and the Provision of Public Goods

Another important question which remains to be answered is how attitudes which are still visible today are connected to developmental outcomes. As already indicated in the previous chapter, what was problematic about communal properties within the military colony was the limited inter-familial exchange and the formation of a vertical type of solidarity, which means a fragmented social life and a culture of distrust. As shown in the previous sections, people in the formal military colony trust their families more and have lower trust in non-family members. In addition, they think that they have to engage in corruption in order to obtain certain benefits, and they are less likely to engage politically (i.e. they are less likely to participate in demonstrations and they are less likely to sign petitions). The lack of trust in others, perceptions about corruption, and lack of political engagement are directly relevant for why people in the former military colony do not have access to public goods today.

Civic engagement is fundamentally the process by which citizens voluntarily engage in activities which signal to the local and national government that they need public goods. In addition, public engagement also allows citizens to monitor the actions of their elected officials and empowers individuals to vote out of office politicians that they are not pleased with. While arguably under-provision of public goods and lack of political engagement are endogenous to each other, the institutional trajectory of the Habsburg military colony indicates that it was under-provision of public goods which was the first in the causal chain leading to further alienation from the central state. Such alienation was further exacerbated by the persistence of communal properties, which permitted limited inter-familial exchange. Therefore, there is a top-down explanation for the low provision of public goods until 1881 with the imperial government intentionally discriminating against the inhabitants of the military colony. The low provision of public goods has a bottom-up explanation after 1881 where the locals failed to coordinate in order to signal to the government that they needed public goods. The bottom-up explanation is corroborated by modern statisticians who investigate the problem of public goods and local government transparency today.

As already mentioned, they argue that locals need to get involved in the process of budget allocation for the provision of public goods (Ott *et al.*, 2018).

The other types of attitudes including risk acceptance, attitudes toward authority, and attitudes toward women are not directly relevant for the provision of public goods. However, they directly derive from the exposure to communal properties and to having been forced to live in rigid family clans for over three hundred years. Such results complement the other findings on the other norms (which are relevant for the provision of public goods) and provide further evidence that there is indeed a legacy of these historical institutions which persists to the present day.

In this chapter I provided evidence for some of the cognitions that are closely connected to the idea of family clans. Both historical evidence and modern surveys indicate that people in the former military colony should feel closer to their families and should trust people outside of their social milieu less. Moreover, closer affinity to family members translates into higher perceived nepotism and corruption. Some evidence suggests that respondents in the former military colony have a more collectivist outlook on life, by disagreeing with statements that effort and intelligence are important in order to succeed in life. There is also evidence for the persistence of risk aversion: modern survey respondents prefer jobs that offer lower payment and higher job security. Similarly, the results also indicate stronger beliefs in the south than in the north that men are better leaders than women and a stronger agreement with the idea that women should do the household chores. Finally, there is some evidence for the negative effect of military colonialism on certain forms of political participation such as getting involved in demonstrations and signing petitions, but there are no obvious effects for voting. However, this chapter has also shown that certain norms and attitudes that historical travelers and scholars could observe in the 1930s and 1940s do not exist anymore. It is no longer the case that people in the former military colony prefer more authoritarian structures or that they have higher respect for authority. Similarly, there is no difference between the former military and the civilian areas today when it comes to trust in formal political institutions such as the government, courts, or the police. This may be less surprising given the multitude of governments and political regimes that followed after the fall of the Habsburg Empire.

7   Beyond the Habsburgs

Frontier zones are not unique to the Habsburg Empire. The fact that the grenzers were products of processes of "internal colonialism" (Scott, 2010, p. 3) makes them very similar to many frontiers throughout time and history. However, the Habsburg military colony was an area that was heavily regulated by the state, which gives it some peculiarity. A variety of charters and laws were passed with regard to the status of its inhabitants. According to Rothenberg (1960b), the military colony in Croatia introduced a highly paternalistic despotism both when it came to the internal social structure and when it came to supporting the absolutist ambitions of the Habsburgs.

Therefore, the grenzers in the military colony were substantially different from the self-governing people of Zomia in Southeast Asia (Scott, 2010), who were beyond the reach of the center. The land of the grenzers in the Habsburg Empire was not the home of the fugitive, mobile population running away from state-making processes and whose mode of existence would become intractable to the state. While originally many of the grenzers were refugees from the Ottoman Empire, once they moved into the Habsburg territory, they would live their life within the strict rules of the Habsburg state. The social structure in the frontier was very hierarchical with the grenzers having a very clear identity, markedly different from that of the Zomia settlers that Scott (2010) describes, whose identities were much more fluid. Therefore, such characteristics reduce the number of cases where the insights from this study can be applied.

The Habsburg military colony is somewhat similar to the military frontier between Spain and France, which acquired a territorial character after 1722, in the context of war and plague (Sahlins, 1989). When the news of the Marseilles plague reached the Cerdanya at the end of July 1720, the Spanish army in control of the valley erected a "sanitary cordon," which was to define formally the territorial boundary of the two states. In around 1722 the Spanish military authorities constructed a line of twenty-seven wooden barracks, most of them on the valley floor. Military occupation entailed royal administration of the entire valley (Sahlins, 1989, p. 65). Specifically, the occupation consisted of the administration of patrimonial revenues and royal dues for villages throughout Cerdanya. While some of the locals were co-opted for the protection of the border by the Spanish who erected the sanitary cordon, military occupation only meant taxation. The Spanish-French border never became a military colony.[1] In addition, the Cerdanya region, where the Spanish military authorities had constructed a line of twenty-seven wooden barracks, was in fact rich: "The relative wealth of the Cerdanya surprised French military commanders from Lieutenant General Roger de Rabutin in 1654, himself born in the fertile Burgundian plains, to the Duc de Noailles, governor of Roussillon in 1678" (Sahlins, 1989, p. 66).

The Anglo-Scottish and Anglo-Irish borders under the Tudors, around the fifteenth century are in certain respects similar to the Habsburg-Ottoman frontier zone. They were also organized like military colonies. Lack of resources is what prevented the Tudors from creating an elaborate defensive system. The border therefore relied much more on the topography of the region, the castles and fortified towns that were already there, and the local population of the region. Ellis (1995, p. 7) argues that "the system of defences and the obligation to maintain watch and ward and to do military service in defence of one's country, as laid down in the statute of Winchester of 1285, was sufficient to exclude petty raiders from the interior." Similar to the Habsburgs, the troops were not professional soldiers, but subjects of the region. Descriptions from 1550 indicate two characteristics which defined the English in those areas: "wildness and negligence" (Ellis, 1995, p. 71), as a result of drastic curtailment of financial and military subventions by the central government, who were much more concerned with ensuring dynastic security. Nevertheless, unlike the Habsburg military colony, the inhabitants of the region were expected to be governed "like Englishmen everywhere, by the course of the common law and the normal institutions of the English government" (Ellis, 1995, p. 7). As argued in the previous chapters, this was not the case with the Habsburg military colony. In addition, unlike the Habsburg military frontier, the delegation of power at the border was given to local magnates (e.g. Percies, Nevilles, Dacres, etc.) to mitigate the weakness of the central government there. Such magnates would formalize their influence through feudal relationships with the peasants and would occasionally rebel against the center.

Military colonies were used extensively in the Roman Empire. During Caesar Augustus (27 BCE to 14 CE), the Roman Empire expanded

---

[1] Sahlins (1989), however, explores how the frontier zone became a place for the growth of nationalism, where the center and the periphery mingled. Identity was perceived through difference and opposition – village against village, Cerdanya against Roussillon, Catalonia against Castile, Spain against France.

its territory and brought troops from the center to its frontiers. This was a period of consolidation of client states in the periphery (Longo, 2018, p. 29). The border was maintained mostly through small auxiliary units, while the legions were placed on the roads between the center and the periphery, acting as mobile military forces. The client states, similar to the military colony in the Habsburg Empire, acted as a buffer area, taking the burden of external attacks until Roman defenses arrived. In fact, Machiavelli in the *Prince* comments on the Roman tactics in the outer provinces arguing that they "sent out colonies, indulged the lesser powers without increasing their power, put down the powerful and did not allow foreign powers to gain reputation there" (Machiavelli, 1996, III, p. 12). It was through the roads emanating from the capital that the Romans were able to establish and maintain control. They continued to be used under Alexander Severus (208–235 CE) in the third century and they were looked down upon by the professional troops. Subsequently, under Diocletian (244–311 CE) and Constantine (272–337 CE) there was a change in their status whereby both the position of a colonist, called *limitanei*, and the plots of land which they controlled became hereditary (Isaac, 1988).

The military colonies that were most similar to the Habsburg ones and which were contemporaneous to them are the Russian and the French examples. The Russians created colonies as early as the sixteenth century and, in this respect, developed at the same time as the Habsburg frontier. The French colonies emerged in the early nineteenth century as an economical method to ensure the security of French settlers within the newly conquered territories in Africa. In the following subsections, I present brief overviews of the logic for creating military colonies, some of the debates around the creation of such institutions, and some details about how such institutions were implemented in Russia and Algeria.

7.1 The Russian Military Colonies

The first documents indicating the existence of Russian military colonies date back to 1524. These were groups of "Cossacks" and constituted buffer populations at the border with neighboring empires such as Poland-Lithuania and the Ottoman Empire. They were also used to prevent Tatar invasions. Originally, the Cossacks were peasants who fled from their place of origin to live together in self-governing communities (Witzenrath, 2007). After decades of negotiation among Poland, Russia, and Turkey, the Cossacks ended up submitting to the Orthodox tsar in 1681. Attempts to reduce them to regular serfs in the seventeenth and eighteenth centuries were met with bitter discontent by the Cossacks, but they kept their allegiance to the tsar.

They continued to be organized in a way to protect the Russian territory against advances by Poland-Lithuania and Tatars (Khodark-ovsky, 2002). They also played a key role in driving the Ottomans out of Crimea in 1783 (Ferguson, 1954; Pipes, 1950; Romaniello, 2012). Overall, there were a few lines of Cossacks throughout the empire. They are represented in Figure 7.1. The first line was the one between the rivers Dnieper and Donets in the territory of what is today central and eastern Ukraine. Originally, these were serfs who ran away from the Poland-Lithuanian Commonwealth and who settled in the region between the two rivers. These were called "Zaporozhian Cossacks" and were meant to protect the empire against raids by the Crimean Tartars. After the uprising of 1648–1657 against Poland-Lithuania, they formed a Cossack state in 1649 – the Cossack Helmanate. It was disbanded in 1764 by the Russian Empire (Khodarkovsky, 2002). Catherine the Great (1729–1796) contributed to the consolidation of the Zaporozhian Cos-sacks by moving more population into the area. Overall, the new inhabitants were Moldavians, Wallachians, Serbs, and Tatars, occupy-ing a vast territory between the rivers Dnieper, Inhulets, Inhul, and Buh (Pipes, 1950).

Military buffer areas continued under Peter the Great (1672–1725), who was responsible for the deployment of Cossacks to the Caucasus mountains, in the Kuban and Terek river regions (Sumner, 1949, pp. 15–16). Peter the Great thought of developing self-perpetuating bodies of military officers in order to solve the problem of having to levy recruits from the civilian population. Military colonies would consist of two types of people: farmers who would do the agricultural work and soldiers who would be ready to fight at any time necessary. In times of peace, the soldiers were supposed to assist other peasants with their work (Bitis and Hartley, 2000, p. 2). He also used the Don Cossacks, located along the homonymous river, in multiple military campaigns.

The region in close proximity to the Caucasus mountains had a special administration as a result of the military deployment by Peter the Great. According to Desprez (1847), the region of the Caucasus moun-tains was made out of bellicose tribes who had been subjected to military service "being unable to do anything better" for centuries (Desprez, 1847, p. 730). The Astrakhan Cossacks formed another division in the Caucasus, which was created as a result of the Russian relocation efforts of 1737 along the right bank of the Volga River from Astrakhan to Cherniy Yar (today's Astrakhan Oblast, Russia). They were initially cre-ated for patrol service along the Lower Volga on the Caspian coasts, on the Southeast Russian border. They were deployed for a variety of military purposes until 1919. The Orenburg and Ural Cossacks were established in the mid-eighteenth century to defend the city of Orenburg and the wider region against Kazak attacks coming from beyond the Ural mountains (Sumner, 1949, pp. 15–16).

Siberian Cossacks were people who settled in Siberia at the end of the sixteenth century as a result of the conquest of this territory. The main Cossack armies in the region were the Sibir, the Semirechye (located in the present-day southeastern Kazakhstan and northeastern Kyrgyzstan), and the Cossacks next to the Baikal Lake, a division created during the nineteenth century, in charge of patrolling the Sino-Russian border. Finally, the Amur Cossacks constituted another military section, created in the mid-nineteenth century with Cossacks from the Baikal region. The Amurs contributed to the suppression of the Boxer Rebellion in China (1899–1901) and the Russo-Japanse War of 1904–1905. Cossacks were exempt from taxes to the state (Desprez, 1847, p. 730). Unlike the serfs in Russia, they enjoyed property rights, with only meadows and pastures being enjoyed collectively. Figure 7.1 displays where Cossack armies were located historically in the Russian Empire.

Generally, the Cossacks were seen as a source of reliable and devoted soldiers. They were therefore different from the regular subjects of the Russian Empire and were part of the tsar's army. After the Crimean War, Alexander II (1818–1881) started to reduce the pressure that the Cossacks were under, as a result of the natural resources discovered in the Don and Kuban regions (Rothenberg, 1966). They continued, however, to be part of the Russian army until the October revolution of 1917.

The most relevant efforts to build military colonies which were very similar to the Habsburg ones and for which there are abundant historical sources date back to the 1800s. Some of these sources do indeed indicate that it was the Habsburg military colonies which provided an inspiration for the Russian ones. For example, in 1810 Alexander I of Russia (1777–1825) considered adopting them throughout the empire, but he did not realize the full importance of such establishments until 1814 when he "appreciated with his own eyes and recognized the glorious merits of the military colonies in Austria" (Desprez, 1847, p. 725). Given the large spread of the empire, professional soldiers would only be able to arrive on time with great difficulty to counteract potential attacks on the western or southern imperial border. By placing such colonies in those strategic locations, the imperial government could buy itself enough time to mobilize the professional army (Desprez, 1847, p. 730). There were four additional reasons according to Ybert-Chabrier (2004, p. 549) which led to the creation of new military colonies by Alexander I: (1) reducing army expenses; (2) ensuring easy recruitment to the army; (3) maintaining agriculture in times of peace and having the troops always ready to act; (4) giving a place of exile to retired and disabled

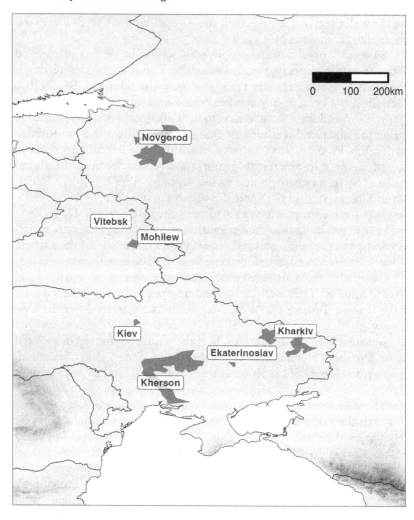

Figure 7.1 Approximate location of Cossack armies in the
Russian Empire from the fourteenth to the twentieth century
Notes: Redrawn based on Rossiyskaya Gazeta (2013); Spring (2003).
Elevation and modern borders in the background.

soldiers. Finally, the goal was to gradually replace the entire professional
Russian army with troops from these military colonies.

Russian nobility did not view the establishment of military colonies
favorably. Nobles frequently circulated narratives portraying such communities as dangerous for the imperial power: "Would it not be
possible that the military colonial government of Novgorod, close to

Saint Petersburg, could they not allow themselves to be corrupted by the political spirit and led astray by the advice of a popular and ambitious general?" (Desprez, 1847, p. 733). Desprez contends that such narratives were ultimately driven by the prospect of nobles losing part of their territory and some of the serfs inhabiting their lands. Such intuition is also confirmed by Bitis and Hartley (2000, p. 324), who cite William A'Court, ambassador to Russia in 1828–32, in mentioning the "control [the military colony] gives to the Crown over the nobility in [...] their own Estates."

Emperor Alexander appointed Count Aleksey Arakcheyev (1769–1834) to bring to fruition his ideas on Russian military colonialism, a count who rose from military ranks where he was a commander to become a general of artillery (Lyall, 1824; Unknown Author, 1828). Once invested with all the confidence of Tsar Alexander, the count decided to build colonies in close proximity to the capital. The places which were designated first for the creation of three divisions of grenadiers for colonization were the districts of Saint Petersburg and Novgorod. Ybert-Chabrier (2004) explains that Arakcheyev's estate was in Gruzino, a place about 60km away from Saint Petersburg. Establishing colonies that were close both to his estate and the imperial capital would allow him to maintain his political influence. The places chosen in close proximity to Saint Petersburg had nothing special: "few inhabitants, infertile, unhealthy [...] apart from the proximity to the capital" (Ybert-Chabrier, 2004, p. 549). By contrast, the places in Novgorod were swampy but not deserted. They featured a long tradition of commerce which continued for a few years after the establishment of the colonies.

Lyall (1824, pp. 22–23) explains the process of militarization: the Russian emperor issued a decree nominating "the crown-villages which are to become military colonies. In the designated villages (which are inhabited by crown-peasants, and consequently are at the Emperor's disposal), the name, age, property, and family of each householder are registered; those who are above 50 years old are chosen to form what is called Master-Colonists." Soldiers from the regular army would be brought to live together with existing farming families. Desprez (1847) describes the difficult situation of professional soldiers when they were separated from their families and were forced to live in unknown farming communities.[2] Receiving communities were expected to tolerate the

---

[2] Desprez (1847) draws the distinction between military colonists and military settlers, who should not be confused: "the soldier serves in active service and gives the surplus of his time on the farm where he lives; the settler [on the other hand], maintains the soldier, with the exception of the equipment and the pay, which remain the responsibility of the treasury" (Desprez, 1847, p. 730).

presence of soldiers on their land while in exchange "were exempted from the tax which they owed to the state and also owned their homes in perpetuity" (Desprez, 1847, p. 730). The reality, however, was different, with soldiers being perceived as "foreigners." They would stop being labeled as such once they married within the local farming community. In order for the locals and soldiers to become one unitary community, and for the distinction between soldiers and settlers not to be made, a few generations would have to pass (Desprez, 1847). Both soldiers and local farming communities would be considered tenant settlers (*hozjaeva*). The farmers would continue to be exclusively dedicated to agriculture, while others would be dedicated to military affairs and only use the surplus of their time for agriculture. In addition, military colonists also had some work obligations toward the state: they had to participate in the repair and construction of roads, bridges, churches, schools, and public buildings. They also had to be involved in other types of work designated by the imperial authorities summing to about two days a week.

Within the designated villages, land was divided into equal portions with colonists enjoying communal property rights. The pastures and meadows would also be enjoyed by everyone as public goods. Each master-colonist would receive about forty acres of land.[3] If the family did not have enough cattle or agricultural tools to survive, they would have to unite their property with that of others. The master-colonist would train to become a soldier himself and would be expected to wear a uniform, march on relevant occasions, use a sabre, and perform military salutes. Similarly, each master-colonist would be expected to support a soldier – an *agriculturist-soldier* (Lyall, 1824, p. 25) (usually, a son, a relative, or a friend who could succeed the military colonists) – and raise a horse which could subsequently be used for the imperial cavalry. The soldier would assist with the cultivation of land, grazing the cattle, or animal husbandry in exchange when free from military duties. Finally, the master-colonist would also support a *reserve*, another son or relative of his. In case the agriculturist was slain in battle, he would be replaced by the reserve. The descendants of the master-colonists, the agriculturists, and the reserves were called *cantonists* from the ages of thirteen to seventeen and would train to become soldiers themselves. Education was a key component of the children located in the colony: all children were taught reading, writing, and arithmetic, in addition to a "sort of catechism containing the duty of a soldier" (Lyall, 1824, p. 28), which would entail the handling of the sword and riding horses.

---

[3] Forty acres of land was the amount which was considered essential for subsistence for every colonial family by the imperial authorities (Ybert-Chabrier, 2004).

The villages designated to become colonies would become military districts or military regiments under the command of a general. If the areas designated to become military colonies were deserted, extensive works would first be conducted to prepare the land for construction. Such works included deforestation, desiccation of marshes, drilling of canals, etc., which cost the empire large sums of money.[4] This is the case for some of the areas in close proximity to Saint Petersburg. The government bore the costs of the military establishments, and came to the aid of the poorest peasants to support their families and their farms in the initial stages (Desprez, 1847, p. 731).

Not all populations exposed to colonization were the same. Some were more resistant to the new military colonial institutions than others. People exposed to military colonialism in the south (mostly Kherson) were Cossacks who already had historical experience with militarization under Peter and Catherine the Great and were important players in the fight against the Ottomans and Tatars. People from other regions were less receptive to such institutions. Ybert-Chabrier (2004, p. 528) describes how the people from the Novgorod area were much more attached to their traditions and resistant to innovations and military discipline. The first military colonial experiments in Novgorod were met with resistance from the local peasants. Locals were dissatisfied with the notion that they had to adhere to the new military rules imposed by the empire, while the fact that they had "to cut their hair and shave their beard, added fuel to the flame" (Lyall, 1824, p. 21). Curtiss (1965) mentions that the restrictions were so severe that even the children were drilled, expected to wear uniforms, and enrolled in the army as soon as they came of age. Such disaffection culminated in the revolt which broke out in Novgorod on July 11, 1831, which "was the expression of a dissatisfaction which dated back to the origins of the colonies" (Ybert-Chabrier, 2004, p. 551). The revolt ended with more than 400 people massacred and it was only the presence of the emperor that quelled it. About one hundred non-commissioned soldiers were tortured for their participation in the revolt, while others were sent to Siberia.

Under Nicholas I of Russia (1796–1855), son of Alexander I, large reforms were brought to the military colonies which had to do with bringing the status of the Russian military colonists closer to that of Russian Crown peasants, abandoning the idea of using the colonies as the only source of military recruitment, and eliminating the separate

---

[4] Ybert-Chabrier (2004, p. 550) estimates that deforestation, desiccation of land, the purchase of animals for the colonists, and the provision of food for the inhabitants during multiple years for one single infantry regiment should have cost the empire around 5 million rubles.

military administration (Ybert-Chabrier, 2004). These reforms were initiated in 1826 and transformed the infantry colonies of Novgorod into soldier districts that would keep their lands from the ancient colonized regiments.

Count Ivan Osipovic Witte (1781–1840) is another key figure in the evolution of military colonialism in Russia together with General Arakcheyev. He enjoyed great favor with both Emperor Alexander I and Nicholas I. He was very successful in his military campaigns against the Ottomans in 1829, which resulted in his promotion to general, and against Poland in 1831. He had extensive military experience as a military volunteer under Napoleon. He returned to Russia in 1812 and fought against Napoleon in two campaigns. He was then put in charge of the military colony of Chuhuiv in 1817, a town situated about 40 km southeast of Kharkiv in the land of the Buh Cossacks. In a similar way to the colonies of Novgorod, locals responded with some resistance to the attempt at militarization, expressing their dissatisfaction about the requisition of land, abolition of old privileges, and the request from the imperial authorities to serve fodder to the horses of the regiment in 1819. Ybert-Chabrier (2004) explains how despite some local resistance, Witte was able to establish two divisions, one of lancers and another one of cuirassiers in Chuhuiv.

In 1818 he was also put in charge of developing cavalry colonies further south in the empire, in the Kherson district. Count Witte followed orders from General Arakcheyev until 1826[5] (Ybert-Chabrier, 2004), when he became a general. The Kherson colonies consisted of four divisions, one of cuirassiers, two of lancers, and one of houssars for a total of about 21,120 men available to fight (Ybert-Chabrier, 2004, p. 553). Ybert-Chabrier (2004) estimates that the military colony covered approximately 3,500,000 hectares with the abundant vegetation ensuring the subsistence of the colonists. The whole colony consisted of about 87,000 men, who were removed from the civilian authority and were supposed to ensure the subsistence or the recruitment of men for sixteen cavalry regiments. Elisavetgrad (today's Kropyvnytskyi in Ukraine) was the only place under civilian administration in the Kherson district.

Russian military colonies were widespread throughout the history of the Russian Empire. They were located north and south of Saint Petersburg, Novgorod, Witebsk, Mohilew, Kharkiv, Kiew, Podolia, and Kherson (Pipes, 1950). As already mentioned at the beginning of this subsection, additional historical colonies were located at the borders with

---

[5] After the death of Tsar Alexander I in 1825, Arakcheyev lost all his positions in the government. This led to his removal from the court and the exile to his estate of Gruzino.

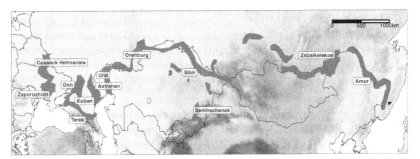

Figure 7.2 Russian military colonies in the Russian Empire in
the nineteenth century
Notes: Redrawn based on Military Encyclopedia (1912). Elevation
and modern borders in the background.

Poland, Austria, and Turkey. Figure 7.2 displays the Russian military
colonies in the mid-nineteenth century.

Arakcheyev is the figure who brought military colonialism to a whole
new level in the Russian Empire, institutionalizing the practice of soldiers "paying close attention to each other's diligence in the performance
of work" (Pipes, 1950, p. 212). The scheme did not last long, however, with many revolts taking place. Moreover, the administration of
these provinces proved costly and did not produce the expected savings. Therefore, the colonies were dissolved as part of the reforms of
Alexander II (1818–1881) (Curtiss, 1965; Ferguson, 1964).

Political and military pundits of the early nineteenth century typically compared the Russian and the Habsburg military frontier systems
and argued that they played an important role in the politics of the
time of the two states. In both cases, the colonies represented a third
of their military strength. Desprez (1847, p.732) estimated that the military colonies in Russia could provide up to 200,000 soldiers, which
represented about a third of its military power in the nineteenth century. Desprez was also comparing the Russian and the Habsburg colonies
when it came to the threat that they posed to the imperial governments:
while they both played a substantial role in foreign wars, "they may
become a source of political danger to the [Russian] autocracy" and
could be "soon a source of difficulty and embarrassment for Austria."
(Desprez, 1847, p. 735).

In a similar way to the Croatian military colony, people did not fully
enjoy property rights: they were effectively tenants of the state without
real "ownership" of land (Bitis and Hartley, 2000) and lived a highly
constrained life despite the appearance of freedom: "nobody can move,
sell not even their waste, without special authorization" (Desprez, 1847,

p. 731) or "the moral constraints imposed by legislation are always excessive and freedom, null" (Desprez, 1847, p. 731). Given the permanent
military jurisdiction and careful military surveillance, community members lived in perpetual discomfort with the state invading and controlling
all aspects of their private life including the ability to move or to sell
property. The means of production were heavily limited and economic
exchanges were hampered by the lack of means of communication.

The lack of freedom of movement together with restrictions on
property and lack of transportation means were important factors
thwarting economic growth according to Desprez. Similar to Maria Theresa and her son Joseph II, Alexander I of Russia (in power between
1801 and 1825) and Nicholas I (reigning between 1825 and 1855) both
attempted to alleviate the situation of the Russian military colonies with
a modicum of success. As a result of some of the reforms, visitors to
the colonies were typically impressed by the regular design of the houses
and by the presence of roads; colonists, however, viewed them as the
result of additional labor constraints by the state, given that they were
achieved with the toils of their labor (Bitis and Hartley, 2000). As a result
of some of the reforms to alleviate poverty, Russian colonies ended up
having hospitals, churches, schools, and even "English-style latrines to
improve standards of hygiene" (Bitis and Hartley, 2000, p. 323). The
schools, however, were much more interested in training future soldiers
than meeting general educational standards.

Many of these accomplishments, however, were illusory. Some local
colonists occasionally tried to hide the true state of the economy. For
example, Desprez explains that the Novgorod colonies were more privileged than other colonies because of their proximity to Saint Petersburg
and exposure to frequent visits from imperial officials. Desprez provides
the example of the official visit by Emperor Alexander in 1824, when:

[. . .] the entire colonial administration was in turmoil. What could be done
to hide from the sovereign the true state of affairs? The neighboring villages
agreed to improve the roads and arranged between them to lend each other men,
children and cattle. This is done regularly at each inspection. So all hands are
busy repairing roads, bridges, public buildings, or even pulling trees in the forests
to plant them along the paths.[6] (Desprez, 1847, p. 732)

The Russian military system constitutes another good example of
an extractive institution, a system whereby local human resources were
extracted to work in enterprises defined by the state. The Cossacks had
more of an informal status in the sixteenth century and were deployed
in the various regions of the empire. Military colonialism solidified more

[6] Translation from French.

as an institution in the nineteenth century under Alexander I. They were very similar to the Habsburg military colonies in that the basic demographic unit was the peasant-soldier, they were originally serfs, and they lived under a communal property rights system. When it comes to applying the theoretical framework proposed, the Russian military colonies do feature the transformation in property rights regime where locals were no longer serfs and enjoyed communal property rights. There is limited exposure to violence and some investment in infrastructure as evidenced by the presence of hospitals, schools, and roads as a result of the reforms initiated by Alexander I. While the last factor should be associated with positive outcomes, its causal effect would be difficult to tease out given its limited longevity and inconsistency – the fact that villages kept being added or removed from the military colonial system. The Russian military colony together with the Habsburg one constituted a model for ensuring the security of the French settlements in North Africa.

7.2   Military Colonialism in French Algeria

Military colonialism went beyond Europe. In order to demonstrate that land-based empires have more elements in common with sea-based empires than one would typically expect, I examine the military colonies which the French created in Algeria. Such institutions were adopted by the French Empire in the early 1800s, following the Habsburg and Russian models (Azan, 1936; Marmont, 1837; Rashid, 1960; Rothenberg, 1966). The idea of military colonies had existed in France, however, for a long time. Before the French Revolution, Colonel Servan (1741–1808) anticipated in a book about the "citizen-soldier" the creation of an army of citizen-soldiers at the frontier of the empire, making the argument that "citizens were born for the defense of their country. They had to be soldiers and the republican spirit, the education, the love of liberty and glory . . . made them natural heroes" (Servan de Gerbey, 1780, p. 11).

French rule in Algeria started in 1830 with the invasion of Algiers and lasted until the Algerian War of Independence of 1962. The very idea of conquering Algeria stemmed from the expansionist ambitions of Charles X (1757–1836), who desired "a new France, which could increase the riches and the power of the mother-nation" (Rouire, 1901, p. 341), similar to Britain. Yet, French authorities were aware that the colonization of Algeria would not be similar to the English establishments in North America and Australia or the Spanish conquest of South America: "all the Algerian soil was occupied, cultivated; the people who possessed it were relatively numerous, had been in contact with Europe for centuries and had partly dominated it; [Algeria] had an advanced civilization, approaching our own [. . .] and was heavily opposed to any idea of assimilation or fusion" (Rouire, 1901, p. 342). Hence, the French were already aware of the resistance that they would encounter from the locals. Yet, they decided to pursue their expansionist ambitions further.

Rouire (1901) identifies three periods in the history of the Algerian conquest by the French in the nineteenth century. The first part is what he calls the "heroic phase" between 1830 and 1842, when the French encountered the highest level of resistance from the locals. The second corresponds to the "colonization period," between 1842 and 1856, which saw colonial settlements on the part of the French. This is also the period of heavy settler mortality as a result of diseases (Rouire, 1901, p. 340). The third period corresponds to the time between 1856 and around 1900, close to the time when Rouire (1901) wrote his piece, and where, for the first time, according to him, the number of French births surpassed the number of French deaths.

The need to create military colonies emerged in the early phase. Within this period, French presence in Algeria only consisted of scattered villages built around posts to protect communication between the capital and other towns where a few military garrisons were stationed. According to Bussière (1853), the population who moved was attracted by the new concessions of land. The first French settlers went to the suburbs of Algiers, followed by Vieux Kouba, Tixeraïn, and Rassauta. After 1835 the French expanded to places like Boufarik, Arba, and Beni Moussa. While the new settlers expected their security to be ensured by the continuous passage of troops, this proved insufficient. Bussière (1853) describes how the farms occupied by the French were being ravaged by Abdelkader (1808–1883), an Algerian religious and military leader who led the struggle against the French colonial invasion after being elected emir of the Algerian western tribes in 1832. Attacks against the French by the local tribes in Algeria were a common occurrence between 1830 and 1842 when the first settlers came in: "For twelve years, thefts, arson, assassinations covered Mitidja with misery, ruins, and blood, and it is with good reason that this period was called the gunpowder period" (Rouire, 1901, p. 358). Fierce fights continued between 1842 and 1846. In this period French authorities created soldier settlements in places where fights were still taking place: they also built houses for the soldiers and roads connecting the military settlements to the civilian ones.

The first political debates surrounding the concept of military colonialism indicate that the Habsburg military colonies in Croatia, Serbia, and Romania constituted a model for the French colonial enterprises in North Africa. This is most obviously demonstrated in an essay called

Experiment on the organization of military borders in Austrian border regiments and considerations on the application of this system to a certain degree, to the organization of French possessions in Africa[7] by A. de Terrasson, a French military official who visited Croatia in 1837. On his visit, he noted some of the characteristics of Croatian locals which made them suitable candidates to become warriors and help defend the empire. He agreed with the descriptions of one of the leading social engineers of the Habsburg military colony – commander Joseph Friedrich von Sachsen-Hildburghausen (1702–1787):

I saw a warring people, courageous, rough, and ignorant, children of nature; who feed on simple and coarse food, and living without culture like the oak in the forest, reached the heights of the first human races; good and savage, but superstitious and full of enthusiasm for military glory, familiar with the perils of combat, and eager to plunder, as a reward for bravery and skill; having few needs, poor in knowledge and enlightenment, of an energy that is not soft and refined, steadfastly attached to national customs and therefore, to their land, faithful to their word and willing to keep their promises; naturally marked with frankness and intrepidity, but which, facing both violence and severe repression for a long time, has become suspicious and obstinate; capable of absolute loyalty and the most unshakable devotion, and yet driven by a desire to try all the might of one's strength transformed into fiery ardor and spirit of revolt.[8] (Von Hietzinger, 1817, pp. 298-299)

Terrasson contended that the local population in Algeria was very similar to the warrior population in Croatia and, as a result, could help defend the French settlements in Algeria. Émerit (1959) describes how applying the Croatian military model to Algeria came in fact from an even earlier time during the Napoleonic Empire; the idea came from a French vice-consul in Fiume who considered splitting Algeria into a civilian and a military zone. The locals would be organized in military regiments, very similar to the Croatian military colonies. Further recommendations entailed replacing the local administrative units in Algeria, the *douars*, with zadrugas, which would become the organizational basis for Arab property (Émerit, 1959, p. 94). Neither Terrasson nor the vice-consul provided details on how the transformation of Algerian society could be achieved.

Other military and political pundits of the time were much more scrupulous in the methodology of colonialism. Marie-Théodore de Rumigny (1835–1848) was a military general who was of the opinion that the local Kabyle population (Berber indigenous group in the north

---

[7] The title in French is *Essai sur l'organisation des frontières militaires en régiment frontière de l'Autriche et considérations sur l'application de ce systeme, a un certain degré, a l'organisation des possessions françaises de l'Afrique*, cited in Émerit (1959, p. 94).

[8] Translation from German.

of Algeria) could and should be used as infantry and cavalry under the leadership of French officials. Together, they could thrive by "combining warrior and agricultural lives" (De Rumigny, 1850, p. 52). In his article published in *Le Spectateur Militaire*, an influential French military journal of the nineteenth century, he answered affirmatively to the following question: "Is it possible to reduce our expenses and to reduce our army, while ensuring the same security, and more importantly, the security of the colonial settlers who want to go and establish settlements?" (De Rumigny, 1850, p. 31). As far as costs were concerned, he estimated that one battalion of 1,000 men would cost in France approximately one million francs in 1850. By contrast, a battalion of 1,000 Kabyle legionaries would cost in the region of 500,000 francs during the first years, while the costs would diminish in the ensuing years if they were to live in self-sufficient communities.

Nevertheless, de Rumigny also drew attention to the perils of getting the local Algerian tribes to submit to French authority. While the French could in the initial stages be successful in overcoming resistance, defeating indigenous armies, and conquering strategic locations, long-term success would require a different approach. One of the tactics to prevent local revolts at least in the short run, according to de Rumigny, would be to place the defeated under the watch of French men of confidence while some of the men from the defeated army could be used as human resources to increase the size of the security forces. However, de Rumigny (1850) did mention that holding control over a long period after conquest was an illusion: "no matter how numerous it may be, [the conquering] army will get mixed and lost within the local population." It was therefore important for the conqueror to win over indigenous forces (De Rumigny, 1850, p. 48).

Part of ensuring long-term French success in Algeria was, according to de Rumigny, adopting military colonies. In the second part of his article, de Rumigny (1850) explained the advantages and relevance of military colonialism for the French imperial project in Algeria, "a system that is practiced since ancient times, and which was successful in all times and climates" (De Rumigny, 1850, p. 44). He therefore proposed the creation of communities commanded by French officials: three legions per province, backed up by two or three battalions and if necessary aided by a proportionally sized cavalry in the designated locations. Every legion would have its designated space, with each company and family of settlers being grouped around the battalion. Having such arrangements would play an important role "to protect the borders and all our possessions, and to contain the rebellious Kabyles who will be surrounded by an armed network until their submission is complete" (De Rumigny, 1850, p. 45).

De Rumigny also proposed a series of incentives to be offered to military colonies: they would receive plots of land, while the leaders of the legions would receive larger portions corresponding to their status. Providing land to military colonists would also have the additional role of enabling them "to feed and clothe one or more soldiers, one or more horsemen, and help meet the needs of the legion" (De Rumigny, 1850, p. 45). The general also explained how soldiers would be chosen and admitted by the legion leaders from the local Kabyle population, who have the natural abilities to become infantry corps: "they are loyal, sober, and hard-working; they are serious and their courage is remarkable. Their ability to create villages, to cultivate the land is obvious, and do not destroy forests the way the Arabs do. They plant trees and know perfectly the art of crops" (De Rumigny, 1850, p. 49). In order to ensure the obedience of the locals, three conditions had to be met according to de Rumigny (1850): (1) that their direct superiors are men whom they admire for their bravery and loyalty; (2) that the French are just and play a guiding role; (3) that the French guarantee the local population freedom of religious practice and expression. With adequate guidance from their chiefs, locals would be able to transform their settlements into small farms.

In the process of joining military colonies, locals would bring their families and agricultural tools with them. The state would be responsible for providing arms and ammunition and one franc per soldier. In the second year, according to de Rumigny (1850), the amount should be reduced to half that price. By the third year, the legions would have acquired sufficient revenue that the salary provided by the state would no longer be necessary. Finally, de Rumigny (1850) recommended that all superior officials (especially the captains) be French unless in rare exceptions an indigenous soldier proved fit for that position. Half of the lieutenant positions could be filled by French and half by locals according to de Rumigny. All the orders would be given in French with an unmentioned expectation that the indigenous colonists would learn French. Beyond such broad recommendations, the general proposed that the local commissions on Algeria should be in charge of the local administration and have the freedom to decide on further logistical matters, following the "*model of the Swedish army, and that of the Russian and Habsburg military colonies, which constitute good models to imitate*" (De Rumigny, 1850, p. 48) (emphasis added).

Other political pundits of the mid-nineteenth century were less enthusiastic about the notion of applying the Croatian and Russian military colonial models to French Algeria. While many agreed that ensuring the security of the French colonists in Algeria should be a priority and that military colonies could play an important defensive role against incursions from local tribes, many were also critical of the idea of emulating the military colonial models from the Habsburg and Russian empires. Desprez (1847) was a diplomat, state counselor, and French publicist (1819–1898) who expressed some skepticism. In a piece published in *Revue des deux Mondes*, a monthly literary, cultural, and current affairs magazine, he wrote:

We thought that the history and the current situation of these establishments could offer us some precious documents which can answer some of the questions raised in the [process of] colonization of Algeria. Yet, if the study of Austria and Russia deserves our attention, it should be because there is something to learn from some [specific] administrative arrangements, as opposed to learning from the whole organization. If we want to organize military colonies on the southern frontier of African France, *these two countries have little to teach us.* It is up to us to draw conclusions about what suits both the spirit of our country and the social circumstances specific to our new conquest. It is therefore important to clearly specify the role of military institutions created by the Austrian policy and the despotism of the tsars, in order to prevent errors which we could make by believing in similarities which are more illusory than real.[9] (Desprez, 1847, p. 735) (emphasis added).

In Desprez's view, the reason why the Russian and Habsburg colonies succeeded has to do with the advantages offered of escaping serfdom and acquiring land. The incentives provided to military colonists in Russia and the Habsburg lands were much more generous, which would have made being part of them much more attractive than in Algeria. Similarly, he was also very skeptical when it came to the natural abilities of the local population to fight, their prior experience of dividing their time between agriculture and military endeavors, the size of the local population who could be included in the local military colonies, and the potential local allegiance.

Do we have readily available, like in Austria, warlike tribes, armed since ancient times for the safety of their fields, and accustomed to wielding the sword and the plow at the same time? Do we have, like in Russia, twenty million state serfs and an army also composed of serfs that we can dispose of at our pleasure? No, we do not have populations that we can constrain, nor tribes that offer themselves voluntarily, and therefore we lack the raw material to the point that we do not even yet have the necessary arms for civilian colonization.[10] (Desprez, 1847, p. 735)

In order to further solidify his position against military colonies, Desprez also pursued a line of reasoning that focused on the economic

---

[9] Translation from French.
[10] Translation from French.

viability of military colonies. In his view, colonial institutions could result in "paralyzing" the individual activity of the peasants. The economic status of military colonists both in Russia and the Habsburg Empire was already in stark contrast to the bourgeoning prosperity of the rest of the imperial territories (Desprez, 1847, p. 724).

Other contemporaneous military commentators raised logistical concerns. Charles-François Aulas de Courtigis, a military officer, wrote a report to the French Ministry of War, dated September 10, 1844, in which he argued that it took Austrian military colonies about fifty years to grow to the point of raising 2,000 fighters and hence getting to a similar level of recruitment in Algeria could take a considerable time. Furthermore, it may not necessarily be realistic, according to him, to expect that the colonists would care much about defending the French territory beyond their plots of land that were allocated for their service (M. de Courtigis cited in Émerit (1959, p. 95)). Auguste Bussière, a literary critic, questioned the very notion of a self-sufficient society made out of farmers and soldiers in a piece published in the *Revue des deux Mondes*. According to him, it would not be sustainable to expect that the farming population would always support the military personnel. If military colonies were successful, one would encounter them much more frequently without state intervention (Bussière, 1853).

Despite all the objections raised, the French went ahead with the creation of military colonies in a way that was much more reflective of the propositions by de Rumigny (1850) and Desprez (1847) than of the critics. In a speech to the French Chamber of Deputies on January 15, 1840, Thomas Robert Bugeaud (1784–1849), Marshal of France and Governor-General of Algeria from 1841 to 1847, argued: "We need military or civilian settlers, whatever you want to call them; but [we need to] organize them militarily as the colonist-warriors in similar countries" (cited in Émerit (1959, p. 95)). Bugeaud had been very impressed with the ability of the Austrians and the Russians to easily levy military recruits and he thought that imperial expenditures could be reduced in this manner in Algeria as well. Once he became governor of Algeria, Bugeaud sent the French government multiple ideas for the implementation of such plans. Despite some resistance from the Ministry of War, he managed to create military colonies with farmer-soldiers living under communal properties: "the army supplied in abundance men who were still young, accustomed to fatigue, acclimatized, having acquired a taste for the country, and brought up to work in the fields" (Bussière, 1853, p. 458).

When Bugeaud came to Algeria in 1841, he created a unitary military corp, made out of 4,000 men, with half of the lower ranks reserved for natives who could in principle advance to higher ranks. The first

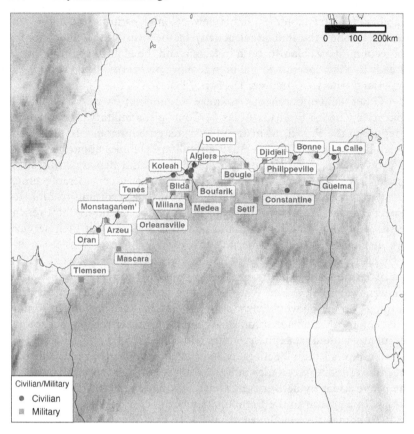

Figure 7.3 French military and civilian colonies in Algeria, 1844
Notes: Drawn based on data from Ministère de la Guerre (1845).

colonies of soldiers were created about 11km away from the city of Oran, in a settlement called Misserghin, where Bugeaud decided to create a fixed military establishment. In a letter to the French Ministry of War, dated November 1837, Bugeaud wrote that in Misserghin he saw "the foundations of a large village," because the settlement was "eminently favorable to the culture of orchards, trees, and also, that of cereals and herds; [...] officers could become owners of the house that they have built and to a certain extent, the adjacent territory" (Yver, 1924, pp. 259–260). Figure 7.3 depicts the main French civilian and military settlements in French Algeria in 1844. These were not stable over time, changing their status from military to civilian quickly.

Indigenous Soldiers in the French Algerian Army

Attempts to recruit soldiers for the military colonies in the empire existed since 1830 with the light infantry of local Kabyle populations and subsequently with the creation of Kabyle military hunters. The first indigenous military divisions appeared in Algiers, Oran, and Bonne. Yacono (1969) explains how according to an ordinance from September 10, 1834, four military squadrons were created with Lieutenant-Colonel Marey-Monge in the lead, a French official "passionate about the life of the indigenous society" (Yacono, 1969, p. 348). From the start, the French took into consideration both military and political aspects in Algeria. It was important for the French to reduce the number of locals who could fight against the imperial authorities through military recruitment, and to establish amicable relations with the local populations. One key aspect related to that is the careful selection of local leaders. For example, Eugène De Monglave, a writer and historian of the early nineteenth century, wrote in a magazine dedicated to French colonial affairs that: "the choice of *thaleb* or *marabout* summoned to run the school is of utmost importance. It is necessary to be under permanent surveillance without a doubt. Watch out for the fanatic! It is important to take precautions and select a man of ours, devoted to our interests, to France, sympathizing with the captain commander" (De Monglave, 1857, p. 148) (emphasis added). Similarly, there were attempts to recruit young men belonging to important indigenous families in exchange for the chance of advancing rapidly to positions of power (Yacono, 1969, p. 364).

Tribe leaders constituted the main way of recruiting locals. Despite occasionally questioning their loyalty, imperial authorities concluded that Algerian chiefs should not be replaced. Historical accounts from military colonels indicate that the French wanted to recruit not only people but also people with horses: for example, Colonel Randon (cited in Yacono (1969, p. 377)) mentioned some good results by "recruiting men with fairly good horses" in the province of Constantine, while in other provinces such as Algiers, the French had to accept "starving" locals. The imperial authorities were also in favor of setting up regimental schools where local spahis[11] could learn French and where French cadres could learn Arabic (Yacono, 1969, p. 354). Similarly, to further incentivize recruitment, the French offered perks to locals such as the possibility of retirement, promotion, and in isolated cases, horses.

---

[11] Spahis were light-cavalry regiments of the French army recruited primarily from the indigenous populations of Algeria, Tunisia, and Morocco. The word derives from the Ottoman word *sipahi*, which means "horsemen."

Finally, the French also decided to be less strict when it came to the military uniforms of the locals.

The basic demographic unit in the Kabyle military settlements was the "smala" or units of approximately 150 families. They were, according to French authorities of the time, areas of land in which native horsemen or spahis established tents for themselves, their families, and their herds. The lands would be cultivated by their children or their parents. The French authorities were very clear in indicating that land within smalas was not to be operated by the entire squadron, but rather, by individual families under a communal property regime. Within the smala, the role of the captain was very important. De Monglave (1857, p. 146) describes it in the following way: "In the garrison or on patrol, his authority only reaches the spahis, while in the smala, his influence goes beyond, to his extended family. This soldier, almost always rich, brings to the territory where the smala is set up, everything that belongs to him, his women, his children, his servants, his horses, his troops. Often his father, his mother, and his brothers, set up their tents near his and live with him as a family unit" (De Monglave, 1857, pp. 146–147). The smalas of spahis were the main method of fighting neighboring bellicose tribes, the most famous of whom were the ones led by Abdelkader. However, some of the smalas proved more effective than others. One of the inspector-generals from the 1860s mentioned how these groups performed the greatest services by surveilling the area along the border with Tunisia, which was populated by many "pillaging tribes" (Yacono, 1969, p. 376).

In subsequent years, multiple legal propositions were made to further regulate the activities of the spahis and Algerian locals more generally. For example, the Regulation of May 1, 1862, indicated that one smala of spahis could not consist of members pertaining to a single tribe while attempts should be made to include as many sons of Arab chiefs as possible within the French squadrons. Multiple articles within that Regulation also specified that French officers should learn Arabic and that they should be helped by military and civilian instructors to transform the smala into a flourishing economy. Children of spahis would receive an education, while the best ones would be admitted to the Arab College of Algiers.

There are few indications about the developmental effects of military colonialism in the French primary sources. This is not surprising, given the much more limited duration of such an institution. Nevertheless, Yacono (1969, p. 378) mentions the agricultural "backwardness" of the areas exposed to military colonialism as a result of a variety of factors. Such factors include lack of tools to be involved in agricultural production; a lack of interest in devoting oneself to agriculture; the limited concessions of land, which were sometimes less than ten hectares, sometimes six, instead of the fifteen or eighteen stipulated by the Regulations of 1862; limited availability of teachers passing on agricultural knowledge, etc. Similarly, Émerit also mentioned that many villages, originally assigned as military colonies, were "deprived of stimuli and ability to enjoy individual profit" (Émerit, 1959, p. 96). In order to remedy the problem to some extent, some of the inspector-generals recommended the settlement of more French families, which in addition to helping foster agricultural development through the transfer of knowledge to the local population would also prevent potential local rebellions.

This was particularly relevant after 1870s when local revolts broke out in Moudjbar, Bou Hadjar, El Tarf, and Aïn Guetta, culminating with the revolt of Mokrani of 1871 – the most important local uprising against France in Algeria since the conquest in 1830. The revolt included more than 250 tribes who rose up and who represented around a third of the population of the country. In order to prevent future rebellions, serious conversations emerged among the higher echelons of the imperial bureaucracy in Paris which focused on resettling families and, more importantly, eliminating the smalas, which were seen as culprits for the revolts (Yacono, 1969, pp. 381–382). As a result of these conversations, the smala ceased to claim the role of model farm for military colonists. In addition, the new military squadron would no longer receive land. Despite such changes in the legal language, the principle of farmer-soldier was maintained.

Exposure to violence in the military colonies seems to have been limited,[12] with most violence exerted by French imperial authorities as a result of disobedience. De Tocqueville (2000) also discusses violence in the French colonial context, his attitude ranging from a defense of the idea of violent submission of the locals in order to "establish a permanent French presence in Africa" (De Tocqueville, 2000, p. xxi) to an account emphasizing the need to contain the excesses of the army. The most famous violent episode in which the colonial French forces were involved is the Dahra cave massacre. Derrécagaix (1911, p. 174) describes it as an episode emulating a previous example of a cave asphyxiation. There was no way for the dissidents to face the French colonial forces in open combat. Therefore, they resorted to the last tactic available to them, which was known from the time of Ottoman rule – hiding in caves. Marshall Pélissier was ordered by Marshall Bugeaud to corall

[12] Arguing that violence has been limited is a comparative statement. When making this statement about Algeria, the point of comparison is Belgian Congo, which "had indeed seen a death toll of Holocaust dimensions" (Hochschild, 1999, pp. 3-4). Assessing the level of violence is important for applying the theoretical framework proposed in Chapter 2.

about 1,000 dissidents from Oulad-Riah and fill the caves with smoke. Clayton (1988, p. 21) explains how "fascines of burning faggots were rolled into the caves' entrances and internal explosions and roof collapses in the caves added to the horror." The news of the massacre reached Paris through a leak from the Ministry of War but the criticism was not loud enough to produce any change to the ways in which locals were treated.

While abundant historical sources exist for the colonization of French Algeria, the Habsburg and Russian military models were applied to other French colonies. In 1818 the French authorities recommended the employment in agriculture of soldiers who finished their terms in France for the colonization of Senegal,[13] following instructions from Colonel Julien Schmaltz (1771–1826). Even before Bugeaud, Schmaltz envisaged a system of small farms with part-time farmers and part-time soldiers who could sign on for fourteen years (Clayton, 1988) with a continuous supply of human resources from among the locals. The plan is described in detail by Schefer (1907):

The garrisons will be supplied initially with soldiers sent [from France], and then by indigenous troops, at least in part, commanded by white officers and sub-officers. This advantageous system which will ease the burden of European troops is highly encouraged. The moment our African colony develops and possesses, as we will see, the first pillars of our current empire, the Restoration government will create the instrument which will allow us to control this empire. The black auxiliary bodies have to form with time the majority of the public force in our establishments in Africa.[14] (Schefer, 1907, p. 208)

Schmalz's plans resulted in the formation of the *1er Bataillon du Sénégal* and later *1er Bataillon d'Afrique*. The two were mostly made up of locals after Paris refused to send any more metropolitan troops, knowing that they would fall victim to diseases. By 1822 about fifty concessions had been arranged with local chiefs according to Clayton (1988) but they were short-lived. Around 1830, the French settlements consisted of "a small group of villages around St. Louis, two up-river trading posts, one post in the Casamance and once on the Gambia river" (Clayton, 1988, p. 51).

The Restoration monarchy (1814–1830) also had expansionist ambitions in Madagascar. Similar to Senegal, there had been a historical French base in Fort Dauphin from 1643 to 1674, and an unsuccessful

---

[13] The French interests in Senegal had been there since the first half of the seventeenth century but they were limited to the coast. Small deployments of soldiers occurred in 1779 but they were unsuccessful as a result of local diseases (Clayton, 1988).

[14] Translation from French.

attempt at colonization in the 1780s. Therefore, past attempts at colonization motivated the French to try once again in the early nineteenth century. The French also wanted a stronger presence in Madagascar as a way to put pressure on the British sea routes to India. By 1819, three forts were established in Fort Dauphin, Titingue, and the island of Sainte Marie with help from metropolitan regiments. Constantly sending troops from France was, however, unsustainable. This is why on December 28, 1820 instructions were given to:

[...] create land for crops in the Sainte Marie island, to help the military colonists which were part of the expedition, to borrow or buy black workers from the local chiefs in Madagascar, and, in this latter case, declared free immediately in exchange for their services; to produce so-called colonial food for the indigenous people, or deliver this food on their own, or to produce food for the military colonists; to attract afterwards in Sainte Marie not only the free Bourbon population, but also other immigrants who would be helpful to call.[15] (Schefer, 1907, p. 217).

The military settlements under the communal property regime were short-lived in Africa – only about eighty years. They constituted, however, the start of the *Armée d'Afrique*, a term which today defines the portions of the French army recruited from French North Africa. The *Armée d'Afrique* would make considerable contributions to French campaigns in Crimea (1854–1856), Italy (1859), Mexico (1861–1867), Indochina (1859–1863), China (1860), and Levant (1860–1861) (Clayton, 1988).

The Habsburg military colony was not an isolated institution specific to the Habsburgs. It developed at the same time as the Russian military colonies and represented a model which the French emulated in many of their colonies in Africa including Algeria, Senegal, and Madagascar. In the Russian case, the Cossacks constituted a buffer population at the border with other empires including Poland-Lithuania and the Ottoman Empire from as early as the fifteenth century and represented an easy way to recruit manpower to fight any other type of Russian war. The colonies that were created in the early 1800s bear much closer resemblance to the Habsburg borderlands after Tsar Alexander I admitted the undeniable "glorious merits" of the military colonies in Austria (Desprez, 1847). Such merits included reducing military expenses, having a permanent place from which to levy army recruits, and having a group of army personnel who are always ready to act. The social engineering behind the Russian military communities also resembles the

---

[15] Translation from French.

Habsburgs, with Russian soldiers being forced to live with local farming families in the settlements designated to become colonies. Farmers would have to feed and generally support the soldiers while the latter would only use their time surplus to help their hosts with agricultural work. Equally, each family was allocated a plot of land which the imperial authorities deemed sufficient in order for individual communities to survive. The Russian military colonies were also different from the Habsburg ones in that the Russian Empire provided a modicum of public goods including education, roads, and investment in the overall public infrastructure.

The French also developed military colonies upon conquering Algeria in the early 1800s as a result of the many attacks by local tribes attacking French settlements. An analysis of the early political narratives surrounding the notion of military colonies reveals that the Habsburg and the Russian frontiers represented the model which the French attempted to emulate. Utilizing local populations entailed large reductions in military expenditures. Unlike the Habsburg and Russian imperial authorities, the French paid much closer attention to questions of loyalty, obedience, and preventing revolts. While around 1830 most of the military colonists were French, the imperial authorities initiated a strategy of incorporating many more locals into the colonies. Despite a large degree of social engineering including elevating the role of captains within local communities, the assignment of land to local families, and restrictions on the homogeneity of military colonies (i.e. preferring multiple different tribes to be part of the same colony as opposed to one single tribe), the French kept the tribe leaders in place as they were aware of their key role in liaising with the imperial authorities to the locals. There are some indications about the negative effects of military colonialism for the development of agriculture in the form of an inability of locals to enjoy individual profit (Émerit, 1959).

Together, the Russian and the French African examples show the wider significance of the Habsburg colonies demonstrating the processes of imperial incorporation, state-making, and the historical mechanisms by which they can leave an imprint of modern outcomes.

Epilogue

Social scientists typically describe the negative effects of colonialism for state and economic development. While many historical episodes do point in a direction which emphasizes oppression and extractivism, some empirical cases indicate that colonialism may not always be associated with negative outcomes. These contradictory results constituted the puzzle behind this project: when is extractivism associated with long-term negative versus positive outcomes? Therefore, in this project I pursued a mode of inquiry focusing on when, how, and why colonialism can affect long-term development.

The question emerged after examining an unlikely contender for an extractive institution: a place situated in Europe which Hechter (1975) or Scott (2010) would potentially label as a case of "internal colonialism," given its geographic proximity to the seat of power. This is the Habsburg military frontier which existed between 1553 and 1881. This place featured institutions which are reminiscent of extractivism like the utilization of local labor force without adequate compensation. At the same time, it was different from typical examples of extractivism in the sense that nothing specific was being extracted (e.g. no crops and no minerals). In order to make sense of the case, I proposed a more capacious conceptualization of extractive institutions in which I separated the process of extractivism from its outcome. As I have shown in Chapter 7, this imperial model is far from being a small isolated institution, specific to the Habsburgs. Military colonialism was a practice which many historical states adopted for cheap recruitment of military manpower and for the defense of the border.

The Russian and the French Algerian military colonies demonstrate that the analysis of the Habsburg frontier has wider significance for the way we understand notions of imperialism, extractivism, and historical legacies. Given their location at the periphery of empires, such cases also force us to rethink border- and state-making. Military colonies are spaces of negotiated sovereignty between the capital and borderland dwellers, who become incorporated into the state as a result of their "web-like" structures (Migdal, 1988). In this book, I investigated at length how such structures which pre-date the state get to be incorporated into the imperial fabric, how they are adopted, repurposed, and how they become part of a new system of rule. The historical strategies of border- and state-making subsequently shaped notions of imperial subjectivity in both inclusive and exclusive terms.

While there are some undeniably negative outcomes associated with extractivism as Chapter 4 demonstrated in the case of military colonies, it is also equally important to examine how imperial institutions continue and potentially reinforce structures already in place during imperial times. Therefore, a major part of this project was also dedicated to historical legacies: understanding how old power structures perpetuate over time, what historical socio-economic processes they unveil after their abrogation, and how they affect the norms and behavior of individuals exposed to them over time. The comprehensive survey of primary and secondary sources and the quantitative analyses based on censuses together with never-before-seen cartographic representations of such data contribute to the aim of providing an accurate picture of imperial borderlands, hoping to be part of a new historical scholarly wave characterized by the adoption of "creative transnational and interdisciplinary approaches to studying the empire" (Judson, 2016, p. 11).

Overview

The book offered a series of cross-disciplinary insights relevant to political science, history, economics, and sociology. Such insights are about state-making, extractive institutions, historical legacies, and Habsburg history.

A major contribution of this book was to develop a coherent theoretical framework explaining the modus operandi of extractive institutions and to describe how they affect the lives of the people exposed to them and those of their descendants. To restate my claims, extractive institutions can affect long-term development through three distinct mechanisms which are part of the process of extraction: historical investment in infrastructure, which can create the basic conditions for subsequent development, changes in the property rights regime, which can further bolster or restrict individual incentives to invest and reap the benefits of one's own labor, and exposure to violence, which can have a detrimental impact on social capital with long-term consequences for development. The worst cases for development are cases where the three meet in one coherent "institutional treatment." Two additional features are equally important. These are the "longevity" and "consistency" of treatment. In order for the effects of violence, removal of property rights, and under-investment in infrastructure to be visible, they need to have lasted for a long time. Absence of property rights for a century should have more of an impact in the long run compared to absence of property rights for a decade. Equally, in order for a historical effect to be seen, it is important for that historical treatment to be uniformly applied and not combined with other treatments or to have periods in which it is applied and periods in which it is not.

I have interpreted the Habsburg military colony as an instance of extractivism and I have described how the institution came about in the sixteenth century as a result of Ottoman attacks. In Chapter 3, I described how the local nobility exerted pressure on the Austrian kings to deploy military troops in the area that is today Croatia and Hungary to protect their lands. This pressure resulted in 1552 in the deployment of military forces who gradually transformed into permanent settlers and who would defend the border in times of need and be involved in agriculture in other times. The costs for supporting the colonies were originally covered by both the landed elites and the imperial coffers while their inhabitants became self-sufficient in subsequent centuries. The sixteenth century is also the time when clear divisions were made between the military and the civilian side of the Habsburg Empire. On the civilian side, the Habsburg Empire continued to share power with the landowners and the Church, while the administration on the military side was appointed by either the king or the nobles.

Land was the main way for the Habsburgs to incentivize the military colonists to stay. People in the Habsburg frontier were escaping the shackles of serfdom to a place where they would receive a plot of land which they could enjoy with their family in exchange for military service. Additional perks included the ability to share booty from the enemy and the ability to choose their own leaders. The military administration of the military colony changed with time. It became more bureaucratized after 1630 with the creation of the War Council in Vienna responsible for proposing generals for the military colony and the administration of justice.

The Habsburg frontier changed its shape with time as the Habsburg territory expanded or contracted. In 1699 it advanced eastward with places that are today in Serbia and Romania becoming part of it. The military frontier also had an important role in preventing the spread of plague starting in 1750 and ending in 1857. Historical documents indicate that the military colony received few public goods from the state. As some of the primary documents suggest, people in the military colony had few schools, had restrictions in place when it came to the expansion of trade and industry, and had few roads. Official documentation from the eighteenth century suggests that any laxity when it comes to those factors (i.e. government investment) would contribute to the desire of the colonists to elevate their status. Multiple subsequent reforms tried to address the asymmetry in development between the civilian and military regions but unsuccessfully.

The last vestiges of the military colonies could be seen at the end of the nineteenth century. First, the military section in Transylvania was abolished in 1859, followed by the Serbian one in 1873, and finally the Croatian one in 1881. The Croatian section of the military frontier provided me with a unique opportunity to investigate the long-term consequences of exposure to such a historical institution. As already mentioned, the case features two important mechanical conditions which make it ideal for tracing legacies: the first condition that is met is that the Croatian section was exposed to military colonialism for over three hundred years; the second condition is that military colonialism was homogeneously enforced, unlike the Transylvanian and the Serbian sections, which were combined with civilian districts.

Historical data allowed me to demonstrate in Chapter 4 some of the socio-economic processes which outlived the military colony. Despite its formal abolition, parts of what was originally the "historical treatment" continued to exist after 1881. An analysis of data measuring land zcu ownership patterns suggested that low land inequality was much more prevalent in the former military colony compared to the civilian area. This was reflected in the higher percentage of landowners with over 100 acres of land, lower percentage of domestic workers, and the higher percentage of small agricultural holders. Such results are not surprising given that large landowners were never permitted to re-emerge. A similar analysis with data from other censuses revealed that communal property rights were also much more prevalent in the first decades after the abrogation of the military colony, which is consistent with the idea of the family clan being the main demographic unit within the military frontier. A variety of historical and modern data capturing access to public goods also indicate that the former military colony continued to have lower railroad and road density, lower access to hospitals, and lower access to sanitation. The pattern of lower access to public goods remained unaltered during the time of the Kingdom of Croatia (1881–1918), Yugoslavia (1918–1945), and communist Yugoslavia (1945–1992) and is also visible today in Croatia.

Family clans were a key component of the military frontier. In Chapter 5, I described how local elites and family clan leaders became part of the state-building project. Family clans existed even before the emergence of the Habsburg Empire as a hegemonic power in the region, but these were adopted for convenience by the imperial authorities:

people could support one another more effectively in the periphery by living in family clans while the whole system was conducive to military obedience. The latter was largely achieved through the collaboration between the military authorities and clan leaders who were the keepers of legitimate politics and justice. They were the ones to receive printed booklets listing the size of the plot of land that they owned, together with the number of days that they owed to the state. In Chapter 5, I described the inner workings of a family clan with an eye on depicting customs and mores which might be related to individual cognitions and attitudes in the long run. In the 1930s, family clans, while on the brink of extinction, still existed. They (still) displayed a strict hierarchy based on sex and age. This was reflected in the household division of labor and the way property was bequeathed. Extensive family clans should be the equivalent of what some neo-Toquevelians would describe as "rich associational life," promoting civicness and good governance (Putnam, 2000; Putnam *et al.*, 1993). I also contended that family clans missed one key ingredient which is relevant for them to lead to positive outcomes: individuals within family clans were not equal. In other words, family clan members lived in communities with high vertical hierarchies, especially based on age and sex.

Family clans lasted much longer in the former military colony. Their longer persistence turned into individual cognitions which are likely the last remnants of the three-hundred-year-old Habsburg institution. In Chapter 6, I tested empirically the persistence of attitudes and norms, using modern data following the Modern Political Economy tradition. The results indicated that people in the former military colony trust their families more and trust other people less. This is consistent with the logic of the importance of the family unit. I also found that in 2016 there was a higher incidence of corruption, which is likely associated with the higher trust in one's family. Trust and supporting one's family could also have meant a higher likelihood of hiring relatives and close friends regardless of their merits and abilities, which according to previous literatures can play a vital role in the development of pervasive corruption (Stinchfield, 2013). I also showed that the variety of rules and regulations governing the colonists' lives likely resulted in more risk aversion. Attitudes toward women which were visible in the 1930s when it comes to inheritance continue to be visible today: people in the former military colony are more likely to agree that men make better leaders and that women should do the household chores. Finally, I have also shown that the descendants of the military colonists are less likely to be involved in particular kinds of political activities including signing petitions and participating in demonstrations. This goes against the predictions by Putnam that a rich associational life is necessarily associated with more "civicness."

The attitudes that were instilled during the institution of military colonialism are likely to have been transmitted over time through inter-generational transmission. Children get to learn about the world and how they should relate to it from their parents. They subsequently update their beliefs based on their lived experience. Suggestive empirical evidence from cohort analyses confirmed stronger beliefs that were associated with military colonialism among older generations. Specifically, older generations have stronger in-out group biases compared to younger generations and are more likely to think that they need to offer bribes to get benefits. While these results may not simply capture the effect of the institution which ceased to exist in 1881, they provide some evidence for the waning effect of attitudes and norms.

The theoretical framework in this book applies to extractive institutions more generally. This could be the extraction of minerals or crops, or the simple extraction of human resources for the variety of projects defined by the empire. Yet, to further illustrate an institution which received very little attention in the social sciences, I continued to focus on military colonialism in the Russian Empire and in the French African colonies. In Chapter 7, I described the role of the Cossacks, a warrior population that was deployed throughout the territory of the Russian Empire from as early as the fifteenth century and ending in the twentieth century. Cossacks were used by the tsars as a buffer zone against neighboring enemies including the Ottomans, Poland-Lithuania, Tatars, the Chinese, etc. They also had a special role within Russia, being freed from serfdom and enjoying property rights, unlike all the other serfs in the empire. I then continued to describe the military colonies which were created in what is today Ukraine and parts of Belarus in the early 1800s for the purpose of potentially replacing the entire Russian army (Ybert-Chabrier, 2004). The types of settlements were very similar to the ones in the Habsburg colony. People lived under communal property rights, and depending on where they were (whether closer to the capital or not), they benefited from some infrastructural investment. There are limited historical accounts about the exertion of violence.

The Habsburg and Russian military colonies constituted models for the military settlements in North Africa under French rule. Military colonies were created to ensure the security of the new French civilian settlements, which continued to be attacked by hostile tribes in the early 1800s. They consisted of both French and indigenous troops. The recruitment of the locals into the French military settlements was very carefully choreographed, with indigenous elites at intermediate levels of authority and with French troops at the top. Leaving some of the local elite chiefs in charge proved problematic as some revolted against the imperial authorities. In a very similar way to the Russian and Habsburg ones, military colonies in Algeria enjoyed communal property rights and had limited investment in infrastructure compared to their civilian counterparts. There is also minimal historical documentation about the use of violence. The adoption of military colonies by a sea-based empire such as France demonstrates the viability of the comparison between sea-based and land-based empires. As the example of military colonialism suggests, some of the hierarchies created between the center and the periphery established overseas have their roots in Europe, which is why the in-depth analysis of the Habsburg military colony and its legacies has important lessons to teach us about imperial rule, institutions, and imperial legacies.

Implications for Other Literatures

The book contributes to the historiography of the Habsburg Empire, to comparative-historical studies on imperialism and state formation, and to research on historical legacies. In the final section, I also reflect on the way we should be thinking about the effects of colonialism.

The Institutional Diversity within the Habsburg Empire

This book contributes to the historical literature on the Habsburg Empire by emphasizing the important legacies of an institution which is well documented in the older regional historiographies but which has eluded generations of historical scholars. It emphasizes how the institutional practices (including property rights, low land inequality, and family clans) helped shape local society in a way that is still visible after these institutions were no longer in place, and whose remains can still be seen today.

Many studies of Central and Eastern Europe have investigated the region as an exceptional place due to its ethnic and religious heterogeneity, but also due to its so-called "backward" economic development (Chirot, 1989). These studies resulted (sometimes unintentionally) in further solidifying the difference between East and West, and reinforcing the sense of normalcy in the West (Judson, 2016; Todorova, 1997; Wolff, 1994). This trend has become apparent again in the recent literature marking the centenary of the outbreak of World War I (Deak, 2014), pathologizing the Austro-Hungarian Empire and suggesting that it was bound to collapse as a result of its ethnic heterogeneity and nationalist conflict.

This trend is in the spirit of the large literature emerging after the collapse of the empire in 1918 which focused on the idea of nationhood (Deak, 2014) and how economic nationalism stood in the way of rebuilding or preserving the trade cooperation among the Habsburg successor states (Hertz, 1925; Jánossy, 2016; Lang, 1934; Pasvolsky, 1928). Nationalist economic policies[1] were unable to facilitate the restructuring that the postwar situation demanded (Berend, 1998; Mosser and Teichova, 1991). The focus on nationhood and economic nationalism pervaded public debates in the twentieth century, which is why, not surprisingly, they left an imprint on both public and academic discourses about the Habsburg monarchy.

Very few works focused on the connection between Habsburg institutions and economic development. The few works that focused on institutions typically examined the institutional drivers of nationalism. For example, works from the 1980s such as the ones by Cohen (1980) and Boyer (1980) investigated socio-political phenomena in Prague and Vienna respectively, attempting to find connections between nationhood and specific Habsburg institutions.[2] Similarly, work in German interrogated the multifaceted ways in which the Habsburg Empire dealt with religious diversity within its realm when it comes to education, legal matters, and census-making (Brix, 1982; Burger, 1995; Stourzh, 1985). These scholars showed how the administration of the empire helped shore up nationalist efforts.

When it comes to borders, the historical literature focused much more on the external borders of the Habsburg Empire (Bérenger, 2013, 2014; Hochedlinger, 2003; Kann, 1957), especially the new demarcating lines included in the peace treaties in the aftermath of World War I, and focused much less on the internal borders of the Habsburg monarchy such as the older lines of separation formed around the military colonies. A study of the Habsburg periphery, as this book demonstrated, revealed interesting processes of both border- and state-making that proved apposite for explaining regional economic growth. In this book, I attempted to go beyond the concept of "backwardness" by offering an in-depth analysis of the social, political, and cultural development of an

---

[1] For example the Romanian, Yugoslav, and Bulgarian governments tended to favor national firms, which came at a considerable cost for the consumer and for the large agricultural sector. In Hungary, such a policy was less extreme, but still had a negative impact on trade and agriculture (Feinstein *et al.*, 2008). Czechoslovakia, despite being one of the highly industrialized places of the former empire, was also affected given its dependence on export markets and the new wave of protectionism within Europe. Poland had a similar fate with fewer markets to export its products to (Feinstein *et al.*, 2008, p. 33).

[2] According to Cohen (1980), national identification was much more contingent on the presence of institutions which would promote such identification. In the case of Germans in Bohemia, these were the dense networks of associations. Boyer (1980) focuses on the emergence of the Social Christian movement as a result of the particularities of the franchise system whereby political power was held by the middle socio-economic groups of Viennese society in the second half of the nineteenth century.

under-explored institution by uncovering a closely connected dialectic between the capital and the self-governed, self-sufficient spaces on the frontier. Communal properties, low land inequality, and family clans are all important institutional components of the monarchy. Such insights add to a more nuanced understanding of the Habsburg borderlands, contributing therefore to the historiography of the Habsburg Empire.

The Tripartite Nature of Extractive Institutions

In showing that extractive institutions can have different modes of operation in ways that are consequential for development, the book contributes to the wide range of studies on imperialism, state formation, and development, in some instances supporting previous findings, while in others providing new insights. For example, the findings are compatible with classic studies by Polanyi (1957) or Wallerstein (1966) in claiming that imperialism caused dramatic transformations which shaped subsequent developmental trajectories. They are also similar to studies investigating the historical causes behind diverging economic pathways as a result of different colonial experiences (Acemoğlu et al., 2001; Kohli, 2004, 2020; Mahoney, 2010). The evidence included in this book demonstrated how states adopt social structures which predate them, how they reproduce over extended periods, and how they become difficult to change. I also tried to move away from the existing literature by arguing that historical empires can affect their successor states in multifaceted ways.

In my theoretical framework, I attempted to interrogate the monolithical mutually exclusive concepts proposed by Acemoğlu et al. (2001), who built on the previous work by North (1990), arguing that the key determinants for long-run development or under-development are protection of property rights and extractive institutions respectively. In the theoretical framework proposed in this book, I described how property rights can in fact be a subset of extractive institutions, by arguing that the extractive goals of the empire can dictate the type of property regime in place. I also went further and unpacked the notion of property rights following the terminology proposed by Schlager and Ostrom (1992), who discuss the right to access, withdraw, manage, exclude, and alienate property. Therefore, I investigated the circumstances under which they can be problematic for development. Communal properties, in the case of all the military colonies described in this book, are cases in which individuals could access, withdraw, and manage, but could not exclude and alienate property. The lack of imperial infrastructural investment and exerting violence onto locals are additional forces which set the developmental trajectory of the military colony on a negative path.

A plethora of studies have investigated how extractive institutions have a negative impact on development, yet few examined the forces behind them that make them problematic. For example, Mahoney (2010) discusses the ambivalent nature of Spanish imperial legacies in Latin America and explores the diverging trajectories of fifteen countries when it comes to present-day development praxis. The argument focuses on the asymmetric way in which colonial institutions allocated resources in ways that were systematically uneven. During its mercantilist phase, Spain settled and heavily colonized places with complex indigenous societies such as the Aztec, Inca, and Aymara empires, which already had developed coercive systems in place for rapid resource extraction. According to Mahoney (2010), it is the *hierarchy of power* and, more generally, patron–client relationships which are a remnant of extractive institutions, and which negatively affected development. His account, however, is difficult to apply in other places where, despite the hierarchies of power, the economies thrived. These are places like Dutch Indonesia where the Dutch invested heavily in local infrastructure including roads and railroads in order to transport extracted crops to the ports. Other cases are the Japanese in Taiwan, who also made extensive investments in the construction of large-scale sugar-processing infrastructure. The British colonial government also established tea and jute plantations in India together with extensive networks of processing plants. Despite the clear and undeniable hierarchies of power of such extractivist experiences, historical investment in infrastructure likely contributed to set the basis for subsequent developmental patterns. For the investment in roads and railroads, this would mean decreasing trade costs, reducing inter-regional price gaps, and increasing real incomes. Therefore, including infrastructural investment within the notion of extractive institutions can help us better understand historical trajectories.

I also argued that the use of violence, which is one key mode of operation of extractive institutions, could have an impact on development. A few studies have investigated the effects of colonial historical violence on long-term development (e.g. Nunn and Wantchekon (2011) or Lowes and Montero (2021)). According to this research, the source of violence matters. If the source is within society, as documented by Nunn and Wantchekon (2011), people end up trusting each other less and become less politically engaged. This should have an indirect effect on economic development, in that the exposure to violence from within the community should reduce "civicness" with nefarious repercussions for development (Putnam, 2000; Putnam *et al.*, 1993). If the source of violence is outside the community such as in the case of Belgian Congo

(Lowes and Montero, 2021), the result should be a more cohesive community, but which is likely politically disarticulated. Such insights are further echoed by the literature which focuses on the formative role of violence in political development (Balcells, 2012; Kalyvas, 2006). By including violence in the theoretical framework, we can have a better grasp of the long-term legacies of imperialism when it comes to individual attitudes and norms.

Historical Processes and Individual-Level Cognitions

The book also contributes to a more fine-grained understanding about how historical institutions impact the present or the mechanisms of transmission. This is consistent with scholarly views contending that in order to provide insights with a higher degree of external validity into the effect of historical imperialism, it is relevant to consider a "broad range of institutions and their associated organizations, including *political arrangements* (e.g., forms of government, policing units, and courts), *modes of economic activity* (e.g., labor systems, trade policies, and types of agriculture), and *sociocultural conventions* (e.g., religious doctrines, entertainment venues, and family structure)" (Mahoney, 2010, p. 23) (emphases added). Scholars in economics were also of the opinion that mechanisms of long-term persistence are likely to involve both formal institutions and cognitions (Alesina and Giuliano, 2015; Greif, 1994; Nunn, 2009).

The analytical framework in this book was inspired by the two dominant intellectual orientations described by Simpser *et al.* (2018): Comparative Historical Analysis and Modern Political Economy. I tried to reconcile the two views in this project by discussing and analyzing both the path-dependent conjunctural socio-economic processes which resulted after the abrogation of the Habsburg frontier and the micro-level cognitions that persisted within the minds of the inhabitants and those of their descendants.

Within the first tradition, the two socio-economic processes which I discussed at length are low land inequality and communal properties. Results obtained from analyses using censuses of the Habsburg successor states indicated that both were much more prevalent on the territory of the former military colony. These were at the core of the institution of military colonialism, in charge of shaping the so-called "state-society relations" (Migdal, 1988): low land inequality represents the product of the elimination of landed elites that took place with the creation of the institution in 1553. Landed elites did not exist at any point until the elimination of the institution. Similarly, communal properties were in place before the emergence of the Habsburg Empire: pastoral economies survived when multiple families congregated and supported each other. These were conveniently adopted by the Habsburgs. Their adoption meant fewer expenses from the center and a greater ability to penetrate society for the purpose of creating obedient subjects ready to defend the empire whenever necessary.

Within the second tradition, I attempted to focus on some of the attitudes and cultural norms that were inculcated by such historical exposure and which might be visible over time. Accounts from travelers to the military colony mostly in the nineteenth century were invaluable to depict specific norms and attitudes which existed during the time of the "historical treatment." Travelers mentioned the importance of family hierarchy for the people in the area, obedience toward military authorities, but also poverty. Subsequent anthropological accounts of the twentieth century were even more informative to get to know the type of "cognitions" that persisted with family clans. The survey of the relevant anthropological historical literature was motivated by my previous finding that family clans were much more likely to exist in what used to be the Habsburg frontier. Such accounts indicated again strict hierarchies based on age and sex which were reflected in everyday interaction and in the way in which inheritance was bequeathed, with women being much less likely to inherit valuable assets. The same anthropological accounts suggested that such attitudes were also waning in the 1930s. To investigate whether such attitudes persisted to the present day, I performed statistical analyses using modern surveys. As already mentioned, people today (likely descendants of the military colonists) trust their family more, trust strangers less, think that they often have to bribe the authorities, are more risk-averse, are less likely to get involved politically, and have views that reflect traditional gender roles. There is limited evidence for a higher respect for authority.

Together, the findings about the socio-economic processes and the individual-level cognitions provide a fuller, fine-grained understanding about how historical institutions can impact the present, with a view to appreciate political orders which "continue to cut deep in places that have yet to escape the [. . .] imperialist yoke" (Simpser et al., 2018, p. 435).

As a last word, it is worth returning to the difficult question of legacies of imperialism for development. As I have already explained, I have started by problematizing the notion that imperialism always has negative consequences for development, being informed by recent findings in the economics literature. As the case of military colonialism has shown, historical imperialist practices can indeed have negative consequences, contributing to what is now commonly regarded as conventional wisdom. But what is more important is understanding the history of the institutions responsible for such patterns, and ascertaining how they trickle down over time and the mechanisms by which they get to have an effect on the present. Some of these institutions are part of historical state-making processes which include vernacular political structures to define imperial projects which last for centuries.

The case of military colonialism provides once again lessons that economic hierarchies created in the era of imperialism cannot be easily changed. Simple policies on the supply side seem to be insufficient to address the economic inequalities which have been in place for a long time. While it is difficult to predict the extent to which citizens can produce sweeping transformations, some grass-root involvement in policy-making will likely yield beneficial results. Territories which used to be imperial borderlands might see a reversal in fortunes with enough citizen participation in a process that is antithetical to past colonialism.

Appendix A   Supplement for Chapter 4

This chapter is a technical appendix to Chapter 4. I present the statistical results in a tabular format that constituted the basis for the results in Chapter 4. The tables offer more extensive details compared to the coefficient plots or the regression discontinuity graphs, including the mean, standard deviation of the main variables of interest, standard errors, R squared, and the size and significance of the Moran's I residual, where applicable.

Regression Discontinuity Assumptions

The key identifying assumption is that all relevant factors besides treatment vary smoothly at the boundary (Keele and Titiunik, 2015, p. 130). That is, letting c_1 and c_0 denote potential outcomes under treatment and control, x denote longitude, and y denote latitude, identification requires that $E[c_1|x,y]$ and $E[c_0|x,y]$ are continuous at the discontinuity threshold. This assumption is necessary for observations located just across the Habsburg civilian side of the boundary to be an appropriate counterfactual for observations located just across the Habsburg military colony. To assess the plausibility of this assumption, Table A.1 examines the following important geographic characteristics: elevation, slope, annual average temperature, annual average level of precipitation, maize suitability (as an example of a crop relevant for the area), kilometers of river, and density of rivers (length of river divided by the area of the municipality).

To be conservative, I treat municipalities as independent observations, as the use of spatially correlated standard errors tends to increase their magnitude (Dell *et al.*, 2018). Columns (1) and (2) of Table A.1 examine elevation and slope, respectively. The point estimates on the military colony side are higher than the mean and statistically insignificant. Columns (3) and (4) show that temperature and precipitation are overall balanced, with a slight difference in temperature but very small compared to the mean. Column (5) documents that suitability for maize is similar on both sides of the boundary. Columns (6) and

Table A.1 *Covariate balance – Geography and historical economic activity*

	Dependent variable								
	Elevation	Slope	Avg. Temperature	Avg. Precipitation	Maize Suitability	Total River Length in km	River Density	Trade Route Density 1450	No. of Trade Centers 1450
	(1)	(2)	(3)	(4)	(5)	(6)	(7)	(8)	(9)
Military Territory	66.542	0.272	−0.420***	4.297	−1,766.755	16.044	56.034*	−0.008	0.003
	(50.589)	(0.331)	(0.151)	(2.729)	(1,382.238)	(14.594)	(33.187)	(0.007)	(0.013)
Mean	211.316	1.477	11.277	112.664	24,569.884	36.719	338.383	0.015	0.005
SD	176.607	1.626	1.074	27.975	5,781.174	51.8	164.846	0.041	0.07
Boundary FE	Yes	Yes	Yes	Yes	Yes	Yes	Yes	Yes	Yes
Region FE	Yes	Yes	Yes	Yes	Yes	Yes	Yes	Yes	Yes
Observations	402	402	399	399	402	402	402	402	402
Adjusted R²	0.327	0.516	0.495	0.872	0.359	0.213	0.117	0.062	0.002

Notes: Coefficients and municipality (opcina) clustered robust standard errors in parentheses from OLS regression. *p<0.1; **p<0.05; ***p<0.01. The unit of analysis is municipality (opcina). See codebook in the appendix for data sources and how the variables were calculated.

(7) indicate that river length flowing through each municipality and river density are balanced, with a slight difference in river density, but very small compared to the mean. Columns (8) and (9) examine the two economic indicators prior to the establishment of the military colony – trade route density and trade center count. Therefore, overall geography and economic factors prior to the establishment of the military colony are balanced. The changes in public goods provision are likely due to political institutions established by the Habsburgs.

An additional assumption that is made in RD designs is no selective sorting across the treatment threshold. This would be violated if individuals with particular traits that are conducive to the provision of public goods and prosperity were more likely to move to one side of the border, leading to a larger indirect effect on public goods. In other words, military colonists might have migrated precisely to escape poverty and low provision of public goods.

In order to provide additional supporting evidence for the assumption of no selective sorting, I also use historical and modern census data on migration patterns. Table A.2 displays the differences in the percentage of out-migrants in 1857 (based on the Austrian Ministry of Internal Affairs (1859)), 1944 (based on a 1944 Catholic parish census – Draganović (1939)), and the net migration rate in 2011 (based on the Croatian Bureau of Statistics (2017)). For 2011, I calculate the net migration rate using the following formula: $1000 \times (I - E) / P$, where I represents the number of people immigrating into the country; E – the number of people emigrating out of the country; and P – the estimated mid-year population. The number of observations differs for the different sources because the units of analysis are different. The unit of analysis for the 1857 census can be city or district (*stadt* or *land bezirke*). The unit of analysis for the 1944 Catholic parish census is parish (*župa*), and given its granularity, it was aggregated at the level of 2011 municipality. Finally, the unit of analysis for the 2011 census is municipality (*općina*).

Migration and sorting along ethnic lines are also unlikely. Historical sources indicate that in the civilian area and in the military colony, people "profess the same beliefs, they speak the same language [. . .] only the population density is higher there [in the military area] and people are more superstitious there, because ignorance is more widespread there" (Perrot, 1869, p. 65). More generally, according to Perrot (1869), the slight differences between the military confines and the civilian area have nothing to do with geography or with people's "races and ethnicities," but rather with the particular institutional conditions that made the military colony different.

In order to further check potential sorting along ethnic lines, I digitized and geolocated a variety of historical and modern censuses:

Table A.2 *Modern and historical selective migration*

	Dependent variable		
	Pct. Out-Migration 1857	Pct. Out-Migration 1944	Net Migration Rate 2011
	(1)	(2)	(3)
Military Territory	1.660	−0.329	−0.211*
	(1.126)	(1.150)	(0.126)
Mean	3.431	3.478	−1.303
SD	3.347	8.802	8.802
Boundary FE	Yes	Yes	Yes
Region FE	Yes	Yes	Yes
Observations	86	313	392
Adjusted R^2	0.088	0.325	0.355

Notes: Coefficients and County clustered robust standard errors in parentheses from OLS regression. *$p<0.1$; **$p<0.05$; ***$p<0.01$. The unit of analysis for the 1857 census can be city or district (stadt) or (land bezirke). The unit of analysis for the 1944 Catholic parish census is parish (zupa) and the unit of analysis for the 2011 census is municipality (opcina). See codebook in the appendix for data sources and how the variables were calculated.

1921 (Yugoslavia Opšta Državna Statistika, 1932), 1931 (Kraljevina Jugoslavija Opsta Državna Statistika, 1940), 1991 (Republika Hrvatska Republicki Zavod Za Statistiku, 1992), 2001, and 2011 (Croatian Bureau of Statistics censuses for 2001 and 2011). The unit of analysis for 1921 is municipality (*opština*) and for 1931 canton (*srez*). For the 1991 census, I aggregated all the 6,694 settlements to the level of 2011 municipalities. While ethnic identity is still important today (being a Serb or being a Croat), the difference in concentration of Serbs and Croats is not statistically different. The percentage of Croats and Serbs in 1921, 1931, 1991, 2001, and 2011 is balanced on the two sides, as illustrated in Tables A.3 and A.4.

Access to Public Goods: Modern and Historical

In this section, I present the results for access to roads and railroads in a tabular format, as shown in Figure 4.6 of the main chapter. The results in columns 1 through 8 show the density of roads and railroads during the existence of the military colony and in the period immediately after the abolition of the military colony, density of roads under communism, and density of roads in modern times. The results confirm indeed that municipalities in the former military colony, on average, had lower access to roads and railroads.

Table A.3 *Historical and modern selective migration by Serbs*

	Dependent variable					
	1921	1931	1991	2001	Change '91–'01	2011
	(1)	(2)	(3)	(4)	(5)	(6)
Military Territory	3.355	4.969	1.805	−1.119	1.795	−0.507
	(3.222)	(5.607)	(2.611)	(2.611)	(1.506)	(2.067)
Mean	19.54	19.112	11.232	5.986	-5.606	6.068
SD	29.782	29.135	20.474	13.732	11.422	14.42
Boundary FE	Yes	Yes	Yes	Yes	Yes	Yes
Region FE	Yes	Yes	Yes	Yes	Yes	Yes
Observations	514	563	425	418	414	423
Adjusted R^2	0.253	0.253	0.350	0.189	0.430	0.200

Notes: Coefficients and robust standard errors in parentheses from OLS regression. *p<0.1; **p<0.05; ***p<0.01. The units of analysis are settlements for the corresponding censuses. See codebook in the appendix for data sources and how the variables were calculated.

Table A.4 *Historical and modern selective migration by Croats*

	Dependent variable					
	1921	1931	1991	2001	Change '91–'01	2011
	(1)	(2)	(3)	(4)	(5)	(6)
Military Territory	−3.331	−4.346	−2.051	1.301	1.795	0.727
	(3.357)	(5.959)	(2.933)	(2.933)	(1.506)	(2.067)
Mean	76.721	77.518	78.696	87.53	9.182	87.457
SD	31.058	30.249	24.29	17.045	12.466	17.657
Boundary FE	Yes	Yes	Yes	Yes	Yes	Yes
Region FE	Yes	Yes	Yes	Yes	Yes	Yes
Observations	514	563	425	418	414	423
Adjusted R^2	0.231	0.255	0.397	0.291	0.430	0.318

Notes: Coefficients and robust standard errors in parentheses from OLS regression. *p<0.1; **p<0.05; ***p<0.01. The units of analysis are settlements for the corresponding censuses. See codebook in the appendix for data sources and how the variables were calculated.

To further show the persistence in the asymmetry of access to public goods, I use data from the former Yugoslavia. Table A.6 investigates differences related to access to hospitals, based on data from Socijalistička Federativna Republika Jugoslavija Savezni Zavod Za Statistiku (1967, 1973). Children are less likely to be born in hospital and pregnancies

Table A.5 *Historical roads and railroads, 1869–2017*

				Dependent variable				
	Railroad Density 1869	Planned Railroad Density 1869	Planned Railroad Density 1884	Thoroughfare Density 1940	Asphalt Road Density 1957	Good Road Density 1957	Residential Road Density 2017	Road Track Density 2017
	(1)	(2)	(3)	(4)	(5)	(6)	(7)	(8)
Military Territory	−0.009***	−0.011*	−0.009*	−0.021***	−0.011*	−0.014**	−0.148***	−0.123**
	(0.003)	(0.006)	(0.005)	(0.007)	(0.006)	(0.007)	(0.046)	(0.059)
Mean	0.007	0.022	0.023	0.047	0.026	0.036	0.439	0.685
SD	0.03	0.049	0.055	0.084	0.075	0.063	0.726	0.665
Boundary FE	Yes	Yes	Yes	Yes	Yes	Yes	Yes	Yes
Region FE	Yes	Yes	Yes	Yes	Yes	Yes	Yes	Yes
Moran eigenvectors	Yes	Yes	Yes	Yes	Yes	Yes	Yes	Yes
Moran's I Residual	−2.323	−2.841	−1.64	−2.354	−2.507	−2.687	−2.708	−2.187
Observations	402	402	402	402	402	402	402	402
Adjusted R²	0.383	0.445	0.298	0.362	0.496	0.355	0.435	0.787

Notes: Coefficients and robust standard errors in parentheses from OLS regression. *p<0.1; **p<0.05; ***p<0.01. The unit of analysis is the 2011 municipality. Data is based on Unknown Author (1869, 1884), Generalstab des Heeres, Abt. für Kriegskarten und Vermessungswesen (1940), Bohinec and Planina (1957), and Open Street Maps. Every regression includes the following covariates: a linear polynomial in latitude and longitude, distance to Zagreb, and boundary segment FE.

Table A.6 *Births and access to hospitals for women, 1964–1970*

	Dependent variable:					
	Pct. Born Hospital 1964	Pct. w/o Professional Help 1964	Pct. Born Dead 1964	Pct. Born Hospital 1970	Pct. w/o Professional Help 1970	Pct. Born Dead 1970
	(1)	(2)	(3)	(4)	(5)	(6)
Military Territory	−11.376*	6.011***	−0.005	−11.770**	5.345***	0.314**
	(6.087)	(1.994)	(0.385)	(4.704)	(1.273)	(0.148)
Mean	65.799	14.486	1.278	79.937	7.186	1.003
SD	22.744	11.255	1.248	16.349	7.02	0.594
Boundary FE	Yes	Yes	Yes	Yes	Yes	Yes
Region FE	Yes	Yes	Yes	Yes	Yes	Yes
Moran eigenvectors	Yes	Yes	Yes	Yes	Yes	Yes
Moran's I Residual	−0.295	−2.78	−0.859	−1.132	−2.478	−2.159
Observations	83	83	83	83	83	83
Adjusted R^2	0.270	0.683	0.133	0.265	0.612	0.069

Notes: Coefficients and robust standard errors in parentheses from OLS regressions. *p<0.1; **p<0.05; ***p<0.01. The unit of analysis is canton (srez). Outcome is measured in 1964 and 1970 according to the census in Yugolslavia.

are less likely to benefit from professional help both in 1964 and later in 1970. Such differences are statistically and economically significant. As already explained in the main chapter, there is a lower percentage of babies born in hospitals both in 1964 and in 1970, and a higher percentage of babies born without professional help.

Low access to public goods can be traced to the modern era. The point estimates in Table A.7 indicate that there are around five percentage points of dwellings which do not have access to water in the former military colony. The coefficient represents approximately half of a standard deviation. The results are similar irrespective of specification, sample selection, and inclusion and exclusion of variables. To save space, I do not report such results.[1]

Table A.7 displays the differences in access to water, access to sewers, and income using the main specification. It indicates that there are more dwellings without access to water or sewers by about five percentage points (columns (1) and (2)) in the former military colony. The effects of the military colony are also visible when it comes to economic prosperity but the results are not as robust. Overall, the point estimates in Table A.7 suggest that population is at higher risk of poverty (using income method) by about three percentage points in the former military colony (which is approximately a fourth of a standard deviation), but these differences are not always significant and are sensitive to model selection.

Socio-Economic Processes: Land Inequality and Communal Properties

Land Inequality

The results in Table A.8 display the regression coefficients for three variables that capture land inequality from the Royal Statistical Central Office in Budapest (1902). The results for all three variables presented

---

[1] The results are robust when (1) including a local linear polynomial in latitude and longitude, (2) including average annual temperature and river density (the two mildly significant geographic covariates), (3) including a local linear polynomial in distance to the boundary, (4) including both latitude and longitude and distance to the military colony border. One concern is that the results may be driven by the district of Zagreb or the municipalities that are part of the Zagreb area (Grad Zagreb or Zagrebačka). The results (5) barely change upon dropping Zagrebačka. Another concern may also have to do with the effect of rivers, which may impose discontinuities in transport costs. Using data from the European Environment Agency, I identify the segments of the border that coincide with rivers and eliminate the municipalities that are closest to those sections of the borders. The procedure therefore (6) limits the sample to municipalities closest to boundary segments that do not coincide with rivers and renders little plausibility to the discontinuity in transport costs imposed by rivers hypothesis.

Table A.7 *Effect of military colonialism on access to water, sewers, and income, 2011*

	Dependent variable:		
	Pct. Dwellings No Water 2011	Pct. Dwellings No Sewer 2011	Pct. People Risk of Poverty 2011
	(1)	(2)	(3)
Military Territory	6.042***	7.021***	3.594***
	(1.076)	(1.126)	(1.387)
Mean	9.181	9.798	24.759
SD	8.548	9.094	12.625
Boundary FE	Yes	Yes	Yes
Region FE	Yes	Yes	Yes
Moran eigenvectors	Yes	Yes	Yes
Moran's I Residual	−1.732	−2.186	−2.642
Observations	393	392	395
Adjusted R^2	0.439	0.472	0.581

Notes: Coefficients and County clustered robust standard errors in parentheses from OLS regression. *p<0.1; **p<0.05; ***p<0.01. The unit of analysis is municipality (opcina). See codebook in the appendix for data sources and how the variables were calculated.

in the first three columns of Table A.8 are statistically and economically significant. On average, there are three percentage points fewer domestic servants in the military colony, which is substantial given that the average mean for the country in 1900 is seven percent. Similarly, the former military colony has fewer large landowners and more agricultural smallholders.

To investigate the effect of large landowners on productivity, I use the data from the Royal Statistical Office in Zagreb (1898) and compile three variables: ratio of carriages to inhabitants, cattle to inhabitants, and horses to inhabitants. The results in Table A.8, columns 4–6, indicate no statistically significant difference between the military and the civilian area, when it comes to these factors.

As far as the persistence of inequality is concerned, the results in column 4 of Table A.9 do not indicate any statistically significant difference in taxed income. The results from 1900 on the ratio of cattle and horses to people together with the taxed income that comes from agricultural yield render little plausibility to a potential mechanism whereby military colonialism affected land inequality, which in turn affected local

Table A.8 *Effect of military colonialism on land inequality, 1900*

			Dependent variable:			
	Pct. Domestic Servants	Log Owners Over 100 acres	Log Agricultural Smallholders	Ratio Carriages to Inhabitants	Ratio Cattle to Inhabitants	Ratio Horses to Inhabitants
	(1)	(2)	(3)	(4)	(5)	(6)
Military Territory	−0.336**	−0.368***	0.418***	0.014**	0.006	0.004
	(0.135)	(0.042)	(0.112)	(0.006)	(0.023)	(0.010)
Mean	0.771	0.333	5.888	0.111	0.495	0.143
SD	1.139	0.56	1.01	0.075	0.232	0.133
Boundary FE	Yes	Yes	Yes	Yes	Yes	Yes
Region FE	Yes	Yes	Yes	Yes	Yes	Yes
Moran eigenvectors	Yes	Yes	Yes	Yes	Yes	Yes
Moran's I Residual	−2.374	−1.593	−1.581			
Observations	472	472	472	2,165	2,165	2,165
Adjusted R²	0.036	0.291	0.392	0.315	0.541	0.774

Notes: Coefficients and robust standard errors in parentheses from OLS regression. *p<0.1; **p<0.05; ***p<0.01. The unit of analysis is county-level administrative unit in Imperial Hungary (járas) for 1900 and settlement in 1895. Data is based on the Royal Statistical Central Office in Budapest (1902); Royal Statistical Office in Zagreb (1898). Every regression includes the following covariates: a linear polynomial in latitude and longitude, distance to Zagreb, and boundary segment FE.

Table A.9 *Effect of military colonialism on land inequality, 1910*

	Dependent variable:			
	Pct. Domestic Servants	Log Owners Over 100 acres	Log Agricultural Smallholders	Log Municipality Income
	(1)	(2)	(3)	(4)
Military Territory	−0.277***	−0.325***	0.683***	0.137
	(0.103)	(0.057)	(0.101)	(0.083)
Mean	0.77	0.339	4.735	8.985
SD	0.985	0.569	1.051	1.03
Boundary FE	Yes	Yes	Yes	Yes
Region FE	Yes	Yes	Yes	Yes
Moran eigenvectors	Yes	Yes	Yes	Yes
Moran's I Residual	−1.781	−1.722	−2.647	
Observations	497	498	493	1,991
Adjusted R^2	0.0004	0.221	0.562	0.595

Notes: Coefficients and robust standard errors in parentheses from OLS regression. *p<0.1; **p<0.05; ***p<0.01. The unit of analysis is county-level administrative unit in Imperial Hungary (jaras) for 1910 and settlement in 1909. Data is based on the Royal Statistical Central Office in Budapest (1913); Hungarian Statistical Office (1915). Every regression includes the following covariates: a linear polynomial in latitude and longitude, distance to Zagreb, and boundary segment FE.

productivity. Instead, the likely mechanism is that large landholders had more power (both political and economic) to put pressure on or lobby the central government to provide public goods such as roads and railroads or invest in public goods because they had much more to gain themselves.

Communal Property Rights

Table A.10 presents statistical results for the difference in communal properties, based on data published by the Royal Statistical Office in Zagreb (1898). The results are highly significant for all four cases: zadrugas take much more space from the municipality area (columns (1) and (2)), and many more people live under communal properties (columns (3)). In addition, they are highly economically significant. As explained in the main chapter, communal properties are larger by about 107 yokes in the military area compared to the civilian area (note that the average communal property size is 436 yokes).

Historical Occupational Structure

The results presented in Table A.11 based on data from Austrian Ministry of Internal Affairs (1859) and the Royal Statistical Central Office in Budapest (1902, 1913) show how occupational structure might have changed within the military colony and outside of it. The number of soldiers is higher in the military colony in 1857, but it ceases to be statistically significant in 1900 and 1910, as shown in columns (4)–(6). While in 1857 there were few civil servants in the military area, this difference is no longer statistically significant in 1900 and 1910, as indicated in columns (1)–(3). The percentage of day workers is lower in the military area: it is negative and significant in 1857 and negative and insignificant in 1900 and 1910. It is also worth noting that many more people start getting involved in agriculture after the end of the military colony, as shown in columns (13)–(15). The percentage of people involved in trade seems to be stable over time, as illustrated in columns (7)–(9).

Alternative Explanations

In this section, I present the main alternative explanation for the persistence of under-provision of public goods in a tabular format. As explained in Chapter 4, I group the alternative explanations in three categories: (1) temporal intermediary treatment factors that could have affected the treatment and the control group differentially; (2) structural treatment factors that could (have) impact(ed) the treatment group simply by being in a border area; (3) alternative mechanisms by which military colonialism affected the way the state behaves in the former military colony.

Temporal Intermediary Factors: Historical Events

Effect of World War II
I compiled a list of all concentration camps that were built by the Ustaša regime, prisoners of concentration camps, and massacre death counts based on historical accounts. The results in Table A.12 indicate no differences when it comes to the number of concentration camps being built, the number of prisoners, and the number of massacres in the two regions, as indicated by columns (3), (4), and (5) of Table A.12. Similarly, it is not the case that Allied powers (US and Britain) bombed one area more than the other (see columns (1) and (2) of Table A.12).

Effect of Yugoslav Wars
The Yugoslav Wars are a series of ethnic conflicts, wars of independence fought in the former Yugoslavia between 1991 to 2001 (Pavković, 2011).

Table A.10 *Effect of military colonialism on communal properties, 1880 and 1895*

	Dependent variable:						
	Pct. People Zadruga Members 1880	Log Area Covered by Zadrugas 1895	Pct. Area Covered by Zadrugas/ Total Area 1895	Log Population in Zadrugas 1895	Pct. People Secretely Parted Zadruga Members 1880	Log Area Coveredd by Secretely Parted Zadrugas 1895	Pct. Area Covered by Secretely Parted Secretely Parted/ Total Area 1895
	(1)	(2)	(3)	(4)	(5)	(6)	(7)
Military Territory	11.737***	0.723***	3.326**	0.560***	4.793***	0.516	1.469
	(4.398)	(0.229)	(1.651)	(0.201)	(0.303)	(0.935)	(0.985)
Mean	11.282	4.364	14.745	3.352	4.001	3.575	7.71
SD	11.285	2.388	18.04	1.984	4.129	2.47	10.538
Boundary FE	Yes	Yes	Yes	Yes	Yes	Yes	Yes
Region FE	Yes	Yes	Yes	Yes	Yes	Yes	Yes
Moran eigenvectors	Yes	Yes	Yes	Yes	Yes	Yes	Yes
Moran's I Test	0.477	0.464	0.52	0.506	0.323	0.372	0.34
Moran Random SE	8.039	1.467	10.322	1.297	2.815	1.786	7.062
Observations	64	2,166	2,166	2,166	64	2,166	2,166
Adjusted R^2	0.334	0.616	0.755	0.605	0.339	0.504	0.574

Notes: Coefficients and county-clustered robust standard errors in parentheses from OLS regression. $^*p<0.1$; $^{**}p<0.05$; $^{***}p<0.01$. The unit of analysis for all columns is village. See codebook in the appendix for data sources and how the variables were calculated.

Table A.11 *Effect of military colonialism on occupational structure, 1857-1910*

	Pct. Civil Service 1857	Pct. Civil Service 1900	Pct. Civil Service 1910	Pct. Military 1857	Pct. Military 1900	Pct. Military 1910	Pct. Trade 1857	Pct. Trade 1900	Pct. Trade 1910	Pct. Day Workers 1857	Pct. Day Workers 1900	Pct. Day Workers 1910	Pct. Agric. 1857	Pct. Agric. 1900	Pct. Agric. 1910
	(1)	(2)	(3)	(4)	(5)	(6)	(7)	(8)	(9)	(10)	(11)	(12)	(13)	(14)	(15)
Military Territory	-0.255***	-0.411	-0.310	5.206***	0.057	0.106	-0.183***	-0.301	-0.402	-0.827***	-0.639*	-0.774**	1.577**	5.012**	7.365***
	(0.079)	(0.254)	(0.226)	(0.532)	(0.193)	(0.136)	(0.030)	(0.213)	(0.246)	(0.099)	(0.388)	(0.387)	(0.772)	(2.052)	(2.170)
Mean	0.973	0.298	0.25	0.973	0.298	0.25	0.227	1.183	1.358	1.124	1.335	2.134	14.785	83.083	81.008
SD	2.184	1.638	1.118	2.184	1.638	1.118	0.402	1.967	1.97	1.375	3.754	4.912	6.987	20.33	20.792
Boundary FE	Yes	Yes	Yes	Yes	Yes	Yes	Yes	Yes	Yes	Yes	Yes	Yes	Yes	Yes	Yes
Region FE	Yes	Yes	Yes	Yes	Yes	Yes	Yes	Yes	Yes	Yes	Yes	Yes	Yes	Yes	Yes
Moran eigenvectors	Yes	Yes	Yes	Yes	Yes	Yes	Yes	Yes	Yes	Yes	Yes	Yes	Yes	Yes	Yes
Moran's I Residual	-1.293	-2.115	-0.945	-2.241	-0.301	-0.363	-1.899	-1.891	-0.956	-2.065	-2.657	-1.138	-1.48	-1.056	-1.223
Observations	77	472	498	77	475	498	77	472	498	77	472	498	77	472	498
Adjusted R^2	-0.048	0.014	-0.009	0.750	-0.008	-0.011	-0.013	0.145	0.062	0.181	0.392	0.190	0.141	0.284	0.301

Notes: Coefficients and cluster robust standard errors in parentheses from OLS regression. *p<0.1; **p<0.05; ***p<0.01. The unit of analysis is county-level administrative unit in Imperial Austria-Hungary (kreis) for 1857, and (jaras) for 1900 and 1910. Data is based on the Austrian Ministry of Internal Affairs (1859); Royal Statistical Central Office in Budapest (1902, 1913). Every regression includes the following covariates: a linear polynomial in latitude and longitude, distance to Zagreb, and boundary segment FE.

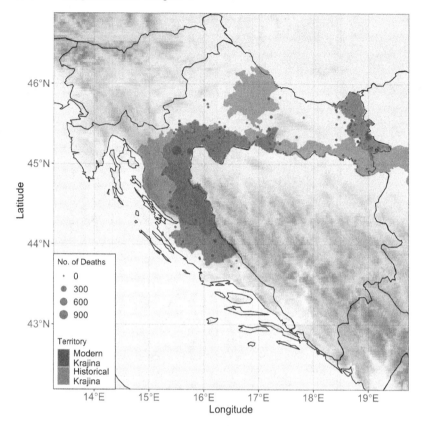

Figure A.1 Historical and modern Krajina

One concern for the validity of the results is that they are driven by the wars in Yugoslavia in the early 1990s. The map in Figure A.1 shows the spread of the Habsburg military border (historical Krajina) and the area of the Republic of Serbian Krajina (modern Krajina). The intersection of the two represents approximately 44 percent of the total area of the Habsburg military frontier zone. In addition, the map also depicts the number of absolute deaths in the Yugoslav Wars based on UCDP data (Sundberg and Melander, 2013), which shows that they were likely to happen both inside and outside of the historical Habsburg military zone and the Serbian occupied area.

To investigate potential material destruction as a result of the war, I use the number of damaged buildings and the extent to which they were damaged. The list of damaged and destroyed cultural monuments in the area comprises the following types of buildings: historic-memorial, civil,

Table A.12 *Alternative explanations: Effect of World War II*

	Dependent variable:				
	Log. No. Bombs	Log. Tons TNT	Log Concentration Camp Count	Log Concentration Camp prisoners	Log Massacre Death Count
	(1)	(2)	(3)	(4)	(5)
Military Territory	−0.220	0.763	−2.428**	−0.439**	0.235
	(0.756)	(0.736)	(0.965)	(0.214)	(0.158)
Mean	0.116	0.186	0.026	0.173	0.305
SD	0.51	0.96	0.14	1.227	1.221
Boundary FE	Yes	Yes	Yes	Yes	Yes
Region FE	Yes	Yes	Yes	Yes	Yes
Observations	402	402	402	402	402
Adjusted R^2				0.027	0.050
Akaike Inf. Crit.	277.675	258.914	105.975		

Notes: Results are coefficients and standard errors from negative binomial models. *p<0.1; **p<0.05; ***p<0.01. The unit of analysis is municipality (opcina). See codebook for data sources and how the variables were calculated.

military/defense, ecclesiastical, sepulchral/cemeteries, sculpture/street furniture. As already explained in the main body of the chapter, the results in Table A.13 confirm that on average the former military colony was in fact less likely to be exposed to the war in Yugoslavia: there are fewer deaths (column (1)) based on data from Sundberg and Melander (2013), a lower number of buildings destroyed based on the gravity of the damage (columns (2)–(7)), or a lower number of buildings depending on their type (columns (8)–(11)).

To further confirm the result about the non-differential effect of WWII and the Yugoslav Wars, Table A.14 does not indicate that the respondents or their families are any more likely to report injury or having had to move because of WWII. There is also no systematic difference in the likelihood of injury during the conflict in Yugoslavia.

Effect of Communist Collectivization and Repression
In order to evaluate the hypothesis about the potential effect of communism, I collected data on the number of cooperatives and the number of households with no cooperative members from the Federal People's Republic of Yugoslavia – Federal Statistical Office (1952a, pp. 10–40). In addition, I also collected data on the number of cooperative plows from the Federal People's Republic of Yugoslavia – Federal Statistical Office (1952b, pp. 15–48). The results displayed in Table A.15 do not indicate any difference in the level of collectivization between the former military colony and the civilian area.

Table A.13 *Alternative explanations: War in Yugoslavia*

						Dependent variable:					
	No. of Deaths	Light Damage 1	Light Damage 2	Light Damage 3	Serious Damage 4	Partial Destr. 5	Complete Destr. 6	Buildings	Churches	Schools	Monuments
	(1)	(2)	(3)	(4)	(5)	(6)	(7)	(8)	(9)	(10)	(11)
Military Territory	−0.821**	−1.402**	−1.028*	−2.187***	−0.732	−1.157*	−0.698	−1.880***	−0.173	−1.378	−2.005***
	(0.385)	(0.681)	(0.544)	(0.597)	(0.720)	(0.678)	(0.825)	(0.676)	(0.587)	(1.256)	(0.529)
Mean	0.303	0.562	1.087	0.617	0.299	0.358	0.194	2.279	0.602	0.072	0.107
SD	0.991	4.698	10.104	4.478	1.96	2.822	1.475	18.417	2.365	0.507	0.761
Boundary FE	Yes	Yes	Yes	Yes	Yes	Yes	Yes	Yes	Yes	Yes	Yes
Region FE	Yes	Yes	Yes	Yes	Yes	Yes	Yes	Yes	Yes	Yes	Yes
Observations	402	402	402	402	402	402	402	402	402	402	402
Akaike Inf. Crit.	408.442	357.676	382.165	329.685	275.538	299.999	214.452	369.014	498.818	151.199	201.818

Notes: Coefficients and standard errors in parentheses from a negative binomial. *p<0.1; **p<0.05; ***p<0.01. The unit of analysis is municipality (opcina). See codebook for data sources and how the variables were calculated.

Table A.14 *Alternative explanations: Wars – perceptions*

	Dependent variable:		
	Injury during WW2	Had to Move during WW2	Injury during Yugoslav Conflict
	(1)	(2)	(3)
Military Territory	0.080	−0.084	0.060
	(0.057)	(0.281)	(0.041)
Mean	0.203	0.094	0.104
SD	0.402	0.292	0.306
Boundary FE	Yes	Yes	Yes
Survey Year FE	Yes	Yes	Yes
Demographic Covariates	Yes	Yes	Yes
Observations	794	42	850
Adjusted R^2	0.096	−0.030	0.056

Notes: Coefficients and robust standard errors in parentheses from Logit. $^*p<0.1$; $^{**}p<0.05$; $^{***}p<0.01$. The unit of analysis is the individual. See codebook for variable descriptions.

Table A.15 *Alternative explanations: Communist collectivization*

	Dependent variable:		
	Total Cooperatives 1950	Households with No Cooperative Members 1950	Cooperative Plows 1950
	(1)	(2)	(3)
Military area	−1.665	−770.969	136.665
	(2.599)	(671.109)	(121.381)
Mean	18.051	831.705	344.226
SD	9.806	1,300.489	550.943
Boundary FE	Yes	Yes	Yes
Region FE	Yes	Yes	Yes
Observations	78	78	93
Adjusted R^2	0.299	0.186	0.311

Notes: Coefficients and robust standard errors in parentheses from OLS regressions. $^*p<0.1$; $^{**}p<0.05$; $^{***}p<0.01$. The unit of analysis is canton (srez). See codebook for data sources and how the variables were calculated.

Results in Table A.16 do not indicate that the communist authorities violently repressed the inhabitants living in the territory of the former colony. The results are based on data from LITS – EDBR (2016).

Table A.16 *Alternative explanations: Perception of communist torture*

	Dependent variable:		
	Torture against Oneself	Torture against Family	Torture against Grandparents
	(1)	(2)	(3)
Military Territory	−0.006	−0.009	−0.020
	(0.008)	(0.031)	(0.018)
Mean	0.003	0.059	0.019
SD	0.058	0.236	0.138
Boundary FE	Yes	Yes	Yes
Survey Year FE	Yes	Yes	Yes
Demographic Covariates	Yes	Yes	Yes
Observations	912	912	912
Adjusted R^2	−0.001	0.078	−0.003

Notes: Coefficients and robust standard errors in parentheses from Logit regression. *p<0.1; **p<0.05; ***p<0.01. The unit of analysis is the individual. See codebook for data sources and how the variables were calculated.

Structural Treatment Factors: Military Colonialism as a Physical Border

The second set of alternative explanations focus on structural factors. The link between military colonialism and economic development could simply be the result of the military colony being placed at the border. As already mentioned, the municipalities that are directly adjacent to the Ottoman/Bosnian border are not included in the analysis with modern outcomes. However, to further mitigate the concern about the effect of the border as a physical space that could be directly correlated with economic output, I pursue two strategies. The first one is to include in the main model a variable that captures the distance to the Ottoman Empire/Bosnia. If the border was indeed connected with economic outcomes, one would expect to see a positive coefficient for the distance to the Ottoman Empire/Bosnia variable. The effect for military colonialism remains significant while the distance to Bosnia variable is in fact negative in both cases, as indicated by the results in Table A.17.

The second strategy is to run placebo tests to ascertain the extent to which running any line (that has the same shape as the line that divided the Habsburg civilian area from the military colony) in a north–south direction would generate a similar effect. The tests suggest that similar results could only be obtained if one moves the border line up to 10–15km. This reinforces the idea that the results are driven by the line

Table A.17 *Alternative explanations: Distance to the Ottoman/Bosnian border*

	Dependent variable		
	Pct. Dwellings No Water 2011	Pct. People at Risk of Poverty 2011	Pct. Less Educated People 2011
	(1)	(2)	(3)
Military Territory	3.129**	6.855***	5.182*
	(1.563)	(1.558)	(2.709)
Military Territory x Distance Bosnia in km	0.036	−0.095***	0.061
	(0.026)	(0.032)	(0.046)
Distance Bosnia in km	−0.076	−0.190***	−0.103*
	(0.051)	(0.037)	(0.056)
Mean	9.181	24.759	43.948
SD	8.548	12.625	13.391
Boundary FE	Yes	Yes	Yes
Region FE	Yes	Yes	Yes
Moran eigenvectors	Yes	Yes	Yes
Moran's I Residual	−1.421	−2.082	−2.132
Observations	393	395	395
Adjusted R^2	0.435	0.566	0.528

Notes: Coefficients and County clustered robust standard errors in parentheses from OLS regression. *p<0.1; **p<0.05; ***p<0.01. The unit of analysis is municipality (opcina). See codebook in the appendix for data sources and how the variables were calculated.

dividing the civilian area from the military colony, located in the middle of the country, as opposed to proximity to the border with the Ottoman Empire/Bosnia. I do not include these results here to save space.

Alternative Mechanisms: Civic Society versus Government

The final set of alternative explanations has to do with alternative mechanisms by which people have lower access to public goods. The results in Table A.18 do not indicate significant differences between the military colony and the civilian area when it comes to ethnic/religious fractionalization in 1921, 1931, 1991, 2001, and 2011. This renders little possibility to the idea that ethnic fractionalization should be connected to economic development.

The second alternative mechanism has to do with the persistence of the military as an occupation in the former colony, which in turn might have distracted the attention of locals from lobbying the government for

Table A.18 *Alternative explanations: Ethnic/religious fractionalization and government transparency*

	Religious Fractionalization 1921	Ethnic Fractionalization 1931	Ethnic Fractionalization 1991	Ethnic Fractionalization 2001	Ethnic Fractionalization 2011	Local Government Transparency, 2016
			Dependent variable			
	(1)	(2)	(3)	(4)	(5)	(6)
Military Territory	0.024	0.035	−0.013	0.007	0.007	0.156
	(0.019)	(0.028)	(0.057)	(0.057)	(0.044)	(0.183)
Mean	0.174	0.175	0.26	0.175	0.172	3.233
SD	0.185	0.183	0.23	0.18	0.183	1.418
Boundary FE	Yes	Yes	Yes	Yes	Yes	Yes
Region FE	Yes	Yes	Yes	Yes	Yes	Yes
Observations	514	561	397	390	390	395
Adjusted R^2	0.210	0.290	0.484	0.401	0.401	0.036

Notes: Coefficients and robust standard errors in parentheses. *$p<0.1$; **$p<0.05$; ***$p<0.01$. The units of analysis are settlements for the corresponding censuses. See codebook in the appendix for data sources and how the variables were calculated.

Table A.19 *Alternative explanations: Involvement in military affairs*

				Dependent variable:	
				Pct. People in	
	Pct. Military 1857	Pct. Military 1900	Pct. Military 1910	Public Service and Army 1931	Pct. Armed Forcces 1991
	(1)	(2)	(3)	(4)	(5)
Military Territory	5.212***	−0.002	0.106	−0.187	−0.177
	(0.457)	(0.033)	(0.138)	(1.113)	(0.132)
Mean	0.973	0.133	0.25	85.556	1.757
SD	2.184	0.804	1.118	10.802	1.032
Boundary FE	Yes	Yes	Yes	Yes	Yes
Survey Year FE	Yes	Yes	Yes	Yes	Yes
Demographic Covariates	Yes	Yes	Yes	Yes	Yes
Observations	77	5,601	498	559	418
Adjusted R^2	0.745	0.012	−0.003	0.267	0.212

Notes: Coefficients and county clustered robust standard errors in parentheses from OLS regressions. *p<0.1; **p<0.05; ***p<0.01. All regressions include a linear RD polynomial in latitude and longitude, a control for distance to Zagreb, and boundary segment fixed effects. See codebook for data sources and how the variables were calculated.

public goods and from being involved in public affairs. As I have shown previously, the difference in percentage soldiers is only statistically significant in 1857. This difference is no longer visible in 1900, the closest census to 1881 – the year of the termination of the military colony. The difference between the military and the civilian area remains insignificant in 1910, 1931, and 1991, as indicated in Table A.19. The third alternative mechanism has to do with the role of local governments or the supply side of the story. As already indicated in the section on socio-economic processes, local elites are much more visible in the area with public goods – the civilian area and less so in the military colony. Finally, results on government transparency visible in column (6) of Table A.18 provide little evidence for the existence of this alternative channel.

Appendix B Supplement for Chapter 6

This chapter is a technical appendix to Chapter 6. I present statistical results in a tabular format that constituted the basis for the results in Chapter 6. The tables offer more extensive details compared to the coefficient plots or the regression discontinuity graphs, including the mean, standard deviation of the main variables of interest, standard errors, and R squared.

Attitudes Stemming from Communal Properties

As discussed in Chapter 6, different kinds of norms and attitudes emerged from the different types of treatments which constituted military colonialism. When it comes to communal properties, these are norms about family socialization and norms about family hierarchy.

Norms about Family Socialization

This section presents the results for the effects of military colonialism on in- and out-group biases and perception about corruption using survey data from LITS. Specifically, I present results for the following hypotheses:

H1a: People in the former military colony trust their family more.
H1b: People in the former military colony trust other people less.
H1c: There should be higher perceived incidence of corruption within the military colony.

The results in Table B.1 provide strong support for the in- and out-group bias hypothesis, with descendants of military colonists being much more trusting of their family members and much less of other people. This is exactly consistent with the very logic of the family clan. When it comes to perception about the incidence of corruption, results also suggest that bribery is much more frequent in the south compared to the north, providing some support to the logic of a persistent effect of the family clans on nepotism and corruption more generally.

Table B.1 *Effect of military colonialism on in-out-group trust and nepotism*

		Dependent variable:			
	Trust Family, 2016	Trust Other People, 2006–16	Bribery Road Police, 2006–16	Bribery Unemployment Benef., 2006–16	Social Security Benef., 2016–16
	(1)	(2)	(3)	(4)	(5)
Military Territory	0.136*	−0.232***	0.245*	0.287***	0.303***
	(0.072)	(0.086)	(0.130)	(0.073)	(0.072)
Mean	4.713	2.828	1.667	1.27	1.305
SD	0.564	1.045	1.001	0.702	0.759
Boundary FE	Yes	Yes	Yes	Yes	Yes
Survey Year FE	Yes	Yes	Yes	Yes	Yes
Demographic Covariates	Yes	Yes	Yes	Yes	Yes
Observations	830	1,817	687	1,738	1,730
Adjusted R²	0.061	0.040	0.156	0.044	0.028

Notes: Coefficients and robust standard errors in parentheses from OLS regression. *p<0.1; **p<0.05; ***p<0.01. The unit of analysis is the individual. Data is based on EBRD LITS 2006, 2010, and 2016. Every regression includes the following covariates: a linear polynomial in latitude and longitude, distance to Zagreb, border-segment fixed effects, age, perception of income, and education. The trust variables range from 1 (complete distrust) to 5 (complete trust). The bribery variables range from 1 (never) to 5 (always).

Table B.2 *Effect of military colonialism on collectivist attitudes*

	Dependent variable:	
	Need Effort and Intelligence to Succeed 2006–16	People are Poor because of Laziness 2006–16
	(1)	(2)
Military Territory	0.004	−0.128***
	(0.043)	(0.024)
Mean	0.564	0.131
SD	0.496	0.337
Boundary FE	Yes	Yes
Survey Year FE	Yes	Yes
Demographic Covariates	Yes	Yes
Observations	1,838	1,838
Adjusted R^2	0.044	0.032

Notes: Coefficients and robust standard errors in parentheses from OLS regression. *p<0.1; **p<0.05; ***p<0.01. The unit of analysis is the individual. Data is based on EBRD LITS 2006, 2010, and 2016. Every regression includes the following covariates: a linear polynomial in latitude and longitude, distance to Zagreb, border-segment fixed effects, age, perception of income, and education. The first variable represents agreement with whether effort, hard work, intelligence, and skills are the most important to suceed in life. The second variable represents agreement with the statement that the reason why there are people in need is because of laziness and lack of will zcu power. Answers can be 1 (agree) or 0 (disagree).

Another important dimension of family clans which is closely connected with in- and out-group attitudes is attitudes toward collectivism. In order to evaluate the persistence of collectivist attitudes, I use the same survey and some of the questions that have previously been used in economics to measure levels of collectivism (Greif, 1994; Gorodnichenko and Roland, 2021). These are disagreement with statements like "Effort, hard work, intelligence, and skills are important in order to succeed in life," or "the reason why there are people in need in your country is because of laziness and lack of willpower." A negative answer to these questions has been used in some literatures as a proxy for collectivist attitudes: in other words, someone who disagrees with the idea that intelligence and skills are important to succeed or someone who disagrees that people are poor because they are lazy should have a more collectivist outlook on life. The hypothesis that I test is the following:

Table B.3 *Effect of military colonialism on risk-taking*

	Dependent variable:	
	Willing to Take Risks 2010–16	Preference Chance Promotion Over Job Security 2010
	(1)	(2)
Military Territory	−0.235 (0.220)	−0.162*** (0.057)
Mean	4.982	1.24
SD	2.559	0.427
Boundary FE	Yes	Yes
Survey Year FE	Yes	Yes
Demographic Covariates	Yes	Yes
Observations	1,692	722
Adjusted R^2	0.129	0.121

Notes: Coefficients and robust standard errors in parentheses from OLS regression. *p<0.1; **p<0.05; ***p<0.01. The unit of analysis is the individual. Data is based on EBRD LITS 2006, 2010, and 2016. Every regression includes the following covariates: a linear polynomial in latitude and longitude, distance to Zagreb, border-segment fixed effects, age, perception of income, and education. The risk variable ranges from 1 – not willing to take risks to 10 – very willing. The job security variable asks the respondent to choose between a high-security job with low chance of promotion (1) and a low-security job with high chance of promotion (2). The setting up a business variable reflects people's responses to the question of whether they have set up a business (1) or not (0).

H2: People in the former military colony have a more collectivist outlook.

The results in Table B.2 provide some support for the persistence of collectivist attitudes. People in the former military colony are much less likely than people in the north to think that people are poor because they are lazy. There is no indication that they are less likely to think that one needs effort and intelligence in order to succeed in life.

Risk and competition avoidance are two additional features that are likely to be associated with family clans. I hypothesize the following:

H3a: People in the former military colony are less likely to take risks.
H3b: People in the former military colony prefer higher job security over higher payment.

Table B.4 *Effect of military colonialism on preference for authoritarian structures*

	Dependent variable:		
	Preference Democracy 2006–16	Preference Planned Economy 2010–16	Authority Questioning 2010–16
	(1)	(2)	(3)
Military Territory	−0.045	−0.075	−0.083
	(0.074)	(0.047)	(0.212)
Mean	2.302	0.331	3.051
SD	0.777	0.471	2.344
Boundary FE	Yes	Yes	Yes
Survey Year FE	Yes	Yes	Yes
Demographic Covariates	Yes	Yes	Yes
Observations	1,750	1,497	1,510
Adjusted R^2	0.019	0.014	0.068

Notes: Coefficients and robust standard errors in parentheses from OLS regression. *p<0.1; **p<0.05; ***p<0.01. The unit of analysis is the individual. Data is based on EBRD LITS 2006, 2010, and 2016. Every regression includes the following covariates: age, perception of income and education. See appendix for details on variables and data sources.

The results in Table B.3 offer support for some of the hypotheses. People in the former military colony are much less willing to take risks as reflected in their preference for higher job security as opposed to a chance of promotion. When it comes to the specific question of willingness to take risks, the effects are not statistically significant, but they do point in the same direction of a lower willingness to take risks.

Norms about Family Hierarchy

The second set of norms which stem from exposure to communal properties are about family hierarchy. For example, one potential cultural trait which could be a direct result of having lived in family clans for much longer and which is discussed by Henrich (2020) as a potential legacy of extended families is conformity. I hypothesize the following:

H4a: People in the former military colony are more likely to prefer authoritarian political structures.
H4b: People in the former military colony are less likely to support the questioning of the actions of authorities.

Table B.5 *Effect of military colonialism on women's roles*

	Dependent variable:	
	Men Are Better Leaders, 2016	Women Should Do Household Chores, 2016
	(1)	(2)
Military Territory	0.272*	0.339**
	(0.160)	(0.163)
Mean	2.344	2.344
SD	1.256	1.256
Boundary FE	Yes	Yes
Survey Year FE	Yes	Yes
Demographic Covariates	Yes	Yes
Observations	881	900
Adjusted R^2	0.027	0.061

Notes: Coefficients and robust standard errors in parentheses from OLS regression. *p<0.1; **p<0.05; ***p<0.01. The unit of analysis is the individual. Data is based on EBRD LITS 2006, 2010, and 2016. Every regression includes the following covariates: a linear polynomial in latitude and longitude, distance to Zagreb, border-segment fixed effects, age, perception of income, and education. The variables capture agreements with the following statements: 1) Men make better political leaders than women. 2) A woman should do most of the household chores. Answers range from 1 – disagree to 5 – agree.

The results in Table B.4 indicate no support for authoritarian structures. There is no difference between the two regions with respect to popular preferences for democracy, preference for a planned economy, or the extent to which authority is questioned.

Attitudes toward women seem to be at the very core of the institution of the family clan. Given the likely legacy on stereotypes about women's role and the available data from LITS 2016, I hypothesize the following:

H5a: People in the former military colony are more likely to think that men make better political leaders.
H5b: People in the former military colony are more likely to think that women should do the household chores.

The results in Table B.5 provide some support for these hypotheses. There is a difference in perceptions about men making better leaders

Table B.6 *Effect of military colonialism on trust in institutions*

	Trust Government 2006–16	Trust Parliament 2006–16	Trust Courts 2006–16	Trust Parties 2006–16	Trust Armed Forces 2006–16	Trust Police 2006–16
Dependent variable:						
	(1)	(2)	(3)	(4)	(5)	(6)
Military Territory	−0.101	0.001	−0.114	−0.050	0.194**	0.054
	(0.085)	(0.086)	(0.096)	(0.087)	(0.081)	(0.095)
Mean	2.283	2.256	2.378	2.047	3.518	3.271
SD	1.073	1.077	1.104	1.01	1.098	1.146
Boundary FE	Yes	Yes	Yes	Yes	Yes	Yes
Survey Year FE	Yes	Yes	Yes	Yes	Yes	Yes
Demographic Covariates	Yes	Yes	Yes	Yes	Yes	Yes
Observations	1,864	1,859	1,849	1,844	1,836	1,862
Adjusted R^2	0.124	0.116	0.059	0.073	0.121	0.070

Notes: Coefficients and robust standard errors in parentheses from OLS regression. *$p<0.1$; **$p<0.05$; ***$p<0.01$. The unit of analysis is the individual. Data is based on EBRD LITS 2006, 2010, and 2016. Every regression includes the following covariates: a linear polynomial in latitude and longitude, distance to Zagreb, border-segment fixed effects, age, perception of income, and education. The trust variables range from 1 (complete distrust) to 5 (complete trust).

Table B.7 *Effect of military colonialism on political participation*

	Dependent variable:				
	Voted Last Local Elections 2006–16	Voted Last Parliamentary Elections 2006–16	Voted Last Presidential Elections 2006–16	Participation Demonstrations, 2006–16	Participation Sign Petition, 2016–16
	(1)	(2)	(3)	(4)	(5)
Military Territory	0.004	−0.044	−0.041	−0.076***	−0.191***
	(0.042)	(0.042)	(0.040)	(0.019)	(0.039)
Mean	0.673	0.729	0.744	0.068	0.365
SD	0.469	0.445	0.437	0.252	0.482
Boundary FE	Yes	Yes	Yes	Yes	Yes
Survey Year FE	Yes	Yes	Yes	Yes	Yes
Demographic Covariates	Yes	Yes	Yes	Yes	Yes
Observations	1,692	1,689	1,697	1,716	1,716
Adjusted R²	0.089	0.067	0.063	0.027	0.117

Notes: Coefficients and robust standard errors in parentheses from OLS regression. *p<0.1; **p<0.05; ***p<0.01. The unit of analysis is the individual. Data is based on EBRD LITS 2006, 2010, and 2016. Every regression includes the following covariates: a linear polynomial in latitude and longitude, distance to Zagreb, border-segment fixed effects, age, perception of income, and education. The voting questions record whether the respondent voted in the last elelections. Answers range from 0 (No) to 1 (Yes). The question on participation in demonstrations or signing of petitions records whether the respondent did any of the two actions in the past – 1 or not – 0.

than women and that women should do household chores. The results are compatible with ethnographic work from the early twentieth century mentioning the subservience of female interests to those of the family clan (Erlich, 1966).

Attitudes Stemming from Historical Under-Provision of Public Goods

A final set of attitudes that derive not so much from family clans but rather from living under an abusive authoritarian empire for over 300 years are attitudes toward the state. I hypothesize the following:

H6: People in the former military colony trust government institutions less.
H7a: People in the former military colony vote less.
H7b: People in the former military colony are less likely to engage in forms of contentious politics such as protests and demonstrations.

The results in Table B.6 provide inconclusive results about the role of military colonialism for institutional trust. The effects are positive and only in one case mildly significant: people trust the armed forces more, which may not be surprising given the military past of the region. Overall, however, there is little evidence on the persistence of distrust in institutions.

When it comes to political participation, the results suggest that people in the former military colony are not necessarily more likely not to have voted in the most recent local elections or in the last parliamentary and presidential elections. The results do point, however, in the direction of a lower probability of participation in demonstrations and a lower likelihood to sign petitions, which is consistent with the conclusions of the literature about the effect of violence on the victims' withdrawal from the political arena (Benard, 1994; Wood, 2006).

Primary Sources

Bautzen Museum. 1762. *Die Bautzener Bilderhandschrift, XXVIII, Trachten Nr. 150.*

Kiepert, Heinrich. 1869. *Völker und Sprachen-Karte von Österreich und den Unter-Donau-Ländern.* MAP. Scale: 1:3,000,000 km. D. Reimer (Lith. Anst. v. Leopold Kraatz), Berlin. University of Chicago Map Collection. G6481.E1 1869 .K5.

Kriegs Archiv Memoirs. 1779. *KA Mémoires XXIII. Joseph II to FM Hadik, Vienna, Dec. 9, 1779.*

Liechtenstern, Joseph M., and Amon, Anton. 1795. *Allgemeine Karte der Oestreichischen Monarchie.* MAP. Scale: 1:2,700,000 km. Herausgegeben von der Kosmographischen Gesellschaft, Wien. University of Chicago Map Collection. G6480 1795 .L5.

Ministère de la Guerre. 1845. *Tableau de la situation des établissements Français dans l'Algérie.* Paris: Imprimerie Royale.

Third Military Survey. 1869. *Franzisco-Josephinische Landesaufnahme [Third Military Survey].* MAP. Scale: 1:25,000km. Österreichisches Staatsarchiv, Vienna.

Unknown Author. 1869. *Die Oesterr: u. Ungar: Eisenbahnen der Gegenwart u. der Zukunft.* MAP. Scale: Unknown. Eigenthum und Verlag von Artaria & Co., Vienna. University of Chicago Map Collection. G6481.P3 1869 .A7.

Unknown Author. 1879. *Die Oesterr: u. Ungar: Eisenbahnen der Gegenwart u. der Zukunft.* MAP. Scale: Unknown. Eigenthum und Verlag von Artaria & Co., Vienna. University of Chicago Map Collection. G6481.P3 1879 .A7.

Unknown Author. 1884. *Die Oesterr: u. Ungar: Eisenbahnen der Gegenwart u. der Zukunft.* MAP. Scale: Unknown. Eigenthum und Verlag von Artaria & Co., Vienna. University of Chicago Map Collection. G6481.P3 1884 .A7.

Von Czoernig, Karl. 1855. *Ethnographie der Oesterrichischen Monarchie.* Vol. 2. Vienna: Kariserlich – Koenigliche Direction Der Administraiven Statistik. University of Chicago Map Collection. DB33.C95.

Primary Sources

Austrian Ministry of Internal Affairs. 1859. *Statistische Übersichten über die Bevölkerung und den Viehstand von Österreich. Nach der Zählung vom 31. October 1857.* Vienna: Herausgegeben Vom K. K. Ministerium Des Innern.

Azan, Paul. 1936. *L'armeé d'Afrique de 1830 à 1852, par le général Paul Azan.* Paris: Plon.

Boppe, Paul 1900. *La Croatie Militaire 1809–1813.* Paris: Berger-Levrault et Cie Editeurs.

Bussière, Auguste. 1853. Le maréchal Bugeaud et la colonisation de l'Algérie: Souvenirs et récits de la vie coloniale en Afrique. *Revue des Deux Mondes (1829-1971),* 4(3), 449–506.

Chenot, Adam. 1798. *Adam Chenot's der Medicin und Philosophie Doctors, gewesenen königl. Sanitäts Physicus in Siebenbürgen hinterlassene Schriften über die ärztlichen und politischen Anstalten bey der Pestseuche.* Wien: Wien Trattner Halle, Saale Universitäts- und Landesbibliothek Sachsen-Anhalt.

Damianitsch, Martin. 1854. *Vorschriften über Militärheirathen.* Vienna: Wilhelm Braumüller.

Damianitsch, Martin. 1861. *Das Disziplinar-Strafverfahren in der k. k. Armee und in der Militärgrenze nach dem neuen Dienstreglement und sonstigen Vorschriften.* Vienna: Wilhelm Braumüller.

De Beaujour, Felix. 1829. *Voyage militaire dans l'Empire Ottoman.* Vol. 1. Paris: Didot Frères.

De Monglave, Eugène. 1857. De L'Influence des Smala de Spahis sur l'avenir de l'Algerie. *Revue de l'Orient et de L'Algérie et de colonies,* 5, 144–150.

De Rumigny, Marie-Théodore. 1850. De l'Éstablissement des colonies militaires kabailes en Algerie. *Le spectateur militaire,* **XLIX**, 31–53.

De Saint-Aymour, Caix. 1883. *Les pays Sud-Slaves de l'Austro-Hongrie (Croatie, Slavonie, Bosnie, Herzegovine, Dalmatie).* Paris: Plon.

Delbrük, Hans. 1900. *Geschichte der Kriegskunst im Rahmen der politischen Geschichte.* Vol. 4. Berlin: Verlag von Georg Stilke.

Demian, Johann Andreas. 1806. *Die Militärgrenze in Kroatien*. Vol. 1. Vienna: Kaulfusz.

Dénes, Edelényi-Szabó. 1928. Magyarország közjogi alkatrészeinek és törvényhatóságainak területváltozásai. [Territorial Changes in the Public Law Components and Legal Authorities of Hungary]. *Statisztikai Szemle*, **6**, 648–714.

Derrécagaix, Victor-Bernard. 1911. *Le Maréchal Pélissier Duc de Malakoff*. Paris: Chapelot.

Desprez, Hippolyte Félix. 1847. Des colonies militaires de l'Autriche et de la Russie. *Revue des Deux Mondes, période initiale*, **19**, 722–735.

Draganović, Krunoslav. 1939. *Opći šematizam Katoličke crkve u Jugoslaviji. [General Schematism of the Catholic Church in Yugoslavia]*. Sarajevo: Izd.Akademije Regina Apostolorum.

Fuller, John F. C. 1925. *British Light Infantry in the Eighteenth Century*. London: Hutchinson.

Heissenberger, Johann. 1872. *Das Disciplinar-Strafrecht im k.k. Heere und in der Militärgrenze*. Vienna: Wilhelm Braumüller.

Hertz, Friedrich. 1925. *Die Produktionsgrundlagen der österreichischen Industrien vor und nach dem Kriege: insbesondere im Vergleich mit Deutschland*. Vienna: Verlag für Fachliteratur.

Hungarian Statistical Office. 1915. *Površina i Katastrálny Čisti Prihod Poreznih Općina Po Težatbenim Vrstima i Razredima. Nakon Katastralnog Izpravka, Provedenog na Temelju Zak. Član. V: 1909. [Area and Cadastral Net Revenue of Tax Municipalities by Claims and Classes. After the Cadastral Correction, Carried out on the basis of the Law from 1909]*. Budapest: Royal Hungarian State Printing House.

Jászi, Oszkár. 1929. *The Dissolution of the Habsburg Monarchy*. Chicago: University of Chicago Press.

K. K. Statistischen Central-Commission. 1830–42. *Tafeln zur Statistik der Österreichischen Monarchie*. Wien: Österreich / Direction der Administrativen Statistik.

K. K. Statistischen Central-Commission. 1849–51. *Tafeln zur Statistik der Österreichischen Monarchie. II. Theil*. Wien: Österreich / Direction der Administrativen Statistik.

Kraljevina Jugoslavija Opsta Državna Statistika. 1940. *Definitvni Rezultati Popisa Stanovništva od 31 Marta 1931 Godine Knjiga IV - Prisutno Stanovnistvo Po Glavnom Zanimanju. [Definitive Results of the Census of March 31, 1931 Book IV: Present Population by Main Occupation]*. Sarajevo: Državna Štamparija.

Lang, Herbert. 1934. *Autarkie und Kriegswirtschaft in der Tschechoslovakei: Die Umschichtung der tschechoslovakischen Wirtschaft, untersucht unter den Gesichtspunkten von Autarkie und Kriegswirtschaft*. Vienna: Kommissions-Verlag von Gelord.

Lopašić, Radoslav. 1884a. *Spomenici Hrvatske krajine*. Monumenta spectantia historiam Slavorum Meridionalium. Vol. 20. Zagreb: Jugoslavenska akademija znanosti i umjetnosti. Edict issued in Linz on September 5, 1538.

Lopašić, Radoslav. 1884b. *Spomenici Hrvatske krajine*. Monumenta spectantia historiam Slavorum Meridionalium. Vol. 20. Zagreb: Jugoslavenska akademija znanosti i umjetnosti. Edict issued in Vienna on June 5, 1535.

Lopašić, Radoslav. 1884c. *Spomenici Hrvatske krajine*. Monumenta spectantia historiam Slavorum meridionalium. Vol. 15. Jugoslavenska akademija znanosti i umjetnosti, 1884–89. Report from Count Gory v. Serin from March 26, 1601.

Lopašić, Radoslav. 1889. *Spomenici Hrvatske krajine*. Monumenta spectantia historiam Slavorum Meridionalium. Vol. 20. Jugoslavenska akademija znanosti i umjetnosti, 1884–89. Report on the Warasdin District from March 7, 1737, Vienna. Issued by Joseph Friedrich zu Sachsen-Hildburghausen.

Lopašić, Radoslav. 1895. *Oka Kupe i Korane. [Around Kupa and Korana]*. Zagreb: Naklada Matice Hrvatske.

Lyall, Robert. 1824. *An Account of the Organization, Administration, and Present State of the Military Colonies in Russia*. London: A. & R. Spottiswoode.

Marmont, Auguste F. L. W. 1837. *Voyage de Monsieur le Marechal de Raguse, en Hongrie, en Transylvanie, dans la Russie meridionale, en Crimee, et sur les bards de la mer d'Azoff*. Paris: Ladvocat.

Military Encyclopedia. 1912. Military Settlements. **6. Vereshchagin. Military Conscription**, 312–640. http://elib.shpl.ru/ru/nodes/1672-t-6-vereschagin-v-v-voinskaya-povinnost-1912. Last checked on July 31, 2021.

Milleker, Felix. 1925. *Geschichte der Banater Militärgrenze 1764–1873*. Pancevo: K. Wittigschlager.

Milleker, Felix. 1926. *Besiedlung der Banater Militärgrenze*. Vrsac: Kirchner.

Mollinary, Anton Freiherr. 1905. *Sechsundvierzig Jahre im Österreich-Ungarischen Heere*. Vol. 1. Zürich: Art. Intitut Orell Füssli.

Pal, Magda. 1832. *Neueste statistisch-geographische Beschreibung des Königreichs Ungarn, Croatien, Slavonien und der ungarischen Militär-Grenze*. Leipzig: Weygand.

Pasvolsky, Leo. 1928. *Economic Nationalism of the Danubian States*. London: Allen & Unwin.

Paton, Andrew Archibald. 1849. *Highlands and Islands of the Adriatic, Including Dalmatia, Croatia, and the Southern Provinces of the Austrian Empire*. Vol. 2. London: Robson, Levey, and Franklyn.

Perrot, George. 1869. L'Autriche d'autrefois et d'aujourd'hui: Les confins militaires et leur législation. *Revue des Deux Mondes, 2e période*, **84**, 38–70.

Radosavljevich, Paul R. 1919. *Who Are the Slavs*. Boston: The Gorham Press.

Rouire, M. 1901. Les colons et l'Algérie: I: la phase héroique de la colonisation. *Revue des Deux Mondes (1829–1971)*, 5(2), 339–374.

Royal Statistical Central Office in Budapest. 1902. *A Magyar Korona Országainak 1900. Évi Népszámlálása 1. A Népesség Általános Leírása Községenkint. [Census of the Hungarian Crown Countries in 1900. General Description of the Population by Municipality]*. Vol. 2. Pest Book Printing Company.

Royal Statistical Central Office in Budapest. 1913. *A Magyar Szent Korona Országainak 1910. Évi Népszámlálása. Második rész. A Nepesseg Foglalkozása és a Nagypari Vallalatok Kozsegenkint. [Census of the Hungarian Crown Countries in 1910. Second Part. Population Occupation and Large Industrial Enterprises.]*. Vol. 2. Printing Press of the Anonymous Society Athenaeum.

Royal Statistical Office in Zagreb. 1898. *Popis gospodarstva i stoke od 31. prosinca 1895. Ergebnisse der Zählung der Landwirthschaftlichen Betreibe und der Viehzählung vom 31 Dezember 1895. [Results of the Farm Census and Livestock Census of December 31, 1895.]*. Vol. 2. Royal Statistical Office in Zagreb.

Schefer, Christian. 1907. *La France moderne et le problème colonial (1815–1830)*. Paris: Alcan.

Schopf, Franz J. 1846. *Archiv für Civil-Justizpflege, politische und kameralistische Amtsverwaltung in den deutschen, böhmischen, galizischen und ungarischen Provinzen des österreichischen Kaiserstaates*. Vol. 1. Graz: Druck und Verlag von J. A Kienreich.

Schwicker, Johann Heinrich . 1883. *Geschichte der österreichischen Militärgrenze*. Vienna: K. Prochaska.

Servan de Gerbey, Joseph. 1780. *Le Soldat Citoyen ou Vues patriotiques sur la manière la plus avantageuse de pourvoir à la défense du royaume*. Neuchâtel: Dans le pays de la liberté.

Seton-Watson, Robert William. 1911. *The Southern Slav Question and the Habsburg Monarchy*. London: Constable.

Sišić, Ferdo. 1918. *Acta Comitialia Regni Croatiae Dalmatiae Slavoniae Volumen V*. Vol. Monumenta Spectantia Historiam Slavorum Meridionalium - 43. Zagreb: Akademijskoj Knjižari Lav. Hartmana. Statuta Valachorum from October 5, 1630.

Socijalistička Federativna Republika Jugoslavija Savezni Zavod Za Statistiku. 1967. *Demografska Statistika 1964. [Demographic Statistics, 1964]*.

Belgrade: Socijalistička Federativna Republika Jugoslavija Savezni Zavod Za Statistiku.

Socijalistička Federativna Republika Jugoslavija Savezni Zavod Za Statistiku. 1973. *Demografska Statistika 1970. [Demographic Statistics, 1970].* Belgrade: Socijalistička Federativna Republika Jugoslavija Savezni Zavod Za Statistiku.

Stopfer, Mathias. 1831. *Erläuterungen der Grundgesetze für die Carlstädter, Warasdiner, Banat, Slavonische und Banatische Militär-Gränze.* Wien: Carl Gerold.

Stopfer, Mathias. 1840. *Lehrbuch über die Grundgesetze der Karlstadter, Warasdiner, Banal, Slavonischen und Banatlichen Militär Gränze.* Graz: J. A. Kienreich.

Szegő, Pál. 1911. *Végváraink szervezete a török betelepedésétől a tizenötéves háború kezdetéig (1541–1593). [The Organization of Our Border Castles from the Turkish Settlement to the Beginning of the Fifteen Years' War (1541–1593)].* Budapest: Rothberger és Weisz Ny.

Thallóczy, Lajos. 1903. *Magyarország Melléktartományainak Oklevéltára (Codex Diplomaticus Partium Regno Hungariae Adnexarum): A horvát véghelyek oklevéltára 1490–1527. [Diploma of the Adjacent Provinces of Hungary (Codex Diplomaticus Partium Regno Hungariae Adnexarum): Diploma of Croatian terminals 1490–1527].* Vol. 1. Budapest: Kiadja a Magyar Tudomanyos Akademia.

Tkalac, Imbro. 1894. *Jugenderinnerungen aus Kroatien: 1749–1823. 1824–1843.* Leipzig: Verlag Von Otto Wigand.

Turković, Milan. 1936. *Die Geschichte der ehemaligen kroatisch-slawonische Militärgrenze.* Susak: Primorski Stamparski Zavod.

Unknown Author. 1828. Russie: Colonies militaires. *Le spectateur militaire,* **XXVII**, 242–253.

Utješenović-Ostrožinski, Ognjeslav M. 1859. *Die Hauskommunionen der Südslawen.* Vienna: F.Manz.

Vaníček, Fr. 1875a. *Specialgeschichte der Militärgrenze.* Vol. 1. Vienna: Kaiserlich-Königliche Hof- und Staatsdruckerei.

Vaníček, Fr. 1875b. *Specialgeschichte der Militärgrenze.* Vol. 2. Vienna: Kaiserlich-Königliche Hof- und Staatsdruckerei.

Vaníček, Fr. 1875c. *Specialgeschichte der Militärgrenze.* Vol. 3. Vienna: Kaiserlich-Königliche Hof- und Staatsdruckerei.

Vaníček, Fr. 1875d. *Specialgeschichte der Militärgrenze.* Vol. 4. Vienna: Kaiserlich-Königliche Hof- und Staatsdruckerei.

Von Hietzinger, Carl Bernh. Edlen. 1817. *Statistik der Militärgränze des österreichischen Kaiserthums.* Vol. 1. Wien: Verlage bei Carl Gerold.

Von Pidoll zu Quintenbach, Carl Freiherrn. 1847. *Einige Worte über die russischen Militär Kolonien im Vergleiche mit der k.k. österreichischen Militär-Grenze und mit allgemeinen Betrachtungen darüber.* Vienna: Druck und Verlag von Earl Gerold.

Yugoslavia Opšta Državna Statistika. 1932. *Definitivni rezultati popisa stanovništva od 31 januara 1921 god. [Final Results of the Census from 31 January 1921].* Sarajevo: Državna štamparija.

Yver, Georges. 1924. *Documents relatifs au traité de la Tafna (1837).* Alger: Jules Carbonel.

Zoričič, Milovan. 1883. *Popis žiteljstva i stoke od 31. prosinca 1880 u Hrvatskoj i Slavoniji. [Population and Livestock Census from December 31, 1880 in Croatia and Slavonia].* Zagreb: Tiskara "Narodnih Novinah."

Secondary Literature

Abramson, Scott F., and Boix, Carles. 2019. Endogenous Parliaments: The Domestic and International Roots of Long-Term Economic Growth and Executive Constraints in Europe. *International Organization*, **73**(4), 793–837.

Acemoğlu, Daron, and Robinson, James A. 2000. Why Did the West Extend the Franchise? Democracy, Inequality, and Growth in Historical Perspective. *The Quarterly Journal of Economics*, **115**(4), 1167–1199.

Acemoğlu, Daron, and Robinson, James A. 2006. *Economic Origins of Dictatorship and Democracy*. Cambridge: Cambridge University Press.

Acemoğlu, Daron, and Robinson, James A. 2012. *Why Nations Fail: The Origins of Power, Prosperity and Poverty*. New York: Crown.

Acemoğlu, Daron, and Wolitzky, Alexander. 2011. The Economics of Labor Coercion. *Econometrica*, **79**(2), 555–600.

Acemoğlu, Daron, Johnson, Simon, and Robinson, James A. 2001. The Colonial Origins of Comparative Development: An Empirical Investigation. *American Economic Review*, **91**(5), 1369–1401.

Acemoğlu, Daron, García-Jimeno, Camilo, and Robinson, James A. 2012. Finding El Dorado: Slavery and Long-Run Development in Colombia. *Journal of Comparative Economics*, **40**, 534–564.

Adamček, Josip. 1984. Problem Krajiškili Buna U Historiografiji [The Problem of the Military Colonial Riots in Historiography]. *Pages 119–140 of:* Pavličević, Dragutin (ed.), *Vojna Krajina: Povijesni pregled, historiografija, rasprave [The Military Frontier: Historical Survey, Historiography, and Articles]*. Zagreb: Biblioteka Znanstvenih Radova.

Agoston, Gábor. 1998. Habsburgs and Ottomans: Defense, Military Change and Shifts in Power. *Turkish Studies Association Bulletin*, **22**(1), 126–141.

Ahram, Ariel I., and King, Charles. 2012. The Warlord as Arbitrageur. *Theory and Society*, **41**(2), 169–186.

Alesina, Alberto, and Giuliano, Paola. 2010. The Power of the Family. *Journal of Economic Growth*, **15**, 93–125.

Alesina, Alberto, and Giuliano, Paola. 2015. Culture and Institutions. *Journal of Economic Literature*, 4(53), 898–944.

Alesina, Alberto, and Rodrik, Dani. 1994. Distributive Politics and Economic Growth. *The Quarterly Journal of Economics*, **109**(2), 465–490.

Algan, Yann, and Cahuc, Pierre. 2010. Inherited Trust and Growth. *American Economic Review*, **100**(5), 2060–2092.

Altić, Mirela Slukan. 2005. Territorial Development and Boundary Determination of the Varaždin Generalate (1630–1771). *Podravina*, 4(7), 7–31.

Amstadt, Jakob. 1969. *Die k.k. Militärgrenze 1522–1881: mit einer Gesamtbibliographie*. Würzburg: Gugel.

Ares, Macarena, and Hernández, Enrique. 2017. The Corrosive Effect of Corruption on Trust in Politicians: Evidence from a Natural Experiment. *Research & Politics*, 4(2), 1–8.

Bachinger, Karl, and Lacina, Vlastislav. 1996. Wirtschaftliche Ausgangsbedingungen. *Pages 51–112 of:* Teichova, Alice, and Matis, Herbert (eds.), *Österreich und die Tschechoslowakei 1918–1938*. Vienna: Böhlau.

Balcells, Laia. 2012. The Consequences of Victimization on Political Identities: Evidence from Spain. *Politics & Society*, 3(40), 311–347.

Banfield, Edward. 1958. *Moral Basis of a Backward Society*. New York: Free Press.

Barkey, Karen. 2008. *Empire of Difference: The Ottomans in Comparative Perspective*. New York: Cambridge University Press.

Bartusis, Mark C. 1997. *The Late Byzantine Army: Arms and Society 1204–1453*. Philadelphia: University of Pennsylvania Press.

Bauer, Michal, Blattman, Christopher, Chytilová, Julie *et al.* 2016. Can War Foster Cooperation? *Journal of Economic Perspectives*, 3(30), 249–274.

Becker, Sascha, Boeckh, Katrin, Hainz, Christa, and Woessmann, Ludger. 2016. The Empire Is Dead, Long Live the Empire! Long-Run Persistence of Trust and Corruption in the Bureaucracy. *Economic Journal*, **126**(590), 40–74.

Beissinger, Mark, and Kotkin, Stephen. 2014. *Historical Legacies of Communism in Russia and Eastern Europe*. New York: Cambridge University Press.

Bellows, John, and Miguel, Edward. 2009. War and Local Collective Action in Sierra Leone. *Journal of Public Economics*, **11–12**(93), 1144–1157.

Benard, Cheryl. 1994. Rape as Terror: The Case of Bosnia. *Terrorism and Political Violence*, 1(6), 29–43.

Berend, Iván T. 1998. *Decades of Crisis: Central and Eastern Europe before World War II*. London: University of California Press.

Berend, Iván T., and Ránki, György. 1960. *The Development of the Manufacturing Industry in Hungary, 1900–1944*. Budapest: Akadémiai Kiadó.

Bérenger, Jean. 2013. *A History of the Habsburg Empire, 1273–1700*. London: Routledge.

Bérenger, Jean. 2014. *A History of the Habsburg Empire, 1700–1918*. London: Routledge.

Berger, Peter. 1990. The Austrian Economy, 1918–1938. *Pages 270–284 of:* Komlos, John (ed.), *Economic Development in the Habsburg Monarchy and in the Successor States: Essays*. New York: Columbia University Press.

Besley, Timothy. 1995. Property Rights and Investment Incentives: Theory and Evidence from Ghana. *Journal of Political Economy*, **103**(5), 903–937.

Besley, Timothy, and Ghatak, Maitreesh. 2006. Public Goods and Economic Development. *Pages 285–303 of:* Banerjee, Abhijit Vinayak, Bénabou, Roland, and Mookherjee, Dilip (eds.), *Understanding Poverty*. New York: Oxford University Press.

Besley, Timothy, and Ghatak, Maitreesh. 2010. Property Rights and Economic Development. *Pages 4525–4595 of:* Rodrik, Dani, and Rosenzweig, Mark (eds.), *Handbook in Economics*. Vol. 5. New York: Cambridge University Press.

Birken, Andreas. 1981. *The Ottoman Empire 1683–1718; 1718–1812; 1812–1881; 1881–1912*. MAP. Scale: 1:8,000,000 km. Tübinger Atlas des Vorderen Orients. Dr. Ludwig Reichert Verlag, Wiesbaden.

Bisin, Alberto, and Verdier, Thierry. 2000. "Beyond the Melting Pot": Cultural Transmission, Marriage, and the Evolution of Ethnic and Religious Traits. *The Quarterly Journal of Economics*, **115**(3), 955–988.

Bitis, Alexander, and Hartley, Janet. 2000. The Russian Military Colonies in 1826. *The Slavonic and East European Review*, **78**(2), 321–330.

Black, Jeremy. 1992. Ancien Regime and Enlightenment: Some Recent Writing on Seventeenth-and Eighteenth-Century Europe. *European History Quarterly*, **2**(22), 247–255.

Blanc, André. 1951. Les Confins militaires Croates au XIX siècle. *Revue des Études Slaves*, **28**(1/4), 111–128.

Blanc, André. 1957. *La Croatie occidentale: Étude de Géographie humaine*. Paris: Institut D'Études Slaves de l'Université de Paris.

Blattman, Christopher. 2009. From Violence to Voting: War and Political Participation in Uganda. *American Political Science Review*, **2**(103), 231–247.

Bohinec, V., and Planina, Fr. 1957. *FLR Jusgoslavia - Motoring Map*. MAP. Scale: 1:800,000 km, Ljubljana, Slovenia.

Boix, Carles. 2003. *Democracy and Redistribution*. Cambridge: Cambridge University Press.

Boix, Carles. 2009. The Conditional Relationship between Inequality and Development. *PS: Political Science and Politics*, **2**(42), 645–649.

Boix, Carles. 2010. Origins and Persistence of Economic Inequality. *Annual Review of Political Science*, **13**, 489–516.

Boix, Carles. 2015. *Political Order and Inequality: Their Foundations and their Consequences for Human Welfare*. New York: Cambridge University Press.

Boix, Carles, and Rosenbluth, Frances. 2013. Bones of Contention: The Political Economy of Height Inequality. *American Political Science Review*, **108**(1), 1–22.

Boone, Catherine. 2014. *Property and Political Order in Africa: Land Rights and the Structure of Politics*. Cambridge: Cambridge University Press.

Booth, Anne, and Deng, Kent. 2017. Japanese Colonialism in Comparative Perspective. *Journal of World History*, **28**(1), 61–98.

Borbála, Bak. 1997. *Magyarország történeti topográfiája. A honfoglalástól 1950-ig. [Historical topography of Hungary. From the Conquest to 1950]*. Budapest: MTA Törtenettudomanyi Intezete.

Bosma, Ulbe. 2007. The Cultivation System (1830–1870) and Its Private Entrepreneurs on Colonial Java. *Journal of Southeast Asian Studies*, **38**(2), 275–291.

Bowler, Shaun, and Karp, Jeffrey A. 2004. Politicians, Scandals, and Trust in Government. *Political Behavior*, **3**(26), 271–287.

Boyer, John W. 1980. *Political Radicalism in Late Imperial Vienna: The Origins of the Christian Social Movement*. Chicago: University of Chicago Press.

Brading, David Anthony, and Cross, Harry E. 1972. Colonial Silver Mining: Mexico and Peru. *The Hispanic American Historical Review*, **52**(4), 545–579.

Brenner, Robert. 1976. Agrarian Class Structure and Economic Development in Pre-Industrial Europe. *Past & Present*, **70**(1), 30–75.

Brix, Emil. 1982. *Die Umgangssprachen in Altöstereich zwischen Agitation und Assimilation: die Sprachenstatistik in den zisleithanischen Volkszählungen, 1880 bis 1910*. Vienna: Verlag der Österreichischen Akademie der Wissenschaften.

Buelens, Frans, and Frankema, Ewout. 2016. Colonial Adventures in Tropical Agriculture: New Estimates of Returns to Investment in the Netherlands Indies, 1919–1938. *Cliometrica*, **10**, 197–224.

Buelens, Frans, and Marysse, Stefaan. 2009. Returns on Investments during the Colonial Era: The Case of the Belgian Congo. *The Economic History Review*, **62**(1), 135–166.

Burger, Hannelore. 1995. *Sprachenrecht und Sprachengerechtigkeit im österreichischen Unterrichtswesen 1867–1918*. Vienna: Verlag der Österreichischen Akademie der Wissenschaften.

Burić, Olivera. 1976. The Zadruga and the Contemporary Family in Yugoslavia. *Pages 117–139 of:* Brynes, Robert F. (ed.), *The Zadruga: Essays by P. E. Mosley and Essays in his Honor*. London: University of Notre Dame Press.

Cagé, Julia, and Rueda, Valeria. 2016. The Long-Term Effects of the Printing Press in Sub-Saharan Africa. *American Economic Jouurnal: Applied Economics*, **8**(3), 69–99.

Canetti-Nisim, Daphna, Halperin, Eran, Sharvit, Keren, and Hobfoll, Stevan E. 2009. A New Stress-Based Model of Political Extremism: Personal Exposure to Terrorism, Psychological Distress, and Exclusionist Political Attitudes. *Journal of Conflict Resolution*, 3(53), 363–389.

Carey, Sabine, Mitchell, Neil J., and Lowe, Will. 2013. States, the Security Sector, and the Monopoly of Violence: A New Database on Pro-Government Militias. *Journal of Peace Research*, **50**(2), 249–258.

Carter, David, and Goemans, H. E. 2014. The Temporal Dynamics of New International Borders. *Conflict Management and Peace Science*, **31**(3), 285–302.

Caunce, Stephen. 1997. Farm Servants and the Development of Capitalism in English Agriculture. *Agricultural History Review*, **45**(1), 49–60.

Cederman, Lars-Erik, Girardin, Luc, and Gleditsch, Kristian Skrede. 2009. Ethnonationalist Triads: Assessing the Influence of Kin Groups on Civil Wars. *World Politics*, **61**(03), 403–437.

Centeno, Miguel Angel. 1997. Blood and Debt: War and Taxation in Nineteenth-Century Latin America. *American Journal of Sociology*, **102**(6), 1565–1605.

Chambers, Jonathan D. 1953. Enclosure and Labour Supply in the Industrial Revolution. *Economic History Review*, 5(3), 319–343.

Chanley, Virginia A., Rudolph, Thomas J., and Rahn, Wendy M. 2000. The Origins and Consequences of Public Trust in Government: A Time Series Analysis. *The Public Opinion Quarterly*, 3(64), 239–256.

Charnysh, Volha. 2019. Diversity, Institutions, and Economic Outcomes: Post-WWII Displacement in Poland. *American Political Science Review*, **113**(2), 423–441.

Charnysh, Volha, and Finkel, Evgeny. 2017. The Death Camp Eldorado: Political and Economic Effects of Mass Violence. *American Political Science Review*, **111**(4), 801–818.

Chirot, Daniel. 1989. *The Origins of Bakwardness in Eastern Europe*. Berkeley: University of California Press.

Christensen, Raymond P., and Yee, Harold T. 1964. The Role of Agricultural Productivity in Economic Development. *Journal of Farm Economics*, **46**(5), 1051–1061.

Clague, Christopher, Keefer, Philip, Knack, Stephen, and Olson, Mancur. 1999. Contract-Intensive Money: Contract Enforcement, Property Rights, and Economic Performance. *Journal of Economic Growth*, **4**(2), 185–211.

Clayton, Anthony. 1988. *France, Soldiers, and Africa*. London: Brassey's Inc.

Cohen, Gary B. 1980. *The Politics of Ethnic Survival: Germans in Prague, 1861–1914*. Princeton, NJ: Princeton University Press.

Coleman, James Samuel. 1990. *Foundations of Social Theory*. Cambridge, MA: Harvard University Press.

Collier, Ruth Berins, and Collier, David. 1991. *Shaping the Political Arena: Critical Junctures, the Labor Movement, and Regime Dynamics in Latin America*. Princeton, NJ: Princeton University Press.

Cooper, Frederick. 1996. *Decolonization and African Society. The Labor Question in French and British Africa*. Cambridge: Cambridge University Press.

Costalli, Stefano, and Ruggeri, Andrea. 2019. The Long-Term Electoral Legacies of Civil War in Young Democracies: Italy, 1946–1968. *Comparative Political Studies*, **6**(52), 927–961.

Croatian Bureau of Statistics. 2017. *Popis stanovništva, kućanstva i stanova 2011. Stanovi prema načinu korištenja. [Census of Population, Households and Dwellings 2011, Dwellings by Occupancy Status]*. Zagreb: Croatian Bureau of Statistics. www.dzs.hr/Hrv_Eng/publication/2016/SI-1586.pdf. Last checked on April 1, 2018.

Curtiss, John Shelton. 1965. *The Russian Army under Nicholas I, 1825–1855*. Durham, NC: Duke University Press.

Cvrček, Tomáš. 2013. Wages, Prices, and Living Standards in the Habsburg Empire, 1827–1910. *The Journal of Economic History*, **73**(1), 1–37.

Dardena, Keith, and Grzymala-Busse, Anna. 2006. The Great Divide: Literacy, Nationalism, and the Communist Collapse. *World Politics*, **59**(1), 83–115.

Davenport, Christian. 2007. State Repression and the Tyrannical Peace. *Journal of Peace Research*, **44**(4), 485–504.

De Tocqueville, Alexis. 2000. *Writings on Empire and Slavery*. Baltimore: The Johns Hopkins University Press.

Deak, John. 2014. The Great War and the Forgotten Realm: The Habsburg Monarchy and the First World War. *Journal of Modern History*, **86**(2), 336–380.

Dell, Melissa. 2010. The Persistent Effects of Peru's Mining Mita. *Econometrica*, **78**(6), 1863–1903.

Dell, Melissa, and Olken, Benjamin. 2020. The Development Effects of the Extractive Colonial Economy: The Dutch Cultivation System in Java. *Review of Economic Studies*, **87**(1), 164–203.

Dell, Melissa, Lane, Nathan, and Querubin, Pablo. 2018. The Historical State, Local Collective Action, and Economic Development in Vietnam. *Econometrica*, **86**(6), 2083–2121.

Deloche, Jean. 1994. *Transport and Communications in India Prior to Steam Locomotion: Volume 1: Land Transport.* Oxford: Oxford University Press.

Dennison, Tracy. 2011. *The Institutional Framework of Russian Serfdom.* New York: Cambridge University Press.

Dennison, Tracy, and Ogilvie, Sheilagh. 2007. Serfdom and Social Capital in Bohemia and Russia. *The Economic History Review*, **60**(3), 513–544.

DiCaprio, Alisa. 2012. Introduction: The Role of Elites in Economic Development. *Pages 1–16 of:* Alice H. Amsden, Alisa DiCaprio, and Robinson, James A. (eds.), *The Role of Elites in Economic Development.* Oxford: Oxford University Press.

Dimitrova-Grajzl, Valentina. 2007. The Great Divide Revisited: Ottoman and Habsburg Legacies on Transition. *Kyklos*, **60**(4), 539–558.

Dincecco, Mark. 2011. *Political Transformations and Public Finances: Europe, 1650–1913.* New York: Cambridge University Press.

Dincecco, Mark, Fenske, James, Menon, Anil, and Mukherjee, Shivaji. 2022. Pre-Colonial Warfare and Long-Run Development in India. *Economic Journal*, **132**(643), 981–1010.

Donaldson, Dave. 2018. Railroads of the Raj: Estimating the Impact of Transportation Infrastructure. *American Economic Review*, **4–5**(108), 899–934.

Donaldson, Dave, and Storeygard, Adam. 2016. The View from Above: Applications of Satellite Data in Economics. *Journal of Economic Perspectives*, **4**(30), 171–198.

Doyle, Michael. 1986. *Empires.* Ithaca, NY: Cornell University Press.

Dray, Stéphane, Legendre, Pierre, and Peres-Neto, Pedro R. 2006. Spatial Modelling: A Comprehensive Framework for Principal Coordinate Analysis of Neighbour Matrices (PCNM). *Ecological Modelling*, **3**(196), 483–493.

Ellis, Steven G. 1995. *Tudor Frontiers and Noble Power.* Oxford: Clarendon Press.

Elson, R. E. 1994. *Village Java under the Cultivation System 1830–1870.* Sydney: Asian Studies Association of Australia.

Émerit, Marcel. 1959. L'influence russe et croate sur la colonisation militaire à l'époque de Bugeaud. *La Revue Française d'Histoire d'Outre-Mer*, **46**(163–165), 85–96.

Engerman, Stanley, and Sokoloff, Kenneth. 2000. Institutions, Factor Endowments, and Paths of Development in the New World. *Journal of Economic Perspectives*, **14**(3), 217–232.

Epstein, Samuel. 1994. Integration of the Cognitive and the Psychodynamic Unconscious. *American Psychologist*, **8**(49), 709–724.

Erlich, Vera. 1966. *Family in Transition: A Study of 300 Yugoslav Villages*. Princeton, NJ: Princeton University Press.

Fabbe, Kristin. 2019. *Disciples of the State?: Religion and State-Building in the Former Ottoman World*. New York: Cambridge University Press.

Fall, Babacar. 1993. *Le Travail Forcé en Afrique-Occidentale française, 1900–1946*. Paris: Karthala.

Federal People's Republic of Yugoslavia – Federal Statistical Office. 1952a. Agricultural Co-Operatives in 1952. *Statistical Bulletin*, 10–40. Year IV, October 1953, Series B-III.

Federal People's Republic of Yugoslavia – Federal Statistical Office. 1952b. Agricultural Machines and Implements 1951. *Statistical Bulletin*. Year IV, September 1952, Series B-III.

Feinstein, Charles, Temin, Peter, and Toniolo, Gianni. 2008. *The World Economy Between the World Wars*. Oxford: Oxford University Press.

Ferguson, Alan D. 1954. Russian Landmilitia and Austrian Militärgrenze. *Südost-Forschungen*, **13**(1), 141–147.

Ferguson, Alan D. 1964. The Russian Military Settlement, 1825–1866. *Pages 107–128 of:* Ferguson, Alan D., and Hamden, Alfred Levin. (eds.), *Essays in Russian Histoy: A Collection Dedicated to George Vernadsky*. Hamden, CT: Archon Books.

Filipović, Milenko S. 1976. Zadruga (Kućna Zadruga). *Pages 268–279 of:* Byrnes, Robert F. (ed.), *Communal Families in the Balkans: The Zadruga: Essays by Philip E. Mosely and Essays in His Honor*. London: University of Notre Dame Press.

Fine, John V. A. 2009. *The Late Medieval Balkans: A Critical Survey from the Late Twelfth Century to the Ottoman Conquest*. Michigan, MI: The University of Michigan.

Forbes, Kristin J. 2000. A Reassessment of the Relationship between Inequality and Growth. *The American Economic Review*, **90**(4), 869–887.

Frankema, Ewout, and Booth, Anne. 2019. *Fiscal Capacity and the Colonial State in Asia and Africa, c.1850–1960*. New York: Cambridge University Press.

Frankema, Ewout, and Buelens, Frans. 2013. *Colonial Exploitation and Economic Development: The Belgian Congo and Netherlands Indies Compared*. Abingdon: Routledge.

Fukuyama, Francis. 2011. Poverty, Inequality, and Democracy: Dealing with Inequality. *Journal of Democracy*, 22(3), 79–89.

Gabora, Liane, and Steel, Mike. 2017. Autocatalytic Networks in Cognition and the Origin of Culture. *Journal of Theoretical Biology*, 431, 87–95.

Gallego, Francisco A., and Woodberry, Robert. 2010. Christian Missionaries and Education in Former African Colonies: How Competition Mattered. *Journal of African Economies*, 19(3), 294–329.

Galor, Oded, and Özak, Ömer. 2016. The Agricultural Origins of Time Preference. *American Economic Review*, 106(10), 3064–3103.

Gardner, Leigh, and Roy, Tirthankar. 2020. *Economic History of Colonialism*. Bristol: Bristol University Press.

Gardner, Leigh A. 2012. *Taxing Colonial Africa: The Political Economy of British Imperialism*. Oxford: Oxford University Press.

Gavrilović, Slavko, and Krestic, Vasilije. 1997. *Građa za istoriju vojne granice u XVIII veku. [Material for the history of the military border in the 18th century]*. Belgrade: Srpska akademija nauka i umetnosti.

Gavrilović, Slavko, and Samardžić, Radovan. 1989. *Građa za istoriju vojne granice u XVIII veku. [Material for the history of the military border in the 18th century]*. Belgrade: Srpska akademija nauka i umetnosti.

Gelman, Andrew, and Imbens, Guido. 2017. Why High-Order Polynomials Should Not Be Used in Regression Discontinuity Designs. *Journal of Business & Economic Statistics*, 37(3), 447–456.

Generalstab des Heeres, Abt. für Kriegskarten und Vermessungswesen. 1940. *Jusgoslawien / Strassennetz*. MAP. Scale: 1:100,000 km. Eigenthum und Verlag von Artaria.

Gerring, John, Ziblatt, Daniel, Gorp, Johan Van, and Arévalo, Julián. 2011. An Institutional Theory of Direct and Indirect Rule. *World Politics*, 63(3), 377–433.

Gilligan, Michael J., Pasquale, Benjamin J., and Samii, Cyrus. 2014. Civil War and Social Cohesion: Lab-in-the-Field Evidence from Nepal. *American Journal of Political Science*, 58(3), 604–619.

Gleditsch, Kristian Skrede. 2007. Transnational Dimensions of Civil War. *Journal of Peace Research*, 44(3), 293–309.

Göllner, Carl. 1973. *Regimenetele Grăniceresti din Transilvania 1764– 1851. [The Border Regiments in Transylvania 1764–1851]*. Bucharest: Editura Militară.

Good, David F. 1984. *The Economic Rise of the Habsburg Empire, 1750– 1914*. Berkley, CA: University of California Press.

Gorodnichenko, Yuriy, and Roland, Gérard. 2021. Culture, Institutions and Democratization. *Public Choice*, **187**, 165–195.

Grandits, Hannes. 2002. *Familie und Sozialer Wandelim ländlichen Kroatien (18–20. Jahrhundert)*. Vienna: Böhlau Verlag.

Granovetter, Mark S. 1973. The Strength of Weak Ties. *American Journal of Sociology*, **78**(6), 1360–1380.

Greif, Avner. 1994. Cultural Beliefs and the Organization of Society: A Historical and Theoretical Reflection Oncollectivist and Individualist Societies. *Journal of Political Economy*, **102**(5), 912–950.

Greif, Avner, and Tabellini, Guido. 2007. The Clan and the Corporation: Sustaining Cooperation in China and Europe. *Journal of Comparative Economics*, **45**(1), 1–35.

Greif, Avner, Milgrom, Paul, and Weingast, Barry R. 1994. Coordination, Commitment, and Enforcement: The Case of the Merchant Guild. *Journal of Political Economy*, **102**(4), 745–776.

Grosfeld, Irena, and Zhuravskaya, Ekaterina. 2015. Cultural vs. Economic Legacies of Empires: Evidence from the Partition of Poland. *Journal of Comparative Economics*, **43**(1), 55–75.

Grosjean, Pauline. 2011. The Institutional Legacy of the Ottoman Empire: Islamic Rule and Financial Development in South Eastern Europe. *Journal of Comparative Economics*, **39**(1), 1–16.

Grzymala-Busse, Anna, and Luong, Pauline Jones. 2002. Reconceptualizing the State: Lessons from Post-Communism. *Politics & Society*, **30**(4), 529–554.

Guardado, Jenny. 2018. Office-Selling, Corruption, and Long-Term Development in Peru. *American Political Science Review*, **112**(4), 971–995.

Guiso, Luigi, Sapienza, Paola, and Zingales, Luigi. 2008. Social Capital as Good Culture. *Journal of the European Economic Association*, **6**(2–3), 295–320.

Guiso, Luigi, Sapienza, Paola, and Zingales, Luigi. 2016. Long-Term Persistence. *Journal of the European Economic Association*, **6**(14), 1401–1436.

Hajdú, Zoltán. 2005. *Magyarország közigazgatási földrajza. [The Administrative Geography of Hungary]*. Budapest–Pécs: Dialóg Campus.

Halpern, Joel M., Kaser, Karl, and Wagner, Richard A. 1996. Patriarchy in the Balkans: Temporal and Cross-Cultural Approaches. *The History of the Family. An International Quarterly*, **1**(4), 425–442.

Hartley, Janet M. 2008. *Russia, 1762–1825: Military Power, the State, and the People*. Westport, CT: Praeger.

Hechter, Michael. 1975. *Internal Colonialism: The Celtic Fringe in British National Development, 1536–1966*. Berkeley, CA: University of California Press.

Heeresgeschichtliches Museum. 1973. *Die K[aiserlich] k[önigliche] Militärgrenze: Beiträge zu ihrer Geschichte.* Vienna: Österr. Bundesverl.

Heine, Steven J. 2008. *Cultural Psychology.* New York: W. W. Norton.

Helmke, Gretchen, and Levitsky, Steven. 2004. Informal Institutions and Comparative Politics: A Research Agenda. *Perspectives on Politics,* 2(4), 725–740.

Henderson, Vernon, Storeygard Adam Weil David. 2012. Measuring Economic Growth from Outer Space. *American Economic Review,* 2(102), 994–1028.

Henrich, Joseph. 2020. *The WEIRDest People in the World.* New York: Farrar, Straus and Giroux.

Herbst, Jeffrey. 2000. *States and Power in Africa: Comparative Lessons in Authority and Control.* Princeton, NJ: Princeton University Press.

Hertz, Frederik. 1947. *The Economic Problem of the Danubian States: A Study in Economic Nationalism.* London: Gollancz.

Hewstone, Miles, Rubin, Mark, and Willis, Hazel. 2002. Intergroup Bias. *Annual Review of Psychology,* 53, 575–604.

Hitchins, Keith. 1985. *The Idea of Nation: the Romanians of Transylvania, 1691–1849.* Bucharest: Editura ştiinţifică şi enciclopedică.

Hoare, Marko Attila. 2006. *Genocide and Resistance in Hitler's Bosnia: The Partisans and the Chetniks.* Oxford: Oxford University Press.

Hochedlinger, Michael. 2003. *Austria's Wars of Emergence, 1683–1797.* London: Routledge.

Hochschild, Adam. 1999. *King Leopold's Ghost: A Story of Greed, Terror, and Heroism in Colonial Africa.* New York: Mariner Books.

Hodža, Milan. 1942. *Federation in Central Europe: Reflections and Reminiscences.* London: Jarrolds.

Hofstede, Geert. 2001. *Culture's Consequences: Comparing Values, Behaviors, Institutions, and Organizations across Nations.* London: Sage Publications.

Hopkins, Antony G. 1973. *An Economic History of West Africa.* New York: University of Columbia Press.

Horel, Catherine. 2009. *Soldaten zwischen nationalen Fronten: die Auflösung der Militärgrenze und die Entwicklung der königlich-ungarischen Landwehr (Honvéd) in Kroatien-Slawonien 1868–1914.* Vienna: Verl. der Österr. Akad. der Wiss.

Horvat, Josip. 1939. *Kultura Hrvata kroz 1000 godina. [Croatian Culture through 1000 Years].* Vol. 1. Zagreb: Tipografija D. D. U Zagrebu.

Hrstic, Ivan. 2017. The Abolition of the Colonate: Long-Term Sharecropping Relations in Dalmatia, 1918–1946. *Agricultural History,* 91(4), 513–535.

Hudson, Valerie M., Bowen, Donna Lee, and Nielsen, Perpetua Lynne. 2015. Clan Governance and State Stability: The Relationship between Female Subordination and Political Order. *American Political Science Review*, **109**(3), 535–555.

Huillery, Elise. 2009. History Matters: The Long-Term Impact of Colonial Public Investments in French West Africa. *American Economic Journal: Applied Economics*, **1**(2), 176–215.

Ingrao, Charles W. 2000. *The Habsburg Monarchy*. New York: Cambridge University Press.

International Court of Justice. 2001 (Mar.). *Case Concerning the Application of the Convention of the Prevention and Punishment of the Crime of Genocide. Croatia v. Yugoslavia. Memorial of Croatia. Volume 5.* www.icj-cij.org/files/case-related/118/18184 .pdf. Last checked on May 19, 2018.

Isaac, Benjamin. 1988. The Meaning of the Terms Limes and Limitanei. *The Journal of Roman Studies*, **78**, 125–147.

Israeli, Raphael. 2013. *The Death Camps of Croatia: Visions and Revisions, 1941–1945*. New Brunswick: Transaction Publishers.

Iyer, Lakshmi. 2010. Direct versus Indirect Colonial Rule in India: Long-Term Consequences. *Review of Economics and Statistics*, **92**(4), 693–713.

Jánossy, Ferenc. 2016. *The End of the Economic Miracle: Appearance and Reality in Economic Development*. London: Routlege. First published in 1971.

Jászi, Oszkár. 1929. *The Dissolution of the Habsburg Monarchy*. Chicago: University of Chicago Press.

Jedwab, Remi, and Moradi, Alexander. 2016. The Permanent Effects of Transportation Revolutions in Poor Countries: Evidence from Africa. *Review of Economics and Statistics*, **98**(2), 268–284.

Johnston, Bruce F., and Kilby, Peter. 1970. *Agriculture and Structural Transformation: Economic Strategies in Late-Developing Countries*. London: Oxford University Press.

Johnston, Bruce F., Kilby, Peter, and Tomich, Thomas Patrick. 1995. *Transforming Agrarian Economies*. Ithaca, NY: Cornell University Press.

Johnston, Bruce F. J, and Clark, William C. 1982. *Redesigning Rural Development: A Strategic Perspective*. Baltimore, MD: Johns Hopkins University Press.

Judson, Pieter M. 2016. *The Habsburg Empire: A New History*. New York: Harvard University Press.

Juif, Dacil, and Frankema, Ewout. 2018. From Coercion to Compensation: Institutional Responses to Labour Scarcity in the Central African Copperbelt. *Journal of Institutional Economics*, **14**, 313–343.

Kaldor, Nicoals. 1955. Alternative Theories of Distribution. *Review of Economic Studies*, **2**(23), 83–100.

Kalyvas, Stathis N. 2006. *The Logic of Violence in Civil War*. New York: Cambridge University Press.

Kann, Robert. 1957. *The Habsburg Empire: A Study of Integration and Disintegration*. New York: Praeger.

Karner, Stefan. 1990. From Empire to Republic: Economic Problems in a Period of Collapse, Reorientation and Reconstruction. *Pages 251–269 of:* Komlos, John (ed.), *Economic Development in the Habsburg Monarchy and in the Successor States: Essays*. vol. 2. New York: Columbia University Press.

Kaser, Karl. 1985. Die Entwicklung der Zadruga in der kroatisch-slawonischen Militärgrenze. *Pages 14–25 of:* Vasić, Milan (ed.), *Der Islamisierungsprozeß auf der Balkanhalbinsel*. Graz: Institut für Geschichte.

Kaser, Karl. 1994. The Balkan Joint Family: Redefining a Problem. *Social Science History*, **18**(2), 243–269.

Kaser, Karl. 1997. *Freier Bauer und Soldat: die Militarisierung der agrarischen Gesellschaft an der kroatisch-slawonischen Militärgrenze (1535–1881)*. Vienna: Böhlau.

Keele, Luke J., and Titiunik, Rocío. 2015. Geographic Boundaries as Regression Discontinuities. *Political Analysis*, **23**(1), 127–155.

Kelly, Morgan. 2019. *The Standard Errors of Persistence*. https://papers.ssrn.com/sol3/papers.cfm?abstract_id=3398303. Last checked on May 26, 2021.

Keynes, John M. 1920. *The Economic Consequences of the Peace*. London: Macmillan.

Khodarkovsky, Michael. 2002. *Russia's Steppe Frontier: The Making of a Colonial Empire, 1500–1800*. Bloomington, IN: Indiana University Press.

Kinglake, Alexander William. 1996. *Eothen or Tales of Travel brought Home from the East*. Evanston, IL: Northwestern University Press.

Klein, Alexander, Schulze, Max-Stephan, and Vonyó, Tamás. 2017. How Peripheral Was the Periphery? Industrialization in East Central Europe since 1870. *Pages 63–90 of:* O'Rourke, Kevin Hjortshøj, and Williamson, Jeffrey Gale (eds.), *The Spread of Modern Industry to the Periphery since 1871*. Oxford: Oxford University Press.

Knack, Stephen. 2007. Measuring Corruption: A Critique of Indicators in Eastern Europe and Central Asia. *Journal of Public Policy*, **27**(3), 255–291.

Knack, Stephen, and Keefer, Philip. 1997. Does Social Capital Have an Economic Payoff? A Cross-Country Investigation. *The Quarterly Journal of Economics*, **112**(4), 1251–1288.

Kohli, Atul. 2004. *State-Directed Development: Political Power and Industrialization in the Global Periphery*. New York: Cambridge University Press.

Kohli, Atul. 2020. *Imperialism and the Developing World*. Oxford: Oxford University Press.

Kohn, Margaret, and Reddy, Kavita. 2017. Colonialism. *The Stanford Encyclopedia of Philosophy*. https://plato.stanford.edu/archives/fall2017/entries/colonialism/. Last checked on December 17, 2021.

Kolossa, Tibor. 1987. A dualizmus rendszerének kialakulása és megszilárdulása, 1867–1875. [The Formation and Consolidation of the System of Dualism, 1867–1875]. *Page 775–865 of:* Katus, László (ed.), *Magyarország története tíz kötetben, 1848–1890. [History of Hungary in Ten Volumes, 1848–1890]*, vol. 6/2. Budapest: Akadémiai Kiadó.

Koroknai, Ákos. 1974. *Gazdasági és társadalmi viszonyok a dunai és a tiszai határőrvidéken a XVIII. század elején. [Economic and Social Conditions in the Danube and Tisza Border Guards in the 18th Century. At the Beginning of the Century]*. Budapest: Akadémiai Kiadó.

Krajasich, Peter. 1974. *Die Militärgrenze in Kroatien*. Vienna: Verb. d. Wissenschaftl. Gesellschaften Österreichs.

Kunicova, Jana, and Rose-Ackerman, Susan. 2005. Electoral Rules and Constitutional Structures as Constraints on Corruption. *British Journal of Political Science*, **35**, 573–606.

Kuran, Timur. 2012. *The Long Divergence: How Islamic Law Held Back the Middle East*. Princeton, NJ: Princeton University Press.

La Porta, Rafael, Lopez-de Silanes, Florencio, Shleifer, Andrei, and Vishny, Robert. 1999. The Quality of Government. *Journal of Law, Economics, and Organization*, **15**(1), 222–279.

Lange, Matthew. 2004. British Colonial Legacies and Political Development. *World Development*, **32**(6), 905–922.

Lange, Matthew. 2009. *Lineages of Despotism and Development: British Colonialism and State Power*. Chicago: The University of Chicago Press.

Lange, Matthew, Mahoney, James, and vom Hau, Matthias. 2006. Colonialism and Development: A Comparative Analysis of Spanish and British Colonies. *American Journal of Sociology*, **111**(5), 1412–1462.

Lazanin, Sanja. 2003. Grof Josip Rabatta i slika hrvatskih krajišnika (kraj 17. i početak 18. stoljeća). [Count Josip Rabatta and a Picture of Croatian Border Guards (Late 17th and Early 18th Century)]. *Migracijske i etničke teme*, **19**(4), 413–432.

Leaf, Murray J., and Read, Dwight. 2012. *Human Thought and Social Organization: Anthropology on a New Plane*. New York: Lexington Books.

Lee, Alexander, and Schultz, Kenneth A. 2012. Comparing British and French Colonial Legacies: A Discontinuity Analysis of Cameroon. *Quarterly Journal of Political Science*, 7(4), 1–46.

Lee, Melissa M. 2020. *Crippling Leviathan: How Foreign Subversion Weakens the State*. New York: Cornell University Press.

Lemarchand, René. 1972. Political Clientelism and Ethnicity in Tropical Africa: Competing Solidarities in Nation-Building. *American Political Science Review*, 66(1), 68–90.

Lesky, Erna. 1957. Die österreichische Pestfront an der k. k. Militärgrenze. *Saeculum*, 8(JG), 82–106.

Lo Iacono, Sergio, and Sonmez, Burak. 2021. The Effect of Trusting and Trustworthy Environments on the Provision of Public Goods. *European Sociological Review*, 37(1), 155–168.

Loewe, Michael. 1986. The Structure and Practice of Government. *Pages 463–491 of:* Twitchett, Denis, and Fairbank, John K. (eds.), *The Cambridge History of China*. New York: Cambridge University Press.

Longo, Matthew. 2018. *The Politics of Borders: Sovereignty, Security, and the Citizen after 9/11*. Cambridge: Cambridge University Press.

Lowes, Sara, and Montero, Sergio. 2021. Concessions, Violence, and Indirect Rule: Evidence from the Congo Free State. *The Quarterly Journal of Economics*, 136(4), 2047–2091.

Lupu, Noam, and Peisakhin, Leonid. 2017. The Legacy of Political Violence Across Generations. *American Journal of Political Science*, 61(4), 836–851.

Lyall, Jason. 2009. Does Indiscriminate Violence Incite Insurgent Attacks? Evidence from Chechnya. *Journal of Conflict Resolution*, 53(3), 331–362.

Macartney, Carlile A. 1937. *Hungary and her Successors: The Treaty of Trianon and Its Consequences 1919–1937*. London: Oxford University Press.

Machiavelli, Niccolo. 1996. *The Prince*. Chicago: University of Chicago Press.

Magas, Damir. 2015. *The Geography of Croatia*. Zadar: University of Zadar and Meridijani Publishing House.

Magocsi, P.R. 2002. *Historical Atlas of East Central Europe*. Seattle, WA: University of Washington Press.

Mahoney, James. 2000. Path Dependence in Historical Sociology. *Theory and Society*, 29(4), 507–548.

Mahoney, James. 2010. *Colonialism and Postcolonial Development: Spanish America in Comparative Perspective*. New York: Cambridge University Press.

Mamdani, Mahmood. 1996. *Citizen and Subject: Contemporary Africa and the Legacy of Late Colonialism*. Princeton Studies in Culture/Power/History. Princeton, NJ: Princeton University Press.

Mann, Michael. 2008. Infrastructural Power Revisited. *Studies in Comparative International Development*, **43**(3), 355–365.

Mares, Isabela. 2017. Inequality and Democratization: An Elite-Competition Approach. *Perspectives on Politics*, **15**(2), 563–565.

Mattingly, Daniel C. 2017. Colonial Legacies and State Institutions in China: Evidence From a Natural Experiment. *Comparative Political Studies*, **50**(4), 434–463.

Mauro, Paolo. 1995. Corruption and Growth. *The Quarterly Journal of Economics*, **110**(3), 681–712.

McNeill, William H. 1964. *Europe's Steppe Frontier, 1500–1800*. Chicago: The University of Chicago Press.

Mead, Margaret. 1976. Introduction: Philip E. Mosely's Contribution to the Comparative Study of the Family. *Pages xvii–xxvii of:* Brynes, Robert F. (ed.), *The Zadruga: Essays by P. E. Mosley and Essays in his Honor*. London: University of Notre Dame Press.

Michalopoulos, Stelios, and Papaioannou, Elias. 2013. Pre-Colonial Ethnic Institutions and Contemporary African Development. *Econometrica*, **81**(1), 113–152.

Michalopoulos, Stelios, and Papaioannou, Elias. 2016. The Long-Run Effects of the Scramble for Africa. *American Economic Review*, **106**(7), 1802–1848.

Michels, Robert. 1915. *Political Parties: A Sociological Study of the Oligarchical Tendencies of Modern Democracies*. London: Jarrold and Sons.

Migdal, Joel. 1988. *Strong Societies and Weak States: State-Society Relations and State Capabilities in the Third World*. Princeton: Princeton University Press.

Mill, John Stuart. 1861. Considerations on Representative Government, in Collected Works of John Stuart Mill. *Page 371–577 of:* Robinson, John (ed.), *Collected Works of John Stuart Mill*. Toronto: University of Toronto Press.

Moačanin, Feodor. 1984. Pokušaji Sporazumijevanja Između Hrvatskog Plemstva I Vlaha Varaždinskog Generalata U 17. Stoljeću. [Attempts at Agreement Between the Croatian Nobility and the Vlach Generalate of Varaždin in the 17th Century]. *Pages 275–302 of:* Pavličević, Dragutin (ed.), *Vojna Krajina: Povijesni pregled, historiografija, rasprave [The Military Frontier: Historical Survey, Historiography, and Articles]*. Zagreb: Biblioteka Znanstvenih Radova.

Moore, Barrington. 1966. *Social Origins of Dictatorship and Democracy: Lord and Peasant in the Making of the Modern World.* Boston, MA: Beacon Press.

Moscona, Jacob, Nunn, Nathan, and Robinson, James. 2020. Segmentary Lineage, Organization and Conflict in Sub-Saharan Africa. *Econometrica,* **8**(5), 1999–2036.

Mosely, Philip E. 1976a. Adaptation for Survival: The Varzic Zadruga. *Pages 31–57 of:* Brynes, Robert F. (ed.), *The Zadruga: Essays by P. E. Mosley and Essays in his Honor.* London: University of Notre Dame Press.

Mosely, Philip E. 1976b. The Distribution of the Zadruga within Southeastern Europe. *Pages 58–69 of:* Brynes, Robert F. (ed.), *The Zadruga: Essays by P. E. Mosley and Essays in his Honor.* London: University of Notre Dame Press.

Mosely, Philip E. 1976c. The Peasant Family: The Zadruga or Communal Joint-Family in the Balkans, and Its Recent Evolution. *Pages 19–30 of:* Brynes, Robert F. (ed.), *The Zadruga: Essays by P. E. Mosley and Essays in his Honor.* London: University of Notre Dame Press.

Mosser, Alois, and Teichova, Alice. 1991. Investment Behaviour of Industrial Joint-Stock Companies and Industrial Shareholding by the Österreichische Credit-Anstalt: Inducement or Obstacle to Renewal and Change in Interwar Austria. *Pages 123–157 of:* James, Harold, Lindgren, Hekan, and Teichova, Alice (eds.), *The Role of Banks in the Interwar Economy.* Cambridge: Cambridge University Press.

Mukherjee, Shivaji. 2018. Colonial Origins of Maoist Insurgency in India: Historical Institutionsand Civil War. *Journal of Conflict Resolution,* **62**(10), 2232–2274.

Mukherjee, Shivaji. 2021. *Colonial Institutions and Civil War Indirect Rule and Maoist Insurgency in India.* New York: Cambridge University Press.

Mukhopadyay, Dipali. 2014. *Warlord, Strogman Governance, and the State in Afghhanistan.* New York: Cambridge University Press.

Muller, Edward N., and Opp, Karl-Dieter. 1986. Rational Choice and Rebellious Collective Action. *American Political Science Review,* **80**(2), 471–488.

Nathan, Noah L. 2019. Electoral Consequences of Colonial Invention: Brokers, Chiefs, and Distribution in Northern Ghana. *World Politics,* 71(3), 417–456.

Nedeljković, Branislav M. 1936. *Istorija baštinske svojine: u novoj Srbiji od kraja 18. veka do 1931. [History of heritage property: in new Serbia from the end of the 18th century to 1931].* Belgrade: Pravni fakultet.

Nedervene Pieterse, Jan P. 1989. *Empire and Emancipation: Power and Liberation on a World Scale.* London: Pluto Press.

North, Douglass. 1990. *Institutions, Institutional Change and Economic Performance*. New York: Cambridge University Press.

North, Douglass C., and Thomas, Robert Paul. 1970. An Economic Theory of the Growth of the Western World. *Economic History Review*, **23**(1), 1–18.

North, Douglass C., and Thomas, Robert Paul. 1971. The Rise and Fall of the Manorial System: A Theoretical Model. *Journal of Economic History*, **31**(4), 777–803.

North, Douglass C., and Thomas, Robert Paul. 1973. *The Rise of the Western World: A New Economic History*. New York: Cambridge University Press.

North, Douglass C., and Weingast, Barry R. 1989. Constitutions and Commitment: The Evolution of Institutions Governing Public Choice in Seventeenth-Century England. *The Journal of Economic History*, **49**(4), 803–832.

North, Douglas C., Wallis, John, and Weingast, Barry R. 2009. *Violence and Social Orders: A Conceptual Framework for Interpreting Recorded Human History*. New York: Cambridge University Press.

Nunn, Nathan. 2009. The Importance of History for Economic Development. *Annual Review of Economics*, **1**, 65–92.

Nunn, Nathan, and Wantchekon, Leonard. 2011. The Slave Trade and the Origins of Mistrust in Africa. *American Economic Review*, **101**(7), 3221–3252.

Oakland, William H. 1987. Theory of public goods. *Pages 485–535 of:* Auerbach, Alan J., and Feldstein, Martin (eds.), *Handbook of Public Economics*, vol. 2. Elsevier.

Ogilvie, Sheilagh, and Carus, A.W. 2014. Institutions and Economic Growth in Historical Perspective. *Pages 403–513 of:* Aghion, Philippe, and Durlauf, Steven N. (eds.), *Handbook of Economic Growth*, vol. 2. Amsterdam, Boston, and London: North Holland.

Olson, Mancur. 1965. *The Logic of Collective Action: Public Goods and the Theory of Groups*. New York: Schocken Books.

Olson, Mancur. 1993. Dictatorship, Democracy, and Development. *American Political Science Review*, **87**(3), 567–576.

O'Reilly, William. 2006. Border, Buffer and Bulwark: The Historiography of the Military Frontier, 1521–1881. *Pages 229–244 of:* Ellis, Steven G., and Esser, Raingard (eds.), *Frontiers and the Writing of History, 1500–1850*. Hannover-Laatzen: Werhahn Verlag.

Ostrom, Vincent, and Ostrom, Elinor. 1977. Public Goods and Public Choices. *Pages 6–49 of:* Savas, Emanuel (ed.), *Alternatives for Delivering Public Services*. New York: Routledge.

Ott, Katarina, and Bajo, Anto. 2001 (June). *Local Government Budgeting in Croatia*. www.internationalbudget.org/wp-content/

uploads/ Local-Government-Budgeting-in-Croatia.pdf. Last checked on May 24, 2021. Institute of Public Finance.

Ott, Katarina, Bronić, Mihaela, Petrušić, Miroslav, and Stanić, Branko. 2018. Budget Transparency in Croatian Counties, Cities and Municipalities (November 2017 – March 2018). *Institute of Public Finance Newsletter*, July, 1–14.

Paige, Jeffrey M. 1997. *Coffee and Power: Revolution and the Rise of Democracy in Central America*. Cambridge, MA: Harvard University Press.

Pálffy, Géza. 2008. Scorched-earth Tactics In Ottoman Hungary: On a Controversy In Military Theory And Practice On The Habsburg-Ottoman Frontier. *Acta Orientalia Academiae Scientiarum Hungaricae*, **61**(1/2), 181–200.

Pálffy, Géza. 2009. Közép-Európa védőbástyája és éléskamrája (1526–1711). [The Bulwark and Larder of Central Europe (1526–1711)]. *Pages 92–115 of:* Ernő, Marosi (ed.), *Európa színpadán. Magyarország ezeréves hozzájárulása az európai közösség eszméjéhez. [On the European stage. Hungary's millennial contribution to the idea of the European community]*. Budapest: MTA Művészettörténeti Kutató Intézete–Balassi Kiadó.

Pálffy, Géza. 2012. The Habsburg Defense System in Hungary Against the Ottomans in the Sixteenth Century: A Catalyst of Military Development in Central Europe. *Page 35–61 of:* Davies, Brian (ed.), *Warfare in Eastern Europe, 1500–1800*. New York: Brill.

Paris, Edmond. 1961. *Genocide in Satellite Croatia, 1941–1945: A Record of Racial and Religious Persecutions and Massacres*. Chicago, IL: American Institute for Balkan Affairs.

Parsons, Talcott. 1937/1949. *The Structure of Social Action*. New York: Free Press.

Pasvolsky, Leo. 1928. *Economic Nationalism of the Danubian States*. London: Allen & Unwin.

Paton, Andrew Archibald. 1849. *Highlands and Islands of the Adriatic, Including Dalmatia, Croatia, and the Southern Provinces of the Austrian Empire*. Vol. 2. London: Robson, Levey, and Franklyn.

Pavković, Aleksandar. 2011. Recursive Secession of Trapped Minorities: A Comparative Study of the Serb Krajina and Abkhazia. *Nationalism and Ethnic Politics*, **17**(3), 297–318.

Pavličević, Dragutin. 1984. *Vojna krajina: provijesni pregled, historiografia, rasprave. [Military Frontier: Historical Review, Historiography, Discussions]*. Zagreb: Sveučilišna naklada Liber.

Pavličević, Dragutin. 1989. *Hrvatske kućne zadruge I. (do 1881). [Croatian House Cooperatives I. (until 1881)]*. Zagreb: Biblioteka znanstvenih radova Sveučilišne naklade Liber i Zavoda za hrvatsku povijest Filozof-skog fakulteta u Zagrebu.

Pavlović, Dobroslav St., and Pavlowitch, Stevan K. 2008. *Hitler's New Disorder: The Second World War in Yugoslavia.* New York: Columbia University Press.

Pecinjacki, Sreta. 1985. *Graničarska naselja Banata (1773–1810). [Border Settlements of Banat (1773–1810)].* Novi Sad: Matica srpska.

Persson, Torsten, and Tabellini, Guido. 1994. Is Inequality Harmful for Growth? *The American Economic Review*, **84**(3), 600–621.

Pierson, Paul. 2004. *Politics in Time: History, Institutions, and Social Analysis.* Princeton, NJ: Princeton University Press.

Pipes, Richard E. 1950. The Russian Military Colonies, 1810–1831. *The Journal of Modern History*, **22**(3), 205–219.

Polanyi, Karl. 1957. *The Great Transformation.* Boston: Beacon Press.

Pollard, Sidney. 1986. *Peaceful Conquest.* Oxford: Oxford University Press.

Pop-Eleches, Grigore, and Tucker, Joshua A. 2017. *Communism's Shadow: Historical Legacies and Contemporary Political Attitudes.* Princeton, NJ: Princeton University Press.

Popescu, Bogdan, and Popa, Mircea. 2022. Imperial Rule and Long-Run Development: Evidence on the Role of Human Capital in Ottoman Europe. *Comparative Political Studies*, **55**(11), 1910–1946.

Probszt-Ohstorff, Günther. 1967. *Die windisch-kroatische Militärgrenze und ihre Vorläufer.* Graz: Historischer Verein für Steiermark.

Przeworski, Adam. 2012. *Democracy and Development: Political Institutions and Well-Being in the World, 1950–1990.* New York: Cambridge University Press.

Putnam, Robert. 2000. *Bowling Alone: The Collapse and Revival of American Community.* New York: Simon & Schuster.

Putnam, Robert D., Leonardi, Robert, and Nanetti, Raffaella Y. 1993. *Making Democracy Work: Civic Traditions in Modern Italy.* Princeton, NJ: Princeton University Press.

Rabbie, Jacob M., and Horwitz, Murray. 1969. Arousal of Ingroup-Outgroup Bias by a Chance Win or Loss. *Journal of Personality and Social Psychology*, **13**(3), 269–277.

Radić, Ante Antun. 1899. *Izvješće O Putovanju Po Bosni I Hercegovini. [Travel Report in Bosnia and Herzegovina].* Zagreb: Jazu. Zbornik za narodni život i običaje Knjiga 4.

Rashid, Asma. 1960. Emir Abd-al-Qadir and the Algerian Struggle. *Pakistan Horizon*, **13**(2), 117–129.

Republika Hrvatska Republicki Zavod Za Statistiku. 1992. *Popis Stanovništva 1991 – Narodnosni Sastav Stanovništva Hrvatske Po Naseljima. [Population Census of 1991 – The National Composition of the Population of Croatia by Settlements]*. Zagreb: Republika Hrvatska Republicki Zavod Za Statistiku.

Rex, John. 2007. *Race, Colonialism and the City*. London: Routledge.

Robinson, James. 2012. Elites and Institutional Persistence. *Pages 29–45 of:* Alice H. Amsden, Alisa DiCaprio, and Robinson, James A. (eds.), *The Role of Elites in Economic Development*. Oxford: Oxford University Press.

Romaniello, Matthew P. 2012. *The Elusive Empire: Kazan and the Creation of Russia, 1552–1671*. London: University of Wisconsin Press.

Rose-Ackerman, Susan. 1999. *Corruption and Government: Causes, Consequences, and Reform*. New York: Cambridge University Press.

Rossiyskaya Gazeta. 2013. From the history of the Cossacks. July 03, 2013. www.rbth.com/multimedia/infographics/2013/07/03/from_the_history_of_the_cossacks_26737. Last checked on July 31, 2021.

Roth, Erik. 1988. *Die planmäßig angelegten Siedlungen im Deutsch-Banater Militärgrenze 1765–1821*. Munich: R. Oldenbourg.

Rothenberg, Gunther E. 1960a. The Origins of the Austrian Military Frontier in Croatia and the Alleged Treaty of 22 December 1522. *The Slavonic and East European Review*, **38**(91), 493–498.

Rothenberg, Gunther E. 1966. *The Military Border in Croatia, 1740–1881: A Study of an Imperial Institution*. Chicago, IL: University of Chicago Press.

Rothenberg, Gunther Erich. 1960b. *The Austrian Military Border in Croatia, 1522–1747*. Vol. 48. Urbana, IL: University of Illinois Press.

Rothenberg, Gunther Erich. 1970. *Die österreichische Militärgrenze in Kroatien 1522 bis 1881*. Vienna: Herold.

Rozenas, Arturas, and Zhukov, Yuri. 2019. Mass Repression and Political Loyalty: Evidence from Stalin's "Terror by Hunger." *American Political Science Review*, **113**(2), 569–583.

Rozenas, Arturas, Schutte, Sebastian, and Zhukov, Yuri. 2018. The Political Legacy of Violence: The Long-Term Impact of Stalin's Repression in Ukraine. *Journal of Politics*, **79**(4), 1147–1161.

Rubin, Jared. 2017. *Rulers, Religion, and Riches: Why the West Got Rich and the Middle East Did Not*. New York: Cambridge University Press.

Rueschemeyer, Dietrich, Stephens, Evelyn Huber, and Stephens, John. 1992. *Capitalist Development and Democracy*. Chicago: University of Chicago Press.

Ruffle, Bradley J., and Sosis, Richard. 2006. Cooperation and the In-Group-Out-Group Bias: A Field Test on Israeli Kibbutz Members and City Residents. *Journal of Economic Behavior and Organization*, **60**, 147–163.

Sahlins, Peter. 1989. *Boundaries: The Making of France and Spain in the Pyrenees*. Oxford: University of California Press.

Sartori, Giovanni. 1970. Concept Misformation in Comparative Politics. *American Political Science Review*, **64**(4), 1033–1053.

Schacher, Gerhard. 1932. *Die Nachfolgestaaten Österreich, Ungarn, Tschechoslowakei und ihre wirtschaftliche Kräfte*. Stuttgart: Enke.

Scheve, Kenneth, and Stasavage, David. 2017. Wealth Inequality and Democracy. *Annual Review of Political Science*, **20**, 451–468.

Schlager, Edella, and Ostrom, Elinor. 1992. Property-Rights Regimes and Natural Resources: A Conceptual Analysis. *Land Economics*, **68**(3), 249–262.

Schultz, Kenneth A. 2017. Mapping Interstate Territorial Conflict: A New Data Set and Applications. *Journal of Conflict Resolution*, **61**(7), 1565–1590.

Schulze, Max-Stephan. 2007. Origins of Catch-Up Failure: Comparative Productivity Growth in the Habsburg Empire, 1870–1910. *European Review of Economic History*, **11**(2), 189–218.

Schulze, Max-Stephan, and Wolf, Nikolaus. 2011. Economic Nationalism and Economic Integration: The Austro-Hungarian Empire in the Late Nineteenth Century. *The Economic History Review*, **65**(2), 652–673.

Schwartz, Shalom H. 1992. Universals in the Content and Structure of Values: Theoretical Advances and Empirical Tests in 20 Countries. *Advances in Experimental Social Psychology*, **25**, 1–65.

Scott, James. 1972. *Comparative Political Corruption*. Englewood Cliffs: Prentice Hall.

Scott, James C. 2010. *The Art of Not Being Governed: An Anarchist History of Upland Southeast Asia*. New Haven: Yale University Press.

Sen, Amartya K. 1999. *Development as Freedom*. Oxford: Oxford University Press.

Shigheru, Sato. 1996. The Pangreh Praja in Java under Japanese Military Rule. *Pages 586–608 of:* Post, Peter, and Touwen-Bouwsma, Elly (eds.), *Japan, Indonesia and the War: Myths and Realities*. Leiden: Brill.

Simmons, Beth. 2005. Rules over Real Estate: Trade, Territorial Conflict, and International Borders as Institutions. *Journal of Conflict Resolution*, **49**(6), 823–848.

Simpser, Alberto, Slater, Dan, and Wittenberg, Jason. 2018. Dead But Not Gone: Contemporary Legacies of Communism, Imperialism, and Authoritarianism. *Annual Review of Political Science*, **21**, 419–439.

Skendi, Stavro. 1976. Mosely on the Zadruga. *Pages 14–17 of:* Brynes, Robert F. (ed.), *The Zadruga: Essays by P. E. Mosley and Essays in his Honor*. London: University of Notre Dame Press.

Slovic, Paul, Finucane, Melissa L., Peters, Ellen, and MacGregor, Donald G. 2004. Risk as Analysis and Risk as Feelings: Some Thoughts about Affect, Reason, Risk, and Rationality. *Risk Analysis*, **24**(2), 311–323.

Soifer, Hillel. 2008. State Infrastructural Power: Approaches to Conceptualization and Measurement. *Studies in Comparative International Development*, **43**(3), 231–251.

Sokol, Hans. 1940. *Die k.k. Militärgrenze*. Vienna: Bergland.

Solimano, Andrés, and Avanzini, Diego. 2012. The International Circulation of Elites: Knowledge, Entrepreneurial and Political. *Pages 53–87 of:* Alice H. Amsden, Alisa DiCaprio, and Robinson, James A. (eds.), *The Role of Elites in Economic Development*. Oxford: Oxford University Press.

Spring, Laurence. 2003. *The Cossacks 1799–1815*. Oxford: Osprey.

Staniland, Paul. 2015. Militias, Ideology, and the State. *Jounal of Conflict Resolution*, **59**(5), 770–793.

Stiglitz, Joseph E. 1983. The Theory of Local Public Goods Twenty-Five Years After Tiebout: A Perspective. *Pages 17–52 of:* Zodrow, George R. (ed.), *Local Provision of Public Services: The Tiebout Model After Twenty-Five Years*. New York: Academic Press.

Stinchfield, Bryan T. 2013. Towards a Theory of Corruption, Nepotism, and New Venture Creation in Developing Countries. *International Journal of Entrepreneurship and Small Business*, **18**(1), 1–14.

Stone, Samuel Z. 1990. *The Heritage of the Conquistadors: Ruling Classes in Central America from the Conquest to the Sandinistas*. Lincoln: University of Nebraska Press.

Stourzh, Gerald. 1985. *Die Gleichberechtigung der Nationalitäten in der Verfassung und Verwaltung Österreichs, 1848–1918*. Vienna: Verlag der Österreichischen Akademie der Wissenschaften.

Sumner, Benedict Humphrey. 1949. *Peter the Great and the Ottoman Empire*. New York: Oxford University Press.

Sundberg, Ralph, and Melander, Erik. 2013. Introducing the UCDP Georeferenced Event Dataset. *Journal of Peace Research*, **50**(4), 523–532.

Szabó, Pál Csaba. 2000. A magyar határőrvidék polgári közigazgatásának újjászervezése (1873–1880). [Reorganizing the Civilian Government of the Hungarian Military Frontier (1873–1880)]. *Comitatus, önkormányzati szemle*, **1–2**(10), 102–118.

Szántó, Imre. 1980. *A végvári rendszer kiépítése és fénykora Magyarországon, 1541–1593. [The Construction and Heyday of the Border Fortress System in Hungary, 1541–1593]*. Budapest: Akadémiai Kiadó.

Tabellini, Guido. 2008. The Scope of Cooperation: Values and Incentives. *The Quarterly Journal of Economics*, **123**(3), 905–950.

Tajfel, Henri, Billig, Michael G., Bundy, Robert P., and Flament, Claude. 1971. Social Categorization and Intergroup Behaviour. *European Journal of Social Psychology*, **2**(1), 149–178.

Tawney, R. H. 1941. The Rise of the Gentry, 1558–1640. *Economic History Review*, **11**(1), 1–38.

Taylor, Alan John Percivale. 1948. *The Habsburg Monarchy 1809–1918: A History of the Austrian Empire and Austria-Hungary*. London: Penguin Books.

Tilly, Charles. 1984. *Big Structures, Large Processes, Huge Comparisons*. New York: Russel Sage Foundation.

Tilly, Charles. 1990. *Coercion, Capital and European States, A.D. 990–1990*. Oxford: Basil Blackwell.

Tilly, Charles. 2003. Armed Force, Regimes, and Contention in Europe since 1650. *Pages 37–81 of:* Davis, Diane E., and Pereira, Antony W. (eds.), *Irregular Armed Forces and their Role in Politics and State Formation*. New York: Cambridge University Press.

Tinta, Aurel. 1972. *Colonizările habsburgice în Banat. 1716–1740. [Habsburg colonization in Banat. 1716–1740]*. Bucharest: Facla.

Tkalac, Imbro. 1894. *Jugenderinnerungen aus Kroatien: 1749–1823. 1824–1843*. Leipzig: Verlag Von Otto Wigand.

Todd, Emmanuel. 1983. *The Explanation of Ideology: Family Structure and Social Systems*. New York: Blackwell.

Todd, Emmanuel. 1990. *L'Invention de l'Europe*. Paris: Seuil.

Todorova, Maria. 1997. *Imagining the Balkans*. New York: Oxford University Press.

Tomasevich, Jozo. 2001. *War and Revolution in Yugoslavia, 1941–1945: Occupation and Collaboration*. Stanford: Stanford University Press.

Tönnies, Ferdinand. 1887/1957. *Community and Society. [Gemeinschaft und Gesellschaft]*. New York: Michigan State University Press.

Triandis, Harry C. 2018. *Individualism And Collectivism*. New York: Routledge.

Trimpop, Rüdiger M. 1994. *The Psychology of Risk Taking Behavior*. London: Elsevier.

Tsai, Lily L. 2007. Solidary Groups, Informal Accountability, and Local Public Goods Provision in Rural China. *American Political Science Review*, **101**(2), 355–372.

Valentić, Mirko. 1984. Hrvatsko-Slavonska Vojna Krajina 1790–1881. [The Croatian-Slavonian Military Frontier 1790–1881]. *Chap. Hrvatsko-Slavonska Vojna Krajina 1790–1881. [The Croatian-Slavonian Military Frontier 1790–1881], pages 57–91 of:* Pavličević, Dragutin (ed.), *Vojna Krajina: Povijesni pregled, historiografija, rasprave [The Military Frontier: Historical Survey, Historiography, and Articles]*. Zagreb: Biblioteka Znanstvenih Radova.

Van Antwerp Fine, John. 1994. *The Late Medieval Balkans: A Critical Survey from the Late Twelfth Century to the Ottoman Conquest.* Michigan: University of Michigan Press.

Van Waijenburg, Marlous. 2018. Financing the African Colonial State: The Revenue Imperative and Forced Labor. *The Journal of Economic History*, **78**(1), 40–80.

Vaníček, Fr. 1875. *Specialgeschichte der Militärgrenze.* Vol. 1. Vienna: Kaiserlich-Königliche Hof- und Staatsdruckerei.

Vlek, Charles, and Stallen, Pieter-Jan. 1981. Judging Risks and Benefits in the Small and in the Large. *Organizational Behavior and Human Performance*, **28**(2), 235–271.

Vogler, Jan P. 2019. Imperial Rule, the Imposition of Bureaucratic Institutions, and Their Long-Term Legacies. *World Politics*, **71**(4), 806–863.

Voigtländer, Nico, and Voth, Hans-Joachim. 2012. Persecution Perpetuated: The Medieval Origins of Anti-Semitic Violence in Nazi Germany. *The Quarterly Journal of Economics*, **127**(3), 1339–1392.

Voitchovsky, Sarah. 2005. Does the Profile of Income Inequality Matter for Economic Growth? Distinguishing between the Effects of Inequality in Different Parts of the Income Distribution. *Journal of Economic Growth*, **10**(3), 273–296.

Vollrath, Dietrich. 2007. Land Distribution and International Agricultural Productivity. *American Journal of Agricultural Economics*, **89**(1), 202–216.

Von Neumann, John, and Morgenstern, Oskar. 1947. *Theory of Games and Economic Behavior.* Princeton, NJ: Princeton University Press.

Vonyo, Tamas. 2018. *The Economic Consequences of the War: West Germany's Growth Miracle after 1945.* London: Cambridge University Press.

Voorhees, Burton, Read, Dwight, and Gabora, Liane. 2020. Identity, Kinship, and the Evolution of Cooperation. *Cultural Anthropology*, **61**(2), 194–218.

Völkl, Ekkehard. 1982. Militärgrenze und Statuta Valachorum. *Pages 9–24 of:* Ernst, Gerhard (ed.), *Die österreichische Militärgrenze: Geschichte und Auswirkungen.* Regensburg: Schriftenreihe des Regensbuger Osteuropainstituts.

Völkl, Ekkehard, and Ernst, Gerhard. 1982. *Die österreichische Militärgrenze: Geschichte und Auswirkungen.* Schriftenreihe des Regensburger Osteuropainstituts. Regensburg, Kallmünz: Lassleben.

Vucinich, Wayne. 1976. A Zadruga in Bileća Rudine. *Pages 162–186 of:* Brynes, Robert F. (ed.), *The Zadruga: Essays by P. E. Mosley and Essays in his Honor.* London: University of Notre Dame Press.

Wagner, Walter. 1973. Quellen zur Geschichte der Milirargrenze im Kriegsarchiv Wien. *Schriften des Heeresgeschichtlichen Museums in Wien*, 6, 284–286.

Waldner, David. 1999. *State Building and Late Development*. Ithaca, NY: Cornell University Press.

Wallerstein, Immanuel. 1966. *Social Change: The Colonial Situation*. New York: Wiley.

Walter, Barbara F., and Snyder, Jack. 1999. *Civil Wars, Insecurity, and Intervention*. New York: Columbia University Press.

Weber, Max. 1864/1947. *The Theory of Social and Economic Organization*. New York: Oxford University Press.

Weber, Max. 1905/1992. *The Protestant Ethic and the Spirit of Capitalism*. New York: Routledge.

Wedeen, Lisa. 2008. *Peripheral Visions: Publics, Power, and Performance in Yemen*. Chicago: Chicago University Press.

Weingast, Barry R., North, Douglass C., and Wallis, John Joseph. 2012. *Violence and Social Orders: A Conceptual Framework for Interpreting Recorded Human History*. New York: Cambridge University Press.

Wessely, Kurt. 1954. *Die österreichische Militärgrenze: Der deutsche Beitrag zur Verteidigung des Abendlandes gegen die Türken*. Göttinger Arbeitskreis Schriftenreihe 43. Kitzingen am Main: Holzner.

Wessely, Kurt. 1973. The Development of the Hungarian Military Frontier until the Middle of the Eighteenth Century. *Austrian History Yearbook*, 9, 55–110.

Wittenberg, Jason. 2006. *Crucibles of Political Loyalty: Church Institutions and Electoral Continuity in Hungary*. London: Cambridge University Press.

Wittenberg, Jason. 2015. Conceptualizing Historical Legacies. *East European Politics and Societies: and Cultures*, 29(2), 366–378.

Witzenrath, Christoph. 2007. *Cossacks and the Russian Empire, 1598–1725: Manipulation, Rebellion and Expansion into Siberia*. New York: Routledge.

Wolf, Nikolaus. 2005. Path Dependent Border Effects: The Case of Poland's Reunification (1918–1939). *Explorations in Economic History*, 42(3), 414–438.

Wolf, Nikolaus, Schulze, Max-Stephen, and Heinemeyer, Hans-Christian. 2011. On the Economic Consequences of the Peace: Trade and Borders after Versailles. *The Journal of Economic History*, 71(4), 915–949.

Wolff, Lary. 1994. *Inventing Eastern Europe: The Map of Civilization on the Mind of the Enlightenment*. Stanford, CA: Stanford University Press.

Wood, Elisabeth Jean. 2006. Variation in Sexual Violence during War. *Politics and Society*, 3(34), 307–341.

Yacono, Xavier. 1969. La colonisation militaire par les smalas de spahis en Algérie. *Revue Historique*, **242**(2), 347–394.

Ybert-Chabrier, Édith. 2004. Hordes faméliques et colons militaires en Russie d'après le baron de La Ruë (1834). *Cahiers du Monde russe*, **45**(3/4), 521–529.

Yeomans, Rory. 2015. *The Utopia of Terror: Life and Death in Wartime Croatia*. Rochester: University of Rochester Press.

Zak, Paul J., and Knack, Stephen. 2001. Trust and Growth. *The Economic Journal*, **111**(470), 295–321.

Index

Printed in the United States
by Baker & Taylor Publisher Services